OUT & ABOUT

Gay Travel Guides

USA
RESORTS AND
WARM WEATHER
VACATIONS

OUT & ABOUT

Gay Travel Guides

USA
RESORTS AND
WARM WEATHER
VACATIONS

Essential Information for Gay and Lesbian Travelers

BILLY KOLBER-STUART AND DAVID ALPORT

HYPERION

NEW YORK

Library of Congress Cataloging-in-Publication Data

Designed by Helene Wald Berinsky

First Edition

10 9 8 7 6 5 4 3 2 1

Library of Congress Cataloging-in-Publication Data

Kolber-Stuart, Billy, 1964–
USA resorts and warm weather vacations : essential information for
gay and lesbian travelers / Billy Kolber-Stuart & David Alport.—
1st ed.

p. cm.—(Out & about gay travel guides)
ISBN 0-7868-8177-1
1. United States—Guidebooks. 2. Gays—Travel—United States—
Guidebooks. 3. Resorts—United States—Guidebooks. I. Alport,
David, 1960– . II. Out & about (New Haven, Conn.) III. Title.
IV. Series.
E158.K64 1997
917.304′929′08664—dc20   96–24613
CIP

ACKNOWLEDGMENTS

~~~~~~~~~~

*O*ur immeasurable thanks to the writers whose original contributions to the *Out & About* newsletter have been adapted for this book, to our subscriber contributors whose comments helped fill in the local flavor, and to our office staff who kept everything moving: Mike Acker, Dr. Frederick Altice, Bob Anderson, Betsy Billard, Alan Brown, Kevin Casey, Mark Davis, Matt Farris, Peter Frank, Fred Gates, Bob Goldfarb, Jerry Gottlick, Bobby Guilmartin, Chris Guly, Richard Gray, Max Harrold, David Heslop, Jack Herzberg, George Hobica, David B. King Jr., Barbara Kolber, Tom Loughlin, Kevin Martin, Matthew Pealer, Greg Plowe, Tim Ribar, Lance Ringel, John Rozzo, Kirk Ryder, David Savage, Xander Shapiro, Vicky Skinner, Paul Spugani, Korky Vann, Stephen Wheelock, Chris Winkle, Joelle Yuna.

Thanks also to our families and friends, for aid and affection, for help and direction, for loyalty, love, and for sooth: Vivian Agura, Eliot and Doris Alport, Matthew Bank, Elissa Barnes, Stephanie Blackwood, John Blair, Rich Campbell, Bob and Alison Cilia, Rick Cirillo, John Clark, Chip Conley, Jim Cottrell and Joe Lovett, Stanley Dalnekoff, Bruce Decker, Gina and Ed Gatta, Nancy Getlan, Michael Goff, Marilyn and Arnold Goldman, Sibyl Goldman, Marcello Giuliani, Jim and Abra Handler, Gary Kadesh, Michael Kaminer, Maureen Kellis-Henry, Stanley Kolber, Bruce Kolber-Stuart, Ron Kraft, Harold Levine, Mark Litwin and Adam Shulman, Eric Marcus, Jim McPartlin, Steve Mendelsohn, Tracey Ober, Kile Ozier, Tanya Pope, Mara Posner,

Gideon Rose and Sheri Berman, Charlie Rounds, Marvin Schwam, Henry Scott, Bennett Shuldman, Lauren Spertus, Norman Stone, Harriet and Ed Vincent, Sara Unrue, Tom Viola, Susan Wilson, Jeff Yarbrough, Barbara Zakin, Pam Zicca.

And thanks to our agent, Barney Karpfinger, and our editor, Rick Kot, whose vision and support brought this book to your shelf.

CONTENTS

OUT & ABOUT

Gay Travel Guides

USA
RESORTS AND
WARM WEATHER
VACATIONS

INTRODUCTION

~~~~~~~~~~~~~~~~

$\mathcal{F}$irst and foremost, we want to thank you for buying this *Out &
About* guidebook. If you are looking to make your vacation more
adventurous, sophisticated, exciting, interesting or gay-comfortable,
you've made a wise selection. When we started the *Out & About*
newsletter in September 1992 with an audience of 123 subscribers, we
had the simple (!?!) goal of delivering issue after issue of relevant, useful, entertaining, and otherwise essential information about travel for
gay consumers. Gay travel wasn't anything new: Gay women and men
have always traveled, and probably always more than their straight
counterparts. But such travel wasn't always considered "gay." Sometimes, it wasn't even fun, as gay travelers could be turned away from
the inn simply for being gay.

Gay Travel Evolution

Times have changed, and time has changed gay travel. More than
twenty years ago, Hanns Ebensten began taking small groups of "dis-

cerning gentlemen" on exotic trips all over the world, and the organized group tour became part of the gay travel experience. More than ten years ago, RSVP Travel Productions chartered its first cruise ship and ran an exclusively gay cruise. (The Islanders' Club, a New York City travel company, ran the very first gay cruise in 1972.) RSVP's success in creating a "gay environment" vacation made it the world's largest gay vacation purveyor, and made the "gay environment" a model for gay vacations.

In the four years that followed the first issue of *Out & About* doors opened to gay travelers in numbers unimaginable a decade earlier. Not only have we witnessed an extraordinary increase in cruises, tours, and resorts devoted primarily or exclusively to gay women and men, but we've seen a parallel increase in the number of mainstream suppliers sensitive to gay issues and interested in making their hotels and tours attractive to the gay market. We've moved past the era when gay travel was defined by lists of bars, bathhouses, and hotels run by "members of the club." The world opened up to gay travel, and the travel industry opened up to the idea of gay singles and couples traveling openly and freely.

Many of our proudest moments at *Out & About* have been in helping catalyze that change. When *Travel & Leisure* and *Condé Nast Traveler* wrote about us, it was the first time the word *gay* had appeared between their covers. Our newsletter and the extraordinary press coverage it received in media such as *The New York Times, USA Today, Time, Forbes,* and on CNN and CNBC have been instrumental in the recognition of gay travel as a legitimate and important niche market for the travel industry.

The Out & About Difference

You'll find that *Out & About* guides differ from other travel books you may have used in the past. They combine gay-specific information with solid travel recommendations and travel-industry insider knowledge. We call our approach "decision empowering" because it is designed to provide the details you need to choose among the ever-increasing number of options available to gay travelers. Our series will help you discover new vacation opportunities and better enjoy familiar ones. While no guidebook can be a perfect match in sensibility for each person who uses it, we're confident that you'll find that the *Out & About* series is best-suited to your needs.

The concept of the "gay traveler" defies simple categorization and includes the full spectrum of travel tastes and styles. We are singles, couples, and groups, men and women, young and old. We travel to popular destinations and off the beaten path, in grand style and on a budget, on short getaways and extended vacations. We travel to explore, to frolic, to visit old friends and meet new ones. We travel to see the world's treasures and history, to broaden our horizons, and to do business. We travel to escape, to retreat, and to indulge. The *Out & About* series is written for the full range of gay travelers and brings a unique understanding of how our particular needs can be accommodated when we travel for any reason.

A Whole New Way to Plan a Vacation

This first book in the *Out & About* guidebook series is devoted to vacation travel for gay women and men. It is unique in its comprehensive approach to choosing, planning, and actually going on vacation. This book is full of great vacation ideas, from big gay group vacations to intimate hideaways. It's also full of great recommendations and some of the best practical travel information available in *any* guidebook.

The destinations we've included in this book are seasonal and year-round, warm weather resort-type areas. This includes some cities like Los Angeles, but not cool-climate cities you might visit on vacation such as San Francisco. You'll find those places in our *North American Cities* guidebook.

We will tell you what you need to know to choose among various suppliers and help you decide whether a gay environment vacation is right for you, and if so, which one. But our emphasis is primarily on the middle ground: independent vacations at gay-popular destinations. Such vacations involve the greatest number of choices among where to stay, eat, play, shop, and what to see and do. We've answered those questions here, and we've answered them in a way that straight guidebooks can't, and other gay guidebooks haven't. Using this book to guide your choices will make your travels more comfortable, enjoyable, and gay, in all senses of the word.

Sex and Sensibility

Our focus is heavily weighted toward hotels and restaurants, since these are the most important components of any great vacation. At the same time, we know that romance and sex are important aspects of all lives—gay and straight—and even more so on vacation. We think of our books as a mainstream travel series with a distinctly gay perspective. Most gay guidebooks have focused on sex, with travel being secondary. We recognize that sometimes our sexual orientation is pivotal in the decisions we make about travel, while at other times, it is barely relevant. You won't find listings here for places where paid or public sex takes place. We're not judgmental about these activities, but they're already amply covered in other books, magazines, and newspapers. What you will find are hundreds of resorts, guest houses, group vacations, and restaurants where you will feel welcome and comfortable as a gay person. You'll also find a full range of gay nightlife and activities, with detailed appraisals and honest evaluations and information that will enable you to choose, plan, and take your best vacations ever.

Thanks for Joining Us

It is our profound hope that someday the entire industry will integrate gay travelers into their planning, training, and marketing to the extent that it makes this series virtually irrelevant. Until that time, you can rely on us to deliver the kind of information you need to make the most of all your travels. Fasten your seatbelts. It's going to be an exciting journey!

HOW TO USE THE
OUT & ABOUT GUIDES

A Note About Accuracy

All guidebooks, even ours, start to become out-of-date before they're even published. While many of our recommendations will be valid for years to come, others are wrong even before the books are bound. This is particularly true for nightlife at destinations with few gay-specific venues. Knowing how to use a guidebook sensibly can help avoid disappointment. Here are a few tips:

1. Use listed prices as a general guide. We've chosen to print actual room rate ranges for hotels and average entrée prices for restaurants instead of the "inexpensive-moderate-expensive-very expensive" in most other books. Expect these to change (usually up about 8% per year).

2. Call for more information. We've listed all relevant phone numbers, as well as those of gay hotlines, local gay publications, Internet Website addresses, and nightclub phone numbers so you can verify if indeed the "Tuesday-Night Shipwreck" party is still the most popular event of the week.

3. Ask the locals. Don't be afraid to check with your hotel concierge, cruise ship director, or flight attendant to verify if the Girl Grill or Boy Bar is still really popular. The odds are in your favor that he or she will know the answer, or will know someone who does.

About Our Guest House Ratings

Out & About's Palm Ratings are the first and only ratings system for gay-specific accommodations. Evaluating the gay guest house resorts of Key West, Ft. Lauderdale, Palm Springs, and Provincetown, they reflect our own opinions, taste, and sensibilities. Cleanliness, professional management, quality furnishings, and attractive setting/decor are the most important criteria for us. We try to describe the most salient of an establishment's characteristics in these areas, because each traveler assigns a different weight to each characteristic. Although we have personally inspected all of the rated resorts, we also rely on supplemental information from *Out & About* newsletter subscribers, travel agents, and local friends to round out our appraisals. Our 5 Palms rating denotes gay or gay-popular accommodations of exceptional quality. Like the AAA Five-Diamond or the Mobil Five-Star awards, the *Out & About* 5 Palms rating indicates an attention to comfort and detail of the highest standard. The ratings are given to hostelries that should not disappoint travelers accustomed to luxury hotels and inns. Four Palms lodgings are also highly recommended and are leaders in the gay accommodations field. The difference between the 3 Palms and 2 Palms categories is small and based more upon subjective criteria than the other category distinctions. Many of these properties offer great value and can be very good choices for less fussy travelers. One Palm "Last Resorts" are places where we'd be willing but disappointed to stay. In the rarest of circumstances, we've listed 0 Palms businesses. These are gay-marketed properties that fail to meet the most basic minimums of cleanliness and comfort.

Out & About Palm Ratings are available only for destinations with a large concentration of gay-specific accommodations. At other destinations, listed properties are all recommended (unless otherwise noted), and our comments reflect their individual merits.

Sexual Temperature

While the atmosphere at any given resort is a function of the guests there at a particular time, our "Sexual Temperature" ratings will help point you to (or from) places that have a sexually charged ambiance. **Low** indicates an often mixed clientele (men/women or gay/straight) and a usually nonsexual environment. **Moderate** or **Medium** suggests the frisky undertone of a double entendre. **High** generally corresponds to any all-male environment, and **Very High** labels places where sexually explicit entertainment is sometimes participatory.

Room Rates

We've listed the full room-rate range, from the lowest rate available in low season to the highest rate charged in high season. Although most properties have a range of rates for each season, don't expect to find high season rates much lower than the maximum listed, except at accommodations with a wide variety of room types. In those places, the high season rate listed may be for a suite or cottage, and standard guest rooms may be much less expensive. Off-season, you may find special discounts and flexible rates. Over holiday periods, you'll probably find minimum-stay requirements.

PRACTICAL TRAVEL ADVICE

*L*iving well is not the best revenge. Traveling well is. Having a lot of money helps, but even those on a budget can sometimes travel as if they'd spent a queen's ransom. Little of the advice that follows is specific to gay travelers, but all of it will make your travel more enjoyable and less expensive. We've chosen to include it in this book because you deserve it, and any advantage it gives you over the traveling fools, straight and gay, who haven't bought our book. This chapter is a collection of insider information, tricks of the trade, and common sense, which seems to depart airports more frequently than planes do. Knowledge is power, manners count (beauty is as beauty *does*, boys and girls), and he/she who dies with the most *redeemed* frequent-flyer points wins. *Bon voyage* and perhaps more important, *Bonne route!*

Transportation

GETTING TO AND FROM THE AIRPORT

With airlines like Southwest keeping airfares in the double-digit range, it is easy to spend more money traveling to and from airports than flying between them. Tokyo taxis may be famous for their outrageous fares, but even here in the States ground transportation can push up the cost of a vacation or business trip. Finding a taxi alternative is the most common route to savings, but our path starts before you even book your trip.

Choose the Right Airport. So many of us (and our travel agents) are accustomed to arriving at the big airports that we forget about alternative airports that may be closer to our destination or offer less expensive ground transportation. Burbank, White Plains, Oakland, London Gatwick, Chicago Midway, and Houston Hobby are just a few examples of airports gaining prominence for their convenient and/or inexpensive ground transportation options.

Use Public Transportation. Many of us shy away from it away from home because we are unfamiliar with the options. The best way to find out about what's available is to call the local Convention and Visitors' Bureau. Its job is to help visitors get into and around its city, and the staff does it well. Public transportation is always a fraction of the cost of a taxi, and rail service options often beat rush-hour traffic.

Use Semipublic Transportation. Many cities have shared-van and flat-rate transportation options that combine some of the convenience of a taxi (door-to-door service, for instance) with some of the savings of public transportation. You can also get the information from the *North American Business Planner,* a publication of the *Official Airline Guides* that most travel agents have. You can call 800-AIR-RIDE for information on the services at the three New York airports, and by all means, if you haven't tried a SuperShuttle, do so the next time you fly to a city it services.

GETTING THE MOST FROM FREQUENT-FLYER PROGRAMS

Frequent-flyer programs are the heart of most airlines' marketing efforts and have allowed thousands of travelers to enjoy free flights, first-class upgrades, and even entirely free vacations. In fact, so many freebees have been given away that the airlines have been reining in the rewards. But opportunities still abound, and the number of ways to earn miles has increased dramatically. If you pay attention to the programs (read the member bulletins!) you can capitalize on the frequent-flyer bonanza.

Concentrate Your Mileage with One Airline. Upper-tier programs are becoming the focus of all frequent-flyer programs, which have been trimming benefits for the least frequent flyers to enhance those of the most frequent, a sort of "We cheat the other guy and pass the savings on to you!" deal. This puts travelers into two groups: those who fly in excess of 20,000 to 50,000 actual flight miles annually, and those who don't. Those who do get bumped into upper-tier programs dubbed Gold, Platinum, Preferred, Elite, Medallion, Premier, and the like. Program benefits include: greater availability of award and upgrade seats; priority boarding, waitlisting, check-in, and reservation lines; more ways and opportunities to upgrade; fewer charges for expedited award processing and ticket changes; and more bonus mileage—in short, all of the goodies. If you don't fly 20,000 actual flight miles annually, you lose not only the fun perks, but possibly your mileage as well: Choose a program in which mileage doesn't expire after three years.

Claim Car and Hotel Bonuses. Program affiliations allow you to earn bonus miles for hotel stays and car rentals; sometimes they don't even require a flight in conjunction. At 300 to 1,500 miles for a single car or hotel transaction, you could earn more miles driving and sleeping than flying. *Inside Flyer* magazine (719-597-8880) is a consolidated source for bonus opportunities for all major and most minor programs.

Claim Affinity Bonuses. You can earn money sending flowers, making long-distance phone calls, investing in money market funds, test driving vehicles, subscribing to magazines, filling out surveys—the list is almost endless. The most popular method is using a charge card, earning a mile or sometimes more for each dollar charged. If you're charging at least $10,000 a year, you should definitely be using an affinity credit card. Diners Club (800-2-DINERS or 303-799-1504) has the most flexible program but the least honored card. American Express (800-327-2177 or 910-333-3211) offers Membership Miles on many of its cards, a special "Rewards Plus" Gold Card, with special benefits and increased earning opportunities for frequent flyers, and the Platinum Card, with an incredible array of benefits for luxury travelers. Almost all airlines have an affiliated MasterCard/Visa program, but beware—these cards have high annual fees and finance-charge rates. If you're carrying a balance, you're not a good candidate for these.

Book Award Travel Early or Late.   Using your earned mileage is not always as easy as it seems. If you want to go to Hawaii or the Caribbean in the winter or Europe in the summer, you need to book almost a year in advance or be prepared to spend double the mileage for awards that are not subject to capacity controls. At the same time, if you have to make a last-minute trip or one that does not include a Saturday-night stay, using your miles may save you from having to buy a full-coach fare.

CAR RENTALS

While we generally pay less attention to car-rental costs since they represent the smallest of our travel expenses, they also happen to be the most variable of travel expenses, affording great savings opportunities if you know how to find them and what you might have to put up with to get them.

Check Out as Many Different Rental Agencies as Possible.   Rates and restrictions vary dramatically. A travel agent who knows how to use his or her computer is a great help here, because with one phone call you can compare the rates of all major and most minor companies— there are frequently as many as 20 at a major airport. Be sure to ask about additional charges for things such as extra days, additional drivers, dropping off at a different location, and excess mileage. Note that agency computers are not well designed for comparing nonairport locations or one-way rentals—you may need to make a few calls. Also, don't assume that your corporate discount number is the lowest rate— Automobile Club rates are usually lower, and most cities offer promotional rates lower still.

Don't Automatically Accept the Loss Damage Waiver.   This is a big moneymaker for rental agencies and is usually sold with a mixture of insouciance and scare tactics—"CDW is optional, sir, but if you decline it you are responsible for the full sticker price value of this two-tone Chevy Lumina, plus lost rental revenues and legal fees. . . ." You may in fact already be covered by your personal or business insurance or your credit card. AmEx, Diners, and most gold bank cards offer some kind of LDW coverage, but be careful—most is *secondary coverage* and has a lot of exclusions.

Return the Car with the Tank Full. Prepurchasing a full or half tank of gas is sometimes a good deal, but if you don't, be sure to return the car with a full tank of gas. You probably didn't read all of the fine print, but in reality you signed away the right to have refueling charges governed by reason or restraint.

Physical and Mental Well-being

SAVING YOUR BACK

Travel can be your back's enemy. Especially as one gets older, the back muscles just aren't what they used to be and injury is common—but you can take preventive measures. Here's some welcome relief in the form of advice, some of which you've heard before (thanks, Mom) that bears repeating.

Before You Leave, Pack Light. The main way people hurt their backs when traveling is by dealing with unwieldy suitcases. Do whatever you can to minimize your baggage weight and your interaction with it. After packing for your trip, unpack everything and cut the number of items in half. Which would you prefer, disk surgery or rewearing an outfit? Don't bring full-size shampoo and toothpaste. Miniaturize! Bring only paperback books (fanatics even rip a book in half for short trips). Choose silk, rayon, and other lightweight fabrics. And for heaven's sake, get a luggage cart *with big wheels*. The Travelpro from Eiffel is the best yet produced—first choice of flight attendants and pilots.

Arriving at the Airport. Although this flies in the face of most advice, check your bags (curbside is best) and let someone else struggle with them for a few hours. It's worth the $1/bag tip—just be sure the destination tag is correct. If you insist on carry-on, be careful using the overhead bins—they can be back killers, even if you have managed to leave behind those extra cocktail dresses. On a long flight, get up and walk around every half hour or so to relieve stress on your back muscles.

When You Reach Your Destination. If you've done in your back, get a massage (most hotels have people on call). Request an extra-firm mattress or a bed board in advance; if you don't get one put the mattress on the floor. Rent a car that you know has comfortable seats, such as a Volvo (sometimes available from Hertz), or try to find the same model you drive at home. When it's time to leave, minimize bending by placing your suitcase on a desk or bureau instead of packing on the bed or a low luggage rack.

SAVING YOUR SKIN

As your body's largest organ, and first line of defense, your skin is accustomed to the harsh treatment that everyday life brings it. But traveling often unleashes a new set of elements to which your body may not be accustomed. Taking care of your skin when you travel will not only help keep you looking young and beautiful, Narcissus, but you'll also feel more comfortable and rested.

Keep It Moist in Flight.　Airplane cabins are dry as the desert. Use moisturizer frequently, and for added comfort, spray water. Evian makes a travel spray, as does H_2O Plus. A small spray bottle (beauty supply stores are a good source for travel-size empty containers) filled with tap water works well, too.

Keep It Protected from the Sun.　Warm weather and ski vacations are a sure way to a sunburn. Bring sunscreen with you, including a gentle but high-numbered SPF for your face.

Avoid Harsh Hotel Soaps.　Many deluxe hostelries offer gentle glycerin soaps and after-bath moisturizers. But from the Hyatt right down to the Red Roof Inn, you're better off bringing your own soaps. A travel-size container of liquid bath/shower gel is probably your best bet.

SAVING YOUR SANITY

Traveling can make anyone edgy. Combine edgy with late, and you've got an almost foolproof recipe for frustration. You career into the airport parking lot, shove the parking ticket in the breast pocket of your jacket, fumble through your wallet for your frequent-flyer number at the check-in counter, and run like O.J. (oops, sorry!) to the gate. Two days later you're on the shuttle bus back to the parking lot, and you have no idea where your ticket or the car keys are. *Aaaaaarrrrrrgh!* Here's the better way.

Keep Things in Place. Your airport parking ticket, house keys, and car-rental contract should always go in the same place, whatever that is. My parking ticket goes in my travel wallet behind my upgrade/discount coupons. My house keys go in the side pocket of my carry-on. My rental contract goes in the glove compartment of the car.

Don't Carry Everything with You. On a blank business card, write all of your frequent flyer/stayer/renter numbers, credit card assistance numbers, and travel agent hotline number. Leave the unnecessary plastic at home. (Make sure your travel agent has all of your critical numbers in your reservations profile—then they are available through the agent or his/her 24-hour hotline number.)

Assemble Separate Travel Toiletries and In-Flight Kits, and Keep Them Ready for Travel. Look for travel-size versions of your favorite products or purchase small containers. Be sure to include occasional-use items such as nail clippers, super glue, Q-Tips, aspirin, and safety pins. Not only will these procedures prevent a little missing item from ruining your day, but you might just be able to save someone else's.

SAVING YOUR SEX LIFE

The "twin bed" problem can wreak havoc on a gay relationship, but it needn't. Aside from staying at a gay hotel or resort, there are a number of ways to help ensure your room is equipped with a king- (or queen!) size bed.

Make Sure Your Travel Agent Requests It at the Time of Booking. This is often possible by computer, but confirmed by phone or fax.

Make Sure that Both of Your Names Appear on the Reservation. This does not happen when a hotel is booked through a travel agency computer, even if both names appear on your itinerary. You can check these things yourself if you reconfirm your reservation a few days prior to arrival. The larger hotel chains such as Holiday Inn and Marriott have "frequent guest programs" that, in addition to rewarding your patronage with free travel, also store your room preferences, including bed type, in their reservation system. Most of these programs are free and have benefits that begin with your first stay. Most Hyatt hotels allow you to complete check-in formalities by phone before arrival. That way, the only things you have to ask the desk clerk for are your keys and a cute bell boy to help with all that luggage.

Money and Property

HOTEL RATES

Now that hotels have discovered inventory yield management, hotel rates are almost as confusing as those of airfares. Supply and demand, sometimes assessed on a daily basis, determine the discount off rack (full) rate. The "weekend rate" was almost unheard of ten years ago, and now virtually every hotel in every business city has one, as a way of filling the rooms that business people vacate at the end of the work week. Don't expect to find any bargains during a city-wide convention or the Super Bowl, or Christmas in the Caribbean. Outside of peak travel periods, there are a few ways to play the hotel rate game and win. Here are three of them:

Always Ask for the Lowest Rate.   Many hotels have a nasty habit of starting with their highest rate and working downward. Don't be intimidated: You may have to spend time working your way down. Ask about corporate rates, weekend rates, and package rates—you may find it cheaper to get a room with parking or breakfast than to get just the room itself! Discounts for students, clergy, teachers, and seniors are often available.

Call or Fax the Hotel Directly, Especially If It Is Overseas.   Stateside reservation offices for foreign hotels are frequently unable to book anything but rack rates. This can be true even at big-name chain hotels. Some hoteliers will offer preferential rates to clients who book directly instead of through a travel agent, saving them the agent commission. This practice is very limited; it seems more common because of travel agents' use of computers and reservation-service intermediaries. In most instances, a travel agent contacting the hotel directly will equal or better your efforts. At many business hotels, travel agencies that specialize in corporate travel may have access to rates up to 30% below the lowest ones you could get on your own.

Check Out (and Into) the New Breed of Discount Hotel Chains. Places such as Red Roof, Fairfield, and Hampton Inns offer new, clean, comfortably furnished rooms near airports and suburban business centers. By maintaining standard designs and features throughout their brand, these places are the McDonald's of hotels: priced like other inexpensive accommodations, with a consistent level of familiar quality.

PHONING HOME

The best ways to save on phone bills while traveling are to pick up the phone less frequently, hang it up more quickly, and send postcards whenever possible. Unfortunately, this advice is of little use for those of us who have to:

1. *Check our answering machines three times a day;*
2. *Check up on lovers, dog sitters, and stockbrokers;*
3. *Let Mom know we haven't been mugged or gotten sick since yesterday.*

If you recognize yourself in one of the above categories, you can reduce the damage with these three tips:

Check Hotel Surcharges.   Many hotels charge for toll-free, local, and long-distance access calls made from your room. Making multiple calls from the same access call or phoning from a lobby pay phone can save you about 75¢ a call.

Compare Overseas Rates.   When calling home from many overseas destinations, you can now use a local or toll-free number to access a U.S. operator and long-distance carrier, such as AT&T USA Direct, MCI Call USA, and Sprint Express. While these services are easier than making coin or phone-card calls, sometimes local services are cheaper; either way, it is always less expensive to have the person you're calling call you back.

Use a Surcharge-free Calling Card.   While most long-distance carriers charge an access fee of 60¢ to 80¢ per call, some charge only for the call itself, at very competitive rates. The *Out & About*/ATN calling card offers some of the lowest rates available, and no per-call access fee. Call 800-929-2268 for an application.

P.S. You could also probably get away with calling Mom collect.

DINING OUT

Unless you're going home to Mother's, traveling inevitably involves eating out. For those of us who cook at home most of the time, the expense of restaurant dining can be daunting. Saving money on meals often involves a combination of equally distasteful options. We confess to having skipped meals, stowed continental breakfast goodies for later consumption, purloined extra chocolate mints off the maid's cart, stocked our minibar from the local supermarket, and even supped at Denny's during their free birthday meal promotion. And while we like that Super Bird Sandwich as much as the next guy, it need not be endured for lack of a larger food budget. Here are some more palatable options.

Get a Transmedia Card.   Transmedia is one of the best dining deals around. The card is accepted at over 15,000 restaurants, mostly in New York, Florida, and California. It offers a 25% discount from the food and beverage portions of your bill for up to six people. There are no usage restrictions beyond maximum table size, and the restaurant list is impressive. While you present your Transmedia card like a credit card at the end of your meal, the charge appears on your MasterCard, Visa, or Discover Card bill, along with a matching credit for your discount. Because the restaurant is not absorbing the discount, the card is warmly welcomed and you won't ever be embarrassed using it. It is available for $50 a year by calling 800-422-5090, although a first-year free membership is available from many organizations. *In Good Taste* is almost identical to the Transmedia program, including the list of participating restaurants and merchants. For information, call 800-444-8872 or 305-534-7900.

Le Card is Another Option.   Le Card is an optional but free feature of the Diners Club card and offers a 20% discount program similar to Transmedia's. The program is currently available in 21 metropolitan areas and growing rapidly. The restaurant selection is decent, and once again, because the discount is handled as an associated credit, you simply present your Diners Club for payment of the full amount, and the discount credit is applied retroactively. We like the discreet nature of this program best. *Dining à la Card* is another program that is invisible to the restaurant and your dining companions. You register your credit card numbers with the company, and any time a charge is incurred on a registered card from one of the participating dining establishments, you earn a 20% cash rebate, mailed to you in a rebate check the next month. You can earn the rebate for your first visit at each restaurant each month, and you earn the rebate on the full amount of your charge, up to $120 rebate per visit. The regular program costs $49/year, although discounted or free Dining à la Card programs are available through some frequent flyer programs (most notably United Mileage Plus), in which 10 miles are credited per dollar spent instead of the cash rebate. Call 800-253-5379 for information.

The Entertainment Card Offers More Limited Benefits.   The Entertainment Card is the oldest and largest dining discount program, appearing under many names, including Adventures in Dining, and available in most major markets. The card is part of a travel coupon book, sold primarily by fund-raising groups and specific to a local area. The books have coupons for dining, accommodations, sightseeing, and shopping. The dining discount is provided as one free entrée with the purchase of one, and while the fine-restaurant selection is mediocre, the fast-food discounts are plentiful, and the other travel offers can pay for the cost of the book many times over. (We would not buy the book for the dining discounts alone.) On our last trip to San Francisco, the Entertainment discount (50%) at the Hilton was the *only* discount available in the entire city. The entire book costs $25 to $30, and includes a form to order up to four additional location books—a good idea if you are a frequent traveler to specific cities. Call 800-374-4464 for the number of the local office near you, which will then direct you to a local charity selling the books or sell you the book itself if that is not possible.

YOUR LUGGAGE

A guy walks up to the check-in counter with three bags. He tells the agent, "I'd like that bag to go to Miami, the blue one to Los Angeles, and the third one I'd like you to hold here for two days and then ship it to me in San Francisco." The agent says, "I'm sorry, sir, we can't do that," to which the traveler replies, "Why not? You did it the last time I checked luggage!"

Although automated baggage tags have greatly reduced the number of misdirected bags, pilferage and damage remain quite common. Many travelers do not realize how vulnerable their luggage is until they are trying to replace it or its contents. Here are some tips for protecting your traveling assets.

Get Good Luggage.   This does not mean expensive fancy luggage. While Louis Vuitton and Hartman bags are well-crafted, they might as well have "steal me" written on them. Look for well-made, less obvious bags—sturdy zippers are the most important feature! Hard-sided luggage provides the most internal protection but is more prone to damage than ballistic nylon soft-sided. Small, nonretractable luggage wheels are notorious for breaking. Waterproof is a good idea, unless you only fly from Phoenix to Palm Springs. Ziploc bags are the perfect luggage accessory for anyone carrying a lot of shampoo, lotions, and the like. We use Tutto luggage, top-rated by *Consumer Reports.*

Don't Rely on Basic Locks to Foil Thieves.   Pilferage of checked luggage is all too common and your basic luggage lock won't prevent it. Luggage straps can help deter theft, and the shrink-wrapping of luggage is appearing as an interesting solution to this problem. But the most effective solution is the simplest: Don't pack valuables in your checked luggage. Period. Not only are they at risk, but most valuables are excluded from airline loss liability.

Make Sure Your Bags Are Checked Correctly to Your Destination, and Know What to Do If They Don't Arrive or Have Been Rifled.   A list of contents is good ammunition when filling out a PIR (Property Irregularity Report), which must be done within 24 hours of arrival. Know that domestically, airline luggage liability is limited to a maximum of $1,250 per bag at actual, not replacement, value; international liability may be even less, as it is based on luggage weight. You are entitled to immediate compensation to replace necessities (necessities generally don't include that outfit you *need* for the Black Party) if your luggage is delayed, although make sure any purchases over $25 are approved *in writing* by the airline. Your credit card may offer free and paid supplementary coverage—worth careful consideration if your clothes are very valuable.

CURRENCY EXCHANGE

Currency conversion fees, whether they are obvious or hidden in a disadvantageous rate, can cost you 2 to 10% of your spending power. Many of us, for expediency's sake, exchange money at airports and hotels. Even if you're just exchanging small amounts, the cost of these transactions can add up to a small fortune. Fortunately, the electronic flow of currency has greatly expanded your options for obtaining foreign money. Not only is the process more convenient, it's now less expensive.

Use Your Bank ATM Card. Cirrus and Plus networks have machines worldwide; call before your departure to see if they are available at your destination, and make sure you have a 4-digit PIN code, since longer codes don't work in all countries. Funds are withdrawn from your account at the bank rate plus 1%. You can't do better, except on the black market. The machines in some countries don't accept bank ATM cards but will issue cash advances on a Visa or MasterCard. If your Visa or MasterCard issuer does not have high cash advance fees, and you are able to pay them back quickly, this can still be cost effective. Make sure you have PIN codes for all your cards before you depart; it can't hurt. American Express cash machines are cost-effective for large withdrawals (which come out of your personal checking account), but cashing personal checks at their offices can be as cost-effective as using an ATM (plus these checks sometimes take weeks to clear).

Be Careful Changing Currency in the United States. It may be cheaper to send the funds by registered mail to a broker in a big city than to rely on your local bank. We use N.Y. Foreign Exchange at 800-346-3924. Many large travel agencies such as American Express and Thomas Cook offer currency conversion as well. While you can purchase foreign currency traveler's checks in the United States, you may be better off buying U.S. dollar checks and exchanging them for foreign currency checks upon arrival. Exchange rates abroad tend to be more competitive.

Don't Use Your Bank for Foreign Drafts. If you need a check drawn in foreign currency for a hotel deposit or similar transaction, you'll find it much cheaper to use a company like Ruesch International (800-424-2923), which charges just a few dollars, than your local bank, which may charge as much as $25. The same is true for cashing checks drawn in foreign funds. While it may take a few weeks to get your funds, you won't pay the steep collection fees of most banks.

Planning Resources

There are a few resources available for gay women and men planning travel. For personalized travel arrangements, a professional travel agent is your best ally. In addition to travel agents, these other sources can provide useful planning information: other guidebooks, visitors' bureaus, community organizations, local publications.

USING A TRAVEL AGENT

A professional travel agent can be your best source of travel advice and assistance. Since travel agents are generally compensated by commissions from travel suppliers, their services are usually free of charge to the consumer. Finding a good travel agent is not easy, as industry pay scales don't usually attract individuals with the kind of computer skills, broad knowledge, and travel experience required for the job. That said, there are many great agents out there, and even a merely competent one can greatly enhance your travel experiences while saving you time and money. There are a few things you can do to improve the level of service you receive from an agent.

1. Be clear about your desire and priorities. If cost is most important, say so.
2. Don't expect your travel agent to know everything. If you've done research, share it with him or her.
3. Agents earn their money on travel they book. Don't pick their brains and then book direct; let them issue tickets you book directly with airlines; and let them book ground arrangements, even if you've made the research calls.
4. Remember him or her when you get back and at holiday time. Your feedback is useful, and your gratitude will be well rewarded.

The International Gay Travel Association (IGTA) is a trade organization promoting gay and lesbian travel. Its membership is primarily travel agents but also includes hotels, airlines, publications, and other travel-related businesses. While an agent's membership in the IGTA is not a guarantee of quality, it does evidence some commitment to the gay market and an involvement in the community of gay travel professionals. The IGTA office can provide you with a list of member travel agencies in your area and lists of member accommodations at many destinations. Call them at 305-292-0217 or 800-448-8550, or fax them at 305-296-6633.

HOTEL RESERVATION SERVICES

Hotel reservation services are usually very familiar with available accommodations at the destinations they serve. They can compare and contrast amenities and locations for you and provide recommendations based on their personal experience and the feedback from previous clients. Most reservations services have preferred relationships with certain hotels. While this may allow them to offer better pricing or amenities at those properties, it also means that they may steer you toward those properties, or away from properties with which they do not have such relationships. We can recommend the following gay-popular services:

South Florida Hotel Network	South Florida 800-538-3616 or 305-538-3616
In Town Reservations	Provincetown 800-677-8696 or 508-487-1883
Provincetown Reservations System	Provincetown 800-648-0364 or 508-487-2021
French Quarter Reservations Service	New Orleans 504-523-1246

OTHER GUIDEBOOKS, MAGAZINES, AND NEWSLETTERS

Two companies, Damron and Ferrari, publish the most widely read gay travel guidebooks. The *Damron Address Book* was the very first gay travel guide and has greatly evolved from its 1964 origins. The book contains comprehensive nightlife listings for over 2,000 cities and towns in the United States, Mexico, the Caribbean, and Canada. The listings are thorough but provide very little subjective information, other than occasional demarcations of supposedly very popular venues. Ferrari's *Places of Interest for Men* is not as good, but their *Places of Interest for Women* benefits from its longer history when compared to *Damron's Women's Traveler.*

Both companies also publish gay accommodations guides. While the information in these books is advertiser provided, they are both helpful resources for travelers with a keen interest in gay-specific accommodations. The full-color photos in the *Damron Accommodations Guide* make it more useful than Ferrari's *InnPlaces.* International travelers have poorer choices. The *Spartacus Guide* is really the only worldwide gay guide, but often worse than no guide at all, since many listings are outdated or misinformed. Its coverage of Germany and northern Europe is its most reliable section. While the *Odysseus Guide* does not cover as much of the world as *Spartacus,* it is a better guide for Greece and Spain. *Gay Europe* (Berkley Publishing Group, New York) by David Andrusia is a fine resource for nightlife and restaurant recommendations. The prose is a bit off-putting, but the selections are well chosen and their descriptions useful.

Many of the gay guidebooks can be ordered from Damron Mail Order (800-462-6654 or 415-255-0404), Lambda Rising (800-621-6969 or 202-462-6969), Catalog X (800-285-8836) or Greenwood-Cooper (800-959-9843).

Three travel periodicals are currently available for gay women and men. *Out & About* is the newsletter that is the original source of much of the information in this guidebook. It is 16 pages long, published 10 times a year, and includes current, nonadvertiser-biased travel advice, including destination information, guest house ratings, news, and tips. Subscribers also receive a free subscription to the *Out & About Calendar,* a quarterly listing of tours, cruises, parties, conferences, and other events of interest to gay travelers. See the inside back cover to order, or reach us by phone (800-929-2268 or 212-645-6922), fax (212-645-6785), e-mail (*outndabout@aol.com*), or mail (8 West 19 Street, #401, New York, NY 10011). *Our World* is a four-color glossy magazine, also published 10 times a year. *Our World* runs travel features about worldwide destinations and a listing of men's and women's tours in each issue. Much of the editorial is advertiser driven or advertiser supplied. Subscriptions are $45 per year; request information by phone (904-441-5367) or mail (1104 N. Nova Rd., #251, Daytona Beach, FL 32117).

The Guide is a monthly publication focused mostly on nightlife and sex clubs in cities around the world. Much of the coverage is geared to New England and the Midwest. Subscriptions are $45 per year; request information by phone (617-266-8557), e-mail (*theguide@guidemag.com*) or mail (P.O. Box 990593, Boston, MA 02199).

VISITORS' BUREAUS

State and city convention and visitors' bureaus are often valuable outlets for local travel information. While they rarely provide gay-specific information, they may be able to direct you to gay community resources. Tourist offices can take up to four weeks to reply to a visitor request, so be sure to leave plenty of time for a response. Phone listings for visitors' bureaus are included in the FYI section of each destination.

GAY COMMUNITY ORGANIZATIONS

Local gay community organizations and hotlines can often answer specific questions that may not be covered by this guide. Numbers are listed in the FYI sections for each destination.

LOCAL GAY PUBLICATIONS

One of the quickest ways to verify the current state of gay nightlife and events in a given city is to compare our listings with those of the local gay newspaper or magazine. Many of these publications will send you a copy in advance of your trip; some are available at A Different Light and Lambda Rising Bookstores in New York, West Hollywood, San Francisco, and Washington, D.C.; and some offer information on the Internet. When in doubt, call clubs directly, particularly to verify special event nights such as "beer busts" and tea dances. Phone numbers for these publications can be found in the FYI section of each destination.

WEB SITES

Visit the *Out & About* web site at http://www.outandabout.com for up-to-the-minute gay travel information and hot links to other gay travel sites.

ESPECIALLY FOR WOMEN

~~~~~~

*I*n many ways, women's travel experiences are very different from those of men. Women traveling together usually don't face the awkward reception or discrimination that men often do, since women have a tradition of traveling with companions in the interest of safety. Sex continues to be a much more significant component in the male travel market, but women's trips evolved from feminist, political and consciousness-raising, and community-building experiences, which are still a significant component of the women's travel marketplace.

There are very few tours, tour operators, and guest houses catering exclusively to the women's market, and those that cater to a mixed market are almost invariably male dominated. In addition, a number of women's tour operators are not lesbian-specific, for they cater to women of all sexual orientations. Most lesbian entrepreneurs cite a lack of sufficient market demand to sustain lesbian-only travel businesses. While many attribute the lack of demand to the lower socioeconomic status of women in general, many factors may contribute: female couples are more likely to have children than male couples; the women's market has fewer advertising media, particularly internationally; and perhaps most important, the women's travel market is not fueled by the same sexual opportunities and sexual marketing that have allowed the men's market to grow.

A number of lesbian-specific and woman-specific tours and events are noted in this section, and throughout this book. In fact, the majority of our listings are not male-, female-, or even gay-specific, but mainstream venues that are particularly friendly, welcoming, or popular with gay women and men. They are restaurants, hotels, and destinations where gay singles and couples can travel comfortably. Whether you favor lesbian-only, women-only, gay-only, or mixed environments, you'll find travel help here, for organized group and independent vacations.

Organized Women's Travel

There are only a handful of women's tour operators, and you'll find them listed in the Organized Travel section (page 332). One company dominates the women's travel market. Olivia Cruises & Resorts grew out of the Olivia Records business, and what began on the simple idea of a "concert at sea" has blossomed into the largest women's travel business. Olivia charters cruise ships and resort villages, and does an excellent job of programming special activities, entertainment, and events.

THE "DINAH"

The women's party scene is dominated by one huge party, oddly enough (or not, if you think about it) built around the Nabisco Dinah Shore Golf Classic in Palm Springs each spring. Although some women come to watch the golf and the LPGA ladies, most come to dance and to lie by the pool. With no political subtext or feminist agenda, the Dinah is a weekend of fun, fun, fun till your momma takes your T-Bird away. The main parties are a joint effort of Club Skirts in San Francisco and Girl Bar in Los Angeles, and while most of the attendees still hail from those two cities, there is a growing attendance from other parts of the country. For more information, call 310-281-1715.

Women's Music Festivals

Every year thousands of women (some of whom have traveled hundreds of miles) camp out, share showers and port-a-potties, stand in line for food that, at best, has been described as "adequate," and then stay up night after night till the wee hours of early morning! Furthermore, they not only do this willingly, but enthusiastically. The attraction? Women's music festivals. Women loyally return to these festivals, where close bonds are formed with others who've made the same pilgrimage. For them, the events take on the flavor of a family reunion, adding to the dogged devotion. The festivals, growing in number and popularity, are entertainment spectacles, educational smorgasbords, craftswomen's showcases, cultural opportunities, and just plain fun.

TOO MUCH OF A GOOD THING

The festivals have grown more and more comprehensive, and it is now common to find workshops on healing, overcoming the "isms," improving lesbian relationships, health and fitness, lesbian politics, parenting, entrepreneurship, spirituality, and older women's issues. Country-western dancing lessons and drumming are frequently offered, and theater experiences can range from distinctly amateur to near-Broadway professional.

Some of the festivals offer too much to choose from, leaving the attendee dizzy with decision-making and gnashing her teeth over missed opportunities. With each event scheduled only once a year, the producers understandably try to provide as great a variety of events as they can so that there is something for everyone. The more eclectic one's tastes, the more difficult it is to narrow down the choices.

LET THE MUSIC PLAY

If one is contemplating attending a women's music festival, there are certain admonitions to heed. "Rustic" is the popular description of the facilities at most festivals, and if one is hypersensitive to heat, careful consideration of the time of year and place of the event is advised. Bare breasts are not a requirement but definitely a widely embraced option available for the duration of the festivals. Everyone is required to share in the workload, and the heat, dust, long lines, and hard ground can be daunting, even for veterans. If that doesn't scare you away, you're in for an almost surreal retreat.

DON'T TREAT ME LIKE A STRANGER JUST BECAUSE WE'VE NEVER MET

Women find that other women who attend the festivals are generally very open, friendly, and happy to be there. This helps create a wonderfully positive atmosphere where lesbians feel liberated, able to live temporarily in a world where everywhere they look there are other lesbians living their lives openly. The festivals create a rarified environment, where one feels free to be who she is without shame, fear, or caution.

There is unanimous agreement among festival goers that attending at least one women's music festival is a "must" for all lesbians. You may find it literally a "once-in-a-lifetime experience," but you might also be hooked like the thousands of women who return and/or travel to other festivals year after year.

EVENT INFORMATION

The Michigan Womyn's Music Festival is the largest women's event, but there many to choose from every summer and fall. For more information and additional listings, see the calendar, or consult the *Women's Traveler* or *Ferrari's Places for Women*.

TRAVELING SINGLE

~~~~~~

ravel brochures are filled with pictures of happy couples enjoying the pleasures of romantic settings and foreign lands. If you're single, it's pretty easy to feel left out. If it makes you feel any better, heterosexual singles are similarly left out. But before you descend into wallowing, there are a number of reasons to be cheerful, and some of them follow in this chapter. Single travelers have more travel options than ever, as tour companies and destinations create programs to cash in on this large market.

Traveling solo has some advantages. Your schedule need not accommodate someone else's needs, and when there's only one seat left on an airplane, you don't have to find an alternate flight. In foreign lands, single travelers are more likely to reap the benefits of interacting with the locals, since it is easier to "shield" yourself when you're traveling as a couple or in a group. But traveling solo has disadvantages as well. The "single supplement" is the greatest of these, the extra charges levied on travelers who aren't sharing the cost of their sleeping accommodations with another traveler. These supplements are a simple matter of economics, not discrimination, particularly now that hotel rooms and cruise-ship cabins are almost exclusively designed for double occupancy.

Although a number of tour companies (gay and straight) try to match single travelers with roommates to provide pricing parity for single travelers, it is a hit-or-miss proposition that often fails—it's hard enough traveling and sharing a room with someone you like, let alone a stranger. Even if the tour company doesn't offer a formal matching program, it's worth letting them know you'd like to share a room—they might be able to accommodate you. The largest gay tour operators base their single rates on shared accommodations, with supplements for single accommodations that can range from 20% to as much as 100% of the share rate.

Economics are just one side of the coin. The other is companionship, which can take many forms. For men in particular, romance (okay . . . sex) is often the goal, and many of the single vacation experiences for men are designed to facilitate such interaction. Travelers looking for congenial companionship also need facilitation, and some solo vacations do a good job of encouraging people to interact with each other. No matter which kind of single traveler you are, or what kind of interaction you're looking for, you'll be disappointed if you expect someone else—the tour operator, guest house manager or other travelers— to make it happen for you. Make the effort to introduce yourself, strike up conversations, say hello to the guy/gal next to you. We can't make it happen for you, either, but we can point you in the right direction.

Looking for Love in all the Wrong Places

If you're looking to get laid, look for maximum density. No, we don't mean "big and stupid," but vacations where you'll meet lots of other like-minded travelers. Consider your options in three varieties: gay-popular destinations, big gay group vacations, and gay events. If you're looking for pleasant company and congenial companionship, look for environments that foster conversation and interaction. Consider your options in three additional varieties as well: gay guest houses, smaller gay group vacations, and gay events. Gay events appear in both places, but travelers looking for companionship should choose events that are activity-based. The gay rodeo, gay softball championships, and gay ski weeks are all good options, as is any event where the participants have a common interest or purpose, or any purpose at all other than just partying.

Gay Vacations/Large Groups

Large gay group vacations can be an ideal option for single travelers since they are specifically designed to provide interaction with a large number of travelers, a vacation setting conducive to interaction, and specific activities to stimulate and facilitate interaction. While those basic elements are pretty consistent across different large group vacations, the subtle differences between those vacations can make a significant difference in your experience. For women, Olivia Cruises is the only company offering regular group departures of 300-plus women. For men, RSVP and Atlantis are the most popular trips, and while there is a lot of overlap in their clientele, their trips are very different. Shy singles may find these large groups intimidating, and sometimes cliques of the young and the restless create an "A-group/B-group" atmosphere that intensifies the effect. Still, for most singles, large groups have the most to offer, including the best share-rate and single supplement programs.

RSVP

RSVP was the first name in gay group vacations, and still the only vacation company offering large gay cruises to the gay market. Their land-based vacation, Club RSVP in Puerto Vallarta, Mexico, has been successful in attracting previous RSVP cruise veterans as well as many new travelers, and a growing percentage of women. (RSVP's recent efforts at marketing to "gay men and lesbians together" have not produced significant numbers of women on cruises.) The cruise vacations offer constant activities, with something for everyone. RSVP does an excellent job of catering to older travelers. Dressing for dinner, floor show entertainment, and the comparatively sedentary pace of life at sea appeal to a more established clientele, who can afford the relatively premium price of an RSVP cruise. RSVP's greatest strengths are organization, entertainment, and genuine concern for each of its guests, and these talents are evident in each type of RSVP vacation. Club RSVP is less expensive, and more inclusive, with an open bar and sports activities included in the price. The beachfront location is beautifully landscaped, with a huge pool, and offers easy access to the nightlife, dining, shopping and activities of Puerto Vallarta and environs. RSVP's smaller boat charters offer a less structured cruise experience, but also less appeal for singles because of the smaller number of guests. RSVP's foray in the women's market is admirable and well intentioned, but we don't foresee it greatly increasing the proportion of women on RSVP trips (still about 5% on cruises; higher at Club RSVP). For singles, the division is probably a good thing. RSVP's Caribbean cruises attract more and younger singles than their European sailings.

Atlantis

Atlantis Events produces a variety of vacation weeks, mostly appealing to a young, active segment of the single male market. Heavily promoted to the circuit party crowd, Atlantis strives to create a high-energy environment in a tranquil vacation setting. Atlantis's first offerings utilized Club Med resorts, offering an unparalleled range of sports activities and some of the most beautiful, secluded beaches in the world. Atlantis has also expanded into cruises, utilizing small vessels like the *Club Med 1* and the *Windsong*, in more exotic destinations like Tahiti and the Mediterranean, which attract a more sophisticated, older and, unfortunately for singles, more coupled clientele. Atlantis has begun using some new resorts, less well known than Club Med, but significantly less expensive, and apparently offering a reasonable facsimile of the Club Med experience. The first such "Club Atlantis" trip was completely sold out, and underway at press time. Active sports and beach lovers will enjoy Atlantis. While there are plenty of older guys and non-jock types on all Atlantis vacations, men who are insecure in the company of bubble-butt beach boys should beware the land-based options. The women who go on Atlantis trips are mostly the kind who like hanging out with the boys. Single women looking for romance should look elsewhere.

Olivia

Olivia Cruises and Tours operates cruise-based and land-based vacations exclusively for women. Their clientele is very diverse, but skews towards politically-correct San Francisco Bay area types, and is less popular with the big city glamour crowd. Of the three companies doing large gay/lesbian groups, Olivia probably does the best job of programming entertainment and events, creating an ideal environment for single women to meet each other. Unfortunately for singles, Olivia's trips are often 80% couples, which can foster too much of that "why are the good ones all married" feeling, but with sold-out trips of 500-600 women, that still leaves over 100 singles to mingle. Consciousness-raising, community-building and friendship-making activities are important parts of an Olivia experience, and they need to hold weight in your decision to go on an Olivia vacation.

Gay Vacations/Small Groups

Small group vacations have a distinct advantage in their ability to provide low-pressure social opportunities. Their distinct disadvantage is in numbers: In a group of 10 to 30 travelers, many or all of whom could be couples, the pickings are slim at best. These vacations are best for those who are more concerned with companionship than romance. If you're content with that, or with the possibility of one-night stands (quasi-commercial or otherwise) in the places your tour visits, small group vacations are a good option for you. Romantic complications are not the only concern for single travelers in small groups. The cost factor is also an issue, as small groups are less likely to offer single share rates, and most likely to have large single supplements. Your enjoyment of a small group vacation is also heavily rooted in your enjoyment of your fellow travelers. Couples know at the very least they can share experiences with each other. Singles can really be on their own if the other tour members are not agreeable.

Different tour operators have different strengths. See the Organized Cruise and Tour chapter at the end of this book for more specific information on the many gay tour operators, and be sure to ask trip organizers who the other participants are likely to be. Some good questions to ask: Are they mostly from one part of the country? Are they mostly singles or couples, older or younger? What do participants tend to do during free time and at night? Do they break into smaller groups, disperse individually or stick together? Consider what kinds of situations would make you uncomfortable, and ask about them.

Gay Events

"Girls just want to have fun" is a truism of the gay-event experience, whether you are a girl of either the genetic or "you go, girl" variety. Events have the largest attendance, the randiest crowds, and the lowest prices. Sex, drugs, and rock and roll can dominate these events, sometimes to the exclusion of any real "quality time" to meet new people and explore new friendships. Women's events, traditionally dominated by the serious political granola lesbians, have begun to include parties that look more like boys' circuit parties. While the women at the Michigan Womyn's Festival are debating the exclusion of "womyn not born womyn," the girls in Palm Springs for The Dinah are debating which party had the hottest go-go girls. The guys' events, some in their second decade, have not evolved much from their original format. The newer events reflect a trend toward more sophisticated production, but even simpler formats: cruise by day, dance by night. Most events are mainly or exclusively skewed to men or women, with the exception of sports events like the gay rodeo or Aspen Gay Ski week, which tend to attract sizable numbers of both communities. Events that have an activity focus provide more quality opportunities for casual interaction, and are better for fostering friendships and romances that last for more than just one night. Events are best for extroverts, who can capitalize on the quantity of participants. Introverts should consider going with a group of friends, and even then, be prepared to make a real effort to meet people. Some events to consider are listed in the Calendar Chapter at the back of this book; you'll find on-going listings in the quarterly *Out & About* Calendar, sent to subscribers and available to all on the *Out & About* web site: http://www.outand-about.com.

Gay-Popular Destinations for Singles

The big gay meccas are generally the best destinations for singles, since they best satisfy the density criteria, and have multiple venues for meeting other singles in various settings. Still, if you keep our criteria in mind, you'll find great singles venues at every destination profiled in this book. Key West (305-294-4603 or 800-535-7797) and Provincetown (800-637-8696) plan special events with particular appeal for singles; call their business guilds for schedule information.

Gay Guest Houses for Singles

Gay guest houses provide an unparalleled environment for gay singles in a strange land. At their best, they offer an ideal location near local nightlife, comfortable common areas to lounge in, and professional management who will help you feel welcome, encourage interaction between guests, and give you the lowdown on the local nightlife. Most of the guest houses we recommend fit this description, and single travelers who stay at these guest houses are rarely found spending an evening alone with room-service dinners and Spectravision. A number of all-male guest houses promote the romantic (okay... sexual) opportunities you'll find on-property. Details on these particularly recommended guest houses for singles are found in their respective destination chapters.

Palm Springs: Cathedral City Boys Club, Desert Palms, Delilah's Enclave, Inndulge, Inn Exile, InnTrigue, The Villa, 550 Warm Sands
Provincetown: Gabriels, The Boatslip, The Ranch
Key West: Oasis, Lighthouse Court, Big Ruby's Guesthouse, Rainbow House
Honolulu: Hotel Honolulu, Mango House
Ogunquit, Ma.: Inn at Two Village Square
Saugatuck, Mich.: Douglas Dunes Resort
Fire Island, N.Y.: Pines Place
Laguna Beach: The Coast Inn
Ft. Lauderdale: Royal Palms, Blue Dolphin
Rehoboth, Del.: Ram's Head Inn, Renegade Motel
Russian River, Cal.: Fifes Resort, Russian River Resort
Los Angeles: San Vicente Inn

SPECIAL CONSIDERATIONS FOR HIV+ TRAVELERS

*E*ven for the seasoned traveler, good preparation is required for a healthy trip. For HIV+ travelers, it is essential. HIV+ travelers have medical and legal considerations to bear in mind. Trip planning should be a collaborative effort between the HIV+ traveler, the health-care provider, and a travel agent, to minimize unnecessary travel risks. A close relationship with a health-care provider and an understanding of potential risks associated with high levels of immunosuppression are important when discussing risks at travel destinations. Travel agents can help ensure safe accommodations if they understand specific travel needs. A careful overview of potential complications will help ensure a safer and more enjoyable travel experience. Since most medical complications experienced by HIV+ persons can be more severe and more difficult to treat, it is important to identify the potential risks and minimize them prior to departure.

Although personal physicians are an important resource, travel clinics offer the most current information on destination-specific health hazards and precautions, and you may locate one through your local health department or university medical center. In addition you or your physician may obtain advice from the Centers for Disease Control and Prevention (CDC) travel hotline 404-332-4555. The majority of preventable medical complications occur among international travelers who visit developing countries. Pre-travel medical advice should be sought at least four to six weeks prior to a trip. Major considerations when obtaining pre-travel medical advice for the HIV+ traveler should include an assessment of underlying health, degree of immunosuppression caused by HIV, necessary medications, travel itinerary, duration of the trip, and the expected access to medical care. Several preventive strategies exist, including a variety of vaccinations, prophylactic antibiotics, and an understanding of how to reduce contact with many infectious agents. In addition, the HIV+ patient should have a full understanding of the potential complications should these preventive strategies fail, so that early diagnosis and treatment can minimize the problems caused by serious infectious agents.

Health Precautions

A variety of vaccinations can prove invaluable for HIV+ travelers and should be administered preferably two to six weeks before travel. Efficacy of these vaccines depends on the status of the immune system of the HIV+ patient; however, the majority of these vaccines have few side effects, and the benefits clearly outweigh the risks. For those who are receiving routine care for HIV infection, the majority of these vaccines are standard (see checklist below). Those that are highly recommended for HIV+ travelers include: (1) pneumococcal vaccine (Pneumovax) to be given every five years; (2) tetanus boosters to be given every five years; and (3) for those without previous exposure, hepatitis A and B vaccine. This series is administered over six months. Influenza vaccine should be given seasonally: October to April if traveling in the northern hemisphere, and April to August if traveling to the southern hemisphere. For those who are traveling to developing countries for more than two weeks, immune globulin should be administered for the prevention of hepatitis A. For those with CD4 counts (T helper cells) greater than (>)200 who are asymptomatic, vaccination for measles, mumps, and rubella (MMR) should be considered if measles antibodies are not present by blood tests. For those spending time in the rural areas of developing countries, vaccination against polio and typhoid should be considered with the inactivated injectable vaccines instead of the live oral ones.

VACCINE CHECKLIST

Vaccine	*Frequency*
pneumococcal	5 years
tetanus/diphtheria (dT)	5 years
influenza	seasonal
hepatitis B	3 injections over 6 months
hepatitis A	2 injections over 6 months
immune globulin	once prior to each trip
measles, mumps, rubella*	once, depending on antibody status
polio	once
typhoid fever	10 years
cholera	not effective but occasionally required

*oral

The World Health Organization eliminated the requirement for cholera vaccine for travelers in 1988; however, some countries will still seek evidence of immunization. Yellow fever vaccines are required for entry by some countries. Yellow fever is a serious viral disease that is transmitted by mosquitoes, primarily in equatorial South America and Africa. For asymptomatic HIV+ persons with CD4 counts >200, yellow fever vaccine is probably safe to administer but should not be given within three weeks of a cholera vaccination. For HIV+ travelers with CD4 less than (<)200, the vaccination should not be given, because of the low but real risk of encephalitis (brain swelling). If possible, immunocompromised travelers should avoid travel to highly affected areas, but if travel is unavoidable, a physician's letter of medical contraindication should be provided to satisfy international health requirements. More important, rigorous mosquito avoidance measures should be utilized to prevent transmission of yellow fever and a number of other serious infections, of which malaria is the most common.

MONTEZUMA'S REVENGE

The most frequent medical complications for all travelers are infections involving the gastrointestinal tract, of which traveler's diarrhea is the best known. Careful planning and avoidance of certain foods and beverages can diminish the risks of this complication. An estimated 16 million people from industrialized nations will travel to developing countries each year, and one-third will develop traveler's diarrhea. Of those affected, approximately one-third will remain in bed, and another 40% will have to curtail their activities. The countries of highest risk are found throughout most of Asia, Africa, the Middle East, and Latin America. Intermediate-risk countries include some Caribbean islands, Japan, China, and most of southern Europe. HIV+ patients, for a variety of reasons, face increased risks of developing symptoms from typical exposures and may have a more severe or protracted course, as well as a decreased response to therapy. Antibiotic prevention with ciprofloxacin is recommended for the HIV+ traveler visiting developing countries. (Some resistance to doxycycline and increased side effects among HIV+ travelers taking sulfa-containing Bactrim make these agents less desirable.) For individuals placed on ciprofloxacin, there may be an increased risk for development of thrush secondary to alterations in native flora. HIV+ patients with CD4 counts <200 may already take Bactrim for PCP prevention. Although recommended for HIV+ people, preventive antibiotic use is dependent upon travel duration, destination, availability of medical services, potential allergies, drug interactions, and the personal preferences of patient and physician.

WATCH WHAT YOU EAT

Since traveler's diarrhea is caused by infectious agents acquired by food and water ingestion, it is prudent to watch your diet as carefully as possible. Tap water and ice from anyplace other than four- and five-star hotels should be strictly avoided, even for brushing teeth. Bottled beverages are preferred, with acidic and carbonated choices offering the greatest safety, but remember they are only as safe as the source from which they are taken. Not all countries have similar standards of disinfection. Milk and milk products (ice cream, cheese, or cream in tea or coffee) must be pasteurized. If questions exist regarding the safety of the drinking sources, it is preferable to heat the liquid to boiling. If heating is not available, iodination or chlorination are the next most effective means of water disinfection, and tablets for these disinfectants may be purchased prior to your trip.

Food can be contaminated by a variety of mechanisms. Leafy vegetables may be contaminated by the soil in which they are grown or during food preparation. In general, foods should be served fresh and hot, preferably in establishments with clean kitchens and bathrooms. It is usually advisable to avoid street vendors and uncooked or undercooked foods. Inquire about restaurants with a reputation for safe food, and when possible, eat in private homes rather than commercial establishments. Swimming in water that is suspected or known to be contaminated by sewage should be avoided, because inadvertent swallowing of water while swimming can lead to infection. For those who develop diarrhea associated with fever, bleeding, and/or severe abdominal pain, medical attention should be sought immediately, since complications may be more rapid and severe among HIV+ travelers.

SERIOUS CONSIDERATIONS

Any trip made by an HIV+ patient who receives intravenous (IV) therapies such as antibiotics, pain medication, parenteral nutrition, or hydration, requires careful and detailed consideration prior to departure. For domestic travelers, there are many home IV therapy companies nationwide that can provide medication, supplies, and nursing support at remote destinations. Physicians offering these services at home can coordinate continuation of services elsewhere. In some cases, it will be important to carry medications and supplies, and a doctor's note detailing the medical need for the supplies is usually necessary. Two-thirds of states have either prescription or paraphernalia laws governing possession of needles or syringes. Disposable ice packs (especially those activated by compression) are useful for medications that require refrigeration but are not practical for extended travel. Consider carrying extra copies of prescriptions for medications with your passport should your baggage become lost or stolen. This may obviate time-consuming frustrations later.

International travel for HIV+ patients receiving IV therapies is problematic. Transportation of narcotics, syringes, or needles can delay and complicate passage through customs. A letter from a physician may help in some countries. Advance contact with the consulate can establish a helpful ally at your destination. Consulates may be able to provide the name of a physician in the foreign country so that precautionary contact can be made prior to leaving. Remember that most international destinations do not accept U.S. insurance coverage, and the HIV+ patient should be prepared to pay for all medical expenses out of pocket. Although international travel poses many barriers for those on a complicated medical regimen, travel is not absolutely prohibited and most physicians will go out of their way to coordinate such activities if they will lead to an improved quality of life.

LOOK BEFORE CROSSING

Additional considerations for HIV+ travelers include discriminatory immigration and travel restrictions. When carrying antiretrovirals such as AZT, DDI, D4T, or DDC, consider carrying them as unobtrusively as possible. Most other medications will not be recognized by customs agents as HIV associated. You should carry a prescription for each medication with you, and those who receive subcutaneous injections as an outpatient need authorization for carrying needles into international destinations.

HELP OVERSEAS

Despite the best preparation, medical problems and emergencies can and do occur during travel, and their risks are undoubtedly magnified in areas where medical attention is less sophisticated or less readily available. Travel insurance, including medical evacuation coverage, is highly recommended for travel in such areas. In addition, American Express and some MasterCard and Visa issuers offer emergency assistance in locating English-speaking doctors or replacing prescriptions. Check for these services and carry their numbers with you (obtain a non-800 number you can call collect from abroad).

MORE INFORMATION

Additional information beyond the scope of this chapter is available from the CDC's hotline (404-332-4555), which operates 24 hours a day. The CDC also publishes "Health Information for the International Traveler" annually, a valuable source of information for compulsive travelers.

Travel Insurance for HIV+ Travelers

Travel insurance covers various kinds of trip cancellations and interruptions, baggage loss, medical emergencies, and death or dismemberment (not the Bobbitt kind) while traveling. You probably have some coverage already, from your existing health insurance, and coverage provided by your credit card issuer when you charge your trip to a credit card. But the major travel insurance component you should attend to is trip cancellation coverage. While there are many variations, trip cancellation insurance reimburses you the nonrefundable payments made for your trip if you have to cancel because of an emergency. (Some policies let you cancel for any reason, but these don't always offer full protection.) Most travel agents sell insurance policies (often more profitable to them than a trip itself!), as do most tour operators. Insurance purchased from or through a tour operator often won't reimburse you if the tour operator goes bankrupt, but most independent policies will. Expect to pay 5 to 7% of your total trip cost for coverage, and be sure to read exclusions carefully, particularly with regard to preexisting conditions. Any statements regarding coverage made to you over the phone should be backed up in writing.

PREEXISTING CONDITIONS

Most policies have a "preexisting condition" provision, which basically means that you are not covered if your loss or expense is the result of an injury or illness present or occurring sixty days prior to and including the effective date of coverage. This is the date your trip begins, except for trip cancellation coverage, which is effective the date you buy the policy.

"Condition present" usually means a condition for which treatment by a licensed physician has been sought or advised or for which symptoms exist that would cause a prudent person to seek diagnosis, care, or treatment. However, a condition is usually covered if it is controlled (not exhibiting symptoms or requiring the adjustment of treatment or medication) throughout the sixty-day period by the taking of medications, and travel restrictions are not advised by a licensed physician. Some policies treat HIV as a preexisting condition, regardless of whether your treatment is controlled as described above, and would not cover cancellation or medical assistance for any related illness. However, in the event of an accident, such as breaking your leg, you could still be covered. It is also important to understand that if you are traveling with a companion, both of you must take out separate policies or a group policy (but *not* a family policy) to be fully covered. If only *you* have a policy, *your* cancellation fees would be covered if *your companion* broke a leg and couldn't travel, but *your companion's* cancellation fees would not.

PREEXISTING CONDITIONS WAIVER

In 1995, Mutual of Omaha began selling a tour and cruise travel insurance policy that waives all preexisting conditions. Travelers qualify for the waiver by purchasing the insurance within 24 hours of the time the initial trip deposit is made and purchasing coverage for the full cost of the trip. The program was available in 44 states at press time. For more information or to enroll, ask your travel agent or call 800-228-9792.

No travel agent, insurance brochure, or newsletter is qualified to define the terms of coverage for you; only the insurer itself, through the certificate of insurance or a dedicated phone service unit, can verify what is and is not covered. By all means buy insurance, but know what is covered before you go. Other insurance providers include Access America (800-284-8300), Worldwide Assistance (800-821-2828), Carefree (800-323-3149) and Travel Guard (800-826-1300); most travel agents offer at least one company's products.

STRAIGHT TRAVEL/GAY CHOICES:
THE GAY CONSUMER'S GUIDE TO MAINSTREAM TRAVEL SUPPLIERS

*I*n 1992, hardly a single major airline, hotel chain, or car-rental firm was actively pursuing gay business or considering its gay customers and employees in creating company policy and marketing programs. In writing about this area of gay travel, *Out & About* has both catalyzed and chronicled the change in mainstream travel providers. Today, many major mainstream travel suppliers address gay travelers, through internal policy, aggressive marketing, and sponsorship of gay organizations and events.

Most of the travel done by gay women and men is not specifically gay-identified: We fly on planes, rent cars, and stay in big hotels undistinguished from the traveling public at large. But our patronage supports companies with widely varying degrees of gay-friendliness.

No mainstream travel supplier has radically changed its product to appeal to gay consumers—just imagine ordering a special "gay meal" on American Airlines: fried green tomatoes for an appetizer, rainbow trout for the entrée, and for dessert, a triangle-shaped Cherry Grove jubilee. But there are four ways a mainstream travel supplier can be more gay-friendly:

Include "Sexual Orientation" in Its Nondiscrimination Policy. Recognizing the rights of its gay employees is a tangible and important step in becoming a gay-friendly company.

Create Parity in Program Benefits between Married Spouses and Gay Couples. For the airline industry, this includes transferability of frequent-flyer awards, membership privileges in private airport lounges, and companion ticket offers. For the car-rental industry, this includes the waiving of additional driver surcharges.

Enter the Gay Marketplace. By placing advertisements in gay media, joining the International Gay Travel Association, and assigning sales representatives to cover the gay market, travel companies demonstrate their recognition of the gay consumer as a valuable client and their willingness to stand up to right-wing criticism.

Sponsor Gay Organizations and Events. From softball teams to the Human Rights Campaign, there are gay- and AIDS-related sponsorship opportunities that parallel the mainstream opportunities sought out by major travel suppliers.

WHAT YOU CAN DO

The pressure exerted on mainstream suppliers from their customers, particularly their elite-level frequent customers, has been the most effective motivating factor for policy change at mainstream suppliers. Your criticism and praise carry a lot of weight in these service-industry businesses. Use customer comment cards and letters to management to express your support of gay-friendly actions and displeasure at homophobic ones. Let the mainstream companies know how their policies, advertising, and programs affect your choice of supplier as a gay traveler. These communications are taken seriously, and one letter can make a difference.

Fly Free, Girlfriend: Rating the Airlines and Frequent-Flyer Programs

Our airline ratings are based primarily on the carriers' frequent-flyer programs, since participation in these programs is so often the determining factor in carrier choice. All frequent-flyer programs are not created equal, and a gay traveler needs to pay very close attention to the specific provisions of each if he or she plans on sharing the benefits of accumulated mileage with his or her SOPWALS (Spouse Or Partner Without Any Legal Status). Most of the airlines have relaxed their award transfer policies since we first rated them in September 1992, but there is still one airline with limited transfer restrictions, and unless you read the program rules very carefully, thousands of miles could go by before you realize you're subject to them.

To further differentiate the airlines, we've rated carriers on their commitment to the gay market and their gay employees. "Commitment" encompasses three major areas: advertising and sponsorship, equal opportunity/discrimination protection, and sensitivity training on HIV issues and the gay market. The final grades are based one-third on award transferability, one-third on commitment, and one-third on the more general frequent-flyer program criteria: ease of earning/redeeming awards, upper-tier benefits, and partner choices.

AMERICAN: Grade A

Transferability.   When first rated, a few of American's bonus awards were legal-spouse limited, but pressure from gay AAdvantage members resulted in a policy change making all awards fully transferable.

Commitment.   Granted, their early HIV sensitivity training was court mandated, but American is the only carrier implementing wide-scale HIV sensitivity training. A corporate communications video was screened for 70,000 employees in advance of the Gay Games telling them that "lesbians and gay men are coming to New York in record numbers. . . . It is critical that they be treated with the respect and dignity they deserve." American is also the official carrier of the San Francisco AIDS Foundation, was the only U.S. carrier to advertise in *Travel Weekly*'s first gay travel supplement, is a member of the IGTA, and is the only carrier with a staff of full-time employees devoted to the gay market. A written policy protects its gay employees from discrimination.

General Benefits.   A solid program with the best general customer service, AA has the smoothest award reservations process.

CONTINENTAL: Grade C

Transferability. All awards are completely transferable, but certificates must be ordered in transferree's name. Elite "spouse upgrade" program has been eliminated.

Commitment. Continental was one of two airlines sponsoring gay travel marts. The airline took a major step in sponsoring the Gay Games, although they backpedaled when describing their sponsorship to pilots and the mainstream press. AIDS is mentioned in flight attendant training. No written policy protects employees from discrimination.

General Benefits. The program and the airline defy mediocrity by being wonderful and awful at the same time. A fantastic array of mileage partners and generous mileage earning are balanced by poor customer service and very limited seat availability for award travel.

DELTA: Grade B–

Transferability. Strangely, Delta added "legal domestic partner" to their restricted list of eligible award transferees. It didn't help flyers who can't get partnership registration, but it did help validate such legislation. Their revamped Skymiles program features fully transferable awards.

Commitment. Delta has steered clear of gay marketing, and while it has had a reputation for homophobia, a written policy protecting its gay employees from discrimination was implemented in February 1994. Some individual base managers have conducted HIV-specific training.

General Benefits. Delta's new program reflects the worldliness of their Pan Am acquisition, with a hint of that ol' southern hospitality in their easy mileage rollover provision. Elite programs are unusually generous.

NORTHWEST: Grade C

Transferability. All awards fully transferable, but new award certificates cannot be transferred by signature without the earning party having to appear at a ticket counter.

Commitment. Northwest is the second airline to join the IGTA and has done some gay-specific test marketing. No special training is in place with regard to HIV and AIDS, but a written policy protects gay employees from discrimination.

General Benefits. KLM is the only major partner, and while they participate more fully in Worldperks than partners in other programs (KLM mileage counts toward upper-tier plateaus), the combined route structures are somewhat limited.

TWA: Grade C-

Transferability. In 1995, TWA finally removed its award transfer restrictions, making its awards fully transferable.

Commitment. No gay-specific marketing, no written nondiscrimination policy, no specific training on HIV or AIDS.

General Benefits. Geared for the international (specifically transatlantic) traveler. A strange collection of partners: Air India, Adam's Mark Hotels, the Flower Club. Free domestic coach awards are not slated to increase from 20,000 miles, and mileage never expires.

UNITED: Grade B

Transferability. All awards are completely transferable.

Commitment. United was the first major U.S. carrier with a written policy protecting its gay employees from discrimination, and the first with a gay employee group, GLUE. Flight attendants' recurring emergency procedures training includes first aid and sensitive care to AIDS patients, and a sales employee has been assigned to the gay market. Also, United was a major sponsor of the 1996 Names Project quilt display in Washington, D.C.

General Benefits. A solid program with the most airline, lodging, car-rental, and cruise partners. Upgrades are tough for non-elite level members.

USAIR: Grade C–

Transferability. While all USAir awards for travel on USAir are transferable, airline partner awards are limited to a companion traveling with the award recipient on an identical itinerary, or spouse, children, parents, stepchildren, stepparents, in-laws, brothers, sisters, grandparents, and grandchildren.

Commitment. No gay-specific marketing, although a proposal was in the works at press time. The company added a written nondiscrimination policy in 1996, but has no specific training on HIV or AIDS.

General Benefits. USAir has a very good range of partners and an upper-tier program that is easily attainable (British Airways miles count toward program plateaus) and very rewarding.

Follow the Lavender-Brick Road: Rating the Car-Rental Companies

Additional Driver fees, the charges that car-rental companies append for more than one driver on a rental vehicle, are a significant revenue source to many car-rental firms and were instituted to compensate for the higher rate of vehicle damage associated with many multiple-driver rentals. The risk is lower in cases where the renters share a business or familial relationship and is customarily waived for legal spouses and fellow employees. This policy ends up discriminating against gay and lesbian couples, who logically present a reduced risk but are still charged the fees in many instances. It's an all-too-familiar scenario for many gay and lesbian travelers, but it's beginning to change. Avis received an *Out & About* Editor's Choice Award in 1994 for being the first car-rental company to waive these fees for same-sex couples. Our ratings of the top car-rental companies have two additional criteria: the companies' commitment to their own gay and lesbian employees, demonstrated by having a nondiscrimination policy, and their commitment to the gay travel market, demonstrated by any gay-specific marketing effort. The results show improvement in some areas—but they also indicate that there isn't a single company that couldn't, to quote Avis's famous motto, "Try harder."

We found no car company doing gay-specific marketing yet, but we do give Avis bonus points for having joined the International Gay Travel Association. Our grading scheme works as follows: Having a policy that either waives fees for same-sex couples or charges everyone (including legal spouses) earns a C rating. Having a written non-discrimination policy or gay-specific marketing raises the grade to B; adding both earns an A. In the absence of a nondiscriminatory additional-driver fee policy, having either of the other two items rates a D. Having none of the three fails.

ALAMO: Grade B

Alamo's additional driver policy is simple and fair: A flat $3 a day at all locations, for all drivers, except where prohibited by law (currently California and Nevada). What's more, the company's application for employment specifically states that they do not discriminate on the basis of sexual orientation, which is particularly relevant for otherwise unprotected workers in its home base of Florida. When asked about targeting the gay and lesbian travel market, Alamo's spokesperson replied, "Not that I know of." Still, with the evenhandedness of both the additional driver and nondiscrimination policies, "Remember the Alamo!" could become a relevant cry to gay and lesbian renters.

AMERICAR/AMERICAN INTERNATIONAL: Grade C

Americar also boasts a meticulously fair policy of $3 a day for all additional drivers. But while the spokesperson for the Florida-based company insisted that "we have all backgrounds, colors, sexual orientations, and religions in our employee mix," their nondiscrimination policy covers "whatever the law dictates"—little consolation for employees in Florida, where Americar is headquartered. As for targeted marketing, the company is admirably blunt: "In our market, price drives everything. That's the only thing that works." Hmm.

AVIS: Grade B–

Avis was the first to waive additional driver fees "if someone is traveling with a life partner or significant other." (The actual policy includes an amusing list of synonymous terms.) The company spokesperson noted with pleasure the "good reaction" this policy change has gotten from gay travelers; he made it clear that the policy was not intended to be "deliberate or specific marketing" to the gay community. He did, however, refer to gays and lesbians as "part of our family" in discussing the broad spectrum of people to whom the company markets without addressing special groups. Nevertheless, the existence of a written nondiscrimination policy for the employee-owned company could not be confirmed.

BUDGET: Grade D–

Budget has a unusual policy. The company waives its fee—an average $8 a day (ouch!)—for "legal spouses only, as defined by states," but "in areas where laws state that sexual orientation must be included (in nondiscrimination) the surcharge is waived." Budget's own nondiscrimination policy does not include sexual orientation, and the company does no targeted marketing either.

DOLLAR: Grade C

Dollar imposes an additional driver fee "in virtually every case," except where a large contract has been negotiated with a single entity such as the federal government. The fee varies depending on location. The company, which has moved from Los Angeles to Tulsa in the last six months, is in the midst of shifting its marketing strategy, too. To date there has been no "narrowcasting," in the words of Dollar's spokesperson, but he added, "It's safe to say if research shows value (in focusing on a group such as gays and lesbians) we'll probably be there." In the meantime, no nondiscrimination policy.

HERTZ: Grade C

The nation's largest car-rental company has a PR operation at its New Jersey base that was consistently courteous, prompt, and thorough in responding to *O&A*'s inquiries. Unfortunately, that's about all it has to recommend it. After harsh criticism in *Out & About,* Hertz spent more than a year defending its gay-discriminatory additional driver fee policy before changing it. Hertz ended the discrepancy not by waiving fees for domestic partners, but by adding them for all additional drivers, including legal spouses. The company states that it does not discriminate based on sexual orientation, but this is not in their written policy, and they do no gay-specific marketing (at least they canned O.J.).

NATIONAL INTERRENT: Grade B

At about the same time Avis made its move on additional driver fees, National Interrent quietly changed its policy to waive fees for couples with proof of domestic partner status from their local governments— admirable in theory, but limited in its practical effect. But the Emerald Aisle has extended itself further since then, now waiving fees for persons with proof of common residence. "The important thing was a strong relationship with the key renter," explained a company spokeswoman. The company has done limited targeted marketing in the gay community. The company has a general policy statement about treating all employees "fairly, in a businesslike manner consistent with the law." Perhaps being based in gay-progressive Minnesota has made National a little complacent on this point.

THRIFTY: Grade C

While primarily a franchise organization, Thrifty does have a policy that marriage will result in no additional driver fee; otherwise, the amount charged varies by location ("It's not a lot," their spokesperson volunteered). Although Thrifty cannot dictate to its franchisees, employees at its corporate national headquarters (Tulsa) are protected by a provision that specifically states that the company does not discriminate on the basis of sexual orientation. "We share that policy with our franchise owners," added the spokesperson, "and hope they would duplicate it." He added that niche marketing is a concept yet to catch on at Thrifty.

One Bed or Two?:
Rating the Hotel Chains

The king-size bed, that vessel of spousal togetherness, is not always a sure bet for gay and lesbian hotel guests who want it. Some couples, upon check-in, are still given the old "Ha ha, look at this, you're booked in a king bed, how silly!" routine. While some of the big hotel chains have changed their policies—in writing and practice—others merely state their good intentions or insist sexual orientation is private and that all guests are treated equally. Whatever. The hotelier's traditional respect of a guest's privacy does little to enhance the stay of a gay or lesbian tourist or businessperson. In fact this tradition, left unaltered, only entrenches outdated notions of the identity and heterosexual orientation of guests. The fact remains that a hotel's ignorance of its gay and lesbian clientele can cut deeply into the sense of comfort so essential to smooth lodging. To guide your lodging choices, we have rated the major hotel chains according to four criteria: equal employment opportunity; award transferability; gay-specific marketing; sensitivity training.

The spectrum of gay-friendliness is quite broad among hotel chains. It ranges from Hyatt's five hotels in the San Francisco area actively pursuing gay clients, to Sandals, the Caribbean chain that bans homosexuals outright. Hyatt and Sonesta, a small company with only a few U.S. locations, are two family-run chains singled out as progressive not only in their everyday handling of guests and employees but also in their less obvious corporate morality. Both are known for philanthropy to the gay and AIDS communities through donations of space and cash. Still, Hyatt has yet to protect its gay and lesbian employees formally from chainwide discrimination.

A new direction was forged at Hilton Hotels after a senior executive made damning statements in 1994 about the prospect of legal same-sex marriages in Hawaii. Under pressure from gay rights groups and individual travelers, Hilton wrote sexual orientation into its Equal Employment Opportunity clause on its standard job application, joined the IGTA, and flipped from bottom to top on the gay-friendly index.

Although most chains insist corporate policies are followed by all their properties, whether franchises or wholly-owned, the reality is that individual hotel locations affect everything, at least somewhat. The hotel industry is just beginning to address the gay marketplace and workforce and will need more specific and direct exposure to gay travelers to realize the changes that have occurred in the airline industry. So applaud Outrigger's membership in the IGTA, and the Hyatt Regency La Jolla's magazine ad with two men in it. And don't let your partner stand at "the gay rack" the next time you check in at a Ritz-Carlton. Step right up to the front desk hand-in-hand, and make sure that the "ladies and gentlemen" behind the desk know that the person sharing your bed ain't no lady—*he's* your lover.

HILTON: Grade B+

Equal Employment Opportunity. After the outcry over statements by a senior executive regarding the court case over same-sex marriages in Hawaii, the chain has worked with proponents of gay rights and changed its equal employment clause to include sexual orientation. The clause is also contained in the employee handbook. The company, with roughly 214 properties, has 70,000 employees. "Things change," says spokesperson Jeanne Datz. "We took this issue very seriously." The executive who made the statements has since been promoted to company president.

Transferability. Hilton's Honors awards are completely transferable.

Gay-specific Marketing. There is no marketing aimed directly at the gay community. Executives have attended gay-sponsored seminars on reaching the gay market.

Sensitivity Training. Hilton's annual half-day training seminar on sexual harassment includes sexual orientation, says Datz. The sessions deal with the sensitivity of gay guests, for instance, checking into a room with one king-size bed, not two beds, or a double-double. Datz urges couples to use the term *king bed* when reserving or checking-in.

HOLIDAY INN: Grade D

Equal Employment Opportunity. The company has a nondiscrimination policy that includes marital status (so that single, or married, people are not discriminated against for those reasons) but does not mention sexual orientation. "It is interpreted to include sexual orientation," says spokesperson Kerri Wightman. Legally, that means little.

Transferability. The frequent-stayer awards are not transferable to anyone.

Gay-specific Marketing. The chain does not target gay media. Individual properties may. IGTA member Holiday Inns are in Tampa, Provincetown, and New York City.

Sensitivity Training. Seminars cover basic guest services but not sexual orientation or HIV/AIDS. "We don't track gay or lesbian guests," explains Wightman. "We would get into more trouble than anything else. That should be none of anyone's business."

HYATT HOTELS: Grade C+

Equal Employment Opportunity. Since the Hyatt Hotels Corporation is a management company, its policies are only recommendations to its individual properties (97 in the United States). Its nondiscrimination policy for hiring does not include sexual orientation, according to spokesperson Linda Eatherton.

Transferability. The company's Gold Passport awards are nontransferable.

Gay-specific Marketing. The chain does no gay-specific marketing. Individual properties, such as the ones in San Francisco, La Jolla, and Chicago have done some direct-mail and gay-friendly marketing. The La Jolla hotel did a brochure depicting men. IGTA member hotels include two in San Francisco, one in L.A., and one in Chicago.

Sensitivity Training. The company's Hyatt University training program strongly advises its properties to learn about diversity and sensitivity to alternative lifestyles, says Eatherton. Further, Hyatt urges its managers to train with Red Cross and United Way programs dealing with HIV/AIDS. "We know that this is being done at the property level," says Eatherton. "It is active and aggressive."

ITT-SHERATON: Grade B

Equal Employment Opportunity. The company's human resources administration guidelines prohibit discrimination based on sexual orientation. However, ITT-Sheraton only owns and manages 59 of 241 ITT-Sheraton properties in the United States. "We can only mandate guidelines to the hotels we own," explains spokesperson Lisa Dickason. "We make recommendations to the others."

Transferability. ITT-Sheraton's Club awards are completely transferable.

Gay-specific Marketing. The chain does no gay or niche marketing. The Sheraton Colony Square in Atlanta hosts the annual Hotlanta festival and the Sheraton New York has hosted large gay and lesbian blocks of rooms and conferences.

Sensitivity training. One of the hotel's suggested training programs covers the Americans with Disabilities Act, which considers HIV/AIDS a disability. Managers are given a role-playing scenario that presents an HIV+ guest.

KIMPTON GROUP: Grade B

Equal Employment Opportunity. The Kimpton Group is based in California and the northwest with 19 properties, including the Triton in San Francisco. The company's hiring policy explicitly forbids discrimination based on sexual orientation.

Transferability. There is no frequent-stayer plan.

Gay-specific Marketing. The chain recently organized a trip for gay travel writers visiting San Francisco. The Triton in San Francisco has put together a gay and lesbian package.

Sensitivity Training. There is no specific sensitivity training. "We have a very savvy staff," says the Kimpton's Sara Ledoux.

MARRIOTT: Grade B

Equal Employment Opportunity. The behemoth of large American hotel chains, with 250 properties domestically, has an affirmative action policy for its employees that includes sexual orientation, according to Marriott's national spokesperson, Geary Campbell. Gay or lesbian candidates are considered part of the workforce the company wants to hire, and once inside, they are afforded legal protection from discrimination based on sexual orientation.

Transferability. Marriott's Honored Guest awards program allows award transfers to anyone the member designates.

Gay-specific Marketing. The chain's advertising targets only mainstream national media.

Sensitivity Training. The company conducts diversity sessions for its employees dealing with alternative lifestyles, sexual orientation, disabilities, and health issues that may exist within the workplace or among the hotels' customers.

OUTRIGGER: Grade A–

Equal Employment Opportunity. This Hawaiian Islands chain, with 29 properties, includes sexual orientation in its equal employment opportunity clause.

Transferability. Outrigger does not have a frequent-stayer plan.

Gay-specific Marketing. The chain has no ads directed at the gay community. It is, however, the only chain surveyed to belong to the IGTA.

Sensitivity Training. Outrigger has ongoing training for its employees combining the Hawaiian culture's traditional welcoming ways with a sense of respect for all people. The process, termed Ke Ano Waa, or the Outrigger Way, applies to relations in the workplace and toward guests. The chain has also conducted AIDS awareness sessions for its workers.

RITZ-CARLTON: Grade C

Equal Employment Opportunity. The company, known for its luxurious accommodations at its 31 properties, does not specify sexual orientation in its equal employment opportunity clause. When asked about it, spokesperson Karon Cullen said that the company does not discriminate and noted the company's motto: "We are ladies and gentlemen serving ladies and gentlemen."

Transferability.   There is no frequent-stayer plan.

Gay-specific Marketing.   There is no advertising aimed at the gay community.

Sensitivity Training.   There is no training dealing directly with the handling of gay guests or HIV/AIDS issues. Cullen said the guests' needs are always paramount but that privacy dictates such issues are not inquired about. "We don't ask about that," she said. "We can't ask that."

Key West, Florida

Key West has always been different from the rest of Florida—or even the rest of the United States. Souvenirs jokingly display the flag of the "Conch Republic," and locals are proud of their defiant, if imaginary, independence. Key West is set at the very end of the Florida Keys, the southernmost point in the United States, just 90 miles north of Cuba. The resort town has long been home to artists, authors, and other eccentrics who migrated there for the quaint, quirky, and very laid-back atmosphere. Quaint and quirky remain the big attraction here, although the affectations of modern tourism have replaced some of the eccentricity with T-shirt shops and big, straight nightclubs. Key West is not primarily a beach resort, for while there are a few big hotels on the beach, the resort's focus is at the other end of town. Duval Street is the main drag, running the length of Old Town and ending at the west end of town, where sunset is a major event every night of the week. The street is a mixed bag of commerce, with great stores and restaurants still nestled among the tourist traps. But walk a few blocks north or south of Duval and you can see (and spend the night in!) some of the charming architectural beauties that embody the seafaring history of the city. Influenced by Bahamian, Cuban, and the Greek Revival style of New England, these structures are a reflection of maritime trade routes, and more than 2,000 of them are on the National Register of Historic Places. More than anything, it is the architecture and foliage of Key West that align it more closely with the Caribbean than with Orlando, and it is this atmosphere that makes Key West such a vacation jewel.

For gay travelers, Key West once reigned as *the* gay vacation mecca, so much so that other resorts are often called "The Key West of the North," or "The Key West of the West" to proclaim their gayness. The development of other gay destinations and vacations has eroded the resort's previous monopoly and eclipsed some of its offerings, particularly nightlife. Key West's reign has also been diminished by the continued influx of daiquiri-guzzling straight tourists who arrive on cruise ships and fill the low-end chain motels on the outskirts of the island.

But all of the elements that earned Key West its reputation are still evident: fine restaurants, a restful, laid-back atmosphere, ample nightlife, and one of the world's largest and most varied collection of gay accommodations.

R&R STILL REIGNS

Despite the "loss" of lower Duval Street to the straight tourist trade, Key West's attractions are plentiful. Days spent poolside or on the beach are truly restful here and lack the attitude of South Beach and the regimen of Provincetown summers. Generations seem to mix more easily in Key West as guest houses attract both young and old. If you avoid the honky-tonk tourist frenzy of lower Duval, you will discover an island of subtle beauty and true tropical charm. Old Town's long, tree-covered streets lined with beautifully restored mansions and decaying conch houses offer a setting quite unlike any of Florida's other tourist centers. Many merchants cater directly to gay patrons, and almost every restaurant welcomes same-sex couples with open arms. The beaches are better elsewhere in Florida, but water sports options abound with many charter boat operations courting the gay community. The nightlife is far behind the trendy offerings three hours north in Miami Beach, but it is friendly and enjoyable. Only rarely does attitude trickle down, and many a romance (both week-long and long-term) has blossomed in Key West's venerable establishments.

GO WITH THE FLOW

In short, Key West offers everything needed for a successful vacation. Don't pack anything dressy (a polo shirt is the most you'll need in the fanciest of restaurants), book yourself into a quaint inn or guest house, rent a bike instead of a moped, and take few expectations except that of relaxation. Chances are you'll quickly settle into the laissez-faire Key West attitude. We know you'll sleep well and eat well; the rest is up to you.

When to Go and How to Get There

You can fly to Key West on commuter aircraft from Miami, Ft. Lauderdale, Tampa, and Naples, via American, USAir, Delta, and Cape Air. The driving route is quite scenic, much of it along ocean causeway. It's about a three-hour trip from Miami, although traffic delays are common on weekends. The drive loses its appeal the second time around, so we recommend driving one way and flying the other. Open-jaw airfares and rental cars without drop-off fees make this easy. It is also possible to arrive in Key West by boat, so long as you're not arriving from Cuba. Contact the Florida Marine Patrol (305-289-2320) for information; advance docking reservations are essential.

As in most of Florida, high season here runs mid-December through mid-April, with school holidays being particularly busy. Summer can be beastly hot and humid and tends to be more popular with Europeans. Spring and fall can be the best times to visit, with good weather and smaller crowds.

Accommodations

Key West has an abundance of charming guest houses, with a large percentage catering to a mixed clientele—either mixed gay/straight, or exclusively gay but mixed men/women. Even the big straight hotels often have a noticeably gay clientele. Many of the guest houses are old structures: high on charm, but not always in the best shape. While there is only one women's guest house, women are welcome at a large number of the listed places. Of these, the Brass Key, Andrew's Inn, The Pier House, and Chelsea House are particularly comfortable for women who want a mixed environment. A number of properties cater exclusively or nearly exclusively to men. While few offer the "very high sexual temperature" environment that is so common in Palm Springs, there is a broader range of environments, appropriate for a broad range of travelers. Lighthouse Court is sexually charged and attracts a young clientele that doesn't mind its spartan furnishings. The Oasis shares the same sexual temperature, but attracts a more sophisticated crowd, including those who choose to play there, but sleep at the Coral Tree, its more deluxe sister property across the street. The Island House tips the scale with a "very high" sexual temperature rating, attracting an older, uninhibited crowd. Whatever your style, you'll find a guest house to match. Because the beach is not the focus here, our ratings reflect a heavy weighting for common areas, pool decks, grounds, and general ambiance. Count on spending a lot of time at the resort, but out of your room. Many properties do not offer in-room phones, and these are specifically noted.

Key Information

FOR LOCATION

We have divided the town into five regions: **Old Town,** the heart of the shopping and entertainment district; **North,** the northern end—removed, quiet, and residential; **Atlantic,** near the Southernmost Point and the Atlantic Ocean; **Gulf,** near the Gulf of Mexico and the sunset; and **Convenient,** close to the heart of Old Town, but north of Elizabeth Street. Nowhere is more than a mile from anywhere else, but the distinction is useful for determining how close to the action you will be.

FOR CLIENTELE

%ST= straight, **EG**= exclusively gay, or **%G**= gay, followed by **%** of **M**en vs. **W**omen. Note that in the partially straight places, this can vary 100% from week to week.

FOR MEALS

CB= continental breakfast; **ECB**= expanded continental breakfast; **FB**= full breakfast; **C**= cocktail hour or hors d'oeuvres of some sort; **WC**= cocktails weekends or only occasionally; **n/a**= not available.

†††††
EXCEPTIONAL

BIG RUBY'S GUESTHOUSE 409 Appelrouth Lane; 305-296-2323 or 800-477-RUBY; $68–200

Newly renovated, Big Ruby's is one of our favorite guest houses in town. Light, airy rooms are nicely decorated and very comfortable. The location just off Duval Street is right in the middle of everything, but the extensive and exotic landscaping helps to create a sense of isolation, even as the throngs march by steps away. A smoothly run operation deserving of its continued high marks. Often booked far in advance.

LOCATION: Old Town **ROOMS:** 17 **NUDE SUNBATHING:** permitted **SEXUAL TEMPERATURE:** moderate **CLIENTELE:** EG/90%M **MEALS:** FB/C

BRASS KEY GUESTHOUSE 412 Frances Street; 305-296-4719 or 800-932-9119; $75–175

Owned by a former Ritz-Carlton employee, and it shows. Extra little touches abound: evening turn-down service, lots of big plush towels, ice tea by the pool—a formula for comfort that works. The pool is small but pretty and the large spa is in a separate area. Located on the edge of Old Town, a six-block walk from the Duval Street masses—a plus for some, a drawback for others.

LOCATION: North **ROOMS:** 15 **NUDE SUNBATHING:** permitted **SEXUAL TEMPERATURE:** moderate **CLIENTELE:** EG/90%M **MEALS:** CB/C

MARQUESA HOTEL 600 Fleming Street; 305-292-1919 or 800-869-4631; $135–275

The finest accommodations in Key West and certainly one of the best small, deluxe hotels in the South. The surroundings are elegant, but the atmosphere is relaxed and the staff highly accommodating. What they lack in refinement they make up for in enthusiasm. The hotel has a loyal gay following, but it is possible you could be the only "family" there. The adjoining Café Marquesa has quickly risen to the top of the local dining scene—a great special-occasion spot.

LOCATION: Old Town **ROOMS:** 27 **NUDE SUNBATHING:** no **SEXUAL TEMPERATURE:** low **CLIENTELE:** 85%ST **MEALS:** none

♈♈♈♈
HIGHLY RECOMMENDED

ALEXANDER'S 1118 Fleming Street; 305-294-9919 or 800-654-9919; $79–214

Charming, high-end guest house on the outskirts of Old Town. Rooms are spotless, nicely decorated, and very comfortable. Pool area is pretty, and some rooms have porches that face the street. A full apartment was recently added, a nice choice for long stays (albeit an expensive one). Definitely a can't-go-wrong-with-this-one choice.

LOCATION: North **ROOMS:** 16 **NUDE SUNBATHING:** permitted **SEXUAL TEMPERATURE:** low **CLIENTELE:** 90%G/mostly men **MEALS:** ECB/WC

CORAL TREE INN 822 Fleming Street; 305-296-2131 or 800-362-7477; $90–175

An attempt at true elegance that only occasionally falls short. Many rooms have balconies and all are impressively furnished. Service is top-notch. Associated with the Oasis across the street. Management was changing at press time.

LOCATION: convenient **ROOMS:** 11 **NUDE SUNBATHING:** yes **SEXUAL TEMPERATURE:** moderate **CLIENTELE:** EG/100%M **MEALS:** ECB/C

LIGHTBOURN INN 907 Truman Street; 305-296-5152 or 800-352-6011, fax 305-294-9490; $98–168

Lovingly restored by its owners, this quirky inn is decorated with treasures and souvenirs from around the world. The pool area is extremely pleasant, and the crowd can be quite eclectic. Rooms have high ceilings and fans, as well as A/C.

LOCATION: convenient **ROOMS:** 10 **NUDE SUNBATHING:** sometimes **SEXUAL TEMPERATURE:** low **CLIENTELE:** 50%ST **MEALS:** FB

OASIS GUESTHOUSE 823 Fleming Street; 305-296-2131 or 800-362-7477; $100–175

A perennially popular choice, the Oasis has extensive sundecks, two pools (one often in use for water volleyball), and a 20-man hot tub.

Rooms are attractively furnished, and service is generally good. Management was changing at press time.

LOCATION: convenient **ROOMS:** 20 **NUDE SUNBATHING:** yes **SEXUAL TEMPERATURE:** high **CLIENTELE:** EG/100%M **MEALS:** ECB/C

PIER HOUSE One Duval Street; 305-296-4600 or 800-327-8340; $175–1,000

The only large hotel with a truly gay following. Staff is very gay-friendly, but the resort is not as involved in the community as it was a few years ago. The resort has a small sandy beach—a rarity on Key West. Ask for a room in the Caribbean Spa Building.

LOCATION: Gulf **ROOMS:** 142 **NUDE SUNBATHING:** no **SEXUAL TEMPERATURE:** low **CLIENTELE:** 85%ST **MEALS:** None

SIMONTON COURT 320 Simonton Street; 305-294-6386 or 800-944-2687; $100–350

This large complex of cottages, inn, and mansion has three pools and trellised brick walkways. Originally built in 1880 as a Cuban cigar factory, the property has been lovingly restored. Cottages have more amenities but less charm.

LOCATION: Old Town **ROOMS:** 23 **NUDE SUNBATHING:** no **SEXUAL TEMPERATURE:** low **CLIENTELE:** 60%ST **MEALS:** CB

✝✝✝

RECOMMENDED

ANDREW'S INN Zero Whalton Lane; 305-294-7730; $98–378

Tucked away on a tiny street, this inn is remarkably intimate and private for its Old Town location. Small, but attractive.

LOCATION: Old Town **ROOMS:** 12 **NUDE SUNBATHING:** permitted **SEXUAL TEMPERATURE:** low **CLIENTELE:** 80%ST **MEALS:** FB/C

AUTHORS OF KEY WEST 725 White Street; 305-294-7381; $65–125

Small, lovely pool area. Some rooms could use renovation, but this is a solid, reasonably priced choice. Each room is named after an author associated with Key West. Has both a loyal gay and straight following.

LOCATION: North **ROOMS:** 17 **NUDE SUNBATHING:** no **SEXUAL TEMPERATURE:** low **CLIENTELE:** 60%ST **MEALS:** CB

COCONUT GROVE 817 Fleming Street; 305-296-5107 or 800-262-6055; $65–200

Comfortable, clean rooms and very friendly, engaging management. Great views from the roof-top decks. Dedicated European following.

LOCATION: convenient **ROOMS:** 22 **NUDE SUNBATHING:** yes **SEXUAL TEMPERATURE:** high **CLIENTELE:** EG/95%M **MEALS:** ECB

CURRY HOUSE 806 Fleming Street; 305-294-6777 or 800-633-7439; $75–135

Attractively furnished and lovingly restored, this nine-room house has a free-form, wood-decked pool. No phones in rooms.

LOCATION: convenient **ROOMS:** 9 **NUDE SUNBATHING:** yes **SEXUAL TEMPERATURE:** high **CLIENTELE:** EG/100%M **MEALS:** FB/C

CYPRESS HOUSE 601 Caroline Street; 305-294-6969 or 800-525-2488; $60–185

Large rooms and a large pool. Needs additional deck space around the pool, and bathrooms could use refurbishing. The facade of this Greek-revival mansion is lovely.

LOCATION: Gulf **ROOMS:** 16 **NUDE SUNBATHING:** yes **SEXUAL TEMPERATURE:** high **CLIENTELE:** EG/100%M **MEALS:** ECB/C

LA TE DA 1125 Duval Street; 305-296-6706 or 800-528-3320; $80–175

Ask to see your room before you commit to it—they run the gamut here. La Te Da is trying hard to be a hot spot again, but there is much room for improvement. Still, the atmosphere has the makings of a fine establishment. Definitely one to watch. On-premise bar has a loyal gay following for happy hour, especially on Friday.

LOCATION: Atlantic **ROOMS:** 16 **NUDE SUNBATHING:** top deck only **SEXUAL TEMPERATURE:** moderate **CLIENTELE:** 50%ST **MEALS:** none

LIGHTHOUSE COURT 902 Whitehead Street; 305-294-9588; $60–225

A very popular place with a loyal and diverse following. Lodging of choice for many of the Miami muscle boys who go slumming in Key West, thus there can be attitude poolside at times. Rooms are clean but many resemble dormlike cubicles. Furniture is strictly utilitarian. There is a café and gym on-premises. A fun place to check out, even if you are not a guest. There has been major ongoing construction around the Lighthouse Court. Inquire when booking.

LOCATION: Old Town   **ROOMS:** 42   **NUDE SUNBATHING:** yes   **SEXUAL TEMPERATURE:** high   **CLIENTELE:** EG/100%M   **MEALS:** none

PILOT HOUSE 414 Simonton Street; 305-294-8719 or 800-648-3780; $75–250

Charm for days. No pool but makes up for it with good location and quaint, romantic décor. All rooms have kitchens.

LOCATION: Old Town   **ROOMS:** 6   **NUDE SUNBATHING:** no   **SEXUAL TEMPERATURE:** low   **CLIENTELE:** 75%ST   **MEALS:** none

PINES KEY WEST 521 United Street; 305-296-7467 or 800-282-PINE; $60–125

Rooms are a little over-the-top, but crowd and management are very friendly. Well-advertised and attracting a big New York contingent.

LOCATION: Atlantic   **ROOMS:** 15   **NUDE SUNBATHING:** permitted   **SEXUAL TEMPERATURE:** high   **CLIENTELE:** EG/90%M   **MEALS:** CB

RAINBOW HOUSE 525 United Street; 305-292-1450 or 800-749-6696; $69–169

Still the only exclusively "womyn's" guest house on the island. Every room is a suite, the pool is attractive, and there is plenty of shaded area for those avoiding the sun.

LOCATION: Atlantic   **ROOMS:** 25   **NUDE SUNBATHING:** permitted   **SEXUAL TEMPERATURE:** moderate   **CLIENTELE:** EG/100%W   **MEALS:** CB

SEA-ISLE RESORT 915 Windsor Street; 305-294-5188 or 800-955-4786; $75–150

Motel-style rooms with low-end furnishings. New management that is intent on constant improvements make this another spot to watch. The pool is large by Key West standards, and there is a small but functional workout room.

LOCATION: convenient   **ROOMS:** 24   **NUDE SUNBATHING:** yes   **SEXUAL TEMPERATURE:** high   **CLIENTELE:** EG/99%M   **MEALS:** CB/WC

SEASCAPE 420 Olivia Street; 305-296-7666 or 800-765-6438; $69–114
Recently restored, this house dates back to 1889. The small garden and Jacuzzi enjoy a quiet atmosphere; furnishings are charming and tasteful. Guest phone by pool.

LOCATION: Old Town   **ROOMS:** 5   **NUDE SUNBATHING:** limited   **SEXUAL TEMPERATURE:** low   **CLIENTELE:** 85%ST   **MEALS:** CB/C

OTHER RECOMMENDED

ATLANTIC SHORES 510 South Street; 305-296-2491 or 800-526-3559; $70–220
A major renovation in 1995 has greatly improved the Shores. It has been freshly painted in bright, deco colors and its rooms have been thoroughly refurbished. It's still a budget operation with a motel-style feel, but now one with style. Additions include a trendy bar that attracts interesting entertainers and a diner that has become a popular breakfast spot. The oceanfront pool area is still host to a popular tea dance on Sunday evenings, and they now show movies on an outdoor screen every Thursday night. This place is trying hard.

LOCATION: Atlantic   **ROOMS:** 71   **NUDE SUNBATHING:** permitted   **SEXUAL TEMPERATURE:** moderate   **CLIENTELE:** 75%G/mostly men   **MEALS:** none

BLUE PARROT INN 916 Elizabeth Street; 305-296-0033 or 800-231-2473; $55–135
A well-kept nineteenth-century Bahamian-style house. Rooms are very small but have charm. Renovated in 1989, and probably due for a refresher soon.

LOCATION: Old Town   **ROOMS:** 10   **NUDE SUNBATHING:** limited   **SEXUAL TEMPERATURE:** moderate   **CLIENTELE:** 50%ST   **MEALS:** CB

CHELSEA HOUSE 707 Truman Street; 305-296-2211 or 800-845-8859; $75–260
Rooms in the 130-year-old house are clean with contemporary furnishings. Clientele is largely straight and European.

LOCATION: Convenient **ROOMS:** 14 **NUDE SUNBATHING:** rarely **SEX-UAL TEMPERATURE:** low **CLIENTELE:** 50%ST **MEALS:** CB

COLOURS KEY WEST 410 Fleming Street; 305-294-6977 or 800-934-5622; $55–185

A 100-year-old house that is well restored. Furnishings are nice, and the atmosphere is very quiet.

LOCATION: Old Town **ROOMS:** 12 **NUDE SUNBATHING:** yes **SEXUAL TEMPERATURE:** low **CLIENTELE:** 90%G/75%M **MEALS:** CB/C

LIME HOUSE INN 219 Elizabeth Street; 305-296-2978 or 800-374-4242; $60–150

Nicely landscaped with a very private feel. Large lovely verandas wrap around this Conch-style mansion. Most rooms have phones.

LOCATION: Gulf **ROOMS:** 11 **NUDE SUNBATHING:** yes **SEXUAL TEMPER-ATURE:** high **CLIENTELE:** EG/100%M **MEALS:** CB/C

WILLIAM HOUSE 1317 Duval Street; 305-294-8233 or 800-848-1317; $85–170

Recently restored in a quirky Deco style. Rooms are large and furnishings quite comfortable. No pool and disappointing sundecks. A must for Deco freaks, but it gets old really fast.

LOCATION: Atlantic **ROOMS:** 10 **NUDE SUNBATHING:** no **SEXUAL TEMPERATURE:** low **CLIENTELE:** 50%ST **MEALS:** ECB

LAST RESORTS

HEARTBREAK HOTEL 716 Duval Street; 305-294-0220; $40–99

Rooms off a hallway that should come with Prozac. Depressing. Well-named. No phones or common area.

LOCATION: Old Town **ROOMS:** 6 **NUDE SUNBATHING:** n/a **SEXUAL TEMPERATURE:** none **CLIENTELE:** n/a **MEALS:** none

ISLAND HOUSE FOR MEN 1129 Fleming Street; 305-294-6284; $65–195

Small, dingy rooms, dirty hallways, even broken glass in places. Ownership was in the process of changing at press time, so maintenance issues may change. Large and cruisy, this place is as close to a bath house as it gets. Prepare for smirks when you tell people you are staying here.

LOCATION: North **ROOMS:** 34 **NUDE SUNBATHING:** encouraged **SEXUAL TEMPERATURE:** very high **CLIENTELE:** EG/100%M **MEALS:** none

NEWTON STREET STATION 1414 Newton Street; 305-294-4288 or 800-294-4288; $50–105

Popular with the leather crowd, rooms are unattractive and a little dingy.

LOCATION: North **ROOMS:** 7 **NUDE SUNBATHING:** encouraged **SEXUAL TEMPERATURE:** very high **CLIENTELE:** EG/100%M **MEALS:** CB

Dining

One of Key West's strongest draws is its wide range of good restaurants. You would expect fresh seafood, but you may be surprised by the abundance of Continental and creative fusion menus. Here are some of our favorites: **Mangia Mangia** (900 Southard Street; 305-294-2469; $12) serves freshly made pasta and features an impressive, award-winning wine list. Ask Elliot to see his list of special bottles. Reasonable prices and romantic outdoor seating make this a real find. Locals lament the fact that their secret is out. Sorry. **Croissants de France** (816 Duval Street; 305-294-2624; $6) offers great crêpes, a fun crowd, and low prices (for Key West). A good choice for the morning after. **Mangoe's** (700 Duval Street; 305-292-4606; $17) is known for pleasant patio dining. Service can be a bit spotty, but the food is consistent and you can watch the crowd parade go by on Duval. Try the omelets at brunch and the pizzas other times. **Kelly's Caribbean Bar & Grill** (303 Whitehead Street; 305-293-8484; $16) is an open-air restaurant and micro-brewery owned by Kelly McGillis of *Top Gun* fame. Located in the original home of Pan American Airways, it's a fun place with a group. **Louie's Back Yard** (700 Waddell Street; 305-294-1061; $27) is a highly acclaimed Key West institution that's worth a visit. It is a bit expensive, and beginning to rest on its laurels a little too much for our taste. Save money—go for lunch instead of dinner. **Café Marquesa** (600 Fleming Street; 305-292-1244; $23) is the place to splurge. Expensive and worth it, serving New American cuisine in a casually elegant atmosphere. Staff is low-key and friendly. **Antonia's** (615 Duval Street; 305-294-6565; $19) is romantic, serving Northern Italian and Continental cuisine. Good special-event spot. Closed at press time because of a fire, we expect it to be open by the time you read this. **Mario City Southern Jungle Watering Hole** (313 Duval Street; 305-293-0039; $20) is a new restaurant with an indoor dining room, umbrella-topped tables outside, and a nice garden bar. Those with a yen for sushi can head to **Origami** (1075 Duval Street; 305-294-0092; $15).

Nightlife

Don't come to Key West expecting world-class nightlife. The options are limited and cannot be compared with Miami or even Fort Lauderdale in terms of size, sophistication, or energy. While the newly rebuilt Copa may generate some excitement, this is decidedly a low-key town—except during Fantasy Fest and Women in Paradise Weeks, scheduled by the Key West Business Guild (see FYI) each fall. At press time, **The Copa** (623 Duval Street; 305-296-8521), Key West's long-standing disco, was still being rebuilt, following a fall 1995 fire that destroyed the original structure. The new club is sure to reign over the local scene when it reopens—probably by the time you read this. **801** (801 Duval Street; 305-294-4737) is a street-front cruise bar. **Bourbon Street** (730 Duval Street; 305-296-1992) is diagonally across the street, currently a happening place catering to a nice mix of ages and tastes. **Saloon I** (Corner Duval Street and Appelrouth Lane; 305-296-8118) is a cruisy bar with a small dance floor and strippers. **Numbers** (1029 Truman Street; 305-296-0333) is a sleazy neighborhood bar with strippers. The **Club International** (900 Simonton Street; 305-296-9230) is called Club I by the locals, and caters to a mixed crowd, but it is very popular with women. **La-Te-Da** (1125 Duval Street; 305-296-6706) had the popular tea dance in its heyday, but is now fairly quiet—it's a nice place for a drink and conversation. For tea dance on Sunday afternoons, head to the **Atlantic Shores Hotel** (510 South Street; 305-296-2491).

Activities

ATHLETIC AND OUTDOOR

Snorkel and **sunset cruises** remain the most popular diversions here. *Floridays* (305-744-8355) is a pristine, gay-friendly 60-foot yacht taking anywhere from 2 to 12 passengers. It is the nicest of the yachts available. Those who are looking for a gay environment (including nude sunbathing) should book the **Clione** (305-296-1433), **Southern Comfort** (305-294-5279) or **Sunshine** (305-296-4608). They don't offer the same level of quality, but they are fun and frisky. **Women on the Water** (305-294-0662) is a lesbian-run sailing and snorkeling tour operator, catering to a mixed clientele. **Mangrove Mistress** (305-294-4213) is a woman-captained 30-foot Tennessee River boat doing snorkel and eco-wilderness charters. For deep-sea fishing, we recommend a half or whole day aboard the **Opportunity** (305-296-4449). For scuba diving, contact **Southpoint Divers** (305-292-9778). The "beach" at Fort Zachary Taylor is increasingly gay to the right end. Head to the **Atlantic Shores Hotel** (510 South Street; 305-296-2491) for pool and ocean swimming, nude sunbathing, and land-based cruising. **Club Body Tech** (1075 Duval Street; 305-292-9683) was formerly the Duval Square Health Club, but is now a branch of one of Miami's gay-popular gyms. It is well equipped.

SIGHTSEEING

The **Conch Tour Train** (305-294-5161) departs from Duval and Front streets every half hour. It is a bit touristy but does provide a broad overview of the town's attractions. The **Old Town Trolley** (305-296-6688) is similar, but a better choice on rainy days. It departs from the Holiday Inn. A new option is the **Duck Seafari** operated by **Duck Tours** (305-296-7252), using an amphibious vehicle to tour the island by land and sea. **Key West Seaplane** (305-294-6978; $159/person) offers day trips to Dry Tortugas, including great views of marine life and shipwrecks, sandy beaches, a tour of the Ft. Jefferson National Monument (a Civil War fort), great beaches, and a two-hour picnic stopover. **Writers' Walk** (305-293-9291) is a one-hour, one-mile guided walking tour of famous literary sites.

It departs from the Heritage House museum on Saturdays, and the Hemingway House on Sundays. **Audubon House and Gardens** (Whitehead Street at Greene; 305-294-2116) was the residence of John James Audubon while he painted the wildlife of the Florida Keys in 1832. The **Ernest Hemingway Home and Museum** (907 Whitehead Street; 305-294-1575) is a palatial Spanish Colonial-style mansion that is still home to 40 cats. Truman's **Little White House** (111 Front Street; 305-294-9991) is now a museum filled with original furniture and artifacts.

SHOPPING

While Key West has its share of tacky souvenir stores and an increasing number of mall chain stores, it also features many arty boutiques and interesting shops. **Leather Masters** (420 Appelrouth Lane; 305-292-5051) sells custom, handmade leather accessories. **Lido** (532 Duval Street; 305-294-5300) sells shorts of all sorts, and the original KWF T-shirts. **Key West Aloe** (524 Front Street; 305-294-5592) stocks natural skin-care products for men and women. **Fast Buck Freddie's** (500 Duval Street; 305-294-2007) is an entertaining Key West institution, an eclectic 5&10. **Island Arts** (1128 Duval Street; 305-292-9909) and the **Guild Hall Gallery** (614 Duval Street; 305-296-6076) are local artists' cooperatives—perfect places to pick up watercolors and other native art in all price ranges. **Towels of Key West** (806 Duval Street; 305-292-1120) sells fine linens and Egyptian cotton robes and towels. They originated the rainbow towel (don't hold it against them). **Whitehead Street Pottery** (1011 Whitehead Street; 305-294-5067) sells porcelain, stoneware, and Raku-fired vessels.

FYI

Southern Exposure (305-294-6303) is the local gay publication, readily available and covering local news and nightlife. The **Key West Business Guild** (305-294-4603 or 800-535-7797) will send you their member directory, provide general information, and tell you of upcoming events, such as Fantasy Fest, Women in Paradise, and the Arts Festival. The **Key West Visitors Bureau** (305-296-3811 or 800-352-5397) provides general tourist information.

Miami (South Beach), Florida

The adage "everything old is new again" certainly applies to the community of South Miami Beach. Once a glittering stretch of luxury hotels and fancy nightclubs and then a seaside ghetto for poor retirees, South Beach has recently undergone a renaissance of grand proportions. Buildings that once sat vacant and crumbling have been purchased and renovated at a dizzying rate. Trendy restaurants and small, funky hotels seem to open weekly. Although there are relatively few gay lodging and dining options, the whole area is so gay-popular that the "mainstream" venues are all gay-friendly, and gay travelers make up a large, if not majority, portion of their business. Although service levels had been a problem, the ever-increasing number of stores, restaurants, and nightlife options meant an increase in quality as well, as businesses operate in an increasingly competitive environment. Most important, the jet set are flocking to the area in droves. Once again, South Beach is earning its reputation as the place to be in south Florida, and as one of the more vibrant seaside communities in the country.

A DIFFERENT KIND OF GAY DESTINATION

While South Beach is still an area in transition, it has all the elements necessary to be classified as a first-rate gay vacation destination. In fact, so attractive are its offerings that South Beach is often mentioned in the same breath as Provincetown, Key West, and Palm Springs. But South Beach is an entirely different kind of gay destination from the more traditional haunts. Where the others are low-key with broad appeal, South Beach is high energy and high fashion. It attracts a fast-lane crowd, including a lot of New Yorkers who commute down each weekend, muscle boys, circuit queens, lipstick lesbians, Madonna wannabees, and everyone in the fashion business. The club scene is cutting edge, and the beach scene looks like the Undergear catalog come to life. Although this can be intimidating to the genetically less fortunate and the steroid free, sophisticated travelers love Miami's unique combination of diverse cultures that collide and fuse together. Overall,

the crowd is certainly mixed, but gays are everywhere and make no effort to hide their sexual identity. It is, all at once, urban like New York
City, laid-back like the Caribbean, and trendy like Los Angeles, with a
European flair thrown in for good measure. All this next to the almost-
white sands and sparkling blue sea that have adorned postcards for
decades.

The center of all the action in South Beach is the Art Deco District.
This square-mile area is made up of 800 buildings between Sixth and
Twenty-third streets and from Ocean Drive west to Lennox Avenue.
(The section of beach most popular with gays is at Twelfth Street.)
While fine examples of the Art Deco style can be found throughout
the district, the majority of the best-preserved buildings line Ocean
Drive. Here, the many brightly colored, newly renovated hotels serve
as a backdrop to a perpetual parade of people. From early in the morning to late, late at night, the sidewalk along Ocean Drive is filled with
a diverse crowd of locals and tourists. From any of the many restaurants and bars that occupy the hotel lobbies, verandas, and sidewalks,
one can watch men in leather cruising up and down the street, young
models on fashion shoots, and a constant stream of tanned bodies
heading toward the beach.

SETTLE IN AND SETTLE BACK

Upon arrival, it is easy for the first-time visitor to become anxious about
the environs. Some visitors worry about the tourist crimes in Miami
proper. Remember that Miami Beach is a separate city from Miami,
and that most crimes have been directed at rental-car drivers near the
airport. While Ocean Drive is certainly a visual feast, some areas only
a block away are seedy and run down. Further, the crowd is so colorful, it can be a bit overwhelming. Parking is very hard to come by in
the area, and if you are checking in to one of the Ocean Drive hotels,
the process of unloading the car can be nerve-racking in the heavy traffic. The best advice is to be patient. After a few hours and several
frozen drinks, you will understand the appeal of South Beach: You can
do everything, you can watch everyone else do everything, or you can
do nothing and still have a good time.

When to Go and How to Get There

The South Beach season runs November through April, although European and Latin American visitors keep coming through the summer months. In addition to the Christmas/New Year's peak travel period, the place is also mobbed for Thanksgiving weekend's White Party at Vizcaya, and the new Winter Party, an AIDS fundraising dance party held on the beach in early March. Summer is definitely off-season, bringing real bargains, high humidity, and slower nightlife.

As an air-transportation hub for Latin America and the Caribbean, Miami is easy to fly into from all over the United States and Europe, but especially from the Northeast. It's about 20 to 30 minutes from the airport to the beach. Taxis and Supershuttles are available. From the airport, a rental car is only recommended if you're going to venture beyond South Beach. Know how to get to the highway before you leave the rental lot, and be sure to read the safety recommendations given with your rental contract. It's often a better plan to rent a car at the beach instead. The very pleasant Fort Lauderdale/Hollywood airport is about an hour from South Beach and offers a lot of additional flight options.

Accommodations

In the early 1990s the accommodations in South Beach were interesting but uneven at best. Fabulous facades were often deceptive fronts for dingy, subpar lodging. Service was erratic, and the truly exceptional hotel was nearly nonexistent. By 1996, style had finally begun to be backed up with substance. Service, while still inconsistent, is much improved, and there really are some great places to stay.

TAP THE DECK, AND THEY'RE ALL GAY HOTELS

Countless lodging choices are available for a gay person in South Beach. Unlike most other areas, one does not have to be overly concerned with choosing an exclusively gay establishment in order to be comfortable and open here. Every hotel seems to welcome gay business and have an openly gay clientele. Further, a significant portion of those trim, pumped young men and women inhabiting the beaches and clubs spend their days or nights working the front desks of the South Beach hostelries. In short, whether you are looking for a small, gay B&B or a large beachfront resort, South Beach has it and, in almost every case, there is no need to feel anxious when requesting one king bed or when holding hands with your partner in the lobby.

LIVING THE HIGH LIFE

DELANO 1685 Collins Street; 305-672-2000 or 800-555-5001, fax 305-532-0099; $130–1,500

Without a doubt, the current hot spot is the Delano, the South Beach outpost of Ian Schrager's group, which brought us the Paramount and the Royalton in New York. The lobby and common areas are stunning but lack warmth and intimacy. The pool area is wonderfully whimsical with lawn furniture set up both around and in the water.

RALEIGH 1775 Collins Street; 305-534-6300 or 800-848-1775, fax 305-538-8140; $139–399

Just north of the Delano, and perhaps a more solid choice, is the Raleigh, a typical 1940s hotel that was lovingly restored and has much of the warmth that the Delano seems to be missing. Most of the rooms are small but well furnished with tropical/Deco furniture and numerous techno gadgets. There are tape, CD, and VCR players in every room, in addition to the standard television. Everything, including the lights, can be controlled with the bedside phone. The staff is friendly and engaging, and the pool area is truly magnificent. A unique outdoor workout area and beach access make this a winning choice. Both the Raleigh and the Delano are on the part of Collins Avenue that is directly on the beach, a few minutes north of the Ocean Drive festivities.

INDIAN CREEK 2727 Indian Creek Drive; 305-531-2727 or 800-491-2772, fax 305-531-5651; $80–190

Indian Creek is serenely nestled between Indian Creek and the Atlantic Ocean at Twenty-eighth street, close enough to the bustling activity but just far enough away to offer quiet solitude. Built in 1936, this 61-room hotel is a real gem, impeccably restored, right down to the original sconces and silverware. The new pool and spacious grounds are an added bonus, reminiscent of a Key West guest house.

THE PELICAN 826 Ocean Drive; 305-673-3373 or 800-7-PELICAN, fax 305-673-3255; $125–280

This hotel is owned by the Diesel Jeans people, and no expense was spared in decorating their 25 rooms, each of which reflects a different theme, such as the Psychedelic, Big Bamboo, Me Tarzan, etc. It is truly incredible (with some French attitude to match), and the perfect place to live out your Carmen Miranda fantasies.

OCEAN FRONT HOTEL 1230–38 Ocean Drive; 305-672-2579, fax 305-672-7665; $125–425

This is a breathtaking hotel, with Mediterranean décor that varies from room to room, including original 1930s English and French furniture. All rooms have VCRs and CD players, some have Jacuzzis and ocean-view balconies. It is in the gay heart of Ocean Drive, directly opposite the gayest part of the beach.

CENTURY BEACH CLUB 140 Ocean Drive; 305-674-8855, fax 305-538-5733; $75–275

Chic, eclectic, and understated, this hotel has a laid-back atmosphere. Room rates include a new-age breakfast buffet, complete with ethereal music. The property is ocean-front, with a garden bordering the sea. Some of the 47 rooms have VCRs and fax machines.

ASTOR 956 Washington Avenue; 305-531-8081 or 800-270-4981, fax 305-531-3193; $115–215

Perhaps our favorite SoBe hotel, the Astor is on the National Register of historic landmarks. Three million dollars were spent renovating the place, which now features marble bathrooms, pool, sunroom bar, glass atrium, custom-made furniture, 25-inch TVs, and voicemail phones.

HOTEL IMPALA 1228 Collins Avenue; 305-673-2021 or 800-646-7252, fax 305-673-5984; $159–369

While not an Art Deco property, this 17-room, 3-suite boutique hotel has style and charm for days. The Impala's architect and designer also helped create Gianni Versace's new villa on Ocean Drive. The rooms have every amenity imaginable, and the service, while intimate and understated, truly is world class. A strong gay management presence ensures that a welcoming environment always prevails.

CASA GRANDE 834 Ocean Drive; 305-672-7003 or 800-688-7678, fax 305-673-3669; $150–1,000
Casa Grande is an understated European-style inn set inconspicuously among the flashy Ocean Drive Deco buildings. The rooms are huge and mostly suites, the décor is beautiful, and the staff is eager to please.

MARLIN 1200 Collins Avenue; 305-673-8770 or 800-688-7678, fax 305-673-0609; $200–325
The Marlin was one of the first deluxe South Beach hotels. While definitely still trendy and inhabited by the model set (Elite has an office here), the tariffs buy more elsewhere.

MORE MODERATE CHOICES

The hotels on Ocean Drive are across the street from the beach, and, like the hotels on the streets behind it, almost all lack swimming pools.

THE CAVALIER 1320 Ocean Drive; 305-534-2135 or 800-688-7678, fax 305-531-5543; $95–350.
THE LESLIE 1244 Ocean Drive; 305-534-2135 or 800-688-7678, fax 305-531-5543; $95–350
Both hotels are excellent moderate choices in this area. Both lobby areas are done in an attractive tropical motif, and the rooms, while small, are bright, clean, and have some artistic flair. The clientele is approximately 50% gay, and the staff is very knowledgeable about gay attractions and events.

THE KENT 1131 Collins Avenue; 305-531-6771 or 800-688-7678, fax 305-531-0720; $65–175
Under the same management as the Cavalier and Leslie, this is a wonderful budget choice right in the heart of the South Beach action. Rooms are clean and well maintained, and, while not exclusively gay, the hotel seems to be predominantly so.

THE COLONY HOTEL 736 Ocean Drive; 305-673-0088 or 800-226-5669, fax 305-532-0762; $99–200

This hotel is one of the most photographed hotels on South Beach and full of beautiful people, many of whom make a living being photographed themselves. The rooms are traditional SoBe retro, and the bar is striking. The lobby is always crowded, making this a fun but hectic choice.

THE PENGUIN HOTEL 1418 Ocean Drive; 305-534-9334 or 800-235-3296, fax 305-672-6240; $63–173

The Penguin is a budget-priced, 44-room Art Deco hotel with a lobby bar.

LILY GUESTHOUSE 835 Collins Avenue; 305-535-9900, fax 305-535-0077; $125–175

With 18 studios and suites in two nicely refurbished buildings, the Lily Guesthouse rooms have kitchenettes, refrigerators, wood floors, and custom room furnishings.

WINTERHAVEN 1400 Ocean Drive; 305-531-5571 or 800-395-2322, 305-538-3337; $55–125

This Art Deco hotel continues to get high marks for its location and rates, and low marks for minimal room decoration and style. Some rooms have been renovated since we last visited, but we haven't seen them yet.

THE KENMORE 1050 Washington Avenue; 305-674-1930, fax 305-534-6591; $49–89
PARK WASHINGTON HOTEL 1020 Washington Avenue; 305-532-1930, fax 305-672-6706; $49–89

These Art Deco hotels share a block-long area with a tropical pool and deck two blocks from the beach, across the street from Twist bar. The Kenmore is the nicer of the two hotels (although the Park Washington was under renovation at press time), with a large 1950s-style lobby. Both properties have mini-refrigerators in the rooms.

EXCLUSIVELY GAY MAY BE THE WAY (OR NOT)

Perhaps because most of the mainstream hotels are so welcoming and accommodating toward gay travelers, it seems that the gay options have not been forced to increase their appeal beyond that of being clean and functional. Unlike Key West, Provincetown, and Palm Springs, South Beach does not feature a large selection of exclusively gay accommodations, and there are none in the deluxe category.

NORMANDY SOUTH non-published address; 305-674-1197, fax 305-532-9771; $70–145

The nicest of the gay offerings is the Normandy South, a traditional guest house in a quiet residential neighborhood somewhat off the beaten path. The décor is slightly quirky and eclectic, but the pool and hot-tub area are beautiful. The entire property is comfortable and definitely smoke-free; clothing is optional. This is probably the best choice for a quiet, restful South Beach vacation, but there have been reports that the staff can be a little rules-oriented.

COLOURS/THE MANTELL GUEST INN 255 West Twenty-fourth; 305-532-9341 or 800-277-4825, fax 305-534-0362; $59–149

A hotel within a condominium complex, Colours is not far from the Normandy and also in a residential area. Rooms are clean, bright, and functional, with typical motel furnishings. There is a large, pretty pool and even a small workout room. The clientele is almost 100% gay and tends to be on the young side. While lacking in charm, this is a solid, consistent operation.

VILLA PARADISO 1415 Collins Avenue; 305-532-0616, fax 305-673-5874; $55–135

The best located of all the so-called gay choices is this small, 17-room hotel in the dead center of the South Beach action. Unfortunately, location is the best thing going for it. The rooms, while large, are somewhat run down. The furniture is 1960s Holiday Inn, and the artwork is laminated photos taped to the wall. Further, the rates seem high compared to what is nearby. The Kent, a few blocks away, is a better choice in the same price range.

BAYLISS 504 Fourteenth; 305-534-0010; $69–95

This small deco hotel is quiet, clean and functional. While lacking in charm, the Bayliss is further inland but still convenient to the gay attractions. The rates are reasonable, and this can lead to many sold-out periods, especially during the winter season. Take note: The sexual temperature seems a little higher here than at similar properties, and the neighborhood a little scarier.

JEFFERSON HOUSE 1018 Jefferson; 305-534-5247, fax 305-534-5247 *51; $60–130

The Jefferson House is a good choice within walking distance of the beach and bars. The staff is friendly and knowledgeable, and the property features a new swim-spa and sundeck.

THE ISLAND HOUSE 715 Eighty-second Street; 305-864-2422 or 800-382-2422, fax 305-865-2220; $49–129

For men only, Island House has eight clean, no-frills rooms and suites on the north side of Miami Beach (the closest gay accommodations to the nude beach at Haulover, about a ten-minute drive from South Beach). Rooms have private baths, remote TVs, phones, and at least a refrigerator. The clothing-optional patio area has a Jacuzzi.

THE EUROPEAN GUEST HOUSE 721 Michigan Avenue; 305-673-6665; $49–89

This is worn, unkempt, and no longer worthy of consideration.

South Florida Hotel Network (800-538-3616, fax 305-538-5858) is a great booking resource for South Beach. Gay owned, the Network represents about 200 hotels and does a great job of matching travelers to appropriate accommodations (it really is the South Beach guru). The agents can find you a room when the city is sold out, there is no charge for their service, rooms can be booked through your travel agent, and the Network also has an inventory of condominium apartments and houses for rent. In addition, **Connection Tours** (305-673-3153 or 800-688-8463) and **ZMAX** (305-532-0111 or 800-538-0776) offer hotel packages for South Beach.

Dining

South Beach's restaurant scene is managing to keep in step with the feverish pace of restoration and renewal that is sweeping the area's hotels and shopping districts—seemingly matching every newly refurbished hotel with another hot new eatery. Almost without exception, these restaurants are struggling to fill the tall order of serving the latest in haute-trend cuisine (any mixture of Pacific Rim/Brazilian/Caribbean food) to the haute-trendy clientele they depend on for continued popularity. Much of this cuisine is the culinary equivalent of runway fashion: flashy and fun, but lacking in substance and utility. At least it won't come back to haunt you like the ill-advised chemise in the back of your closet. The best food in town can be found at **Pacific Time** (915 Lincoln Road; 305-534-5979; $16), serving pan-Pacific cuisine. The **Strand** (671 Washington Avenue; 305-532-2340; $12), **Palace** (1200 Ocean Drive; 305-531-9077; $11) and the always-open **News Café** (800 Ocean Drive; 305-538-6397; $10) are good see-and-be-seen places. **China Grill** (404 Washington Avenue, at Fifth Street; 305-534-2211; $35/family style) is an epicenter of the celebrity dining scene. Like its Manhattan sibling, it serves Pacific Rim Moderne cuisine, and manages to be intimate despite its enormity. **Lucky Cheng's** (1412 Ocean Drive; 305-672-1505; $15) is the South Beach annex of the kitsch Manhattan Cantonese restaurant famous for its Asian drag queen waitstaff. The bar runs along one wall, lighted cleverly with a row of inverted Chinese paper parasols, and is a good perch from which to watch the exuberant nightly drag show, even if you're not dining there. **Nemo Restaurant** (100 Collins Avenue; 305-532-4550; $22) feels like a chic Mediterranean port restaurant, serving an adventurous mix of surf and turf, and Pacific Rim and South American flavors abound. **Caffe Torino** (1437 Washington Avenue; 305-531-5722; $10) recalls Miami Beach's supper-club past, with its solid white décor and roomful of circular tables filled with toasting models, performers, and professional party-goers. Monday night drag shows round out the *Goldfinger* feeling. **Swirl** (1049 Washington Avenue; 305-534-2060; $8) serves a *tapas*-like menu of munchies. It's a popular hangout, very camp, very hip—people sometimes dance in their courtyard. **Yuca** (501 Lincoln Road; 305-532-9822; $20) is a sunny, expansive restaurant that serves a sophisticated and inventive array of Caribbean and South American cuisine, ideal for late afternoon *tapas* and cocktails after a day at the beach, or *meriendas* (in-between meals snacks) served from 3:00 P.M. to 5:00 P.M. The **Colony Bistro** (736 Ocean Drive; 305-673-6776; $20) is also very popular. Off Ocean Drive, try the **Lazy Lizard** (646 Lincoln Road; 305-532-2809; $8) for good, cheap Southwestern cuisine, **Barrio** (1049 Washington Avenue; 305-532-8585; $9) for Mexican, **Lulu's** (1053 Washington Avenue; 532-6147; $8) for the crowd, and **Escopazzo** (1311 Washington Avenue; 305-674-9450; $15) for Northern Italian. **Joe's Stone Crab** (227 Biscayne; 305-673-0365; $15) is a venerable institution, taking no reservations and only open mid-October to mid-April. The stone crab is divine, but the wait can be hell. Equally difficult to get into is the Gloria Estefan–financed **Larios on the Beach** (820 Ocean Drive; 305-532-9577; $9), serving good Cuban food, and **Bang** (1516 Washington Avenue; 305-531-2361; $30) serving Madonna and other fashionable locals. The **Blue Door** restaurant at the Delano Hotel (see Accommodations) has already developed a reputation for excellent food (somewhat of a rarity in South Beach) and a selective reservation policy (unfortunately all too common). Note: Many restaurants in the area automatically add a 15% gratuity to all checks.

Nightlife

South Beach is home to some of the hottest nightclubs in the world. Things swing five nights a week, with crowds of locals and tourists partying like it's 1999. Appropriately, the artist formerly known as Prince had a place here, but it's gone like his old name. The bar scene suffers a bit from the huge emphasis on clubs, dancing, and partying, but you don't need a gay cruise bar to cruise in Miami. The cafés and bars along Ocean Drive create a nearly constant cocktail atmosphere. The **Palace Bar & Grill** (1200 Ocean Drive; 305-531-9077) is right across from the gay beach and the prime spot for a late-afternoon pick-me-up. The **Hollywood Juice Bar** (704 Lincoln Road; 305-538-8988) is the perfect place to pick up an after-workout drink or cruise the constant stream of after-workout boys.

No nightlife scene changes faster than the one in South Beach. Even the weekly bar rags have a hard time keeping up with the constantly opening venues. Those that follow were accurate at press time, which is only slightly more useful than being accurate in 1980. Be sure to check the local nightlife magazines, which may also have changed by the time you arrive. **Café Torino** (see Dining) hosts a drag show on Monday nights. Tuesday and Wednesday are pretty slow. Thursday night is Latin night at **Kremlin** (727 Lincoln Road; 673-3150). **821** (821 Lincoln Road; 305-534-5535) is popular until midnight playing hits from the 1970s. **Arena** (1235 Washington Street) is popular late on Saturday nights, as is **Warsaw** (1450 Collins Avenue; 305-531-4555), which draws a smaller crowd all other nights. Sunday nights the crowd is split between **Amnesia** (136 Collins Avenue; 305-531-5535) from T-time until midnight, **Liquid** (1439 Washington Avenue; 305-532-9154), and **Warsaw** from 10:00 P.M. on. **Twist** (1057 Washington Avenue; 305-538-9478) is the most popular cruise bar, popular before and after the peak dance club hours. The **Loading Zone** (1426A Alton Road, behind Domino's and Subway; 305-531-5623) is a serious Levi's/leather bar. **Orchid** (1475 Collins Avenue) is the women's club. At press time, South Beach was without an after-hours disco. Expect another club to take up the 3:00 A.M. to 10:00 A.M. slack on Friday and Saturday nights. Despite the pervasively sultry and gay-friendly atmosphere, don't continue or consummate dance-floor romance on the beach. It is closed at night, and the police use infrared surveillance equipment to control drug-related and other illegal activity.

Activities

ATHLETIC AND OUTDOOR

If the scene on the sand makes you feel somewhat deflated, you can catch a quick muscle pump at **Body Tech** (1253 Washington Avenue; 305-674-8222), or **Gridiron** (1676 Alton Road; 305-531-4743), attracting a rougher-edged crowd. **The David Barton Gym** (at the Delano Hotel; 305-674-5757) caters to the chic gym-bunny crowd. Though a car tends to be a burden, especially if you're just in for the weekend, you may want to rent a bicycle from **Cycles on the Beach** (713 Fifth Street; 305-673-2055) or a scooter from **Scooters on the Beach** (1131 Fifth Street; 305-531-7777).

SIGHTSEEING

Most gay tourists in Miami confine their exploration to the Art Deco architecture and bikini-clad sights along Ocean Drive. But in case of rain or cold weather, you'll be glad to know there are plenty of historical and cultural activities to enjoy in the area. **Vizcaya** (3251 S. Miami Avenue; 305-250-9133) was the palatial estate of James Deerling, the International Harvester magnate, although it is better known today as the home of Thanksgiving's White Party, a shining star on the gay party circuit. Built in 1916, the mansion is furnished with impressive antiques and artwork, and is set amidst 10 acres of formal gardens. Thirty-four of the 70 rooms are open to the public. The **Bass Museum of Art** (2121 Park Avenue; 305-673-7533) is a diminutive museum with a small but good permanent collection. It is housed in an Art Deco building adorned with carved nautical features. Also notable for its architecture, the **Center for the Fine Arts** (101 W. Flagler Street; 305-375-1700) is part of the Metro-Dade Cultural Center, a huge Spanish-style complex designed by Philip Johnson. The museum emphasizes art of the Americas produced in this century. The **Wolfonsian Foundation Gallery** (1001 Washington Avenue; 305-531-1001) houses a 50,000-piece collection of Art Deco and Art Nouveau decorative and fine arts. The **Historical Museum of South Florida** (101 W. Flagler Street; 305-375-1492) is also part of the complex, chronicling the history of south Florida's settlement. Many *Flipper* episodes were filmed at the **Miami Seaquarium** (4400 Rickenbacker Causeway; 305-361-5705), which now hosts 15 live marine shows daily, featuring dolphins (yes, they still have one named Flipper), performing seals, and a killer whale named Lolita.

SHOPPING

SoBe is home to great clothing and housewares shopping; if you're a shopaholic, you might not have time for the beach. The **Lincoln Road pedestrian mall** was renovated in early 1996 and is *the* place to ply your plastic. If you find yourself short of sufficient beach and disco wear, head straight to **GW** (718 Lincoln Road; 305-534-4763), which bills itself as the place to buy all "gay necessities," such as clothing, cards, and books. **Whittal & Schon** (1319 Washington Avenue; 305-538-2606) has interesting, funky clothing.

FYI

Hot Spots is the established local gay nightlife publication, listing current happenings and special events. It's free and available at most clubs and some shops. *Scoop* and *TWN* can also be useful. *Wire* is a good publication for party ads, and *Pride* has a comprehensive list of things to do. *South Beach Magazine* is the local glossy lifestyle publication. The **South Beach Business Guild** (718 Lincoln Road; 305-534-4763) is the gay chamber of commerce. The **Gay/Lesbian Community Center** (1335 Alton Road; 305-531-3666) operates a drop-in center and can answer some questions by phone. On-line information can be found on the Internet at *http://sobe.com.*

Ft. Lauderdale, Florida

All it took was a simple open-container law enforced in 1986 to knock Ft. Lauderdale off the Spring Break map. Now that the rowdy crowd of collegiate beer guzzlers has sought other shores, Ft. Lauderdale has grown up and is luring more sophisticated, adult visitors with its unique combination of South Florida attractions. Ft. Lauderdale offers a wide range of accommodations, and an even wider array of things to do. The main attractions are straightforward: a broad, long white sand beach; warm, blue ocean water; and easy accessibility from all over, especially the Northeast corridor.

For gay travelers, Ft. Lauderdale is more popular than ever. Long in the shadow of Key West and more recently Miami, Ft. Lauderdale is on the verge of becoming a gay vacation mecca. It is home to a sizable gay population, a gay-friendly local government, a growing number of businesses catering to gay tourists, and a good mix of tourist attractions. Ft. Lauderdale is often thought of as an "alternative" to Miami, Key West, Orlando, and Palm Beach, and it is second to all of those destinations in one way or another: Its nightlife is less exciting than that of Miami, its gay guest houses less beautiful than Key West's, its major attractions are second to those of Orlando, and its shopping and dining are not quite as enticing as those of Palm Beach. But coming in at #2 on all of those criteria makes Ft. Lauderdale the overall winner as a resort destination, and it is the rich variety of a Ft. Lauderdale vacation that makes the city a shining star on the gay travel horizon.

FRIENDLY AND FUN FOR (ALMOST) EVERYONE

For better or worse (probably for better), Ft. Lauderdale is not Miami. If you're looking for the "A-gay" high life—drug-frenzied dancing, celebrity-haunt hotels, and bronzed, muscle-bulging boys—you won't find it here, and you won't be happy staying here and driving back and forth to play in Miami. Ft. Lauderdale is a kinder, gentler, and less intimidating kind of gay destination, more popular with older gays, suburban gays, and midwestern gays. The nightlife has a local, friendly feel and is spread throughout the area. Speaking of spread out, driving is a virtual necessity, and while you'll rarely spend more than 15 minutes getting anywhere, you'll find a strictly limited number of venues within walking distance of your lodging, no matter where you stay.

THE LAY OF THE LAND

Ft. Lauderdale boasts miles of navigable inland waterways that wind through palatial estates, citrus groves, and west to the exotic Everglades. The city began as a fort during the Seminole Wars of the 1830s, and then in 1893 Frank Stranahan opened a trading post and ferry service across the New River. The railroad also arrived in the 1890s and began the tourist trade. Overshadowed by Miami and Palm Beach, Ft. Lauderdale remained a sleepy little town until the 1920s when a developer dug out canals and began offering waterfront real estate. Called the "Venice of America" by some, Ft. Lauderdale offers canal-side dining and water taxi transportation evocative of the Italian tourism capital. The city has renovated its beachfront and also added a river walk along the New River near Las Olas Boulevard. The river walk has helped revitalize the downtown historic area and is anchored by a new theater and museum complex. Here open-air fairs, festivals, and art shows vie for the attention of weekend visitors and locals. Curbside parking and sidewalk dining have transformed Las Olas into a walking street, with some of the best shopping and dining the city has to offer. The city is split by the Intracoastal waterway, and businesses on the beach side of the split refer to their addresses as "Ft. Lauderdale beach." While there is a lot of renovation and rebuilding going on "on the beach," the aquatic limitation on expansion has meant that most new development is west of the Intracoastal.

WHERE THE BOYS (AND GIRLS) ARE

For years, Ft. Lauderdale has offered a broad range of gay nightlife, and it continues to do so, with big club, neighborhood bar, and specialty environments for just about everyone, including popular options for women and older men. But the bars and clubs are just part of the destination's gay appeal. The city is home to ten gay guest houses, including the Royal Palms, one of the best gay resorts in the world. The city doesn't have a gay commercial neighborhood or strip, although many gays live in the residential neighborhoods of Victoria Park and Wilton Manors, and it does have gay-popular restaurants, gay stores, a gay gym, and two gay beach areas: one opposite N.E. Eighteenth Street, where the dunes and oat grass are, and one across the road from Seville Street, in front of the McDonald's (You *do* deserve a break today!). What the city lacks in "gay cultural immersion," it makes up for with a huge range of mainstream attractions and diversions, almost universally gay-friendly.

When to Go and How to Get There

High season is December through April, and you will find the beaches and pool decks filled with sun seekers primarily from the northeast, but including a large contingent of Canadian and European visitors as well. While the summer can be very hot and humid, the late spring and fall are pleasant and offer great deals on hotels and airfare. Ft. Lauderdale's International Airport is very pleasant to travel through and continues to gain new service, most notably Southwest Airlines, which started service in January 1996. As an alternative, Miami International is about 45 minutes south, offering an even larger array of nonstop destinations, particularly to Latin America and the Caribbean. (Miami's airport often feels as if it's *in* Latin America.) Rental cars are plentiful and cheap, and drop-off charges are almost unheard of statewide.

Accommodations

MAINSTREAM HOTELS

The city has a few good mainstream choices, most notably those that follow:

MARRIOTT HARBOUR BEACH 3030 Holiday Drive; 954-525-4000 or 800-222-6543; $119–365

This is the only true beachfront resort, and while it does a lot of convention and meetings business, it offers a true resort experience, with tennis courts, a large pool, and a health club.

HYATT REGENCY PIER 66 2301 S.E. Seventeenth Street Causeway; 954-525-6666 or 800-233-1234; $199-249

The other luxury spot in town, the Hyatt's facilities and location are not equal to the Marriott's, although the Hyatt has spa facilities.

RADISSON BAHIA MAR BEACH RESORT 801 Seabreeze Boulevard; 954-764-2233 or 800-333-3333; $149-179

Just across from the beach and tastefully decorated in "nouvelle Floridian" décor with an open and airy feel, the Radisson has facilities that include a fitness center and tennis courts.

THE RIVERSIDE HOTEL 620 E. Las Olas Boulevard; 954-467-0671 or 800-325-3280; $89-149

Built in 1936, the place is still charming with its terra-cotta and wicker decor and is located amidst the Las Olas shopping, dining and entertainment scene.

GAY-SPECIFIC CHOICES

🌴🌴🌴🌴🌴
EXCEPTIONAL

THE ROYAL PALMS 2901 Terramar Street; 954-564-6444 or 800-237-PALM, fax 954-654-6443; $125-175

With 10 rooms just two blocks from the beach, the Royal Palms rates our highest praise. The rooms and suites are tastefully decorated, with TVs, VCRs, CD players, irons, safes and mini-refrigerators. The service is the epitome of professional and friendly, with a lot of unexpected touches. The pool and gardens form a beautiful tropical oasis: lush, aromatic, romantic, and clothing-optional. A stay here is reason enough to visit Ft. Lauderdale.

CLIENTELE: 99%G/99%M

🌴🌴🌴🌴

HIGHLY RECOMMENDED

KELLY'S GUESTHOUSE 1909 S.W. Second Street; 954-462-6035, fax 954-522-2764; $50–170

Heavily marketed to a German/leather crowd, Kelly's is under brand-new ownership and may start more mainstream gay marketing. The 13 units are spread throughout the private compound, with handsome gardens, fountains, and wood decks. Most have fully equipped kitchens, all have TVs, private phones, and patios. The décor is simple yet sophisticated, VCRs are available on request, as are leather sheets. Two cautions: Maid service is every other day, and Kelly's is located at the edge of a bad and inconvenient neighborhood.

CLIENTELE: EG/100%M

🌴🌴🌴

RECOMMENDED

BAHAMA HOTEL 401 N. Atlantic Boulevard; 954-467-7315 or 800-622-9995, fax 954-467-7319; $49–195

The Bahama Hotel is not a gay hotel but has a more significant gay following (25 to 40%) than any of the other mainstream hotels. Rooms are clean and simply furnished, although some feature special touches, such as canopy beds. All have TVs, phones, safes, and views of the ocean. The large scallop-shaped pool hosts a weekly schedule of water aerobics; other amenities include turn-down service, coin-op laundry, off-street parking, a small spa, bicycles, and **The Deck** restaurant. The property will have completed significant renovations by press time.

CLIENTELE: 65%ST

SAINT SEBASTIAN GUEST SUITES 2835 Terramar Street; 954-568-6161 or 800-425-8105, fax 954-568-6209; $59–99

Calling itself "the other fabulous gay guest house on Ft. Lauderdale Beach," this property strives to emulate the Royal Palms next door, and does so to some extent. The grounds are nicely landscaped, the staff friendly, and the rooms well-provisioned—many include kitchens with matching dishes. Continental breakfast is provided in the morning and complimentary beverages are provided in the afternoon. A wheelchair-accessible room is planned.

CLIENTELE: EG/100%M

LA CASA DEL MAR 3003 Granada Street; 954-467-2037 or 800-739-0009, fax 954-467-7439; $65–140

Just 300 feet from the beach, La Casa del Mar is a Mediterranean-style resort with 10 units. The building courtyard is quite tasteful and elegant, and the pool area is pretty, but not completely private. The rooms are less attractive. All are "themed," but only the "Monet" room is thematically complete. All rooms have TVs, VCRs, telephones, re-frigerators or kitchenettes, and one full and one twin bed. Rates include a full American breakfast and afternoon wine and cheese.

CLIENTELE: 90%G/Mixed MW

THE PALMS ON LAS OLAS 1760 E. Las Olas Boulevard; 954-462-4178 or 800-550-POLO, fax 954-463-8544; $70–145

This resort offers a very central location and tropical gardens, just one mile from the beach and one-half mile from the shops on Las Olas. The rooms do not live up to their claim of "Ft. Lauderdale's Finest Guest Suites," although they are generally clean and attractive. Grounds are spacious and attractively landscaped; rates include con-tinental breakfast.

CLIENTELE: EG/100%M

ⵜⵜ

OTHER RECOMMENDED

ADMIRAL'S COURT 21 Hendricks Isle; 954-462-5072 or 800-248-6669, fax 954-763-8863; $50–145

Under new management, the Admiral's Court offers 37 rooms and an 18-slip dock. Both of the two pools offer crowded decks, and one overlooks the street. Maintenance is below average.

CLIENTELE: 70%G

THE BLUE DOLPHIN 725 N. Birch Road; 954-565-8437 or 800-893-BLUE, fax 954-565-6015; $60–110

Just a short walk from the beach, the Blue Dolphin offers 16 motel-style rooms and suites on two floors surrounding a large pool. All units have TVs, phones, and a refrigerator or kitchenette, and the staff is friendly and dedicated. The pool area is clothing optional and completely enclosed, but not particularly spacious or attractive.

CLIENTELE: EG/100%M

KING HENRY ARMS 543 Breakers Avenue; 954-561-0039 or 800-205-KING; $43–94

Just 300 feet from the ocean, the King Henry Arms offers 12 rooms and suites with TVs, phones, and refrigerators. Furniture is of the eclectic thrift-store variety, and maintenance is below average. A new fence creates privacy from the street.

CLIENTELE: EG/Primarily M

LAST RESORTS

BIG RUBY'S 908 N.E. Fifteenth Avenue; 954-523-7829; $30–135

Rooms are a bit dowdy, but the small pool courtyard is lushly landscaped. Rates include extended continental breakfast and a happy hour. All rooms have TVs, refrigerators, and microwave ovens, but only half have phones. We've heard mixed reports about management.

CLIENTELE: EG/100%M

MIDNIGHT SEA 3005 Alhambra Street; 954-463-4827; $49–129

They tore down the original Midnight Sea and moved across the street. They still need to start all over again.

CLIENTELE: EG/Mostly M

Dining

Ft. Lauderdale's dining options are numerous and varied, including more than its share of high-quality, high-value restaurants. **Mark's Las**

Olas (1032 E. Las Olas Boulevard; 954-463-1000; $23) is one of the hottest spots in the city, sporting the kind of creative cuisine and décor one would expect in trendy Miami. Book well in advance for weekend nights. **Mangos** (904 E. Las Olas Boulevard; 954-523-5001; $12) is also on Las Olas, offering al fresco dining, seafood, steaks, and live dance music (attracting a mixed gay/straight dance crowd). Another trendy, popular spot on Las Olas is **Mario's** (1313 E. Las Olas Boulevard; 954-523-4990; $18) with an Italian menu and live jazz. A more casual, relaxed atmosphere can be found at the small, but brightly painted **Victoria Park Restaurant** (900 N.E. Twentieth Avenue; 954-764-6868; $16), which features a French Caribbean–folk menu and is very gay-popular. Their specialty is pork loin Jamaica-style. **The Down Under** (3000 E. Oakland Park Boulevard; 954-563-4123; $20) offers traditional Continental dining with an exceptional wine list, and waterfront setting, but catering to a mostly older, straight couple crowd. The waterfront **California Café** (Pier 66, Seventeenth Street Causeway; 954-728-3500; $23) is a more hip alternative, serving an eclectic, multicultural menu, featuring hardwood-grilled entrées, great seafood, and excellent service. **Primavera** (830 E. Oakland Park Boulevard; 954-564-6363; $20) is stuck in a strip mall, but don't let its location fool you. The décor is handsome, and the food is the city's best authentic Italian. **Café Seville** (2768 E. Oakland Park Boulevard; 954-656-1148; $14) offers a genuine Andalusian menu and atmosphere behind its shopping center exterior. **Rainbow Palace** (2787 E. Oakland Park Boulevard; 954-565-5652; $17) is another strip-mall denizen, whose interior reveals a pleasant surprise—elegant Chinese food. For Northern Italian in a formal Italian atmosphere, head to **Il Tartufo** (2400 E. Las Olas Boulevard; 954-767-9190; $20). **San Angel** (2822 E. Commercial Boulevard; 954-772-4731; $18) offers genuine nouvelle Mexican cuisine, featuring delicate, regional taste sensations in lieu of the usual Tex-Mex fare. Late-night breakfast at **Lester's Diner** (250 State Road 84; 954-525-5641; $5) includes waitresses with beehive hairdos and assorted late-night crazies, all at no extra charge! **The Deck** (401 N. Atlantic Boulevard; 954-467-7315; $9) at the Bahama Hotel offers the best breakfast on the beach, and will have completed the indoor expansion of its restaurant by the time you read this. The city has three exclusively gay restaurants, none truly outstanding: **Tropics** (2000 Wilton Drive; 954-537-6000; $12) is by far the best of the three, serving moderately priced, decent American food, with a very pleasant atmosphere and popular piano bar. The food is more erratic at **Legends** (1560 Wilton Drive; 954-467-2233; $12), sometimes good, sometimes awful. **Chardee's** (2209 Wilton Drive; 954-563-1800; $12) is popular with an older crowd, but more for its happy hour than its food. If you eat there, stick with the prime rib—it's palatable.

Nightlife

Ft. Lauderdale has a full spectrum of nightlife options, with over 40 gay bars and clubs in the area. Nightlife here is on the early side, with some popular afternoon tea dances and most clubs shutting down at 2:00 A.M. **The Copa** (Federal Highway and S.E. Twenty-eighth Street; 954-463-1507) is the long-reigning dance club, very popular on Friday and Saturday nights, and one of the few after-hours clubs. It runs special events weekly—check the gay nightlife guides for a current schedule. The **Stud** (1000 W. State Road 84; 954-525-7883) is its main competition, busiest Saturday and Sunday. **Club Cathode Ray** (1105 E. Las Olas Boulevard; 954-462-8611) is the popular yuppie hangout, busy most nights, packed on weekends, especially Sunday tea dance, and busiest for Monday-night beer bust. The **Club Caribbean** (2851 N. Federal Highway; 954-565-0402) is also popular on Sunday afternoons, attracting a sleazy crowd. The **825** (825 E. Sunrise Boulevard; 954-524-3333) also has a reputation for sleaze, this one earned for strippers and hustlers. The **End-Up** (3521 W. Broward Boulevard; 954-584-9301) is open late and is a favorite haunt for off-duty bartenders from other bars. **Chardees** (2209 Wilton Drive; 954-563-1800) is one of the most popular bars in town, catering to older (sixties to eighties) men and their admirers. The place is jam-packed for Friday happy hour. **I-Beam** (3045 N. Federal Highway; 954-561-2424) is also popular for happy hour, catering to a broad range of men—twenties to seventies, with three bars, videos, and music playing low enough to talk. Tuesday nights are busy for karaoke. The **Gold Coast Bar & Grill** (2471 E. Commercial Boulevard; 954-492-9222) is also a popular happy-hour spot. **The Eagle** (1951 Powerline Road; 954-462-6380) caters to the usual Eagle leather crowd but is not as popular as the **Ramrod** (1508 N.E. Fourth Avenue; 954-763-8219), the most popular leather/Levi's bar. Their Thursday night "battle of the bulge" contest is heavily attended. **The Otherside** (2283 Wilton Drive; 954-565-5538) and **Electra** (1600 S.E. Fifteenth Avenue; 954-764-8447) are the most popular spots for women, although the Copa attracts a good number of women to their dance floor.

Activities

ATHLETIC AND OUTDOOR

Naturally the Atlantic Ocean and beach are the main attractions in Ft. Lauderdale. One gay beach section runs between Castillo and Valencia streets and the other is at the dunes opposite N.E. Eighteenth Street. The city maintains several parking lots just west of State Road A1A. While the beach is a busy place during the day, don't forget to take a quiet, romantic stroll along it at either sunrise or sunset. Thrill seekers, on the other hand, can enjoy parasailing, jet skiing, and other water sports at **Bill's Sunrise Boat Rental** (301 Seabreeze Boulevard, just off Las Olas near the oceanfront; 954-467-1316; and 2025 E. Sunrise Boulevard; 954-462-8962) or one can scuba or snorkel one of three reefs that lie just offshore. For those seeking a uniquely Floridian activity, go west from Ft. Lauderdale to **Everglades Holiday Park** (Griffin Road and U.S. 27; 954-434-8111) and take an airboat tour of the Everglades and catch the alligator show and wildlife exhibits. Other interesting wildlife experiences can be found at **Butterfly World** (3600 W. Sample Road; 954-977-4400), where you can walk among thousands of live butterflies, and **Flamingo Gardens** (3750 Flamingo Road, Davie; 954-473-2955), with its 60 acres of gardens and half acre "free-flight" aviary. Ft. Lauderdale has a number of gay-friendly gyms, but all are predominantly straight. They include the **Zoo** (3001 S.E. Fifth Street; 954-525-7010; $10/day; $25/week), **World Gym** (1440 N. Federal Highway; 954-566-4750; $8/day; $30 week), **Bally's Scandinavian** (750 W. Sunrise Boulevard; 954-764-8666; Bally's members only) and the **Downtown Gym** (713 E. Broward Boulevard; 954-462-7669; $8/day; $22/week). The **Club Ft. Lauderdale** (400 W. Broward Boulevard; 954-525-3344; $6/day) is primarily a bathhouse, but has many gym members who use the limited but well-maintained gym equipment, swimming pool, and sundecks. The

Art Deco–style beach promenade is popular for running and Roller-blading. **Ft. Lauderdale Frontrunners** (954-566-8413): Call for information on organized gay running groups and events.

SIGHTSEEING

The new **Museum of Science and Discovery** (231 S.W. Second Avenue; 954-462-4115) offers hands-on science exhibits and an IMAX theater. The **Broward Center for the Performing Arts** (201 S.W. Fifth Avenue; 954-462-0222) is a modern architectural triumph, including a 2,500-seat theater with exceptional acoustics and drawing top-name entertainment. It, along with the **Parker Playhouse** (707 N.E. Eighth Street; 954-764-0700), regularly hosts nationally touring productions. The **Stranahan House** (335 S.E. Sixth Avenue; 954-524-4736) on the banks of the New River offers a restored glimpse of the 1890s home of the city's founder. The **Museum of Art** (Andrews Avenue and E. Las Olas Boulevard; 954-763-6464) has an interesting permanent collection and a good mix of traveling shows. The **Graves Museum of Archaeology and Natural History** (481 S. Federal Highway, Dania; 954-925-7770) covers a broad spectrum of ancient cultures and artifacts, from Columbia to Egypt to prehistoric Florida. And if you haven't seen enough men in bikinis on the beach, head for the **International Swimming Hall of Fame** (1 Hall of Fame Drive; 954-462-6536) where two swimming pools are home to youthful Olympic hopefuls and the Speedos of Greg Louganis and Mark Spitz are on display. Many of Ft. Lauderdale's attractions are accessible by water—hire a **Water Taxi** (954-565-5507 or 954-467-6677), call it a *vaporetto,* and enjoy the *dolce vita* afloat.

SHOPPING

The small specialty shops and stores along Las Olas Boulevard in downtown Ft. Lauderdale are coming back to life after several sleepy years. Art galleries, antique shops, and clothing stores, along with restaurants, have grown in number over the past couple of seasons. Gay-themed businesses flourish. **Audace** (813 E. Las Olas Boulevard; 954-522-7503) features an extensive collection of designer men's swim and underwear from around the world. **J. Miles Clothing** (954-462-2710), a favorite shop for sportswear, clubwear, gift items, and unusual novelty T-shirts, was relocating at press time. **Grand Central Sta-**

tionery (1227 E. Las Olas Boulevard; 954-467-2998) has cards and gifts, and **Outbooks** (1239 E. Las Olas Boulevard; 954-764-4333) stocks gay and lesbian books and gifts. For Italian designer clothes at discount prices, try **Vogue Italia** (Men: 1018 E. Las Olas Boulevard; 954-763-5255; Women: 831 E. Las Olas Boulevard; 954-462-7143). **Under Wraps** (823 E. Las Olas Boulevard; 954-522-2227) sells vintage 1920s to 1940s women's clothing, including some made out of chenille bedspreads. You'll find unique, artful gifts and housewares at **Elements** (1034 E. Las Olas Boulevard; 954-525-5754). The best selection of swimwear is located at **Trader Tom's** (912 N. Federal Highway; 954-763-4630) where a wall of 5,000 men's bikinis and several thousand more on racks await. For those shoppers into excess, the world's largest outlet mall—2.2 million square feet, over 200 stores— is **Sawgrass Mills** (Sunrise Boulevard and Flamingo Road; 954-846-2350). In addition to some large discount anchor stores (**Marshalls, T.J. Maxx**, et al.) and the usual slew of shoe stores, you'll find **Donna Karan, Fendi, Fossil**, and **Neiman Marcus** outlets, and **Off Fifth**, the Saks Fifth Avenue clearance store. In addition, the **Galleria Mall** (2414 E. Sunrise Boulevard; 954-564-1015) offers shoppers the standard retail shopping experiences, anchored by **Neiman Marcus, Dillards, Saks Fifth Avenue, Lord & Taylor**, and **Burdines**. For leather and toys, try **Fallen Angel** (3045 N. Federal Highway; 954-563-5230). **Catalog X** (850 N. E. Thirteenth Street; 954-524-5050) calls Ft. Lauderdale home, with a retail outpost of their large gay catalog business.

FYI

Gay weekly magazines like *Hotspots* (also on the Internet at *http://covebbs.com*) and *The Scoop* are freely available at gay clubs, restaurants, and retail establishments, with complete club event information. The **Broward Gay & Lesbian Community Center Hotline** (954-563-9500) will answer questions and provide referrals. General tourist information and brochures are available from the **Greater Ft. Lauderdale Convention & Visitors Bureau** (200 E. Las Olas Boulevard, Suite 1500; 954-765-4466 or 800-356-1662). You can get *free travel directions and tourist assistance* in the greater Ft. Lauderdale area by calling 954-527-5600 or #333 from a cellular phone (305-557-5600 or #444 in greater Miami).

Orlando, Florida

Are you going to see the Mouse or not? Orlando is Disney and all the family vacation hoopla that surrounds it. Which isn't to say that you will feel out of place without kids, but that if you're going to Disney, you must be prepared for the middle-American masses who will be there with you. *Rule 1:* Money spent to increase privacy and decrease transportation time is well spent. *Rule 2:* Avoid school vacations. *Rule 3:* Don't come without a sense of humor. Orlando's gay scene is busy and active, with a good mix of locals and tourists. The annual unofficial "gay day" at Walt Disney World (the first Saturday in June), which is sponsored by local gay and lesbian organizations, has expanded into a four-day weekend event, but it has not changed the nature of gay Orlando the other 361 days of the year. Unless you're coming for Orlando's big gay weekend, plan your trip around the theme park activities, and season it with gay nightlife.

When to Go and How to Get There

Orlando is busy year round, and even the heat and humidity of summer can't keep the crowds away. During school vacations, it is impossibly busy. Some of the best times are the weeks before and after the weeks that include major holidays. Orlando's International Airport is one of Florida's busiest, but discount fares can still be elusive. Be sure to check out air-inclusive packages, especially for the on-site properties. Some of the biggest tour operators are **Certified Vacations** (800-233-7260 or 954-522-1440), which sells vacations under their own name, as well as under the American Express, Delta Dream Vacations, and Men on Vacations names, and the **Walt Disney Travel Company** (800-327-2996 or 407-828-3232). Travel agents are a good source of help with Disney bookings, and special rates and services are available for Disney stockholders, AAA members, and American Express Cardmembers. Orlando is an easy drive from most resort areas on the east and west coasts of the state, and if you're combining a stay in Orlando with a stay on the coast, it's easy and cost-effective to fly into one city and out of another, taking advantage of free car-rental drop-off throughout the state.

Accommodations

It's well-known that a large percentage of the people employed in the hotel industry in Orlando are gay, making most of the resort hotels gay-friendly, at least from a staff perspective. "Gaydar" can usually pick out concierges, front-desk clerks, and guest-services employees who should be able to make your stay more comfortable. Doing the Disney thing can be greatly facilitated by staying on-site at one of the **Disney Resorts** (800-647-7900 or 407-934-7639 for the properties' central reservations). Each resort is "themed" to ensure continuity with the Magic Kingdom's various "worlds."

THE YACHT AND BEACH CLUBS near EPCOT; 407-934-8000 for Beach Club; 407-934-7000 for Yacht Club; $240–250

Twin hotels adjacent to each other near EPCOT center, each designed according to its respective motif. Sharing a 25-acre lake and a host of recreational and health facilities, these two properties are our choice for tasteful surroundings and full amenities.

THE CONTEMPORARY near the Magic Kingdom; 407-824-1000; $215–245

Its dramatic calling card is the monorail that snakes right through its 90-foot atrium lobby, as well as two Olympic-size swimming pools and three restaurants.

DIXIE LANDINGS near EPCOT; 407-934-6000; $129

Our pick for the best value. The plantation-theme resort is divided into a "Mansion" or the cabinlike "Bayou" buildings. There are a few pools on-site, along with a handy bike-rental center.

The much-talked-about **Swan** and **Dolphin** hotels, designed by Michael Graves, made us queasy from the mélange of colors and patterns, and the **Grand Floridian** is best suited to those who have an irrepressible antebellum itch. All hotels off-site should be considered a cost-saving measure, with the exception of the first three listed:

THE PEABODY ORLANDO 9801 International Drive; 407-352-4000 or 800-732-2639; fax 407-351-0073; $230–290

The sister hotel to the Memphis original, this one has the familiar ducks paddling around in the lobby fountain and the elegant Dux restaurant.

HYATT GRAND CYPRESS RESORT 1 Grand Cypress Boulevard; Lake Buena Vista; 407-239-1234 or 800-233-1234; $185–240

An impressive luxury hotel on 1,500 acres, with 146 private villas overlooking a Jack Nicklaus–designed golf course, a mammoth free-form pool, and a world-class health club.

ORLANDO MARRIOTT WORLD CENTER World Center Drive; 407-239-4200 or 800-621-0638; fax 407-238-8991; $134–164

Also features a complete health club, tennis courts, and four pools.

MARRIOTT RESIDENCE INN 7975 Canada Avenue; 407-345-0117 or 800-227-3978; fax 407-352-2689; $74–144.

An all-suite property convenient to the attractions.

Remember, anywhere you stay will be primarily straight, with two exceptions:

PARLIAMENT HOUSE MOTOR INN 410 N. Orange Blossom Trail; 407-425-7571; $44

Both reviled and beloved, the Parliament is a no-frills, threadbare motel that hops around the clock, thanks to its five bars (see Nightlife), a coffee shop, a lake, and poolside recreation areas that host an all-day happy hour. Overnighters shouldn't plan on getting much sleep at this integral part of Orlando's gay scene.

A VERANDA B&B, 115 N. Summerlin Avenue; 407-849-0321 or 800-420-6822; fax 407-872-7512; $89–169

This gay-friendly B&B is made up of five historic cottages surrounding a tropical courtyard, located in downtown Orlando. Each cottage has its own private entrance, private bath, cable TV, and phone with answering machine.

Dining

Unsurprisingly, Orlando is not a dining capital. Almost all of the best restaurants are in hotels, but there are a couple of gay-popular eateries in other areas outside the resort complex. Inside Disney World, EPCOT has the best variety of restaurants. **Coral Reef** in the Living Seas Pavilion isn't bad for seafood, and in the World Showcase, there's a restaurant for every country presented. **Les Chefs de France** comes the most highly recommended, and the atmosphere at the **Marrakesh** restaurant is complete with belly dancers and live music. **Hemingway's** (at the Hyatt Grand Cypress; 407-239-1234; $25) is the best restaurant in town, serving continental and upscale American cuisine in a dramatic, cliffside setting overlooking the hotel's lagoon. **Chatham's Place** (7575 Dr. Phillips Boulevard; 407-345-2992; $25) serves the best fish in town in a casual but chic atmosphere. **Dux** (at the Peabody Hotel; 407-352-4000; $35) is the most elegant dining room in the city, serving a globally influenced, inventive cuisine. **Arthur's 27** (in the Buena Vista Palace; 407-827-3450; $26) serves surf or turf continental in an elegant dining room. About 30 minutes from Disney, you'll find **Le Cordon Bleu** (537 W. Fairbanks Avenue, Winter Park; 407-647-7575; $22), an unassuming French restaurant with superior food and service in a faux country farmhouse setting. Before dinner have a drink in the adjoining **Harper's Tavern**, an authentic 1950s retro-bar said to have been the first gay hangout in the area, though not anymore. **The Bubble Room** (1351 S. Orlando Avenue, Highway 17–92, Maitland; 407-628-3331; $18) is about as campy as a restaurant can get. Bring your lover and ask to sit in the Tunnel of Love boat or the giant birdcage. In the midst of the kitsch, the food is surprisingly good American steak-house fare. Don't skip dessert, and keep an eye out for particularly attractive Bubble Scouts (waiters). The **Beeline Diner** (in the Peabody; 407-352-4000; $11), serves the city's best nachos 24 hours a day, as well as other moderately priced dishes. A handful of gay-popular restaurants are convenient to the bar scene. **The Thornton Park Café** (900 E. Washington Street; 407-425-0033; $14) is in Orlando's gayest residential area and serves seafood and Italian specialties. **Moorefields** (123 S. Orange Avenue; 407-872-6960; $15) serves healthy Continental to a lesbian and gay clientele—especially popular with women. **Dug Out Diner** (at the

Parliament House; 407-425-7571, ext. 711; $6) is a gay diner in the
Parliament House complex.

Nightlife

Orlando's bar scene is afflicted by gigantism, like everything else in this
town. Two gay entertainment complexes (one named, appropriately
enough, **The Complex**) offer a multitude of gay entertainment options.
Not exactly E-ticket, but sometimes a lot of fun. Too bad the sailors are
gone, though—the Naval Training Center was closed down a few years
ago. Thursday nights are when locals whoop it up on **Pleasure Island**,
the entertainment complex of Disney World. **Mannequins** disco has the
highest gay presence on that night, although there are other bars and
restaurants worth checking out. **The Club** (578 N. Orange Avenue; 407-
426-0005) is Orlando's biggest and best dance club, hopping with
hunks on Wednesdays and Saturdays. Other bars are included inside,
and for the smoke-sensitive, it has a sophisticated ventilation system so
no "smoke gets in your eyes." **The Complex** (3400 S. Orange Blossom
Trail) comprises three bars in addition to the **New Image Fitness Center** (see Activities): **City Lights Cabaret** (407-422-6826), a drag and
dance bar; the **Loading Dock** (407-857-1609), a men's bar with a box-
car "backroom"; and the **Orlando Eagle** (407-843-6334), a men's
leather bar. **Parliament House**'s (see Accommodations) complex includes two bars: **Powerhouse** (407-425-7571) is the video/dance bar
attracting a young crowd, and the **Stable** (407-425-7571) is a C/W bar.
Thursday night is **Twirl** at **The Edge** (100 W. Livingston Street; 407-
839-4331), another mammoth dance bar attracting a youngish crowd
for its DJ-spun techno-house raves and early drink specials. Early
evenings belong to the **Cactus Club** (1300 N. Mills Avenue; 407-894-
3041), where a more professional crowd gathers after work to play pool,
cruise, and hang out. By 11:30 P.M., most have moved on, either to
Southern Nights (375 S. Bumby Avenue; 407-898-0424), also packed
for its Sunday tea dance, or the **Phoenix** (7124 Aloma Avenue; 407-
678-9220) in Winter Park or back to the Parliament House. **Uncle
Walt's** (5454 International Drive; 407-351-4866) is a gay men's bar
convenient to the resort hotel area, popular with a thirties to forties

crowd. **Faces** (4910 Edgewater Drive; 407-291-7571) is the local women's bar, but you'll find plenty of women dancing at the mixed **Southern Nights** (above).

Activities

ATHLETIC AND OUTDOOR

Orlando abounds with outdoor fun, thanks to the gazillion facilities provided by the area's resort hotels. Virtually every one will have more than one Olympic-size pool, numerous tennis courts, a health club, a jogging track, and golf courses. Disney World's **River Country, Typhoon Lagoon**, and **Blizzard Beach** are fun for those wanting to spend the day wet and soaking up rays, while enjoying an occasional water slide or river run. Tennis players should call the **Disney Racquet Club** (407-824-3578) for court reservations, partner referrals, and lessons. **New Image Fitness Center** (3400 S. Orange; 407-420-9890) is the only gay gym. It's open 24 hours, and even though there are no private rooms or pornography, it attracts a bathhouse crowd late at night. There are five **Bally's** in Orlando, and four have spa facilities that attract a gay clientele. The one at 4850 Lawing Lane (407-297-8400) is particularly popular; all require a Bally's membership or affiliated hotel referral. Just north of the Kennedy Space Center (reached via State Highway 50) is **Playalinda Beach**, the area's gay stretch of shoreline. The north end of the beach is popular with (mostly straight) nudists, and just beyond is the gay section.

SIGHTSEEING

Believe it or not, the Magic Kingdom and EPCOT center are only the beginning of Orlando's many family-oriented attractions. **Disney–MGM Studios** (within WDW, just south of EPCOT; 407-824-4321) and **Universal Studios Florida** (1000 Universal Studios Place; 407-363-8000 or 800-232-7827) are neck-and-neck rival theme parks, both with movie-based thrill rides and actual movie and television production on-site. While visiting both theme parks might be hard to justify, you can make your decision based on which studio's films you love more. **Disney–MGM** has the "double barrel" of two studios' worth of films and attractions on its side, including a Backstage Tour, the **Great Movie Ride** (whisking visitors through such films as *Singin' in the Rain, Raiders of the Lost Ark, The Wizard of Oz*, and other classics) and the **Twilight Zone Tower of Terror**, a free-fall scream ride that begins in an old hotel. **Universal Studios Florida** has the best rides, and is less emphatic on cinema history than **Disney–MGM**. The **Back to the Future** ride is the most jolting and heart-racing, and the **Alfred Hitchcock: The Art of Making Movies** attraction offers an absorbing glimpse into the tricks and techniques behind Hitch's most famous films. **Sea World** (7007 Sea World Drive; 407-351-3600) is worth a full day for Pisceans and their admirers. Among the day's highlights are **Mission Bermuda Triangle, Wild Arctic, Shamu**, and the world's largest marine zoo. Intellectuals will be pleasantly surprised by the educational focus of Sea World's activities. Or, you can get into the water and be a dolphin yourself at **Wet 'N' Wild** (6200 International Drive; 407-351-1800 or 800-992-9453). The wave pool is for would-be surf dudes, re-creating some decent breakers, and the giant water roller-coaster ride is worth the wait. **The Kennedy Space Center** (46 mi. east on State Highway 50; 407-452-2121) is the main launching pad for most U.S. space missions and gives an interesting two-hour bus tour throughout the complex, including the launch pad and astronaut training facilities. The IMAX film, *Destiny in Space,* plays at the Spaceport USA wing. **Church Street Station** (129 W. Church Street) in old downtown Orlando was once a pair of decrepit hotels. Now the pair has been restored (to the tune of most generic, renovated warehouse districts nationwide) into a noisy, straight complex of karaoke saloons, cutesy restaurants, and specialty boutiques with names like Phineas Phogg's Balloon Works. Locals might recommend the area, but gay couples will probably not feel comfortable in this eighteen-to-twenty-five-year-old hetero nightlife area.

SHOPPING

Belz Factory Outlet World (5401 W. Oak Ridge Road; 407-352-9600) is the largest outlet center of its kind in the world, with 180 brand-name merchants in a huge, multi-mall complex. The one bummer is that they don't have a J. Crew. **Out & About Books** (930 N. Mills Avenue; 407-

896-0204) is the main lesbian/gay bookstore, and a good resource for literature on gay goings-on in town. Go ahead and buy the Mouse ears; then put the plastic away until you get home.

FYI

The Triangle (714 E. Colonial Drive; 407-425-4527) is the monthly gay paper. **Orlando/Orange County Convention & Visitors Bureau** (407-363-5800). The **Gay & Lesbian Community Services** (407-THE-GAYS) can provide local referrals and information.

Florida's West Coast:

TAMPA, ST. PETERSBURG, SARASOTA, FORT MYERS, NAPLES

The stereotypical view that West Florida is primarily a destination for Canadians and the retired is not entirely unearned. Retirement communities abound, and at times, Canadian plates outnumber Floridian ones on the road. The population, especially in the coastal beach communities, is decidedly older than in other areas of the state and traffic seems to move noticeably more slowly. There are golf courses everywhere you look, and cafeteria restaurants are popular. This is not all bad. The more relaxed pace of the gulf coast can be a nice alternative to frantic Miami, and the mature nature of the area can be a blessed relief after Orlando's plethora of young families and screaming children. This is definitely a center for rest, relaxation, and sun worship, and best suited to couples traveling together. The single set looking for nightlife and action will probably feel a little stir crazy.

Although you will find some gay nightlife and accommodations here, the real attractions of the west coast are the beautiful white sand beaches and the warm, calm waters of the Gulf of Mexico. It seems the farther south you travel, the more conservative the natives. Gay visitors looking to let it all hang out should look east. Those who are looking for someplace peaceful and genteel will find a lovely vacation on Florida's west coast, and just enough gay nightlife to remind you that we are indeed everywhere. West Florida has few gay-specific or gay-marketed properties, and those that do exist offer limited facilities and amenities. On the other hand, West Florida's mainstream resorts offer some of the finest accommodations in the country, but are not especially gay-comfortable, catering primarily to hetero couples and families. Calculate your priorities and budget, and choose accordingly.

When to Go and How to Get There

Tampa is one of Florida's largest cities and offers easy air access to the entire west coast of the state. Most of the low-cost airlines serving Florida fly into Tampa, resulting in reasonable fares across the board. It is often dramatically cheaper to fly into Tampa rather than Sarasota, Fort Myers, or Naples. The 1996 addition of Southwest Airlines to the market has increased the availability of low-priced airfares. High season in the Tampa area runs from early November to sometime in April. Rates for everything go up during this time period and prime accommodations can be very hard to come by. Further, there are many weekends in the middle of the winter when there is not a rental car to be found. Be sure to book early.

FYI

West Florida's gay publications are currently *Contax* and *Watermark*. *Support Inc.* (813-332-2272) offers gay information and referrals in the Fort Myers area. The *Gay Information Line* (813-586-4297) offers similar information in the St. Petersburg area. For general travel information, contact the following chambers of commerce and convention and visitors' bureaus: **Naples Chamber of Commerce** (3620 North Tamiami Trail; 941-262-6141), **Fort Myers Metropolitan Chamber of Commerce** (1365 Hendry Street; 813-334-1133), **Tampa Convention & Visitors Bureau** (111 Madison Street; 813-223-1111 or 800-826-8358, ext. 75), **Sarasota Convention & Visitors Bureau** (655 N. Tamiami Trail; 941-957-1877 or 800-522-9799), **St. Petersburg Convention & Visitors Bureau** (One Stadium Drive; 813-582-7892 or 800-345-6710).

TAMPA/ST. PETERSBURG

Tampa is the largest city in this area, with a bustling economy and big-city diversions. Across Tampa Bay you'll find its sister city, St. Petersburg, and St. Petersburg beach.

Accommodations

Downtown Tampa is convenient for nightlife, and is less than an hour from the beach.

GRAM'S PLACE GUEST HOUSE 3109 Ola Avenue North; 813-221-0596; $45–100
The only Tampa lodging option marketing itself to the gay community. This quirky but comfortable B&B is located in a transitional working-class neighborhood within ten minutes of all major night clubs. There is a quaint deck area with a new hot tub, and the proprietor is enthusiastic and willing to offer suggestions and assistance.

The nicest of the mainstream hotels is the **Hyatt Regency** (2 Tampa City Center; 813-225-1234 or 800-223-1234, fax 813-273-0234; $79–194), but if you're here for the beach, you're better off staying on the other side of Tampa Bay. St. Petersburg and nearby beach towns are about 40 minutes from downtown Tampa, and while there is very little gay-specific nightlife in this area, there are several gay-friendly lodging options, including the **Sea Oates and Dunes** (12625 Sunshine Lane, Treasure Island; 813-367-7568; $295–595/week), a popular lesbian-owned ten-room motel convenient to the beach. Clientele is mixed gay/straight.

THE BARGE HOUSE 3112 Pass-A-Grille Way, St. Petersburg; 813-360-0729; $61–85
Caters exclusively to professional women, with two guest rooms and a cottage.

CAPE HOUSE 2800 Pass-A-Grille Way, St. Petersburg; 813-367-6971; $60
Offers three rooms in a charming and homey Cape Cod house within walking distance to the gay beach. Clientele is mixed gay women/men.

Non-gay lodging choices in this area include the **Don Cesar Resort** (3400 Gulf Blvd, St. Petersburg Beach; 813-360-1811 or 800-637-7200, fax 813-367-6952; $175–1,000), a wonderfully restored Mediterranean-style mansion set on a beautiful beach, and the **Renaissance Vinoy Resort** (501 Fifth Ave., N.E., St. Petersburg; 813-894-1000 or 800-468-3571, fax 813-894-1970; $179–319), a huge, convention-style resort that has all the typical luxury amenities and services centered around a restored landmark building.

Dining

Fresh local seafood is king here, and you'll find it prepared in all styles. Most fine dining is in the Continental and Nouvelle American modes. Restaurants listed are straight, unless otherwise indicated. You'll find one of Tampa's notable restaurants even before your plane lands. **CK's** (Tampa International Airport, 8th Floor; 813-879-5151; $19) serves imaginative cuisine in a revolving setting that offers views of the airport traffic and downtown skyline. **Mise en Place** (420 W. Kennedy Boulevard; 813-254-5373; $15) is located right across from the University of Tampa. Despite the French name, the food is cutting-edge American bistro. They are also open for lunch. **Bern's Steak House** (1208 S. Howard Avenue; 813-251-2421; $22) took top honors in the *Wine Spectator*'s 1996 rating of steak houses. Count on a great steak and an amazing wine list. The decor is different, and a touch heavy-handed, in each of the five dining rooms; dessert is enjoyed upstairs in private glass booths. Head to Ybor City if you're hankering for Cuban food. The **Silver Ring Café** (1831 East 7th Avenue; 813-248-2549) is an old-fashioned luncheonette, serving the best Cuban sandwich (essentially a sub, hero or hoagie, by another name) in the area. **Fins** (8000 West Gulf Boulevard, Treasure Island; 813-367-1724; $10) is a Caribbean-style cafe that is part of the gay Bedrox complex on Treasure Island.

Nightlife

The nightclubs have recently been in a state of flux, so consult the local papers when you arrive. **Howard Avenue Station** (3003 N. Howard Avenue; 813-254-7194) is an established and popular disco/nightclub, especially crowded for its Sunday night strip shows. **Tracks/El Goya** (1430 E. Seventh; 813-247-2711), is in Ybor City, Tampa's nightlife district. **Tracks** is known for lavish drag shows and frequent concerts, but has lost some of its luster as the dance palace of choice. Ybor City, two miles from downtown, is full of popular bars and restaurants. It gets a bit loud and raucous on the weekends, but is worth a visit. The **Cherokee Club** (1320 Ninth Avenue; 813-247-9966) is also in Ybor City, catering primarily to women. They feature live DJs and entertainment, and the best nightclub decor in town. **Angel's Lounge** (4502 South Dale Mabry Highway South; 813-831-9980) is a male strip bar, popular on Wednesday nights. **City Side** (3810 Neptune Street; 813-254-6466) is good for happy hour, attracting a "gentlemen's crowd" of local business people, and particularly popular on Monday. **Club 2606** (2606 N. Armenia Avenue; 813-875-6993) is the local leather/Levi's bar, with a leather shop on site, in case you forgot to pack your chaps. Enjoying a great deal of popularity right now is **Parthenon** (802 E. Whiting Street; 813-273-8788), a go-go boy-infested dance club that is only gay on Friday nights. At the beach, **Bedrox** (8000 West Gulf Boulevard; Treasure Island; 813-367-1724) has a beach bar, a Caribbean cafe, a live music lounge called **Gothic Java**, and a high-tech disco called **Club Rox**. To the north is the **Pro Shop** (840 Cleveland Street, Clearwater; 813-447-4259), a 20-year-old institution in Clearwater, with a large bar and a diverse clientele.

Activities

ATHLETIC AND OUTDOOR

Metro Flex Fitness (2511 Swann Avenue; 813-876-3539; $7/day) is Tampa's gay gym, with a full range of free weights, equipment and aerobics classes. Tampa's beach playground is across the bay in St. Petersburg and Treasure Island. **Bedrox** (8000 W. Gulf Boulevard, Treasure Island; 813-367-1724) is a gay bar and restaurant complex with the largest private gay beach in the state. This stretch is *the* gay beach serving the Tampa area, although Pass-a-Grille Beach has a gay section below Eighth Street.

SIGHTSEEING

West Florida's most popular attraction is **Busch Gardens/The Dark Continent** (3000 East Busch Boulevard; 813-987-5082), a huge African-themed amusement park with interesting zoo areas, several roller coasters, and assorted other thrill rides in addition to a working beer brewery. But high culture is also readily available along the coast. The **Tampa**

Museum of Art (600 N. Ashley Drive; 813-223-8130) is known for its collection of 19th-century Japanese art. The **Henry B. Plant Museum** (401 W. Kennedy Boulevard; 813-254-1891) on the University of Tampa campus is filled with memorabilia from the opulent Moorish-style Tampa Bay Hotel of the 1890s. The **Salvador Dali Museum** (1000 Third Street S., St. Petersburg; 813-823-3767) is a modern facility housing an impressive collection of 94 oils and over one thousand other original Dali works from 1914 through 1980.

SHOPPING

The **Shops at Harbor Island** (601 S. Harbor Island Boulevard; 813-223-9898) is an upscale indoor mall; **Old Hyde Park Village** (1509 W. Swann Avenue; 813-251-3500) offers similar upscale options in a historic, outdoor setting. **Fairground Outlet Mall** (6302 E. Buffalo Avenue; 813-621-6047) is the local outlet mall. If you're in the market for stogies, head to **Tampa Rico** (in Ybor Square, Eighth Avenue and Thirteenth Street; 813-247-6738), selling hand-rolled cigars in the mall that was built in the former cigar factory. **Tomes & Treasures** (202 S. Howard Avenue; 813-251-9368) is the local lesbigay bookstore.

SARASOTA

Farther south and much less touristy than the St. Petersburg area is Sarasota, a well-known destination for rich retirees. This area abounds in fine restaurants, good shopping, and deluxe hotels. The beaches are also some of the most beautiful in the world.

Accommodations

HOLIDAY INN LIDO BEACH 233 Ben Franklin Drive; 941-388-3941 or 800-892-9174; $99–179

This solid, moderately priced option, a typical HI operation with a peerless location—is just around the corner from St. Armands Circle, the toney shopping and dining area, and just across the street from beautiful Lido Beach, the north end of which is Sarasota's gay beach area.

THE RESORT AT LONGBOAT KEY CLUB 301 Gulf of Mexico Drive; 941-383-8821 or 800-237-8821, 941-383-0359; $145–610

A good choice, set right on the beach in the middle of a gated resort community. Amenities include the standard pool, many tennis courts, and two golf courses. Rooms are very spacious and tastefully decorated in light earth tones.

NORMANDY INN 400 N. Tamiami Trail; 941-366-8979 or 800-282-8050; $45–110

A good gay-oriented budget choice, and with mirrors on the ceilings, is only the slightest bit sleazy. It is in walking distance of many good restaurants, and only two miles from the best beaches.

Dining

Carmichael's (1213 N. Palm Avenue; 941-951-1771; $22) specializes in wild game, served in a restored landmark 1920s home. **Ristorante Bellini** (1551 Main Street; 941-365-7380; $16) serves moderately priced, authentic northern Italian food.

Nightlife

While not a gay nightlife mecca, the town has several club options. **Bumpers** (1927 Ringling Boulevard at Main Street; 941-951-0335), also known as Club X, has a large dance floor and is gay on Thursday and Saturday nights. **HG Roosters** (1256 Old Stickney Point; 941-346-3000) is a small, intimate happy hour bar that tends to attract an older clientele.

Activities

ATHLETIC AND OUTDOOR

Lido Beach (Benjamin Franklin Drive) is a great place to sun, and attracts a lot of gays to its north end.

SIGHTSEEING

The **Marie Selby Botanical Gardens** (811 South Palm Avenue; 941-366-5730) are in the heart of the city, with 15 gardens of exotic botanicals, including an amazing orchid center. Near the airport, you'll find the **John & Mable Ringling Museum of Art** (811 South Palm Avenue; 941-355-5101), a 66-acre tribute to the circus impresario who helped forge Sarasota's cultural identity. Even more impressive than the Rubenses and El Grecos is Ringling's mansion, Ca'd'Zan, modeled after the Doge's palace in Venice. The Circus Galleries are a collection of memorabilia and displays that chronicle the early days of the famous circus. The performing arts are alive and well in Sarasota. The **Van Wezel Performing Arts Hall** (777 North Tamiami Trail; 941-953-3366) hosts theater, music, and dance companies from all over the world in their seashell-shaped performance hall. The **Sarasota Opera House** (61 N. Pineapple Avenue; 941-953-7030) hosts major performers from Europe and the United States.

SHOPPING

St. Armand's Circle is the Rodeo Drive of west Florida, with more than 100 stores and restaurants catering to the country club and window-shopping sets.

FORT MYERS/NAPLES

South of Sarasota lie Fort Myers and Naples, both home to even more year-round retirees and winter visitors, more golf courses, and more beautiful beaches. Neither Fort Myers nor Naples is particularly known for its gay offerings or accepting nature, although Naples has a small gay beach.

Accommodations

Naples is home to several world-class hotels.

THE RITZ-CARLTON NAPLES 280 Vanderbilt Beach; 941-598-3300 or 800-241-3333, fax 941-598-6690; $145–595

Set on 20 acres and reeks of old money and class. The resort has a very formal air to it and the staff is as polished as they come. Rates run from high to astronomical, but the restaurant is wonderful, the beach is beautiful, and rooms are posh.

REGISTRY RESORT 475 Seagate Drive; 941-597-3232 or 800-247-9810, fax 941-597-3147; $125–675

Slightly more reasonable and a little less fabulous than the Ritz-Carlton, this well-run, beautifully maintained resort comes with a golf course, 15 tennis courts, and a great pool with waterfall.

Dining

The Oasis (2222 McGregor Boulevard, Fort Myers; 941-334-1566) is a too cool, popular women-owned/run restaurant, serving breakfast and lunch daily—sandwiches, omelets and the like. **The Velvet Turtle** (1404 Cape Coral Parkway, Fort Myers; 941-549-9000; $13) is gay-popular, serving American cuisine in an elegant but casual atmosphere. The **Chef's Garden** (1300 Third Street S., Naples; 941-262-5500; $24) serves award-winning, creative, gourmet cuisine in an upscale bistro setting. Upstairs, **Truffles** (1300 Third Street S., Naples; 941-262-5500; $11) has a more casual atmosphere and menu, with pastas, dinner salads and similar light fare.

Nightlife

The **Bottom Line** (3090 Evans Avenue, Fort Myers; 941-337-7292) is a two-floor complex with a main show bar and dance floor, game room, and karaoke bar. Drag and strip shows provide entertainment; a cover charge is levied on weekends. The alternative bar is called **The Alternative** (4650 Cleveland Avenue, Fort Myers; 941-277-7002), with two bars, a gift shop, and small dance floor. Their happy hour runs 3–9 P.M., but their big draw is karaoke. Both clubs cater to a mixed lesbian/gay crowd. The **Office Pub** (3704 Grove Street, Fort Myers; 941-

936-3212) is a small, no-attitude neighborhood bar. **The Galley** (509 Third Street S., Naples; 941-262-2808) is the only game in Naples, with a small dance floor, and a surprisingly young crowd, considering the town's median age.

Activities

ATHLETIC AND OUTDOOR

Lowdermilk Park (corner of Banyan Drive and Gulf Shore Boulevard in the 2200 block), is the gay-popular beach in Naples, especially during the week. The **Naples Fitness Center** (1048 Castello Drive, N., Naples; 941-262-1112; $11/day) is the gay-popular gym. Near Fort Myers, the beaches of **Sanibel** and **Captiva** offer unparalleled opportunity for collecting sea shells. Stormy weather and a falling tide are the best conditions for this activity, which draws serious collectors and novices alike.

SIGHTSEEING

Fort Myers pays tribute to another West Florida resident at the **Thomas A. Edison Winter Estate and Botanical Gardens** (2350 McGregor Boulevard; 813-334-3614). The estate includes the two houses that Edison lived in, a museum of his inventions, his winter laboratory, and his exotic and scientific gardens.

SHOPPING

If you didn't have time to go to Sanibel Island and collect them yourself, the **Shell Factory** (2787 N. Tamiami Trail, North Fort Myers; 941-995-2141) is the world's largest shell shop, with every imaginable shell souvenir that money can buy. The charming town of Naples offers some truly upscale beach boutique shopping.

Rehoboth Beach, Delaware

This Delaware beach community is a resort town marked by a wide expanse of beach, tree-lined streets, and old houses. During the summer months, the town comes alive as the population swells to roughly 50,000—about 12 times the winter population. Rehoboth is most popular with gays from Washington, D.C., who escape the capital to frolic by the sea. The resort reflects D.C.'s conservatism and preppiness to some degree, and offers, like Provincetown, a more wholesome, less sexually focused retreat than Palm Springs or South Beach. You can expect to be charmed by the boardwalk, seaside shops, good restaurants, and fun nightlife.

There has been some tension in Rehoboth between the local year-round residents, who include a high proportion of straight retirees, and the burgeoning summer population, which includes a high proportion of urban gays. This is sometimes perceived as a straight-gay conflict, but gay women and men are treated well overall and eagerly welcomed by the straight and gay business communities alike. Rehoboth offers gay beaches, nightlife, and accommodations from inns and B&Bs to motels. With good restaurants, tax-free shopping, and an accessible and busy gay social scene, it's a happening place.

When to Go and How to Get There

You can reach the Rehoboth Beach area by air by flying into the Ocean City/Salisbury, Maryland, Airport. The airport is less than an hour from Rehoboth Beach. By train, Amtrak stops in Wilmington, Delaware, which is about a 90-minute car ride to Rehoboth Beach. Most visitors arrive by car, from nearby cities. Lewes, Delaware, is less than 10 miles north of Rehoboth and is reachable from Cape May, New Jersey, on the 70-minute **Cape May-Lewes Ferry** (609-886-9699 or 800-643-3779; $18/car and driver). Rehoboth is approximately 120 miles southeast of the nation's capital, 120 miles south of Philadelphia, and 200 miles south of New York City. Once you're there, you can park your car and walk, bike, or Roller-blade, except for trips to the Renegade, North Shore Beach, or the outlet shops. Rehoboth is another resort that is at least partially open all year, but really only popular in the summer. Room rates in season may be as much as double the rates off-season.

Accommodations

Rehoboth has a number of gay-marketed guest houses, and one recommendable gay-friendly, mixed-clientele hotel. You won't find any excess of charm here—indeed, the town boasts mostly unremarkable architecture, more typical of the suburbs than a seaside resort town.

SILVER LAKE 133 Silver Lake Drive; 302-226-2115 or 800-842-2115; $60–160

The best of the bunch, Silver Lake is an 11-room, gay-owned B&B in a quiet setting overlooking Silver Lake and the ocean. An expanded continental breakfast is served each morning, and all rooms have private baths and cable TV. It caters primarily to men, with women welcome. It's a 10-minute walk from Poodle Beach, and also has two-bedroom apartments available that will accept pets.

SHORE INN 703 Rehoboth Avenue; 302-227-8487 or 800-597-8899; $45–130

A gay-owned B&B with 14 rooms, the Shore Inn is located about a mile from the beach and five blocks from the edge of downtown bars and restaurants.

SAND IN MY SHOES Canal and Sixth streets; 302-226-2006 or 800-231-5856; $71–145

A lesbian-owned 12-room guest house, Sand in My Shoes caters primarily to women, with men welcome. A generous, full breakfast is included, and guests are welcome to use the bicycles as well as the gas grill and hot tub in the backyard. A common room has a grand piano and a VCR with a well-stocked tape library. Pets and children are welcome here.

REHOBOTH GUEST HOUSE 40 Maryland Avenue; 302-227-4117; $55–120

Rehoboth Guest House is conveniently located a block and a half from the boardwalk (but a good 15 minutes from Poodle Beach) and has been gay owned and operated for the last 25 years, catering to gay men, lesbians, and gay-friendly straights. A continental breakfast is offered in the sunroom each morning.

BEACH HOUSE B&B 15 Hickman Street; 302-227-7074; $50–154

This aptly named B&B is about four blocks from Poodle Beach, with 10 large rooms and simple but pleasant décor. The two least expensive rooms have shared baths.

RAM'S HEAD INN RD 2 Box 509, County Road 275; 302-226-9171; $90–140

This inn is a men-only B&B a few miles outside of town, with nine rooms, an in-ground heated pool, cabana with service bar, gazebo hot tub, full gym, sauna, sundeck, library, lounge, and tape library. Breakfast is served, and an open bar is provided from 12 noon to 4:00 P.M. It has the highest sexual temperature of the properties listed here.

RENEGADE 4274 U.S. Highway 1; 302-227-1222; $35–120

A 10-minute drive from the beach, this gay motel is notable because it is also home to the main dance club. It is the place to stay if you want to sleep near the heart-of-the-action.

BRIGHTON SUITES 34 Wilmington Avenue; 302-227-5780 or 800-227-5788; $59–199

This a gay-friendly mainstream 66-room hotel has spacious rooms, each with a wet bar.

Dining

Rehoboth offers an impressive array of world-class cuisine, at world-class resort-town prices. You won't be wanting for a good meal, but you may be wanting for a higher credit line. Few moderately priced choices exist, although plenty of inexpensive, touristy low-brow eateries are available for those who left home without it. If you're in the market for upscale dining, you may have trouble choosing among the large number of excellent possibilities. **Blue Moon** (35 Baltimore Avenue; 302-227-6515; $22) has been voted one of the top 10 restaurants in the state by the *Delaware News Journal* for its Asian-influenced American cuisine. It has a romantic fireplace and a lively and gay bar. **A Chef's Table** (10 Henlopen Junction Mall; 302-227-6339; $23/meal) serves a prix-fixe dinner of truly creative and delicious New American cuisine. **La La Land** (22 Wilmington Avenue; 302-227-3887; $21) serves eclectic creative cuisine in a romantic atmosphere. **Chez La Mer** (210 Second Street; 302-227-6494; $22) offers continental-style cuisine indoors and on their rooftop. Entrées include sautéed soft-shell crabs, filet mignon, as well as a limited vegetarian menu. They have been cited by the *Wine Spectator* for their wine list. The outdoor patio is surrounded by a bamboo garden. **Back Porch Café** (59 Rehoboth Avenue; 302-227-3674; $24) serves creatively prepared fresh food including fish, beef, lamb, pork, and game. With indoor and outdoor seating a half block from the beach, reservations are recommended. **Square One** (37 Wilmington Avenue; 302-227-1994; $20) serves California cuisine in a bright, California-Mediterranean dining room displaying contemporary art. **The Captain's Table** (Highway 1; 302-227-6203; $15) is not in the best location but serves very good food. Their nouvelle continental menu, originally prix fixe, is now expanded but still limited. **Celsius** (50 Wilmington Avenue; 302-227-5767; $20) is very popular and very small, with a fun, jovial (noisy) atmosphere and a creative menu. **Cloud 9** (234 Rehoboth Avenue; 302-226-1999; $14) is under the same ownership with a similar menu, but less inexpensive and more fun, with almost a bar type of atmosphere (it has a popular bar attached)—good for either fine dining or a quick, short meal.

Less pricey (under $25/person/meal) but still very popular and very good are the following: **Mano's** (10 Wilmington Avenue; 302-227-6707; $13) specializes in steaks and seafood. With upscale, casual, white-linen dining and affordable prices, it's the closest gay-owned restaurant to the water. Reservations are highly recommended. **Sydney's Side Street** (25 Christian Street; 302-227-1339; $17) offers Cajun and Creole food accompanied by live jazz nightly. The **Iguana Grill** (52 Baltimore Avenue; 302-227-0948; $12) serves decent Southwestern cuisine—brunch is their most popular meal. **Dos Locos** (42 1/2 Baltimore Avenue; 302-227-5626; $12) offers very good Mexican food and patio dining. **Adriatico Ristorante & Café** (Baltimore Avenue and N. First Street; 302-227-0789; $16) serves huge portions of classic southern Italian dishes. **Dream Café** (26 Baltimore Avenue; 302-226-2233) is very gay-popular and serves good sandwiches. Just look for the giant teacup. **Cuppa Jo** (39 Baltimore Avenue; 302-226-9220) is a popular gay coffeehouse, with outdoor (only) seating, open late and located right next to the Lambda Rising bookstore.

Nightlife

The Blue Moon (35 Baltimore Avenue; 302-227-6516) is the happy hour of choice, packed with the après sun crowd from 4:00 to 6:00 P.M. daily. **Renegade** (4274 U.S. Highway 1; 302-227-4713), Rehoboth Beach's only gay and lesbian dance club, features a video bar, a C/W bar, and a disco bar. Women's tea dance is every Saturday from 4:00–7:00 P.M. Men's tea dance is on Sunday during the same hours. The Renegade is open seven days a week from 11:00 A.M.–4:00 A.M. There is also a swimming pool and a restaurant on the premises. Rehoboth has an active and popular house party circuit, with many parties open to the public. To locate weekend house parties, check out *The Underground*, talk to a seasonal renter, or look for flyers being selectively distributed on Poodle Beach on Saturday afternoons.

Activities

ATHLETIC AND OUTDOOR

The gay beaches are the big attraction here, and you'll find two of them: **North Shores**, which is mostly frequented by women and older men, and **Poodle Beach**, just south of the Boardwalk, near Queen Street. Additional entertainment is found strolling the mile-long boardwalk complete with games and amusements. If you don't find what (or who) you're looking for on the beach, chances are you'll find it (or them) at **The Renegade**, Rehoboth's only dance club. Bicycles are a popular form of transportation here, and you can rent them locally. Try **Wheels Bi-**

cycle Shop (318 Rehoboth Avenue; 302-227-6807) or **Marilee Bike** (70 Rehoboth Avenue; 302-227-5534).

SIGHTSEEING

Rehoboth is really an escape from sightseeing. If you feel the need for something educational, cultural, or historic, head back to Washington, D.C.

SHOPPING

You'll find a smaller outpost of D.C.'s **Lambda Rising** (39 Baltimore Avenue; 302-227-6969) bookstore in town, a good place to pick up the local gay papers and get acquainted with the local activity. They are open 10:00 A.M. to midnight, seven days a week. **Splash** (15 N. First Street; 302-227-9179) sells fashionable men's clothes. The **Glass Flamingo** (46 Baltimore Avenue; 302-226-1366) sells furnishings, arts, and collectibles, with an emphasis on Deco and items from the fifties. **Stone Heart** (29 Baltimore Avenue; 302-226-2249) sells an eclectic assortment of contemporary fine arts and crafts. Over 150 brand-name outlet stores make Rehoboth a major national tax-free shopping destination.

FYI

Rehoboth has two local papers providing gay information. *The Underground* is a good source for nightlife special-event information. *Letters from Camp Rehoboth* (39 Baltimore Avenue; 302-227-5620) is published biweekly in season (mid-April to mid-November) by Camp Rehoboth, a nonprofit community service organization that promotes cooperation and understanding between gay and lesbian residents and visitors, and the local community at large. A good reference guide to the area is the **TripPak** (P.O. Box 9285, Richmond, VA 23227; 800-595-4404; $9.95), which includes comprehensive destination information, as well as discount coupons for establishments here and in Washington, D.C. The **Chamber of Commerce** (302-227-6181) can also be a helpful source.

Fire Island, New York

A spit of barrier beach along the southern shore of Long Island, 32 miles long and as little as 200 yards wide, Fire Island is home to a string of distinct and diverse communities, only two of which, Cherry Grove and Fire Island Pines, are predominantly gay. Just 90 minutes from Manhattan, Fire Island remains relatively undeveloped and unspoiled. There are no cars, no cable TV, few bars, fewer stores, and precious little to do that doesn't revolve around the simple pleasures of the seaside or the kindness of strangers. Unlike other gay meccas such as Provincetown and Key West, Fire Island has not been developed for the short-term visitor. This is both a blessing and a curse. Planning a vacation here is difficult and expensive. But overcome those obstacles, and you'll enjoy the island's legendary attractions. The seemingly endless beach, uncrowded even on the busiest weekends, and the scenic rolling boardwalks and dense vegetation near the bay create a unique rustic beauty. Superimpose a gay social scene of great density, creativity, and stamina, and you have a summer retreat that is both worlds away from the pressures of everyday life, and right at the heart of gay culture.

THE PINES VERSUS THE GROVE

Despite their proximity, the Grove and the Pines are not interchangeable. While tourists may move easily between the two by water taxi ($4 one way) or beach walk (20 minutes), summer residents rarely do so. The Pines pictures itself as more upscale and professional. True or not, it can be a severe dose of New York attitude by the sea. (It is often joked that the Pines is a community of 10s . . . looking for 12s.) Whether the atmosphere is attributable to xenophobia or narcissism, only Miami has a comparable excess of muscle-bound, chest-shaved, self-absorbed boys. More and more women are choosing to summer here, but they are still a small minority. The Grove takes itself less seriously. The visible crowd is a bit older and diverse, there's more camp than high design, there are many more lesbians, and the restaurants are consistently better. Most of the A-list parties are in the Pines; most Grove residents are thankful for that. Unfortunately, the Grove is increasingly attracting straights, particularly day-trippers, who can make the tea dance at the Ice Palace a bit less comfortable.

PARTY HARD, SLEEP LATE

What the island lacks in welcome and accommodation for tourists, it makes up for in environment and scale. The expansive beach and automobile-free boardwalks are the essence of peaceful retreat. Watching the sunset from the end of a dock, or watching man and man's best friend frolicking in the surf at sunrise, will make you feel rejuvenated. And you may need that energy. Because you could also watch the sunset from the balcony at high tea, and the sunrise in the same place, after having danced all night at the Pavilion. The party opportunities here are unequaled, and most are open to the public, or at least to anyone who knows about them. The party scene in the Pines is daunting for a first-time single visitor. If you don't have a host on the island, the best way to visit is to rent a house with a group of friends.

The boys in the Pines are slaves to fashion and routine. We can't help you get dressed, but this simple schedule should at least put you in the right place at the right time.

Friday 4 P.M.: Get out of the city, any way you can afford. The LIRR offers an opportunity to make friends before the island attitude is fully developed.

5:30: Arrive Sayville. Get out of the train, have $2.00 ready to hand to the jitney driver. Listen to conversations, but avoid joining in. You may pick up some private party information.

6:00: Ferry to the Pines. First signs of weekend relief. If you're traveling by yourself, wait to get on the ferry (get a drink, make a phone call). Stragglers attract the most attention, and you will have an opportunity to survey the crowd before choosing a seat.

6:30: Arrive in the Pines. Go to the Pantry (grocery store). Buy supplies for dinner, or just pretend to. Good opportunity to scope.

8:00: High tea begins. Don't show up before 8:04, arrive by 8:06 for a good banquet seat (sit on the railing, feet on the seat).

9:59: Leave tea for dinner. Only day trippers, Boatel boys, and the really desperate stay past the official end of tea (10:00 P.M.).

Midnight: Optional cocktails at the Island Club. Serious all-night party boys should still be disco-napping.

2:00 A.M.: The Pavilion is now in full swing. This is not about cocktails. Late night at the Pavilion is about debauchery and dancing with your friends or housemates, not meeting new people. Stay until you have to leave.

6:00: Suddenly morning. Good time for a sunrise walk home on the beach.

Saturday Noon: Crack of noon: Time to think about getting out of bed, lunch by someone's pool or at the Blue Whale, a veritable viewing stand.

1:00: To the beach. Play kadeema. Stroll and scope. Read the *New York Times*, *Vanity Fair*, or gay fiction.

4:00: To the gym. Go with a partner.

6:00: Go home. Shower. Shave (this can be a whole-body, whole-house affair). Apply balms, salves, and scents.

8:04: Same as last night.

Sunday when you get up: Buy the Sunday *Times* off the dock, relax, and read. If you're going home, a modest amount of whining is in order; if you're staying, modest gloating is favored instead.

If you have straight friends, you may be invited to spend time in one of Fire Island's many other communities, such as Davis Park, Fair Harbor, or Ocean Beach. Beware—these communities are separate and distinct from one another, and transportation between them is limited to walking the beach and expensive, infrequent water taxi service.

When to Go and How to Get There

Fire Island is only in season during the summer, starting slowly in late April, and tapering off by early October. It is busiest weekends, from Memorial Day to Labor Day. New York's Gay Pride weekend (the last one in June) is slow, but the following Fourth of July weekend is particularly busy and traditionally attracts a large contingent from Los Angeles. "Morning Party" weekend, the Gay Men's Health Crisis benefit party in mid-August, is the most crowded of the summer. If you've got the bucks, fly from midtown Manhattan ($139–159 each way;

Eastway (800-882-9646). Otherwise, like everyone else, drive, ride the bus, or take the train. The **Islanders/Horizon** bus (212-255-8014; $20 one-way) has been running for 30 years, with a limited number of departures but a more pleasant experience than the **Long Island Rail Road** (718-217-5477; $7–10 one-way), which runs almost hourly from Penn Station in Manhattan and Jamaica Station in Queens (near La Guardia and Kennedy airports) to Sayville, New York. At the rail station, you pick up a minivan ride ($2) to the ferry. The ferries (**Sayville Ferry**: 516-589-0810; $10 round-trip) run almost every hour in season—passengers and pets only—no cars (parking is available across the street for $7/day, or slightly further down at **Lands End Marina** for $5/day). If you're flying in, check out **Islip Airport**—it's a 15-minute cab ride from the ferry by **Colonial Taxi** (516-589-3500).

Accommodations

One reason Fire Island has so few tourists is an intentional lack of hotels and guest houses.

PINES PLACE 516-597-6162; $100–250/night

Located in the Pines, this B&B offers rooms on a nightly and weekly basis, and while it's expensive, it's your best option. They have moved from their original location to a house with a pool on the other side (east) of the harbor, with six rooms (four with private bath) and ocean views. Additional accommodations are often available through them as well.

THE BOATEL 516-597-6500; $150–200

Offers 27 rooms with rudimentary accommodations, cinder-block walls, cheap furniture, and shared baths. It is well located on the harbor between the Pavilion and the Blue Whale, has a pool in the back amidst the Island Gym, and caters to a young, frisky crowd.

If you can get a group together, rent a house for a week through **Pines Harbor Realty**: 516-597-7575, **Bob Howard**: 516-597-9400, or **Island Properties**: 516-597-6900. If you decide to rent a house, be prepared to spend from $300–1,000 per person, per week, depending on how fabulous and crowded the house is. Fire Island is geared for summer residents, not tourists, so there are few lodging options. Choices in the Pines are exceptionally limited.

THE CHERRY GROVE BEACH HOTEL Bay View Walk, 516-597-6600; $69–199, 57 rooms
A bit more respectable than the Boatel, and it has a large pool. It is part of, and right adjacent to, the Ice Palace, the Grove's entertainment complex.

There are a few other guest houses here, most notable (and noticeable):

BELVEDERE Bayview Walk, 516-597-6448; $80–200, 38 rooms
A rundown Venetian architectural phantasmagoria, better to look at than stay in.

CAROUSEL GUEST HOUSE 185 Holly Walk, 516-597-6612; $70–175, 11 rooms
A better choice for lodging, although we've had mixed reports on the service (a bit rules-oriented) and the breakfast (skimpy).

Dining

There really is not a decent restaurant in the Pines. The deli counter at **Peter's Meat Market** in the Pines Pantry is often the best food (doesn't that say it all?), although you can do pretty well if you stick to the simple menu items at the **Yacht Club**, and slightly better at the ambience-free **Island Club Bistro**. The restaurants in Cherry Grove (20 minutes by foot from the Pines or $4 by water taxi) are better, though still hardly worth the money—**Top of the Bay** offers a reasonable facsimile of fine dining. **Yougottawanna** and **Michael's** offer more casual fare.

Nightlife

Nightlife here is pretty simple. In the Grove, cocktails happen on the bay at **Cherry's**, followed by dancing at the Ice Palace. On weekends, the Ice Palace is also popular for afternoon tea dance, although this is an increasingly straight affair. In the Pines, there is **Tea**, every night 8:00–10:00 P.M., on the upper deck of the Pavilion. The absence of the word *dance* is not a typo: the legendary tea dance doesn't really exist anymore, although the Blue Whale occasionally tries to revive the legend with a 6:00–8:00 P.M. Classic Tea that is populated mostly by weekend day-trippers. The **Pavilion** reopens as a disco at midnight on weekend nights (and occasionally mid-week) and the music blares until 8:00 or 9:00 A.M. The cover charge runs $5–15, depending on the DJ. The **Island Club**, upstairs, behind the Pavilion, offers dancing, cocktails, a piano bar, and pool table. It gets going earlier, has no cover, and is particularly popular on Friday nights. There are fundraising parties most weekends in the Pines, and even more private cocktail parties, some of which require invitations, but most of which become free-for-alls. Ask around at tea, and keep your eyes out for little invitations. Otherwise, just follow the packs of boys fresh from the shower at 6:00 P.M. Tell the hosts that you're a friend of David's, and he told you to meet him there. (No one knows last names here—you'll be safe as long as you're not crashing a ticket- or guest-list-controlled private party, which is rare, but not unheard of.)

Activities

ATHLETIC AND OUTDOOR

Fire Island is all about the outdoors, although there are surprisingly few ways to enjoy it. There are no boat or watersports rental facilities in the Pines or the Grove. Bicycle riding and Roller-blading are also impractical on this part of the island. There is a tented gym in the Pines ($10/day), and volleyball, Frisbee, Boogie-boarding, and Kadeema are all popular on the beach. Fishing and clamming are rarely practiced by visitors, yet both activities will attract a great deal of attention. Bluefish are a common catch on the ocean side. All you need to go clamming is the desire. Walk out into the bay, dig around the sandy bottom with your feet, pick up things that feel like clams, and hope they are!

SHOPPING

Shopping facilities are limited, although you will be amazed by the breadth of inventory at the **Pines Pantry** and the **Pines Hardware** store. A few gift and clothing stores are available if you forgot your Calvin Klein boxer briefs or need a new swimsuit or Fire Island sweat-shirt. Couture is represented by **Raymond Dragon**'s store in the Pines, famous for the namesake designer's form-hugging club and swim fash-ions. Shopping only becomes a great activity after Labor Day, when the end-of-season sales start and real bargains abound.

SIGHTSEEING

Forget about museums, walking tours, and historical monuments. The major sights here are all two-legged, and they'll parade for you day and night. If you have the stamina, take a walk down the beach to **Sunken Forest**, a unique and fascinating National Park Service forest a few miles west of the Grove.

FYI

General and gay information on Fire Island is not readily available, and finding someone to answer your questions is often a challenge. Locals are the best reference, and if you're renting a house, you'll find a ready reference in your realtor. If you're staying at Pines Place, you'll find your hosts there are also in-the-know. Don't count on any assistance from the surly desk staff at the Boatel. ATMs were installed in the Pines in 1996. A $3 service charge is added to each $100 maximum with-drawal.

Provincetown, Massachusetts

It's hard not to love Provincetown, or P'town as anyone who has been there calls it. Nowhere else on earth will you find so many gay women and men, crossing all age, race, and social strata, having such a good time, all summer long. P'town is easy to reach, by car, ferry, or plane from Boston. Once you get there, you have a great range of lodging options, including some of the best gay guest houses in the world. If you love lobster and clam chowder, you'll think you're in heaven, but the town also offers a full range of dining options, sure to please even the most discriminating palates. By day there's the beach, shopping, historic and cultural offerings, bike paths, art galleries, and the classic tea dance every afternoon. By night you can catch cabaret acts by nationally known performers or indulge in fun, affordable nightlife for men and women.

Provincetown is located at the very tip of Cape Cod. The Cape is famous for its Atlantic Ocean beaches and great sand dunes, although the town of Provincetown itself is more adjacent to the ocean than on it— fronting Cape Cod Bay with water views but no real beach to speak of. It stretches east and west from its center, but is only a few blocks wide, creating a column of activity that runs down Commercial Street. Its proximity to Boston makes it particularly popular with Beantown denizens and other New Englanders, but visitors come from all over. The town has a distinctly New England feel, enhanced by fresh ocean breezes and namesake Cape Cod architecture. Life here is fairly wholesome for a big gay resort—bars close at 1:00 or 2:00 A.M., there's not much of a drug scene, and few if any of the guest houses offer the sexual playground atmosphere that is common in Palm Springs and Key West. It's not prudish, just a bit more innocent than Fire Island. You can find romantic isolation here—settling into a quaint guest house with a good book and/or lover, but you need to do so at the west or east end of town, or off-season.

CREATURES OF HABIT

In the summer, P'town is busy all week long, and especially so on the weekends. Although a lot of straight tourists come to town for the day, you'll never feel uncomfortable holding your lover's hand on **Herring Cove**, the gay beach, or **Commercial Street**, the main drag through town. You'll see lots of openly gay couples doing so. The social schedule runs like clockwork in the summer. The whole town seems to come together for tea dance every afternoon at 4:00 P.M., migrate to after-tea at **The Pied**, and then dissipate for dinner. Those who aren't ready for bed when the bars and clubs close at 1:00 or 2:00 A.M., head to **Spiritus Pizza** and hang out, spilling into the street and slowing traffic. It's a fun summer ritual, easy to repeat daily, but not essential to enjoying this definitively gay destination. Provincetown is a perfect destination for anyone who wants to take a step back to a simpler time. It recalls the kind of summer when the world was really yours from June until September. It's a real gay community without feeling like a ghetto, and it's the best of New England—quaint, charming, friendly, and fun.

When to Go and How to Get There

P'town is becoming a year-round resort, with more and more guest houses, restaurants, and stores staying open into or through the winter months. Although choices are limited in the winter, a lot of couples come to enjoy sweatshirted walks on the beach and snuggling by a real wood fire. The town is at its busiest during the summer, with July and August offering the best weather. Although the social activities dwindle rapidly after Labor Day, early fall offers great bargains in accommodations and shopping, and occasional Indian Summer temperatures. You can drive from Boston by taking the Southeast Expressway (I-93) south to Route 3 and then to Route 6, but beware the police in Truro, who have nothing better to do than stop cars, even for minor offenses. Driving time from Boston is about two hours, five from New York (barring bad traffic—Rt. 6 can be painstakingly slow, and there's no alternative). You can take the ferry from Boston on **Bay State Cruises** (617-723-7800). Trip time is 2 1/2 hours. Our favorite way is to fly on **Cape Air** (800-352-0714). Joint fares are available from many cities, with easy connections in Boston, particularly from USAir and Continental. The Cessna flight takes 25 minutes and offers great views, especially at sunset.

Accommodations

On the whole, it's hard to beat Provincetown's collection of gay, straight and mixed guest houses. The focus is more on genuine New England charm than resort-style facilities and amenities. You won't find many pools or extensive landscaping, but you will find a lot of quaint rooms and friendly hosts. Very few of the guest houses offer sexually charged environments, so we have replaced the "Sexual temperature" category with a "Quaint" category. Quaint is probably the least normative of any of our categories—the word literally means "odd in an old-fashioned way," and many of the places with medium to high Quaint ratings are just that, but others are compelling in a different manner that we can't quite define. They are certainly attractive and charming—just not in an odd, old-fashioned way. Regardless, "quaint" is not necessarily an indication of quality.

A NOTE ON ACCOMMODATIONS

Many of the houses here are old. Very old. Hundreds of years old. You'll find a lot of steep stairs, tiny or nonexistent closets, very little air conditioning, and some head-bumping potential on low-ceilinged staircases. If any of these particular items are problematic for you, be sure to ask when making reservations. Unless otherwise noted in the descriptions, all of the guest houses offer continental breakfast. **Provincetown Reservations System** (508-487-2021 or 800-648-0364) and **In Town Reservations** (508-487-1883 or 800-677-8696) are reservation services offering booking assistance for almost all Provincetown accommodations (including condo and house rentals), with each service handling a few properties exclusively. Both can be good resources when rooms are tight or if you're having a hard time choosing among the many options.

Amenities (air conditioning, TV, VCR, phone) listed in uppercase apply to all rooms; lowercase listings apply only to some rooms.

🌴🌴🌴🌴🌴

EXCEPTIONAL

BRASS KEY 9 Court Street; 508-487-9005 or 800-842-9858; fax 508-487-9020; $60–200

Owner Michael MacIntyre is a Ritz-Carlton alum and it shows. From the elegant yet comfortable furnishings, to the thoughtful amenities, to the professional, hard-working, and gracious staff, this is a class act and our first-choice house in town. A huge hot tub, nicely landscaped brick pool deck, phones in each room, and ideal location are all great. If the rooms had ocean views, we'd never leave. At press time, the owners of the Brass Key had purchased the Haven House, and were awaiting final approval to incorporate two of its buildings and its pool into the Brass Key complex.

WATER VIEW: slight **CLIENTELE:** EG/85%M **QUAINT:** high **ROOMS:** 12 **AMENITIES:** AC, TV, VCR, PHONE, fan **MEALS:** CB

BRADFORD GARDENS INN 178 Bradford Street; 508-487-1616 or 800-432-2334, fax 508/487-0191; $105–185

A real New England Colonial with hardwood floors, chenille bedspreads, beautiful wallpaper and appointments. Spectacular gardens, full breakfast, and a relaxed quiet atmosphere. Town houses are more modern, but in keeping with the feel of the main house.

WATER VIEW: distant **CLIENTELE:** EG/85%W **QUAINT:** high **ROOMS:** 19 **AMENITIES:** tv **MEALS:** FB

BEACONLITE 12/16 Winthrop Street; 508-487-9603, 800/696-9603, fax 508/487-9603; $40–160

With darker colors that give an English country-house feel, the house is elegant and well-run under new management of previous guests who liked the place so much they bought it. 16 Winthrop, also trading under the name Beaconlite, is more colorful and eclectic, but also very attractive.

WATER VIEW: none **CLIENTELE:** EG/70%M/30%W **QUAINT:** medium-high **ROOMS:** 15 **AMENITIES:** TV, AC, FANS **MEALS:** CB

ᛏᛏᛏᛏ

HIGHLY RECOMMENDED

BENCHMARK INN AND ANNEX 6–8 Dyer Street; 508-487-7440 or 888-487-7440, fax 508-487-3446; $65–225

Still in the renovation stage at press time, the Benchmark Inn is conditionally rated four-palms, based on the reputation and plans of its owners. Formerly the Christopher Inn, the Benchmark Inn is now under the same ownership as the Monument House and the Ranch, and plans to offer the highest level of service and amenities. Some rooms have exceptional water views; the eight annex rooms share common facilities but will offer a lower standard of amenities.

WATER VIEW: limited but excellent   **CLIENTELE:** 90%G/60%M/30%W
QUAINT: high   **ROOMS:** 15   **AMENITIES:** ac, TV, vcr, phones   **MEALS:**
ECB/CB

FAIRBANKS INN 90 Bradford Street; 508-487-0386 or 800-FAIRBNK, fax 508-487-3540; $50–175

Four-poster and sleigh beds, a lot of fireplaces, wide-plank floors, and a charming collection of antiques and reproductions work together to complete the feel of this restored 200-year-old captain's house. A convenient but quiet location is a plus.

WATER VIEW: none   **CLIENTELE:** EG/70%M/30%W   **QUAINT:** high
ROOMS: 15   **AMENITIES:** TV, vcr, AC, fan, PHONE   **MEALS:** ECB

LAND'S END 22 Commercial Street; 508-487-0706; $82–250

Layer upon layer of antiques, luxuriant plants, and artifacts make the place spectacularly unique in an *Addams Family* kind of way. Views are as impressive as the over-the-top décor. Friendly management.

WATER VIEW: excellent   **CLIENTELE:** Mixed G/S 60%G   **QUAINT:** unratable   **ROOMS:** 16   **AMENITIES:** FAN   **MEALS:** CB

PLUM'S 160 Bradford Street; 508-487-2283, $78–99

Victorian antiques, flowers, and potpourri come together to make this the most romantic women's house. A full gourmet breakfast awaits when you've awoken from your Laura Ashley dreams.

WATER VIEW: none **CLIENTELE:** EG/100%W **QUAINT:** high **ROOMS:** 5 **AMENITIES:** FAN **MEALS:** FB

SIX WEBSTER 6 Webster Place; 508-487-2266 or 800-693-2783, $55–200

One of the six oldest homes in P'town, this house offers the intimate colonial feel of old New England. Antiques, fireplaces, nine-person Jacuzzi, an ideal location, and friendly management make Six Webster a favorite.

WATER VIEW: none **CLIENTELE:** EG/90%G/75%M **QUAINT:** high **ROOMS:** 9 **AMENITIES:** TV, phone, FAN, ac **MEALS:** CB

SOMMERSET HOUSE 378 Commercial Street; 508-487-0383 or 800-575-1850, fax 508-487-4746; $55–115

A restored Victorian with a pleasant mix of antique and newer traditional furniture. Water views from the garden and a wide range of prices are attractive.

WATER VIEW: good **CLIENTELE:** 50%G **QUAINT:** medium-high **ROOMS:** 14 **AMENITIES:** FAN **MEALS:** CB

TRADEWINDS 12 Johnson Street; 508-487-0138, fax 508-487-9484, $55–130

Rich-colored walls, tiled baths, and Ethan Allen–elegant furnishings give Tradewinds an air of civility and charm, just slightly short of the character of the other houses in this category. The outdoor whirlpool and brick deck are joined by a new deck off the second floor.

WATER VIEW: some **CLIENTELE:** EG/75%M **QUAINT:** medium **ROOMS:** 16 **AMENITIES:** TV, VCR, fans **MEALS:** CB

WHITE WIND INN 174 Commercial Street; 508-487-1526, fax 508-487-3985; $60–165

High ceilings and Berber rugs complete the old New England feel of this gracious mansion. Their veranda is the ideal spot for watching the tea parade between the Boatslip and the Pied.

WATER VIEW: some **CLIENTELE:** EG/80%G/60%M/40%W **QUAINT:** high **ROOMS:** 19 **AMENITIES:** TV, ac, fans **MEALS:** CB

†††
RECOMMENDED

AMPERSAND 6 Cottage Street; 508-487-0959; $51–116

A Greek revival house, with a blend of contemporary and antique furnishings that works quite well. The sundeck has a view of the harbor; the location is just far enough west to be removed yet not inconvenient.

WATER VIEW: some   **CLIENTELE:** 95%G/80%M/20%W   **QUAINT:** high
ROOMS: 12   **AMENITIES:** tv, FAN   **MEALS:** CB

BOATSLIP 161 Commercial Street; 508-487-1669 or 800-451-7547; $110–150

Recently renovated rooms make this heart-of-the-action place an attractive option for men who want to be on top of the action (literally—tea dance is held here). Small private patios provide excellent views of the waterfront scenery and scene.

WATER VIEW: excellent   **CLIENTELE:** 95%G/90%M   **QUAINT:** low
ROOMS: 45   **AMENITIES:** TV, fans   **MEALS:** CB

CHECK'ER INN 25 Winthrop Street; 508-487-9029, or 800-894-9029, $75–100

A friendly comfortable atmosphere is the greatest selling point, but the rooms are quite nice, and the landscaping is very pretty (even our green-thumbed Aunt Lillian never had such beautiful house plants!).

WATER VIEW: none   **CLIENTELE:** EG/99%W   **QUAINT:** low   **ROOMS:** 8
AMENITIES: none   **MEALS:** CB

THE COMMONS 386 Commercial Street; 508-487-0358, 800-487-0784; $60–135

A charming set-up, much improved since its days as the Oceans Inn.
WATER VIEW: none   **CLIENTELE:** 90%G/50%M/50%W   **QUAINT:**
medium   **ROOMS:** 16   **AMENITIES:** TV, fan, ac   **MEALS:** CB

GABRIEL'S 104 Bradford Street; 508-487-3232 or 800-969-2643; $50–150

Immensely popular as the largest and most playful house for women. Recent additions include a hot tub, sauna, and workout and steam rooms. Guest rooms each have a theme dedicated to a noteworthy woman, some are slightly dark and odd-shaped.

WATER VIEW: none   CLIENTELE: EG/99%W   QUAINT: low   ROOMS: 20
AMENITIES: PHONE, TV

HERITAGE HOUSE 7 Center Street; 508-487-3692, $40–85

Airy, light, pretty, and friendly, the big rooms here are a good value. Common areas include a charming veranda and an in-tune piano that once accompanied Judy Garland at the Provincetown Playhouse. One drawback: all rooms share four baths.

WATER VIEW: distant   CLIENTELE: EG/60%W/40%M   QUAINT: high
ROOMS: 13   AMENITIES: none   MEALS: ECB

HAVEN HOUSE 12 Carver Street; 508-487-3031 or 800-261-2450, fax 508-487-4177; $45–100

Recently purchased by the owners of the Brass Key, the Haven House is in transition as parts of it, including the pool, are shifted to the Brass Key complex. We expect the remaining rooms to provide clean, comfortable, well-run and affordable accommodations.

WATER VIEW: none   CLIENTELE: EG/97%M/3%W   QUAINT: low
ROOMS: 7   AMENITIES: TV, AC   MEALS: CB

LAMPLIGHTER INN 26 Bradford Street; 508-487-2529 or 800-263-6574, fax 508-487-0079; $45–159

Under new ownership, the Lamplighter has updated its décor and upgraded its services to include an expanded continental breakfast and nightly turndown service. The hilltop location in the west end affords nice views. Attractive landscaping, off-street parking, and a rooftop deck round out the amenities.

WATER VIEW: some   CLIENTELE: 90%G/75%M/25%W   QUAINT: medium   ROOMS: 10   AMENITIES: TV, ac, PHONE, fan   MEALS: ECB

MONUMENT HOUSE 129 Bradford Street; 508-487-9664 or 800-942-1542, fax 508-487-3446; $39–99

Renovated and nicely furnished, added touches include fresh flowers and fresh pastries from the attached pastry shop. Rates include free parking.

WATER VIEW: none   CLIENTELE: 90%G/50%M/50%W   QUAINT: medium   ROOMS: 4   AMENITIES: TV, FAN   MEALS: CB

NORMANDY HOUSE 184 Bradford Street; 508-487-1197 or 800-487-1197; $40–145

Lovely, though not extraordinary décor, but the main attraction is the setting. Perched above the harbor, the Normandy offers the best view east of Land's End. From the roof deck to the large hot tub, the sight lines are spectacular.

WATER VIEW: excellent **CLIENTELE:** 90%G/60%M/40%W **QUAINT:** medium **ROOMS:** 8 **AMENITIES:** phone, TV, VCR, AC **MEALS:** CB

ROOMERS 8 Carver Street; 508-487-3532, $55–130

Quality antiques, tasteful décor, and spacious rooms and gardens have made this inn popular.

WATER VIEW: some **CLIENTELE:** 98%G/90%M/10%W **QUAINT:** high **ROOMS:** 10 **AMENITIES:** TV, FAN **MEALS:** CB

ROSE AND CROWN 158 Commercial Street; 508-487-3332, $45–130

A garage sale fantasy come true. Lots of interesting stuff to look at, more kitschy than the elegant Land's End. On the heart of the main strip, the place is relaxed and fun.

WATER VIEW: none **CLIENTELE:** EG/75%M/25%W **QUAINT:** high **ROOMS:** 8 **AMENITIES:** tv, FAN **MEALS:** CB

SANDPIPER BEACH HOUSE 165 Commercial Street; 508-487-1928 or 800-354-8628, fax 508-487-6021; $57–135

A turreted Victorian right next to the Boatslip, whose facilities are available to guests at no charge. Some rooms have private balconies, most have bay views, all have private baths.

WATER VIEW: very good **CLIENTELE:** Mixed G/ST **QUAINT:** medium-high **ROOMS:** 13 **AMENITIES:** TV, ac, PHONE, fan, vcr **MEALS:** CB

SHIREMAX 5 Tremont Street; 508-487-1233, $30–90

Features include large rooms, a quiet west-end location, and tasteful, though sometimes quirky décor. Well-maintained and named for the resident Samoyed-Husky dogs.

WATER VIEW: none **CLIENTELE:** 95%G/80%M/20%W **QUAINT:** medium-high **ROOMS:** 9 **AMENITIES:** tv, vcr, FAN **MEALS:** ECB

THREE PEAKS 210 Bradford Street; 508-487-1717 or 800-286-1715; $55–115

A classic Victorian with mostly reproduction furnishings and a wrap-around porch. The place is tasteful, quiet, and friendly. Off-street parking is provided.

WATER VIEW: none **CLIENTELE:** 90%G/50%M **QUAINT:** high **ROOMS:** 7 **AMENITIES:** TV, ac, fan **MEALS:** CB

WATERMARK INN 603 Commercial Street; 508-487-0165, fax 508-487-2383; $65–290

Rooms are open and airy, furnished in an Ikea-modern style. The real attraction is the waterfront location. Waterfront rooms open directly onto the 80-foot beach deck.

WATER VIEW: excellent **CLIENTELE:** 50%ST **QUAINT:** low **ROOMS:** 10 **AMENITIES:** PHONE, TV, FAN **MEALS:** none

WATERSHIP INN 7 Winthrop Street; 508-487-0094 or 800-330-9413, fax 508-487-2797; $29–147

With a décor that has a somewhat nautical theme, the place is simply but tastefully decorated. Comfortable common room and friendly service.

WATER VIEW: none **CLIENTELE:** 85%G/70%M/30%W **QUAINT:** medium **ROOMS:** 18 **AMENITIES:** tv, FAN **MEALS:** CB

WEST END INN 44 Commercial Street; 508-487-9555 or 800-559-1220, fax 508-487-8779; $65–179

This Greek Revival is quite pretty, tastefully decorated, and located in the quiet west end of town. Rooms are larger than average, and a full breakfast is included.

WATER VIEW: some **CLIENTELE:** EG/85%M/15%W **QUAINT:** medium **ROOMS:** 7 **AMENITIES:** TV, VCR, FAN **MEALS:** FB

OTHER RECOMMENDED

BULL RING WHARF 381 Commercial Street; 508-487-3100; $50–175

This is Cape Cod circa 1950. In any other setting, this furniture might elicit a "yuck," but somehow with the exposed beams and the seafront setting, it works. All apartments (minimum seven-night stay), be sure to get one in the old building with a water view.

WATER VIEW: very good **CLIENTELE:** 80%G/50%M/50%W **QUAINT:** high **ROOMS:** 16 **AMENITIES:** TV, FAN **MEALS:** none

CAPTAIN'S HOUSE 350A Commercial Street; 508-487-9353 or 800-457-8885; $40–119

Clean and comfortable, the décor is unremarkable but nice. Alley location off Commercial is convenient yet quiet.

WATER VIEW: some **CLIENTELE:** 85%G/85%M/15%W **QUAINT:** low-medium **ROOMS:** 19 **AMENITIES:** TV, FAN

CARL'S GUEST HOUSE 68 Bradford Street; 508-487-1650 or 800-348-2275, $30–100

Friendly, clean, and basic, with a lot of silk flowers. Pleasant sundeck and living room. Popular with Europeans.

WATER VIEW: none **CLIENTELE:** EG/99%M **QUAINT:** low **ROOMS:** 14 **AMENITIES:** tv, FAN, ac, vcr **MEALS:** coffee & tea

COAT OF ARMS 7 Johnson Street; 508-487-0816, or 800-224-8230; $35–75

The house is decorated in an eclectic souvenirs-of-the-world motif. All rooms are shared bath; a player piano with ample collection of music is an unusual highlight.

WATER VIEW: none **CLIENTELE:** EG/99%M **QUAINT:** high **ROOMS:** 19 **AMENITIES:** FAN **MEALS:** CB

CHICAGO HOUSE 6 Winslow Street; 508-487-0537 or 800-733-7869; $49–142

Homey and friendly, the house has a deserved reputation for attentive yet informal service. Rooms are average in size and decor; the location is residential but just steps away from the action.

WATER VIEW: none **CLIENTELE:** EG/80%M **QUAINT:** low **ROOMS:** 13 **AMENITIES:** tv, FANS **MEALS:** CB

REVERE GUEST HOUSE 14 Court Street; 508-487-2292, 800-487-2292; $30–100

Very small rooms, but tastefully decorated with a real New England feel. Friendly service and free parking.

WATER VIEW: none   **CLIENTELE:**   75%G/65%M/35%W   **QUAINT:** medium-high   **ROOMS:** 7   **AMENITIES:** tv, vcr, FAN, ac   **MEALS:** CB

THE BUOY 97 Bradford Street; 508-487-3082 or 800-487-2400; $30–95
Above average though unremarkable furnishings. The place is clean, pleasant, and well-located.

WATER VIEW: none   **CLIENTELE:**   99%G/50%M/50%W   **QUAINT:** medium   **ROOMS:** 9   **AMENITIES:** tv, ac   **MEALS:** CB

ANCHOR INN 175 Commercial Street; 508-487-0432 or 800-858-2657, fax 508-487-6280; $75–110
Grandly beautiful exterior, but virtually charmless interior, save some classic touches like the blue-embroidered name on the towels. New management is in the process of procuring antique furniture for some of the rooms, which should be a big help. Water views are marred only by the parking lot.

WATER VIEW: close to excellent   **CLIENTELE:** 50%G 50%ST   **QUAINT:** medium   **ROOMS:** 26   **AMENITIES:** TV   **MEALS:** CB

DEXTER'S INN 6 Conwell Street; 508-487-1911; $50–85
The house is mostly nondescript. A Spiegel catalog look and an unattractive location keep the place from rating higher.

WATER VIEW: none   **CLIENTELE:** mixed   **QUAINT:** low   **ROOMS:** 15   **AMENITIES:** TV, AC   **MEALS:** CB

HALLE'S 14 West Vine Street; 508-487-6310; $50–95
A new addition to P'town, Halle's has a green-and-white décor that is very pleasant. The west-end location and apartments-with-kitchen setup are good for those who crave a good night's sleep and don't need to change outfits six times a day.

WATER VIEW: none   **CLIENTELE:** 98%G/90%W   **QUAINT:** moderate   **ROOMS:** 4   **AMENITIES:** TV   **CB:** none

LADY JANE'S INN 7 Central Street; 508-487-3387; $60–80
Newly constructed in 1986, the inn is a classic Cape Cod–style building with unusual modern amenities such as individually con-

trolled thermostats, private entrances, and closet space. An uninspired common room and broken-shell courtyard round out the amenities.

WATER VIEW: none **CLIENTELE:** EG/99%W **QUAINT:** low-medium
ROOMS: 10 **AMENITIES:** TV **MEALS:** CB

THE RANCH 198 Commercial Street; 508-487-1542 or 800-942-1542, fax 508-487-3446; $29–79

Clean, small rooms with names like Stud Stall and Bull Pen, the Ranch caters to a leather/bear crowd. Nothing fancy, just a central location, friendly atmosphere, and a Colt Studios feel. Under new ownership; no breakfast, only morning coffee is provided.

WATER VIEW: none **CLIENTELE:** EG/100%M **QUAINT:** medium
ROOMS: 20 **AMENITIES:** FAN **MEALS:** coffee

RICHMOND INN 4 Conant Street; 508-487-9193; $35–100

Clean, basic, recently restored but low on charm.

WATER VIEW: none **CLIENTELE:** 90%G/80%M **QUAINT:** high **ROOMS:** 15 **AMENITIES:** FAN **MEALS:** CB

DUSTY MILLER 82 Bradford Street; 508-487-2213; $40–110

Small rooms are furnished with a mixture of wicker/Pier 1–type furniture. The front porch would be a great resting spot if it weren't overlooking a busy intersection. Pets are welcome.

WATER VIEW: some **CLIENTELE:** 90%G/90%W **QUAINT:** low **ROOMS:** 13 **AMENITIES:** tv, ac, FAN **MEALS:** coffee & tea

LAST RESORTS

CROWN & ANCHOR 247 Commercial Street; 508-487-1430; $50–95

Very faded charm of a 1950s-style New England inn, maintained with not much more than an occasional new coat of paint. Swimming pool and bar open in season.

WATER VIEW: very good **CLIENTELE:** 90%G/80%M **QUAINT:** low
ROOMS: 26 **AMENITIES:** PHONE, tv **MEALS:** none

LOTUS GUEST HOUSE 296 Commercial Street; 508-487-4644, fax 508-487-3733; $35–100

Very disappointing; only the heart-of-the-action location will be attractive to some. The very last resort.

WATER VIEW: some   CLIENTELE: 90%G/60%M   QUAINT: low   ROOMS: 13   AMENITIES: FAN

MOOR'S MOTEL 59 Provincelands; 508-487-1342 or 800-842-6379; $40–90

Definitively low-grade motel digs, mitigated by a spectacular view of the marshlands and value pricing.

WATER VIEW: excellent   CLIENTELE: 70%G/50%M   QUAINT: low   ROOMS: 32   AMENITIES: PHONE, TV, FAN   MEALS: CB

SEA DRIFT 80 Bradford Street; 508-487-3686; $30–70

An old-style guest house for men, all units are shared bath with simple and dated furnishings.

WATER VIEW: none   CLIENTELE: EG/100%M   QUAINT: low   ROOMS: 18   AMENITIES: FAN   MEALS: CB

Dining

P'town has a full range of casual to formal dining. Many of the restaurants emphasize seafood, but there is also a strong gourmet presence in town. We've listed our favorites in town—be sure to hit at least one of them during your stay. **Front Street** (230 Commercial Street; 508-487-9715; $17) serves continental cuisine with seating in wood-paneled booths. **Sebastian's Waterfront** (177 Commercial Street; 508-487-3286; $14) is a casual but stylish beachfront hot spot, featuring huge portions, moderate prices, and a late-night menu. **The Red Inn** (15 Commercial Street; 508-487-0050; $22) offers traditional New England dining in a charming Federal atmosphere. **The Lobster Pot** (321 Commercial Street; 508-487-0842; $16) is a definitively traditional New England seafood restaurant, on the water and very good, but very touristy and straight. **The Martin House** (157 Commercial Street; 508-487-1327; $20) serves new American cuisine in a quaint setting with harbor views. Good vegetarian specialties, better than ever, and your best choice in winter. **The Moors** (Bradford Street at Route 6; 508-487-0840; $17) has a dark, timbered dune-shack atmosphere and serves American and Portuguese food. **The Mews Restaurant** (429 Commercial Street; 508-487-1500; $17/10 café) offers excellent continental cuisine, Southern California ambiance, and great service. The upstairs café is more casual. **Pepe's Wharf** (371–373 Commercial Street; 508-487-0670; $21) offers American seafood and Portuguese specialties in a formal waterfront setting. **Gallerani's** (133 Commercial Street; 508-487-4433; $15) is the place for casual, Northern Italian cuisine. **Lorraine's** (229 Commercial Street [rear]; 508-487-6074; $14) is a local favorite, chef-owned, warm and welcoming bistro with a modern, surprising, and delightful Mexican menu. **Café Edwige** (333 Commercial Street [2nd floor]; 508-487-2008; $18) was always good for breakfast and now offers an innovative dinner menu fusing Mediterranean, Latin American, and Asian cuisines. **Dancing Lobster** (9 Ryder Street; 508-487-0900; $13) is a stylish simple wharf trattoria with an open kitchen, harbor views, and only eight tables. A real find, but they don't take reservations. The **Post Office Café** (303 Commercial Street; 508-487-3982; $8) is a gay-family-values version of Denny's: eggs, burgers, and an occasional drag queen.

Nightlife

Most of P'town's nightlife has been the same for years. While there is some variation each year, late night at the A-House and tea dance at the Boatslip really anchor the dance scene. Things get going (and end) on the early side here, running from tea dance until 1:00 or 2:00 A.M. when the discos close. Those who aren't ready to call it a night might be invited to a private after-party but are most likely to be found on the street in front of Spiritus Pizza. In addition to Boston disco bunnies, summertime also draws top-name gay and gay-popular performers to Provincetown. Some are one-night-only gigs, but many are extended runs.

The A-House (6 Masonic Street) is a year-round complex of three bars in a 1700s inn (the Atlantic House), with a dance bar, disco, quaint little bar, and upstairs leather/Levi's bar. **Back Street** (9 Carver Street) is the name of a popular disco more commonly called the Gifford House, which is where it is located. **The Boatslip** (151 Commercial Street) has a very popular gay and lesbian afternoon tea dance (3:30–6:30 P.M.) with small enclosed dance floor and much posing on the waterfront deck. Nightly dance themes include slow dancing and C&W. **Larry's Bar** (177 Commercial Street) is a very friendly, smaller bar—popular with both locals and visitors—located just past the foot of Court. Larry, formerly of the Boatslip, is the very popular bartender. **Kitty's** (Shankpainter and Court) is a small women's bar in a location formerly known as the Love Shack. **The Pied Piper** (193A Commercial Street) is a harborside dance bar with beachfront dock offering some of Provincetown's best DJs. Very popular gay male and lesbian after-tea tea dance beginning at 6:30 P.M. In the evenings, the Pied (nobody ever uses its formal last name) is the most popular lesbian hangout, and a great place to play pool. **Vixen** (336 Commercial Street; 508-487-6424) is another popular lesbian dance bar. The **Crown & Anchor** has been attempting to build a clientele for its dance floor and may succeed by the time you read this. Consult *Provincetown Magazine* or *In Newsweekly* for cabaret, performance, and special event schedules.

Activities

ATHLETIC AND OUTDOOR

Many gay visitors to P'town are slaves to the social schedule: Cruise the beach or Commercial Street until midafternoon, then tea dance, after-tea at the Pied, dinner, dancing, and hanging out at Spiritus Pizza after the clubs close. But there's a lot more to do in P'town and the adjacent Cape Cod National Seashore. The **Cape Cod National Seashore's Bicycle Trails** cover some amazing terrain: towering dunes, eerie scrub pine, and the whitecapped ocean. Rent a bike at **Arnold's** (508-487-0844), where you can also get a free map. There are over five miles to ride in the Provincelands Reservation alone, most not very strenuous, with additional trails in other parts of the National Seashore. The **Dolphin Fleet** (offices located in the Chamber of Commerce Building at the head of the P'Town Pier, 800-826-9300) and the **Portuguese Princess** (508-487-2651) offer sunset whale-watch cruises. The **National Seashore Visitors Center** (Race Point Road, 508-487-1256) offers a number of interesting ranger-led hikes (all free) that explore the seashore's flora, fauna, and history. There's also a gift shop where you can buy the best postcards in town, as well as maps and books. **Get a beach-fire permit.** This is perhaps one of the most romantic things you can do in Provincetown. Buy something to grill, or just some sandwiches and a thermos full of lemonade or sangria, bring your own firewood, and as the sun sets on nearly deserted Race Point Beach, hug someone tight and enjoy one of the most magical evenings you'll ever have. Permits are given in limited numbers on a first-come basis, but usually aren't hard to get because so few people know about them. **Long Nook Beach** in Truro is a spectacle of dune and surf that is officially open only to Truro residents, but you can bicycle there and enjoy it no matter where you're from. One of the best beaches on the Cape, maybe in the United States, Long Nook is dramatic and private, and even has an au natural section if you walk far enough to the right. The **Atlantic White Cedar Swamp Trail** at the Marconi Station in Wellfleet (off Route 6, follow signs) offers a 1.25-mile self-guided nature walk. The Marconi Station is where the first wireless transmission from the United States to Europe was sent on January 18, 1903. The **Provincetown Gym** (170 Commercial Street; 508-487-2776) is small but has all the equipment you need for a pre-tea muscle pump. **Mussel Beach** (56 Shank Painter Road; 508-487-0001) is also a small gym, with fewer women and more cruising.

SIGHTSEEING

The **Pilgrim Monument** is the tallest all-granite structure in the United States, built in 1910 and affording a 360-degree view from its stairway-accessed summit. The adjacent **Provincetown Museum** (508-487-1310) chronicles the town's history.

SHOPPING

Commercial Street is the place. Walk one end to the other, and find a great assortment of resort and casual clothing, art, jewelry, and souvenirs.

FYI

Provincetown has two gay publications in season. *Provincetown Magazine* (508-487-1000) and Boston-based *In Newsweekly* (617-426-8246). The **Provincetown Business Guild** (800-637-8696) can let you know the annual schedule for Women's Week, Single Men's Weekend, and other special events.

Ogunquit, Maine

Popular with actors and artists in the 1920s, Ogunquit has long been a refuge for gay women and men. Ogunquit is the Indian name for "beautiful by the sea" and it lives up to its reputation in every way. This picturesque coastal town boasts a quiet, restful atmosphere, making it a popular resort for gay women and men in the Northeast. While Ogunquit is not exclusively gay, it is a place where gay and straight mix comfortably. Maine is one of a handful of states with a good record on gay rights legislation, and while its citizens (gay and straight) may be more conservative and reserved than those in southern New England, they have proven themselves committed to the true ideal of "liberty and justice for all." Ogunquit offers three miles of beach with good surf and soft sand, and plenty of open space during the week. On summer weekends, a slew of visitors fill the beach and town, creating a festive atmosphere that offers just enough excitement and diversion to satisfy those Energizer Bunny types who can't slow down enough to enjoy flying a kite and playing gin rummy. Although Ogunquit is short on the rainbow flag-waving that makes Provincetown such an obviously gay community, it has enough gay residents, visitors, and businesses to keep you feeling welcomed and entertained.

The grand old wooden hotels that played host to Ogunquit's early visitors were replaced by high-end motels in the 1960s, and more recent development has added condos, art galleries, restaurants, and boutiques. In the summer, open-sided trolleys shuttle visitors between the village, the beach, Perkins Cove, and Route 1 establishments. The village and nearby towns of Wells, York, and Kennebunkport offer quaint sightseeing, shopping, and dining that are the stuff of your Pepperidge Farm–scented vacation dreams. Ogunquit is old New England with open arms for the modern gay traveler.

When to Go and How to Get There

Ogunquit is very much a seasonal resort. The time to visit is from early May to October. Most shops and businesses close after Columbus Day weekend. Ogunquit is easily accessible by private car or public transportation. By car, Ogunquit is just a few miles off Interstate 95 (the Maine Turnpike). You can either take the Wells exit and drive south on U.S. Route 1 or you can take the York exit and go north on Route 1. (Route 1 is Main Street in Ogunquit.) The town is less than an hour south of Portland and less than an hour and a half north of Boston. A car is not really necessary once you're there, so you might consider flying into Portland International Jetport on USAir or Delta, or taking the bus to Portsmouth, New Hampshire. **All Season Taxi** (207-646-1126) offers service from either port. You can easily move between Ogunquit and its coastal neighbors on seasonal bus service run by **Coastal Connection** (207-282-5408) servicing the towns from York to Kennebunkport.

Accommodations

Ogunquit has many gay-friendly inns and motels, and a few gay-popular ones. Many have shared baths, and almost all are closed in the winter. Expect simple but charming in the New England style and you won't be disappointed.

THE YELLOW MONKEY 168 Main Street; 207-646-9056; $40–115

Forty-two guest rooms, a large Jacuzzi, a fitness room, and a sundeck on top of the roof. The Yellow Monkey is the most well-known gay-popular place to stay in Ogunquit. Continental breakfast is served each morning. Rooms are decorated with antique furniture.

HERITAGE OF OGUNQUIT P.O. Box 1295, Ogunquit; 207-646-7787; $45–75

This four-room B&B is lesbian-owned (and women-popular) and is ten minutes by foot to the beach and town. There are five acres of woods behind the guest house to ensure serenity, an outdoor deck, and common room with VCR, TV, microwave, and toaster oven.

INN AT TWO VILLAGE SQUARE 135 Route 1; 207-646-5779; $35–120

Eighteen guest rooms have air conditioning and color TVs; 14 of those have private baths. Open through Columbus Day, the Inn draws a mixed gay and lesbian clientele, and features an expanded continental breakfast, heated pool, and hot tub.

ROCKMERE LODGE 40 Stearns Road; 207-646-2985; $60–135

A charming guest house with a mixed clientele, beautiful pool and garden, wrap-around porch and a great view.

GAZEBO Route 1; 207-646-3733; $65–105

A great 1865 Greek Revival farmhouse, open year-round, with a pool and antique furnishings. Most rooms have private baths, and the clientele is mixed gay/straight.

CLIFF HOUSE Shore Road; 207-361-1000, fax 207-361-2122; $95–175

A large, straight resort complex set on 70 ocean front acres with spectacular views. Rooms in Cliffscape, opened in 1990, are the nicest, with furnished balconies and traditional room furnishings. The crowd skews heavily toward seniors and families.

Dining

Most of Ogunquit's restaurants cater to a mixed or primarily straight clientele. The **Porch Café** (Shore Road and Ogunquit Square; 207-646-3976; $9) serves good American fare to a largely gay clientele (it's attached to the Front Porch Bar), often accompanied by live piano music. **Roberto's Italian Cuisine** (82 Shore Road; 207-646-8130; $12) is a chef-owned trattoria specializing in traditional Southern Italian cuisine. It is relatively gay-popular, as is **Poor Richard's Tavern** (Shore Road; 207-646-4722; $14), serving great lobster stew and other hearty fare in a charming old house. **Barnacle Billy's** (Perkins Cove; 207-646-5575; $13) serves up mouthwatering seafood overlooking the harbor. In addition to steamers and lobster rolls, you can select your own Maine lobster weighing in at up to four pounds; mobbed in the summer with no reservations accepted. **Arrows** (Berwick Road; 207-361-1100; $27) serves "Innovative American" cuisine in a 1765 colonial farmhouse overlooking an expansive country garden, which provides the restaurant with fresh produce. Arrows also makes its own pasta, cures prosciutto, and bakes its own breads and pastries. The clientele is a good mix of gay and straight, the wine list is the largest in the state, and you can count on one of the best meals in the region. Reservations are recommended. **Hurricane** (Perkins Cove; 207-646-6348; $17) has a lovely view of the ocean and a very large wine list. The kitchen is noted for specialties such as Maine lobster chowder, black bean soup, lobster rolls, grilled portobello mushroom salad, steamed mussels, Maine lobsters, plank-roasted haddock, veal chop, and grilled swordfish. Reservations are highly recommended in season; open year round. **Gypsy Sweethearts** (18 Shore Road; 207-646-7021; $14) serves a great gourmet breakfast of inspired egg dishes, and also serves a good dinner.

Nightlife

The Club (13 Main Street; 207-646-6655) is the only dance bar in Ogunquit. It caters primarily to men, although women are welcome. The Club has a video lounge upstairs. Every Sunday there is a tea dance that goes from 4:00 to 8:00 P.M., with a $1.75 bottled-beer special. Every Labor Day, the bar holds an annual Speedo contest on the beach where a new "Mr. Speedo" is honored. An alternative is **The Front Porch** (Ogunquit Square, near Shore Road; 207-646-4005), a piano bar/lounge featuring cabaret singers every other Wednesday in season, with a piano player other days. You can grab a bite to eat downstairs at **The Porch Café**, which serves burgers and seafood at moderate prices. Both clubs are open through Columbus Day.

Activities

ATHLETIC AND OUTDOOR

The beach is a prime attraction here, and you'll find the gay section about 200 yards north of the main entrance. **Marginal Way** is a mile-long beachfront walk that leads to Perkins Cove. The nearby town of Wells is home to the **Rachel Carson National Wildlife Refuge** (off Route 9; 207-646-9226), a one-mile nature trail through white pine forest and a salt marsh. Bike riding is both scenic diversion and practical transportation.

SIGHTSEEING

Perkins Cove is a fishing cove that may look familiar—its foot bridge is one of the most frequently depicted scenes in the state. Its weathered fish shacks are home to nearly 50 restaurants and shops, and the boats here offer fishing and excursion trips. The **Ogunquit Museum of American Art** (Shore Road; 207-646-4909) is an impressive stone-wood-glass structure displaying the work of nationally recognized artists with an emphasis on local talent. The **Ogunquit Playhouse** (Route 1; 207-646-5511) has staged big-name summer-stock productions since 1933. **Kennebunkport**, the summer home of George and Barbara Bush, is a popular nearby tourist destination.

SHOPPING

Just a short ride south on Route 1 in **Kittery** you will find **outlet stores** for J. Crew, Polo/Ralph Lauren, Crate and Barrel, Eddie Bauer, and Timberland, just to name a few. In the town of **Freeport**, which is also along Route 1, you will find Banana Republic, Bass Shoes, Calvin Klein, Reebok, Nike, Patagonia, Cole Haan, Gap, and Donna Karan, as well as L.L.Bean, which is open 365 days a year, 24 hours a day. On Route 1 in Wells you'll find a cluster of antiquarian bookstores, the largest of which is the **Douglas N. Harding Map & Print Gallery** (Route 1; 207-646-8785) with 4,500 square feet of old and rare books, maps, and prints.

FYI

Although the Boston gay papers carry some Ogunquit advertising and event listings, you won't find any extensive coverage of the local scene. The **Ogunquit Chamber of Commerce** (P.O. Box 2289, Ogunquit, ME 03907; 207-646-2939) operates an **Information Center** (207-646-5533) on Route 1 just south of Ogunquit village. It is open all week Memorial Day through Labor Day, and weekends through Columbus Day.

Saugatuck, Michigan

Just two hours from Chicago and four from Detroit lies one of the Midwest's busiest summer gay getaways. Saugatuck, originally an artists' village, is a quaint but bustling town located on the sandy shores of eastern Lake Michigan. There are few remaining vestiges of Saugatuck's early history, and today it attracts a wide range of summer visitors, from families to bikers, who cohabit the town relatively peacefully. Saugatuck and the surrounding cities of South Haven, Douglas, and Holland are home to a community of weekend regulars, whose abodes range from elaborately restored vacation homes (see the February 1993 issue of *Metropolitan Home* for a feature on them) to overnight sailboats and yachts. The *Wall Street Journal* called it the gayest little town in the Midwest, and while its status as a gay resort is still a controversial attribute to its residents, the local gay boys and girls who escape there each summer will be glad to welcome you, and incidences of homophobia are rare.

The gay scene is relatively concentrated in a small number of venues—the beach by day, Douglas Dunes by night, and a main drag of shops and restaurants. The Blue Star Highway runs through the compact town and across the lake/river bridge into the sleepier neighboring community of Douglas. Neither town is exceedingly charming, overdeveloped, or gay-monopolized, but together they offer a quiet, low-key, gay summer experience, wholesome and fun for the whole gay family.

When to Go and How to Get There

Saugatuck is a four-seasons resort, but really only gay-popular in the summer. The closest airport is Grand Rapids, about a 40-minute drive. Most visitors drive from the Chicago/Detroit areas, and you can, too. From Chicago, take 90/94 to 31 to Saugatuck/Douglas exit. From Detroit, take 96 to 196 to Saugatuck exit or 94 to 131 to 89 (back roads).

The drive is about 2 1/2 hours from Chicago and 3 1/2 from Detroit. Once you're in Saugatuck, driving to the beach is the most expedient way to get there, but it isn't the only method. Another route is to shmooze your way aboard ship and join the daily flotilla of sailboats, houseboats, and yachts that navigate down the winding channel, past downtown Saugatuck, and into Lake Michigan. Once out of the harbor and onto the lake, many of the boats anchor just off the private beach and a party of fellow sailors and visitors from shore turns the afternoon into a social event.

Accommodations

Many accommodations are in the town of Douglas, just across the river from Saugatuck.

DOUGLAS DUNES RESORT 333 Blue Star Highway, Douglas; 616-857-1401; $42–125

The main gay resort in town, on 14 acres. It has 10 cottages, 22 motel rooms and 3 suites, in addition to a pool, bars, and disco. Douglas Dunes Resort is mostly gay men, some gay women.

KIRBY HOUSE B&B 294 W. Center, Douglas; 616-857-2904; $65–135

A Queen Anne Victorian with seven rooms, pool, and sundeck. It was for sale at press time, casting doubt on its future gay-friendliness.

ALPEN HAUS B&B 41 Spring Street, Douglas; 616-857-1119; $45–75

A mixed gay-straight B&B, with six rooms and lovely appointments.

PINES MOTEL 56 South Blue Star Highway; 616-857-5211; $35–84

Convenient, clean, and cheap.

DRIFT-WOODS COTTAGES 2731 Lakeshore Drive, Fennville; 616-857-2586; $65–200

Offers lakeshore cottages about 10 minutes from Saugatuck, with a mostly female clientele.

DEERPATH LODGE 616-857-3337; $70-100

Offers women travelers three guestrooms on a secluded 45 acres.

CAMP IT CAMPGROUNDS 6635 118th Avenue, Fennville; $10-15/day; 616-543-4335

Caters to the tent and RV set.

Dining

Saugatuck has a number of gay-popular eateries averaging $9. **Café Sir Douglas** (333 Blue Star Highway, Douglas; 616-857-1401), at the Douglas Dunes Resort, serves dinner only, to a decidedly gay clientele. **Restaurant Toulouse** (248 Culver Street; 616-857-1561) serves excellent country French cuisine in a romantic atmosphere. Open for lunch and dinner, reservations recommended on weekends. The **Kalico Kitchen** (329 Ferry Street; 616-857-2678) offers big breakfasts and late-night dining—open 24 hours on weekends. **Ida Reds Cottage** (645 Water Street; 616-857-5803) serves a great breakfast/brunch in town. **Marro's Italian Restaurant** (147 Water Street; 616-857-4248) serves pizza and standard Italian fare to a mixed crowd. **Global Bar & Grill** (215 Butler Street; 616-857-1555) also caters to a mixed crowd, but has a fun, local tavern atmosphere and good, casual gourmet menu.

Nightlife

By night, the action centers around the **Douglas Dunes Resort** (333 Blue Star Highway, Douglas; 616-857-1401). This gay complex has a front bar/disco, a cabaret lounge, and a patio bar. Most of the action occurs out on the patio deck, which may or may not be connected to the fact that the music in the disco is at least three years old. It is tacky, but a lot of fun. On occasion, particularly the occasion of the big three holiday weekends, the place can get very crowded.

Activities

ATHLETIC AND OUTDOOR

Evenings in this casual resort community revolve around multicottage group dinners, sunset cruises, and an occasional A-list party. Daytime activities revolve around the beach. **Oval Beach**, just a mile down the road from town, is the place to be. Park at the far north end of the parking lot ($3). From there, spread out your beach towel directly in front of the volleyball court and join the local boys. Another option is to pay an additional $5 to attain access to a half-mile stretch of private beach. The private beach allows sun worshippers to bring along pets and alcohol, as well as sport "limited" swimwear. Beach access laws allow public access of 10 feet along all waterways, so most boys opt for the public beach and twice daily sashay down the private beach shoreline to model their summer swimwear and say hello to those strolling in the reverse direction. The nearest gym is **Flex** (474 Century Lane; 616-396-2901 $7/day), located in Holland, about 10 minutes away.

SIGHTSEEING

Climb **Mt. Lookout** for a great panoramic view of Saugatuck and Lake Michigan. Tour the **S.S. Keewatin,** a 1907 Great Lakes ferry boat that is permanently docked in the harbor. The **Red Barn Playhouse** (63rd Street at Blue Star; 616-857-7707) offers summer stock theater. Scenic dune rides are a popular activity for visitors. Call **Saugatuck Dune Rides** (6495 Washington Road; 616-857-2253) for information. **Harbor Village** (Blue Star Highway and Union Street; 616-857-2107) offers a ship museum and boat rides.

SHOPPING

In downtown Saugatuck, you'll find a variety of shops. **2nd Home** (146 Butler Street; 616-857-2208) has a great selection of home furnishings. **Hoopdee Scootie** (133 Mason Street; 616-857-4141) sells novelties, gay gifts, and trinkets. **The Casual Man & Woman** (133 Butler Street;

616-857-2665) is the place for casual men's and women's clothing (no surprise). Just across the bridge in downtown Douglas, you'll find some interesting art galleries, including the **Joyce Petter Gallery** (161 Blue Star Highway, Douglas; 616/857-7861), selling the work of national and regional artists, and the **Out of Hand Gallery** (36 Center Street, Douglas; 616-857-1420), specializing in fine art and watercolors by Michigan artists. If you're around on the last Sunday of the month, check out the **Allegan Antique Fair**, a 25-minute drive away. It's filled with local gay cottage owners searching for tchotchkes for their little gay cottages.

FYI

You'll find events schedules and ads for the Douglas Dunes in the gay magazines in Chicago (*Gay Chicago;* 312-327-7271) and Detroit (*Metra;* 313-543-3500). General travel information is available from the **Saugatuck Information Booth**, located at Culver and Butler Streets, and open on weekends from Memorial Day to Labor Day. The **Saugatuck Area Business Association** (616-857-3133) publishes a handy member directory, which you can pick up at member businesses or the information booth.

Russian River, Guerneville, California

"The River," as local San Franciscans call it, has begun to catch on with gay and lesbian travelers from the far reaches of the country. Russian River is a more rustic summer location than the other destinations in this book. Visitors to the area will find a gay wilderness retreat focused on the shores of the river, but close to the heart of California's urbane and stylish wine country, which increases its appeal for those who are less at ease with nature. Just as life on Fire Island is defined by the New Yorkers who use it as a regular weekend getaway, life on the river is defined by the San Franciscans who overwhelmingly dominate the summer population here. As a result, the Russian River area reflects San Francisco's multicultural mix and liberal P.C. politics. The emphasis here is on the great outdoors, with river and forest scenery being the primary attraction. The river offers canoeing, sandy beaches, and waterhole swimming. The forest creates a perfect setting for enclaves of privacy—well utilized by the abundance of cabin accommodations, outdoor hot tubs, and clothing-optional sundecks. You'll find a lot of tented and vehicle camping, and a laid-back, unaffected atmosphere that can be refreshing or disappointing, depending on your perspective. Although it's never fair to generalize, compared to other resort denizens, the crowd here is likely to include more women who are lesbians with a capital *L*, fewer men who shave (chests or chins), a high percentage of pierced body parts, and a low incidence of too-good-to-talk-to-you attitude. You definitely don't have to be a granola-crunchy-Haight-Ashbury homosexual to enjoy Russian River, but it doesn't hurt.

Travelers of all ages enjoy the river. At the larger resorts, you'll find the full range of twenties to sixties. In town, you'll see singles and couples enjoying the nightlife, though homeowners often elect to spend their nights at home with friends. (They may, however, sneak in a cocktail while dashing out to the Safeway for more salad fixings!) Special weekends for women and leathermen occur each spring and fall, upping the action ante, and women's weekends dramatically change the usual male-dominated demographics. Yes, there are beautiful bodies, but the "scene" is relaxed and less a cult of muscles than the scene in

Fire Island or P'town. Pretensions fall quickly when the most popular cologne is Deep Woods Off and the most popular swimming hole is co-ed and clothing-optional. If sleeping under the stars is more your speed than dancing until dawn, the Russian River resort area is for you.

At the heart of the Russian River communities is the town of Guerneville, surrounded by the towns of Forestville, Rio Nido, and Monte Rio. Heavy floods in the winter of 1995 caused millions of dollars in damage, but thanks to good insurance policies, most businesses came back better than ever, with much-improved shops and guest houses.

Life at the river is definitely not a fashion show. Warm, sunny days call for shorts, T-shirts, sandals, and a swimsuit (mostly optional). Cool nights call for jeans and sweatshirts, with a tank top layered underneath if you're thinking about kicking up your heels. Bug spray is a good idea, especially for those who will be camping out, and sunscreen is a must for the fair skinned.

When to Go and How to Get There

Russian River is a seasonal resort, most popular in the summer because of its outdoor focus. Although it doesn't shut down for the winter, off-season visits are definitely about peace and quiet, and are more popular with straight visitors. The River is a very easy 90-minute drive from San Francisco. The most direct route is to take Highway 101 North to the River Road exit and then go west for approximately 18 miles to the Russian River towns of Rio Nido, Guerneville, and Monte Rio. If you choose to fly, the closest airports are Sonoma County, Oakland, and San Francisco. Bus service is an option, leaving from San Francisco to Santa Rosa. The carrier is **Golden Gate Transit** (415-453-2100).

Accommodations

In keeping with the outdoorsy nature of the area, most of the hostelries in the area feature spacious, woody grounds and relatively unadorned rooms. All listings are Guerneville unless noted.

THE FERN GROVE INN 16650 River Road; 707-869-9083 or 800-347-9083; $69–259

Features cottage accommodations, all with color TVs, some with living rooms, fireplaces, and/or VCRs. A continental breakfast is served each morning, and there is a swimming pool on the premises. Fern Grove Inn sits on eight acres of redwoods within walking distance to town. Clientele is an easy mix of gay and straight.

HIGHLANDS RESORT 14000 Woodland Drive; 707-869-0333; $40–105

Situated on four acres of redwoods, this resort serves a large gay and lesbian clientele with 16 guest rooms, some cabins with fireplaces, and a clothing-optional pool and hot tub.

RUSSIAN RIVER RESORT or "Triple R"; 16390 Fourth Street; 707-869-0691 or 800-417-3767; $40–90

Open year round, with 24 renovated rooms featuring private baths and color TV. Many rooms have wood-burning stoves. The property features a heated pool, hot tub, and the Mill Street Grill, serving breakfast, lunch, and dinner.

PARADISE COVE RESORT 14711 Armstrong Woods Road; 707-869-2706; $65–135

This gay-owned resort is in its twelfth year, drawing a good mix of men and women. With 15 rooms, it is surrounded by flowering plants and palm trees, which lend a tropical feel. All rooms have private baths and most have cable TV and fireplaces. Continental breakfast is served only on weekends and holiday mornings.

THE WILLOWS 15905 River Road; 707-869-2824; $49–129

Has been around for 20 years and serves a mostly gay and lesbian clientele. The 13-room lodge sits on five acres overlooking the river. A large main room with a fireplace is open to guests. An expanded continental breakfast is offered. Guests can also use the full kitchen downstairs. Canoes are available.

HUCKLEBERRY SPRINGS P.O. Box 400, Monte Rio; 707-865-2683 or 800-822-2683; $145

Hosts a gay and straight clientele in four guest cottages on 56 acres. Guests can enjoy a full breakfast in a solarium overlooking a garden, and a California-style dinner on Wednesday and Saturday nights for $25 per person. Added features include a swimming pool, a massage cottage, an outdoor Japanese landscaped spa with a hot tub, and a dramatic view. Each room comes with a VCR, color TV, and coffee maker.

HIGHLAND DELL INN 21050 River Road, Monte Rio; 707-865-1759 or 800-767-1759; $75–225

This well-appointed turn-of-the-century house is on the river in nearby Monte Rio and is one of the most deluxe options in the area. The clientele is mostly gay, and the atmosphere is quiet and serene.

Dining

Burdon's Restaurant (15405 River Road; 707-869-2615; $15) offers affordable continental cuisine including prime rib, chicken, pasta, and seafood. Closed Tuesday and Wednesday. **Breeze Inn Bar-B-Que** (15640 River Road; 707-869-9209; $7) is often considered the best barbecue in northern California. Women-owned, it serves ribs, chicken, and smoked turkey, bottles its own barbecue sauce, and delivers on a three-wheel motorcycle. **Brew Moon Coffee** (16248 Main Street; 707-869-0201) serves salads, bagels, pastries, and gourmet coffees. Also women-owned, it features singers and musicians in the summer. **Sweet's River Grill** (16251 Main Street; 707-869-3383; $12) dishes up California cuisine in an outdoor setting. Sonoma lasagna, Thai mushroom burrito, and garden burgers are just some of the featured entrées. **Baghdad by the Green** (19400 Hwy. 116, Monte Rio; 707-865-2454; $15) is a woman-owned and operated restaurant serving French and Continental cuisine. **Lalita's Cantina and Restaurant** (16225 Main Street, 707-869-3238; $8) is a colorful Mexican restaurant, women-owned with a mixed clientele. Special events including karaoke, guest singers and musicians enliven the atmosphere.

Nightlife

Taking a moonlight stroll through the woods followed by a soothing hot tub under a starry sky is the Russian River's greatest nightlife, but there are plenty of other options for those who prefer cocktails or dancing or looking for a companion for that moonlight stroll. The **Rainbow Cattle Company** (16220 Main Street; 707-869-0206) is a Guerneville bar located in the middle of town. You'll find a mix of gay women and men enjoying pinball machines, two pool tables, and music that ranges from rock to C&W. A popular happy hour offers reduced price drinks from 5:00 to 8:00 P.M. daily. **Molly Brown's Saloon** (14120 Old Cazadero Road; 707-869-0206) is a popular C&W club. **Fifes** (16467 River Road; 707-869-0656) is a popular night spot, with a piano bar, patio and C&W dance floor. The **Triple R Resort** (16390 4th Street; 707-869-0691) is party headquarters, mostly male-oriented, with a lot of events—fundraisers, pool parties, and the like.

Activities

ATHLETIC AND OUTDOOR

The list of things to do at the river is exhaustive. Though most visitors choose to spend their day sunbathing in close proximity to the water, lunch needn't be your most taxing activity. Hiking, canoeing, horseback riding, golf, cycling, and paddleboating are just some of the diversions available within minutes of most lodging. The **Armstrong Redwoods State Reserve** (1700 Armstrong Woods Road; 707-865-2391) offers picturesque hiking among spectacular redwoods, just five minutes from downtown Guerneville. Guerneville itself offers varied shopping, from books to crystals. Many resorts offer river access. If yours doesn't, you can pay a day-use fee at another resort, or use public or secluded beaches. The beach in Guerneville is mostly straight but friendly—a lot of kids and activity. Smaller beaches at the resorts or Wohler Bridge are popular with gays; ask a local or the staff at your resort for directions to these and the more secluded, clothing-optional beaches. **Mike's Bike Rental** (16442 Main Street; 707-869-1106) rents bikes by the hour, half day, or full day. **Burke's Canoe Trips** (8600 River Road, Forestville; 707-887-1222) offers a full-day rental for $30; reservations are a must.

SIGHTSEEING

Countless Northern California attractions are within an hour's drive of Guerneville. The **vineyards** of Sonoma County are just 20 minutes away; Napa is about an hour away. The nearby **Sonoma** and **Marin** coasts offer dramatic views and fresh oysters. For movie buffs, **Bodega Bay**, the scene of Tippi Hedren's showdown with *The Birds*, is right near many state beaches and nature preserves. **Clear Lake** and the mud baths of **Calistoga** are both about an hour away.

SHOPPING

Guerneville has some quaint shops, but save your plastic until you're back in San Francisco. Wine lovers can buy vineyard-direct in Sonoma and Napa valleys.

FYI

The **Russian River Chamber of Commerce** (16200 First Street; 707-869-3533) can also offer assistance, including the dates of the annual **Leather** and **Women's Weekends,** the **Russian River Jazz Festival,** and other special-event weekends. The **Russian River Region Visitors' Bureau** (800-253-8800) is knowledgeable about gay events. **Russian River Wine Roads** (707-433-6782 or 800-648-9922) organizes wine-related activities throughout the year.

Palm Springs, California

In the dead of winter, when the East Coast is buried under three feet of snow, and Florida is experiencing a "freak cold spell" (seemingly an annual possibility these days), there's one gay destination you can count on for heat. Just a two-hour drive from L.A. or San Diego, Palm Springs is a hot destination in both senses of the word. With a lot of gay guest houses and a unique amalgam of attractions, this warm, dry-desert climate draws visitors from all over the world, especially from nearby Southern California communities. A marketing-aggressive group of guest-house owners helped put Palm Springs on the map as a gay resort, and while they have sometimes overhyped the place, they have done a great job of creating a destination where you can enjoy a wide range of gay and nongay vacation activities.

As Highway 10 approaches Palm Springs, the billboards on the side of the road are your only indication that a resort community awaits to break the low desert monotony of your drive. Turning off the highway, Palm Springs soon appears like the Technicolor Emerald City at the end of the Yellow Brick Road. *City,* however, is a misnomer—despite extensive development, Palm Springs still feels like a small town, with only 50,000 permanent residents and no tall buildings. Although Palm Springs has become the golf capital of the world, it is the natural hot springs that originally spurred the area's development. (You can still enjoy the springs in town at the Spa Hotel.) Set at the foot of the San Jacinto mountains, the desert scenery is dramatic, and many resorts are designed and landscaped to take advantage of the spectacular views.

Palm Springs' greatest calling card is its weather. Although it is too hot for our tastes in the summer, it's great the rest of the year. With 330 days of sunshine annually, the skies are almost always clear and the days warm to hot. It's never humid and muggy, and at night, the temperature often drops 30 degrees—providing cool relief and offering additional wardrobe options. The climate is ideal for golf and tennis, and no other gay-popular destination has such extensive facilities for enthusiasts of those two sports. Most of the big mainstream resorts are built around golf and tennis facilities, with paid access privileges for nonguests. The mountain offers hiking and camping for those who enjoy their outdoors a bit rougher, and a tram ride to its summit for those who want to exercise just their eyes. Nonathletic types will appreciate Palm Springs' most participatory sport: lounging. Rest and relaxation top the list of daily activities, and if you like the idea of lying by a pool and looking at the mountains, you'll love Palm Springs.

The large gay presence in Palm Springs is belied by the predominantly straight environment. The area actually consists of five contiguous communities: Palm Springs, Cathedral City, Rancho Mirage, Palm Desert, and Indian Wells, all of which have extensive facilities and developments catering to retirees, second homes, and tourists. Gay life is limited almost exclusively to Palm Springs and Cathedral City. The largest concentration of gay guest houses is in the Warm Sands area of Palm Springs, followed by San Lorenzo, and then Cathedral City, which is also home to much of the gay nightlife. Palm Canyon Drive (Highway 111) is the main drag, running parallel to Freeway 10 through the five communities. It goes one-way south through downtown, with Indian Canyon Drive running north. Other than the cluster of gay resorts in the residential Warm Sands and San Lorenzo areas, most of the gay businesses are spread throughout the area, and even the clustered ones are well camouflaged, hidden behind nondescript facades and identified by small "private resort" signs on their walls. One exception is the small cluster of gay businesses that has developed on **East Arenas Road** in downtown Palm Springs. This concentration of rainbow-flag-flying stores, restaurants, and bars could be the beginning of a new gay visibility in the city. The large number of gay retirees (Palm Springs has the largest Prime Timers chapter in the country) and second-home weekend regulars is more likely to socialize privately than in the nightclubs. The geographic sprawl and the lack of a gay neighborhood makes encounters with these locals and their guests less likely than in more localized gay resorts.

While many aspects of the area invite comparison to other gay resorts, such comparisons form an incomplete picture of the Palm Springs experience. Palm Springs is a perfect long-weekend winter getaway for anyone whose primary interest is relaxing in the sun. It has a broader array of facilities than most gay resorts, but fewer gay-specific options. It does not have Miami's nightlife, Key West's dining, or Provincetown's culture, but it does have enough high-quality gay-specific offerings to fashion a fun vacation. If you stay at a gay resort, you can enjoy a very gay vacation of the laid-back and low-key variety. Jaded New Yorkers expecting *hot, hot, hot* will find that only in the weather (and often the bodies), but with a little attitude adjustment, they should still manage to have a great time. Much of the Palm Springs gay experience is sexually oriented. Many of the guest houses are at the high end of the "Sexual temperature" scale, and the trend is moving even further in that direction. That trend has fueled the growth in Palm Springs' popularity, but it has not limited the broad range of lodging options available. If you're a guy looking to get lucky, Palm Springs is well suited to help you achieve your goal. But the heavily advertised image of Palm Springs as a place for guys on the make is just one side of this multifaceted destination, which is truly a vacation playground almost anyone can enjoy.

When to Go and How to Get There

Most visitors to Palm Springs drive in from Los Angeles or San Diego, and it is at least a two-hour drive from either city. There is air service into Palm Springs, mostly shorter flights from West Coast destinations such as Seattle and San Francisco, and commuter service from Los Angeles, which connects to flights from all over. If you fly in, you will need to rent a car to get around.

Palm Springs' high season runs from mid-October through late April. It gets beastly hot in the summer, but it doesn't close down—many resorts remain busy throughout the year. The city hosts two of the biggest annual gay parties: Dinah Shore Week for women, and the Easter Weekend White Party for men. The women's event in particular overruns the town—the "mostly men" resorts become "women only" for a few days, and lesbians can be seen all over town strolling, shopping, and, oh yeah, watching the golfers.

Accommodations

The best news about the Palm Springs guest houses is that they continue to get better and better. There are ample choices among the new, renovated, and expanded guest houses. At the same time, two resorts that were previously rated 1 Palm have gone away: The **Whispering Palms** was purchased by **Inn Exile,** and seamlessly integrated into their compound. The **Desert Knight** is reopening as **Hot Desert Knights,** with a much-needed overhaul. While the **Smoke Tree Villa** will no longer cater exclusively to women, the **Enclave** now will—giving the **Bee Charmer** a run for its honey. The resorts that were under construction when we visited are listed as unrated, and references to sexual temperature and clientele are projected.

THE LAPS OF LUXURY

None of the gay accommodations in Palm Springs rates 5 Palms. This is not to say that there aren't some excellent choices, only that no single property combines all of the attributes necessary to earn our highest praise. The places rating 4 Palms are grouped together, but they all have very different appeal. Harlow Club and Abbey West are the classiest operations, but both are a bit reserved and haughty. Inn Exile also has some attitude, but of a different variety. The property and the crowd tend toward young, hunky, and hip, and the management strives to keep it that way. The management of InnTrigue has set a great tone—welcoming, professional, friendly, hard-working, and fun. While the rooms of their new addition are a work-in-progress, their new grounds are expansive and very attractive. The Hacienda en Sueño has a hyper-to-please management. The décor is a bit dated, but the rooms and grounds are very spacious, and full kitchens, barbecues, and unique honor pantry are very compelling for those who really want to retreat.

FROM PALACES TO DUNGEONS

The gay accommodations still range from elegant to dumpy, from small, 4-room houses to 44-room compounds, from prudish retreats to iniquitous playgrounds. Your choice of accommodations is more crucial here than at most destinations, and our ratings and comments are geared to helping make sure you end up at the resort that is right for you. While our Sexual Temperature category should help guide you to a comfortable and suitable environment, remember that the atmosphere at any given resort is a function of the guests who are staying there at any particular time. Many of the guest houses have a reputation for being sexually charged, but there are options at all ends of the scale. If you're going for **Dinah Shore** or **Easter Weekend,** you'll find it much more convenient to stay at the events' host hotels, which have included the Marquis, the Riviera, and the Wyndham. Although many attendees lodge elsewhere and just hang out by the host hotels' pools, if you're going for the action you might as well stay in the middle of it. One more note about temperature: Outdoor misting is essential for summertime sunbathing. Virtually all resorts have it—those that don't are noted.

IF YOU'VE BROUGHT YOUR MOTHER-IN-LAW

While Palm Springs is home to some great gay resorts, it also has a wealth of great straight resorts, and those who are looking for extensive resort facilities (and those traveling with their mothers-in-law) may prefer to stay in one of them. Our favorites include the **Hyatt Grand Champions** (44-600 Indian Wells Lane, Indian Wells, 619-341-1000 or 800-223-1234; $99–279), with exceptional golf and tennis facilities, and **The Ritz-Carlton** (68-900 Frank Sinatra Drive, Rancho Mirage, 619-321-8282 or 800-241-3333; $165–275), with a magnificent view of the valley but no golf course on the premises. Downtown, the **Hyatt Regency Suites** (285 N. Palm Canyon Drive; 619-322-9000 or 800-223-1234; $99–239) is attached to the Desert Fashion Plaza, and has begun marketing its two-room suites to gay women and men. The **Spa Hotel** (100 N. Indian Canyon Drive; 619-325-1411 or 800-854-1279; $134–209) actually has hot springs on the premises and a casino. If you're seriously into the spa thing, stay further out of town at **Two Bunch Palms** (67425 Two Bunch Palm Trail, Desert Hot Springs; 619-329-8791 or 800-472-4334; $120–570), the fabulously exclusive retreat of Hollywood's rich, famous, and strung-out.

OTHER KEY INFORMATION

See the section, About Our Guest House Ratings, page 7, for an explanation of our Palms and Sexual Temperature ratings. All rooms have televisions, phones, and VCRs unless noted specifically. All resorts are in Palm Springs, except those denoted CC in their addresses; these are in Cathedral City.

FOR MEALS:

FB= full breakfast; **CB**= continental breakfast; **L**= lunch; **WC**= cocktail hour or hors d'oeuvres of some sort.

EXCEPTIONAL

None. Yet.

HIGHLY RECOMMENDED

ABBEY WEST 772 Prescott Circle; 619-325-0229 or 800-554-3828; $88–250

From the marble entry to well-appointed rooms, this is a class operation, with a Hollywood-glamour feel that borders on pretentious. If you think the square-back Cadillac Seville is the epitome of class, you'll love it here. The new dark green walls and carpets are a bit, well, dark for our tastes. Sundeck does not have misting.

ROOMS: 16   **NUDE SUNBATHING:** private patio only   **SEXUAL TEMPERATURE:** low   **CLIENTELE:** mostly men   **MEALS:** in-room CB

HACIENDA EN SUEÑO 586 Warm Sands Circle; 619-327-8111 or 800-359-2007; $125–165

Spacious grounds, attentive hosts, and a country-house atmosphere (belied only slightly by the chrome-and-mirrors décor) make this a most welcoming place. All units have private patios (some small) and access to an honor pantry for groceries and late-night cravings, and a lot of amenities, including bicycles and gym passes. Not exceptionally stylish, but quiet and private.

ROOMS: 7 **NUDE SUNBATHING:** yes **SEXUAL TEMPERATURE:** low **CLIENTELE:** EG/100%M **MEALS:** none

HARLOW CLUB HOTEL 175 E. Alameda Street; 619-323-3977 or 800-223-4073; $135–220

Truly deluxe, luxurious, elegant, and tasteful, the place deserves to have attitude, but may occasionally cross the line. Nearer to downtown than the gay nightlife, with gym facilities on-site and lunch catered by Mortimer's. The atmosphere is polite, with nude sunbathing restricted and overt sexual activity frowned upon.

ROOMS: 15 **NUDE SUNBATHING:** roof deck only **SEXUAL TEMPERATURE:** low-medium **CLIENTELE:** EG/100%M **MEALS:** B/L

INNDULGE 601 Grenfall Road; 619-327-1408 or 800-833-5675; $69–99

This is hot new comer, with tastefully renovated rooms, a spectacular view, and very attractive pool/yard landscaping. The hard-working, professional management has spent a lot of money improving this large, well laid-out property, and it shows.

ROOMS: 18 **NUDE SUNBATHING:** yes **SEXUAL TEMPERATURE:** high **CLIENTELE:** EG/100%M **MEALS:** CB/C

INN EXILE 960 Camino Parocella; 619-327-6413 or 800-962-0186; $75–114

With spacious, attractive accommodations and gym facilities on-site, its status as a nudist resort doesn't make it a sexual playground—indeed we saw more swimsuits here than at most other resorts. The resort and its brochure are slick, and the crowd is skewed toward yuppie and humpy, with a bit of attitude. Rooms have their own answering machines.

ROOMS: 9 **NUDE SUNBATHING:** all areas **SEXUAL TEMPERATURE:** high–very high **CLIENTELE:** EG/100%M **MEALS:** B/L

INNTRIGUE 526 Warm Sands Drive; 619-323-7505 or 800-798-8781; $75–135

By acquiring the large property behind it, InnTrigue has created one of the most attractive resort environments. Spacious rooms have simple, elegant furnishings—rooms in the acquisition wing feature vintage Deco bath and kitchen tiling. Professional, friendly management wins high praise from a loyal clientele.

ROOMS: 28   **NUDE SUNBATHING:** yes   **SEXUAL TEMPERATURE:** high   **CLIENTELE:** EG/100%M   **MEALS:** CB/C

✝✝✝
RECOMMENDED

ALEXANDER RESORT 598 Grenfall Road; 619-327-6911 or 800-448-6197; $55–99

Serene, spacious grounds and tastefully decorated rooms. Casual and friendly. Lack of air conditioning can be a problem. Bicycles available.

ROOMS: 8   **NUDE SUNBATHING:** yes   **SEXUAL TEMPERATURE:** medium   **CLIENTELE:** EG/100%M   **MEALS:** B/L

AVANTI RESORT 715 San Lorenzo Road; 619-325-9723 or 800-572-2779; $49–109

Spacious grounds and lush landscaping are attractive. A large collection of fruit-bearing citrus trees is particularly notable. Rooms are relatively modern and comfortable.

ROOMS: 14   **NUDE SUNBATHING:** yes   **SEXUAL TEMPERATURE:** medium   **CLIENTELE:** EG/100%M   **MEALS:** CB

CAMP PALM SPRINGS 722 San Lorenzo Road; 619-322-CAMP or 800-793-0063; $69–189

A very friendly place, with attractive, Southwestern décor. Grounds are not particularly attractive, but quite spacious. They make a point of promoting their sexual temperature rating and attract a middle-age crowd with low attitude.

ROOMS: 24   **NUDE SUNBATHING:** yes   **SEXUAL TEMPERATURE:** high   **CLIENTELE** EG/100%M   **MEALS:** B/L

THE COLUMNS 537 Grenfall Road; 619-325-0655 or 800-798-0655; $59–94

Small and quiet, all rooms have been recently remodeled in California contemporary style and have VCRs. The resort has a low profile, but management is solid.

ROOMS: 7 **NUDE SUNBATHING:** yes **SEXUAL TEMPERATURE:** medium-high **CLIENTELE:** EG/100%M **MEALS:** CB

DESERT PARADISE HOTEL 615 Warm Sands Drive; 619-320-5650; $75–135

Casually elegant, beautifully landscaped, furnished in Southwest pastels, and excellently maintained. New management is friendly.

ROOMS: 12 **NUDE SUNBATHING:** yes **SEXUAL TEMPERATURE:** medium-high **CLIENTELE:** EG/100%M **MEALS:** CB

DELILAH'S ENCLAVE 641 San Lorenzo Road; 619-325-5269 or 800-621-6973; $80–100

All rooms have been refurbished with a Southwestern motif and have VCRs; half have modern kitchens. Small but pretty pool area (nonmisted) with simple, stylish patio furniture. Friendly, private, and very nice, it's the nicest choice for women.

ROOMS: 13 **NUDE SUNBATHING:** yes **SEXUAL TEMPERATURE:** low-medium **CLIENTELE:** EG/100%W **MEALS:** CB

HOT DESERT KNIGHTS 435 Avenida Olancha; 619-325-5456 or 800-256-7938; $79–89

A complete renovation has revived what was the 20-year-old Desert Knight, the first gay resort in the area. The resort is specializing in a male nudist clientele. It has a pool but no spa and offers day-use passes for $10.

ROOMS: 8 **NUDE SUNBATHING:** yes **SEXUAL TEMPERATURE:** high **CLIENTELE:** EG/100%M **MEALS:** CB

INNTIMATE 556 Warm Sands Drive; 619-778-8334 or 800-695-3846; $60–108

This small resort is furnished with an Asian motif, exhibiting a greater sense of style than most other resorts in the area. In Warm Sands, but lacking the convivial atmosphere of its larger neighbors.

ROOMS: 4 **NUDE SUNBATHING:** yes **SEXUAL TEMPERATURE:** low-medium **CLIENTELE:** mostly men **MEALS:** kitchen kit

MIRAGE/VISTA GRANDE/ATRIUM 574 Warm Sands Drive; 619-322-2404 or 800-669-1069; $79–165

The Mirage is the newest of these three related resorts. It features a large rock grotto with a walk-through waterfall, gym facilities, barbecue area, and spacious rooms with full kitchens. It is connected to the Vista Grande, whose ordinary but clean rooms surround a pool with a view of the mountains. The Atrium is across the street, quieter, with a Jacuzzi and lush tropical gardens. The friendly management and shared facilities of the three resorts make this one of our favorite options among the cruiser resorts.

ROOMS: 20 **NUDE SUNBATHING:** yes **SEXUAL TEMPERATURE:** high–very high **CLIENTELE:** EG/100%M **MEALS:** CB

SAGO PALMS 595 Thornhill Road; 619-323-0224; $65–110

Small but very well maintained. Pleasant, low-key atmosphere, a charming garden, and a small gym. Most rooms have kitchens, some have fireplaces.

ROOMS: 6 **NUDE SUNBATHING:** yes **SEXUAL TEMPERATURE:** medium-low **CLIENTELE:** EG/100%M **MEALS:** CB holidays only

TRIANGLE INN 555 San Lorenzo Road; 619-322-7993 or 800-732-7555; $94–189

Three blocks from downtown with nice, large rooms featuring TVs, VCRs, and CD players. The grounds are small but romantic. The friendly atmosphere and professional management make this a good choice.

ROOMS: 9 **NUDE SUNBATHING:** yes **SEXUAL TEMPERATURE:** medium **CLIENTELE:** EG/100%M **MEALS:** CB

THE VILLA 67-670 Carey Road, CC; 619-328-7211 or 800-845-5265; $45–118

Originally built by Elizabeth Arden, this resort sits on 2 1/2 acres of nicely landscaped grounds. Very popular for locals; all of the in-room showers look out on plant-filled atriums. On-site bar and deli, middle-age crowd, and some women.

ROOMS: 44 **NUDE SUNBATHING:** no **SEXUAL TEMPERATURE:** medium **CLIENTELE:** mostly men **MEALS:** CB

CANYON BOY'S CLUB 960 N. Palm Canyon Drive; 619-322-4367 or 800-295-2582; $49–89

A large resort set around a 50-foot pool, just north of downtown. The sauna and steam room are popular, and the resort is quite private, despite its main-drag location. In-house all-male video channels are provided in lieu of VCRs, and the décor is new and pleasant. One of the best values in town.

ROOMS: 32 **NUDE SUNBATHING:** yes **SEXUAL TEMPERATURE:** high **CLIENTELE:** EG/100%M **MEALS:** CB

OTHER RECOMMENDED

ARUBA HOTEL SUITES 671 S. Riverside Drive; 619-325-8440 or 800-84-ARUBA; $69–194

Located at the edge of downtown, with large suites good for long stays. Nicely landscaped and well-managed, but the décor is straight from the set of the *Golden Girls*.

ROOMS: 10 **NUDE SUNBATHING:** yes **SEXUAL TEMPERATURE:** low **CLIENTELE:** mostly men **MEALS:** none

THE BEE CHARMER 1600 East Palm Canyon Drive; 619-778-5883; $52–97

Discreet and pleasant, with a Southwestern flair, this women's resort ranks just behind Delilah's enclave for facilities, but has built a reputation for friendly management. No VCRs or misting.

ROOMS: 12 **NUDE SUNBATHING:** topless **SEXUAL TEMPERATURE:** low **CLIENTELE:** EG/100%W **MEALS:** CB

COYOTE INN 234 S. Patnecio Road; 619-322-9675 or 800-269-6830; $59–125

The newly furnished rooms are above average, and the landscaping is pleasant, but the place seems a bit removed, both geographically and atmospherically.

ROOMS: 7 **NUDE SUNBATHING:** yes **SEXUAL TEMPERATURE:** low **CLIENTELE:** EG/100%M **MEALS:** CB

CATHEDRAL CITY BOY'S CLUB 68-369 Sunair Road, CC; 619-324-1350 or 800-472-0836; $69–125

A large property sharing management with the Choices nightclub, the resort is being marketed as a frisky, playground environment. RV parking and day privileges are available; closed-circuit adult video in lieu of VCRs.

ROOMS: 22 **NUDE SUNBATHING:** yes **SEXUAL TEMPERATURE:** very high
CLIENTELE: EG/100%M **MEALS:** CB

DESERT PALMS INN 67-580 E. Palm Canyon Drive, CC; 619-324-5100 or 800-801-8696; $49–109

Updated motel rooms in two wings face a lawn and pool area that bustles with a young crowd that comes to hang out here, regardless of where they're staying. Management keeps changing frequently. This is the "heart of the action" place—a great place to hang out but less so to stay. Rooms do not have VCRs.

ROOMS: 29 **NUDE SUNBATHING:** no **SEXUAL TEMPERATURE:** high-medium
CLIENTELE: mostly men **MEALS:** none

EL MIRASOL VILLAS 525 Warm Sands Road; 619-327-5913 or 800-327-2985; $105–260

Very quiet, spacious grounds with dense and beautiful foliage, two pools, and a spa. The new ownership has made improvements throughout the property. Bicycles and gym passes round out the amenities.

ROOMS: 15 **NUDE SUNBATHING:** at one pool **SEXUAL TEMPERATURE:** low
CLIENTELE: mostly men **MEALS:** CB/L

550 WARM SANDS 550 Warm Sands Drive; 619-320-7144 or 800-669-0550; $49–110

Casual, clean, and small, with as frisky a daytime atmosphere as one could find in a legitimate establishment. In-house video in lieu of VCRs; phones are only available in the office. Nudity is encouraged and practiced by the management.

ROOMS: 6 **NUDE SUNBATHING:** all areas **SEXUAL TEMPERATURE:** very high **CLIENTELE:** EG/100%M **MEALS:** CB

SMOKE TREE VILLA 1586 E. Palm Canyon Drive; 619-323-2231; $75–85

Under new ownership at press time, the property will now be marketed as a male resort instead of its previous women-only policy. The resort has a simple, New England-y feel and mixed prospects.

ROOMS: 10   **NUDE SUNBATHING:** yes   **SEXUAL TEMPERATURE:** low-medium   **CLIENTELE:** men   **MEALS:** CB

WARM SANDS VILLAS 555 Warm Sands Drive; 619-323-3005 or 800-357-5695; $40–99

A nice layout and view are the high points of this resort, which suffers from some maintenance failings. Furnishings are just average, and rooms are a bit dark. Much of the yard is covered in Astroturf.

ROOMS: 26   **NUDE SUNBATHING:** yes   **SEXUAL TEMPERATURE:** high   **CLIENTELE:** EG/100%M   **MEALS:** C

LAST RESORTS

CABANA CLUB 970 Parocela Place; 619-320-1300, 800-669-9276; $39–145

With five one-bedroom units in an old building, this feels more like an apartment than a resort, and a bit creepy at that.

ROOMS: 5   **NUDE SUNBATHING:** yes   **SEXUAL TEMPERATURE:** low   **CLIENTELE:** mostly men   **MEALS:** CB

LE GARBO INN 287 W. Racquet Club Drive; 619-325-6737; $50–125

You must really "want to be alone," because no one we know would stay here. The rooms aren't bad, but the location is very far north, and the place has been deserted most of the times we've visited.

ROOMS: 5   **NUDE SUNBATHING:** yes   **SEXUAL TEMPERATURE:** low   **CLIENTELE:** mostly women   **MEALS:** CB

CASA ROSA 589 Grenfall Road; 619-322-4143 or 800-322-4151; $49–140

In need of a renovation, the place appears to suffer from a lack of conscientious management. The Warm Sands location is a plus, but we'd pick any of its neighbors first.

ROOMS: 8   **NUDE SUNBATHING:** yes   **SEXUAL TEMPERATURE:** low   **CLIENTELE:** mostly men   **MEALS:** CB

UNRATED

SANTIAGO 650 San Lorenzo Road; 619-325-1487; $89–119

This choice property on San Lorenzo could be a real winner. Just opened at press time, it is promising to be Palm Springs's most exotic resort. The size and layout are inviting.

ROOMS: 23 NUDE SUNBATHING: yes SEXUAL TEMPERATURE: high CLIENTELE: EG/100%M MEALS: CB/L

Dining

Dining in Palm Springs is a mixed bag. For the most part, the "gay" restaurants are either not very good, or not very gay. The best restaurants in town are not very gay at all, with one notable exception. **Shame on the Moon** (69-950 Frank Sinatra Drive, RM; 619-324-5515; $17) has reopened in Rancho Mirage, featuring excellent, creative cuisine, a dimly lit, elegant but not stuffy environment, great service, and reasonable prices, with a 50/50 gay/straight clientele. It topped every local's list of recommendations and ours too. **Mortimer's** (2095 N. Indian Canyon Drive, PS; 619-320-4333; $16) is also gay-popular, a little Deco-fruffy for our tastes, but the food is good and their private dining rooms (à la *Funny Girl*) should be fun when they open. The other gay restaurants are casual places—try **The Desert Palm Café** (67-670 E. Palm Canyon Drive, CC; 619-324-3000; $14) for breakfast, lunch or a late-night weekend snack. The **Rainbow Cactus Café** (212 S. Indian Canyon Drive, PS; 619-325-3868; $10) is convenient to downtown and a cluster of gay businesses. **Red Tomato** (36-650 Grove Street [at Highway 111], CC; 619-328-7518; $11) is good for pizza and ordinary pasta dishes. **Richard's Restaurant** (68-500 Highway 111, CC; 619-321-2841; $13) overpromises and doesn't deliver on fine dining. **Edgardo's Café Veracruz** (233 S. Indian Canyon Drive; 619-864-1551; $11) isn't gay-specific but offers great, inexpensive "Mescamerican-Mayan-Huasteco-Aztec" cuisine." Of the straight restaurants, **Bangkok Five** (69-930 Highway 111, RM; 619-770-9508; $15) remains on our list for excellent Thai cuisine and **Blue Coyote Grill** (445 N. Palm Canyon Drive, PS; 619-327-1196; $14) offers good

Southwestern cuisine. **Wally's Desert Turtle** (71-775 Highway 111, RM; 619-568-9321; $26) is probably the nicest formal restaurant in town, with reservations, jacket, tie, and a fat wallet required. For a great diner-style breakfast, head to **Michael's** (68-665 Highway 111, CC; 619-321-7197) or **Bit of Country** (418 S. Indian Canyon Drive, PS; 619-325-5154), for hash browns, griddle cakes, and eggs any style in big portions.

Nightlife

Palm Springs doesn't have cutting-edge nightlife, but it does have a full range of bar and club options, for men and women, busy and fun on weekends. It also has a large number of gay periodicals reporting on it. The *Bottom Line* is the well-established, biweekly magazine, sporting a glossy, full-color cover, extensive listings, and maps, as well as community news and information. A number of new guides also provide information on the local scene. *Megascene* is useful for its news and editorial content. *David* and *Lifestyle Too* are more limited, while the *Desert Daily Guide* is published weekly and provides a nightly run-down of special events and themes at the various clubs and bars. It's an excellent resource for tourists. **C. C. Construction Company** (68-449 Perez Road, CC; 619-324-4241) is still the most popular dance bar, closely followed by **Choices** (68-352 Perez Road, CC; 619-321-1145). **Delilah's** (68-657 Highway 111, CC; 619-324-3268) is the place for women, with a popular happy hour. **Streetbar** (224 E. Arenas Road, PS; 619-320-1266) is a popular cruise bar and hangout, downtown near the Rainbow Cactus and Moonlighting. **JP's** (1117 N. Palm Canyon Drive; 619-778-5310) is further north, with pool tables, darts, pinball, and a back room. The **Tool Shed** (600 E. Sunny Dunes Road, PS; 619-320-3299) caters to a Levi's crowd, while **Wolf's Den** (67-625 Highway 111, CC; 619-321-9688) strives for a hard-core leather and chains atmosphere—but who can wear all that hide in the heat? **Friends** (68-981 Highway 111, CC; 619-328-7612) opened as a nonalcoholic dance club in the former Daddy Warbucks space, but was fighting the city over a licensing issue at press time. **Two Gloria's** (2400 N. Palm Canyon Drive, PS; 619-322-3224) is a popular piano bar–restaurant.

Activities

ATHLETIC AND OUTDOOR

If you view Palm Springs's diversions as sunbathing breaks, you'll find plenty to do. While the area boasts a few high-end shopping malls, it is off-price, outlet, and discount shopping that are the major attraction. Outdoors, you will find world-class golf and tennis, with both resort-based and public facilities. The course at **La Quinta** is a favorite, with spectacular vistas (and, unfortunately, prices to match). The **Oasis Water Park** (1500 Gene Autry Trail, PS; 619-325-7873) features a new water slide called the Black Widow, and 15 other water attractions, complete food service, and private cabana rentals. It is open daily from mid-March through Labor Day and on weekends in September and October. **Joshua Tree National Monument** (Highway 62 to Joshua Tree; 619-367-7511) is a full-day trip from Palm Springs but offers a beautiful view of the natural desert environment. **Gold's Gym** (4070 Airport Center Drive; 619-322-4653; $10/day) is the best workout facility in the area, and many gay guest houses offer complimentary passes. Members of other Gold's Gym facilities get 7 complimentary days' use of the gym each year.

SIGHTSEEING

If you don't have the time to get to Joshua Tree, consider a visit to the **Living Desert** (47900 Portola Avenue; 619-346-5694), a 1,200-acre reserve in Palm Desert. The scenic **Aerial Tramway** (Highway 111 at Tramway Road; 619-325-4227) offers spectacular views from the top of Mt. San Jacinto, 8,516 feet above the valley.

SHOPPING

Palm Springs's discount, outlet, and off-price shopping is hard to miss. You'll pass a large collection of **outlet stores** on I-10, twenty minutes before you get to Palm Springs. A new collection of **discount stores** is on Highway 111, at the edge of Rancho Mirage and Palm Desert. You'll find more upscale (though equally generic) shopping across the highway there, and at the **Desert Fashion Plaza** (123 N. Palm Canyon Drive) downtown, anchored by Saks Fifth Avenue. You'll find clothes more suited for gay men at **R&R Menswear** (333 N. Palm Canyon Drive, PS; 619-320-3007) and a decent selection of "gently worn" clothes for men and women sold on consignment at **Patsy's** (4121 E. Palm Canyon Drive, PS; 619-324-8825), open Thursday through Sunday.

FYI

The Bottom Line (1243 Gene Autry Trail, #121-122, PS; 619-323-0552) is the biggest periodical in the desert. The **Desert Daily Guide** (870 San Lucas Road, PS; 619-320-3237) publishes a weekly night-by-night rundown of entertainment options. Both are readily available at gay businesses. The **Desert Business Association** (P.O. Box 773, PS; 619-323-5000 or 325-1978) is an association of local gay businesses. The **Desert Women's Association** (SCWU, P.O. Box 718, CC; 619-778-1189) publishes the DWA newsletter. **Prime Timers of the Desert** (P.O. Box 3061, PS; 619-328-3326) is the country's largest chapter of this social club for mature men and their admirers. The **Palm Springs Desert Resorts Convention & Tourist Bureau** (69930 Highway 111, Suite 201, RM; 619-770-9000) publishes a *Gay Guide to Palm Springs,* basically their general tourist guide with gay-specific accommodations.

Southern California Coast:

LOS ANGELES, LAGUNA BEACH, LONG BEACH, SAN DIEGO

"Go west" was a popular theme for gay women and men long before the Village People and Pet Shop Boys turned it into a gay anthem, and California is the most gay-populous state, with major communities in San Francisco, San Diego, and Los Angeles. No other U.S. vacation destination has greater mystique than California, and the southern California coastline offers unique treasures and pleasures for the gay traveler. Ironically, it is only the weather that undermines southern California's beach offerings: While the area is sunny all year round, it is really only in the summer that you can count on beach weather. As a summer destination, the climate is ideal: warm without being humid, cooler at night. But even during the winter, southern California offers something no other resort destination can: two major gay meccas and a stretch of beach connecting them.

When to Go and How to Get There

As noted above, southern California's weather is pleasant all year, and although May and June are often foggy, July and August are peak beach season. Southern California offers numerous airport options. Los Angeles and San Diego are the most obvious choices, but the John Wayne Airport in Orange County can be a convenient alternative, particularly for Laguna, as Burbank can be for Malibu.

LOS ANGELES

Johnny Carson called it eighty suburbs in search of a city, and indeed you can come to Los Angeles and never see downtown. L.A. is a state of mind, a shrine of pop culture and holistic nutrition, a place where everyone loves the outdoors but sees it mainly from his or her car. Its heartbeat pulses in Beverly Hills and Malibu—it throbs in West Hollywood. It's one huge movie set where the bit players have car phones and the stars have car-phone fax machines. You may find it hard to imagine why anyone would have to receive a fax in his or her car, but if you can understand this need, you will know the essence of L.A.

—*Out & About*, October 1992

The more things change, the more they stay the same. Despite an earthquake, fires, and the O. J. trial, Los Angeles remains more L.A.-like than ever. As a tourist destination, Los Angeles has an unparalleled number of intriguing attractions, belied by a sometimes monotonous sprawl of suburban strip-mall boulevards. L.A.'s appeal derives from the devil-may-care attitude that's virtually required to live life on a tectonic fault line. It's manifested in the glitz of the entertainment business, the concept of shopping as retail therapy, the splendor of year-round sunny weather, and the speed with which hip, new, and now become "so five minutes ago." Even if you're not normally glamorous by nature, it's easy to pretend here. Wear dark glasses. Tip big. Double park. Run late. Make a lot of phone calls. For the gay tourist, it's easy to get stuck in West Hollywood—not necessarily a bad thing, considering the concentration of gay and gay-friendly hotels, dining, shopping, and entertainment. But while the gay community is well established in West Hollywood and Silver Lake, the westward march continues, with a growing gay presence in the beach communities, particularly Santa Monica. Your warm-weather vacation would be incomplete without spending some time on the coast—and we mean really *on* the coast. Live L.A. like a local and you can't have a bad time. You might, however, find yourself needing a car phone—maybe even a car fax.

For this book, we have covered two areas of Los Angeles: West Hollywood, and the beach centered around Santa Monica. West Hollywood is gay Los Angeles, and Santa Monica is L.A.'s trendy neighborhood at the moment, home to an increasing number of gay residents, but a limited number of gay establishments. Beverly Hills, Westwood, Century City and Bel Air are convenient communities between the two, mostly straight, but filled with popular tourist venues, and convenient to most business and recreation destinations.

Accommodations

L.A. has one great gay guest house, and plenty of gay-friendly establishments in and around West Hollywood and West L.A. in all price categories. West Hollywood and Beverly Hills are a 20-minute drive to the beach (or up to 45, with bad traffic), and an hour from the far reaches of Malibu. The beach also has a number of great places to stay.

GAY-SPECIFIC

THE SAN VICENTE INN 837 N. San Vicente Boulevard; 310-854-6915; $59–109

West Hollywood's only gay guest house, offering great value in tasteful, comfortable accommodations, one block from the heart of the action on Santa Monica Boulevard. It has 18 units and an attractive, lushly landscaped pool deck. Rooms feature their own direct-dial phone numbers and answering machines—perfect for the cell-phone impaired.

THE CORAL SANDS 1730 N. Western Avenue; 213-467-5141

L.A.'s long-standing gay (men only) hotel, popular, with a bathhouse atmosphere, and not recommendable as a legitimate lodging establishment.

THE WHITTIER HOUSE B&B P.O. Box 1799, La Marinda; 310-941-7222; $65–90

A delightful and pretty lesbian-run gay guest house near Disneyland, offering full breakfast, afternoon tea, and a 12-person Jacuzzi.

WEST HOLLYWOOD (WEHO)

FOUR SEASONS 300 Doheny Drive; 310-273-2222 or 800-332-3442, fax 310-859-3824; $260–355

maintains its reputation for top-notch service in this demanding town. Right on the edge of Beverly Hills, it is the perfect gay work/play address.

THE ARGYLE 8358 Sunset Boulevard; 213-654-7100 or 800-225-2637, fax 213-654-9287; $170–1,200

is west Hollywood's splashiest hostelry, with its historic Art Deco design, luxurious rooms, and private-club atmosphere.

THE RAMADA WEST HOLLYWOOD 8585 Santa Monica Boulevard; 310-652-6400 or 800-845-8585; $85–125

With its Pop Art décor, this Ramada is a far cry from your average one; its gay-central location is the prime draw.

THE WYNDAM BEL AGE 1020 N. San Vicente Boulevard; 310-854-1111 or 800-996-3426, fax 310-854-0926; $175–500

Low-key but ornate, this all-suite hotel is well-located and very gay-popular. The sweeping view from its rooftop whirlpools and garden is magnificent.

LE MONTROSE 900 Hammond Street; 310-855-1115 or 800-776-0666, fax 310-657-9192; $165–475

is noted for its plush suites and high-tech in-room amenities. Popular with gays and music-industry types.

THE HOLLOWAY MOTEL 8465 Santa Monica Boulevard, WeHo; 213-654-2454; $40–60

offers clean budget accommodations at the corner of La Cienega and Santa Monica boulevards. It's popular with erotic video actors.

COASTAL AREAS

THE LOEWS SANTA MONICA BEACH HOTEL 1700 Ocean Avenue, Santa Monica; 310-458-6700 or 800-243-1166, fax 310-458-2813; $205–435

Lavish and sophisticated, the hotel has terrific ocean views and cascades down toward the ocean from its street-level lobby.

THE GEORGIAN 1415 Ocean Avenue, Santa Monica; 310-395-9945 or 800-538-8147, fax 310-451-3374; $135–275

Offers great value on the beach, in recently restored, intimately elegant digs.

SHUTTERS ON THE BEACH 1 Pico Boulevard, Santa Monica; 310-458-0030 or 800-334-9000, fax 310-458-4589; $230–350

With its New England feel and beachfront location, this is one of our favorite hotels here.

MALIBU BEACH INN 22878 Pacific Coast Highway; 310-456-6444 or 800-462-5428; $135–275

Shoe-horned into a busy stretch of the Pacific Coast Highway, this is the only hotel right on the beach in Malibu, with great views. Each well-appointed room has a private ocean-front balcony; most have fireplaces as well.

MIRAMAR SHERATON 101 Wilshire Boulevard, Santa Monica; 310-576-7777 or 800-325-3535, fax 310-458-7912

Offers spectacular views, garden bungalows, a bi-level health club, heated pool, and a convenient location.

THE CHANNEL ROAD INN 219 W. Channel Road, Santa Monica; 310-459-1920, fax 310-454-9920; $95–210

Just a block from the beach, this three-story Colonial inn has authentic nineteenth-century details. Expanded continental breakfast is provided, as are afternoon tea, evening wine, and bicycles. Rooms 2, 8, and 12 have water views.

THE MANSION INN 327 Washington Boulevard; 310-821-2557 or 800-828-0688, fax 310-827-0289; $79–125

Gay-friendly, just two blocks from the beach in Marina del Rey.

THE VENICE BEACH HOUSE 15 Thirtieth Avenue; 310-823-1966, 310-823-1842; $85–165

Offers nine charming guest rooms in an elegantly restored bungalow-style home.

BEVERLY HILLS/CENTURY CITY/BEL AIR

THE HOTEL BEL-AIR 701 Stone Canyon Road, Bel Air; 310-472-1211 or 800-648-4097, fax 310-476-5890; $315–495

Exudes true class at every turn. Nothing nouveau or trendy here, it's an oasis of privacy and civility for those who don't need reinforcement to know they're special.

THE BEVERLY HILLS HOTEL 9641 Sunset Boulevard; 310-278-1487 or 800-283-8885, fax 310-281-2902; $275–350

A famous landmark, recently overhauled but retaining its original style and cachet. It has a bit of a resort feel and a lot of nostalgia for the old Hollywood.

THE BEVERLY PRESCOTT 1224 S. Beverwil Drive; 310-277-2800 or 800-421-3212, fax 310-203-9537; $139–185

Fast becoming a hotel of choice for sophisticated travelers seeking affordable luxury. It's located a few long blocks from the commercial heart of Beverly Hills.

Dining

L.A. is a town that likes to eat out, and while its restaurants may not attain the culinary excellence found in San Francisco, the range of dining options, the number of predominantly gay venues, and the abundance of unique settings and atmospheres make for very exciting eating. The prices listed are average entrée prices.

VERY GAY

Mark's (861 N. La Cienega Boulevard; 310-652-5252; $12) is one of the best restaurants, attracting a heavily gay dinner crowd, with a stunning staff to equal the food. Reservations are generally respected with short waits. Fun to go with groups of two to four, though many tables are too central and crowded, given the amount of "yoo-hooing" that takes place. The **Cobalt Cantina** (616 N. Robertson Boulevard; 310-659-8691 and 4326 Sunset Boulevard; 213-953-9991; $13) has a second, original location in Silver Lake. Both are very gay-popular; the West Hollywood branch was the premier A-gay dining spot at press time, with long waits on weekend nights. **The Shed** (8474 Melrose Avenue; 213-655-6277; $17) is the most recent addition to the very gay restaurant scene. The ambiance is a bit darker and more subdued than the previous two, and the food more expensive and intricate. **Muse** (7360 Beverly Boulevard; 213-934-4400; $16) is fashionable without being a scene, except on Friday nights, when it becomes a popular hangout for Hollywood's gay movers-and-shakers. The dining room is airy and understated, the service is attentive and the food is very good, creative, and interesting. **Capone's** (8277 Santa Monica Boulevard; 213-654-0658; $13) has a more casual atmosphere, is gay-owned, and is almost exclusively gay-patronized, serving Euro-California cuisine. Two bars and a piano extend the appeal beyond mealtime. **Figs** (7929 Santa Monica Boulevard; 213-654-0780; $12) is a comfortable, popular, homey restaurant, serving home-style meals to a nontrendy crowd. **Who's on Third** (8369 W. Third Street, WeHo; 310-651-2928; $7) is a postmodern coffee shop serving great breakfasts—very gay-popular despite the horrendous waits on weekends. **Club Café** (at World Gym, 8560 Santa Monica Boulevard, WeHo; 310-659-6630; $5) serves tasty, healthy, and filling post-workout cuisine. The cafe is open to the public, so you don't need to be a gym body or even look like one to eat there. **Benvenuto** (8512 Santa Monica Boulevard, WeHo; 310-659-8635; $10) is popular for its romantic, candle-lit patio and creative (but pricey) wood-baked pizzas. **Café D'Etoile** (8941 1/2 Santa Monica Boulevard, WeHo; 310-278-1011; $12) is always busy and has a diverse, if not unusual menu, including steak, seafood, and cottage pie. **Café La Bohème** (8400 Santa Monica Boulevard, WeHo; 213-848-2360; $20) caters to an elegant mixed crowd, with an eclectic menu and velvet drapes, as its opera-queen name suggests. **Basix** (8333 Santa Monica Boulevard; 213-848-2460; $7) is a semi–open-air café drawing a crowd for morning coffee. Votive candles and a light, inexpensive menu make it a fine choice for a casual dinner as well. **French Quarter Restaurant** (7985 Santa Monica Boulevard, WeHo; 213-654-0898; $9) has long been a major gay landmark, but it resembles a Disney World Food Pavilion and can be equally scary. Better food and crowds can be found elsewhere, but it remains gay-popular at all hours.

UNUSUAL ATMOSPHERE

Dar Maghreb (7651 Sunset Boulevard; 213-876-7651; $24) is a posh, authentic Moroccan restaurant where you can sit on pillows and eat with your fingers. **Inn of the Seventh Ray** (128 Old Topanga Canyon Road; 310-455-1311; $20) serves gourmet organic cuisine in a rustic, serene wooded canyon. **Yamashiro** (1999 N. Sycamore Avenue; 213-466-5125; $23) is one of the prettiest restaurants in Hollywood, with great views. Unfortunately, it is a bit touristy, and its food is not as exceptional as its setting. **Orso** (8706 W. Third Street, WeHo; 310-274-7144; $16) is very celebrity- and gay-popular. The patio is the best place to sit, day or night. Feel free to order off-menu vegetarian dishes—k.d. lang does! **Caioti** (2100 Laurel Canyon Boulevard, Hollywood; 213-650-2988; $12) is Laurel Canyon's place for pizza in a hippie-groovy-glamour mode. We spotted Sandra Bernhard here, eating alone. It figures. **Canter's Deli** (419 N. Fairfax Blvd; 213-651-2030; $10) is a 24-hour deli/coffee shop. It is the center of the universe at 3:00 A.M. Filled with people of all persuasions, including its fair share of homos, supermodels, and slackers. **Maurice's Snack 'n' Chat** (5549 W. Pico Boulevard; 213-930-1795 or 213-931-3877, $11): The phone number is no longer a secret, nor is the appeal of this down-and-dirty soul-food mecca.

AT THE BEACH

Patrick's Road House (106 Entrada [at Pacific Coast Highway], Santa Monica; 310-459-4544; $6) is everything a roadside, beachfront greasy spoon should be. **The Reel Inn** (18661 Pacific Coast Highway, Malibu; 310-456-8221; $13; also 1220 Third Street, Santa Monica; 310-395-5538) is a casual, oilcloth-type place with great, moderately priced seafood, just across the highway from the beach. **Figtree Café** (429 Ocean Walk, Venice; 310-392-4937) offers beachfront dining along the Venice parade of people. The menu is light and wholesome. **Granita** (23725 W. Malibu Road, Malibu; 310-456-0488; $23) is Wolfgang Puck's eatery at the beach. Stylish, tasty, and expensive—a great place for special occasions. Sit outside if you can. **Ivy at the Shore** (1541 Ocean Avenue, Santa Monica; 310-393-3113; $25) is elegant, and full of celebrities enjoying salads, Maui onion rings, and crabcakes. **Chinois**

on Main (2709 Main Street, Santa Monica; 310-392-9025; $23) is another Wolfgang Puck creation, serving glamorous Chinese-French-California food. **Rebecca's** (2025 Pacific Avenue, Venice; 310-306-6266; $20) gourmet Mexican cuisine and mean margaritas attract a trendy, stunning, and, alas, mostly straight crowd. **Babalu** (1001 Montana Avenue, Santa Monica; 310-395-2500; $10) has décor as zany as the multicultural cuisine (Caribbean-Italian-Mexican-Asian-Southwestern) it serves. The food is great and the atmosphere very casual. **Zen Zero** (1535 Ocean Avenue, Santa Monica; 310-451-4455; $22) serves family-style (huge entrées), offers French/Asian cuisine by the former chef of Chinois on Main. **A Votre Santé** (1025 Abbot Kinney Boulevard, Santa Monica; 310-314-1187; $11) serves up affordable, healthy fare—the dairy-free pancakes are amazing. **Riva at Loews Santa Monica Beach Hotel** (1700 Ocean Avenue, Santa Monica; 310-458-6700; $22) is known for its extravagant buffet and sweeping ocean view.

Nightlife

The gay social scene in Los Angeles is eclectic, ranging from pretty buffed boys in West Hollywood, to an artsy, ethnic, and leather crowd in Silver Lake. It's also venue-varied, set not only in bars and clubs, but in coffeehouses, restaurants, beaches, health clubs, and even supermarkets. For many gay tourists, West Hollywood, or WeHo as it is increasingly referred to, is the beginning, middle, and end of a visit to gay L.A. But gay women and men live all over Los Angeles, and while other communities don't have WeHo's gay density, they do have a lot to offer the gay visitor. **A Different Light** (8853 Santa Monica Boulevard; 310-854-6601) is the best place to pick up the many local gay publications covering nightlife and lifestyles. *Edge* and *fab!* are the best sources for men, while the *Lesbian News (LN)* and *Los Angeles Girl Guide* are the best for women. You'll also find San Diego and Orange County publications here, all for free. While the nightlife is not as variable by day of the week as it is in New York or San Francisco, it is wide-ranging, and these publications all do a good job of covering it.

West Hollywood's biggest clubs cater to the young, muscular, and good-looking, making the city a contender for attitude capital of the world, and not always friendly or comfortable. There are, however,

plenty of places where those who fall further afield of that narrowly defined gay ideal will be more comfortable, and we've noted them here.
The youngest gays face the harshest reality—the legal drinking age of
21 is rigorously enforced, although some places have special 18 to 21
functions. Be sure to have photo I.D. with you no matter how old you
look. Most clubs also charge a $5–12 cover on weekends.

THE CLUBS

As in any major city, there is no one club to which all gay men or lesbians gravitate. The social scene is dictated by taste, attitude, age, and
often day of the week. Despite its "big boys, big attitude" aura, most
tourists visiting L.A. will at least want to check out the WeHo scene, and
first on the list is **Rage** (8911 Santa Monica Boulevard; 310-652-7055).
With its shirtless, muscular crowd, it is the most popular dance club/bar
most nights of the week. Down the street and one block east is **Micky's**
(8857 Santa Monica Boulevard; 213-657-1176), which attracts a similar but younger crowd. **Axis** (652 North La Peer Drive; 310-659-0471—
formerly Studio One) is mixed men and women most nights, but a
major hub for lesbians on Friday nights. **Probe** (836 N. Highland Avenue; 310-281-6292) is technically in Hollywood, but its after-hours-
to-dawn, serious drug/party scene attracts a lot of hard-core West Hollywood gym boys to L.A.'s longest running weekly dance club on
Saturdays. **Circus Disco** (6655 Santa Monica Boulevard, Hollywood;
213-462-1291) caters to ethnic crowds. Tuesday is Pink Feather Lounge,
catering to Latinos. Thursday is Gay Afro-American night. Fridays it's
hot Latin men. **Pump** (at the El Ray Theatre, 5515 Wilshire Boulevard;
213-243-5221) is a Sunday-night dance party catering to muscle boys,
drag divas, and a host of other locals. Be sure to check *Edge* or *fab!* for
regular but quickly changing dance parties and events. At press time,
promoter Jeffrey Sanker's monthly Sunday-night party at **House of Blues**
was the "don't miss" dance event, but the quest for the next great thing
sweeps out the old and rings in the new on a regular basis.

THE BARS

If you're not into dancing, **Revolver** (8851 Santa Monica Boulevard,
WeHo; 310-550-8851) is probably your best bet. It's busy most nights,

with video screens playing campy music videos and TV excerpts, women-friendly, but not especially women-popular. For the tougher types, the very dark **Spike** (7746 Santa Monica Boulevard; 213-656-9343) attracts a dare-me, Levi's and leather clientele on Fridays. **The Eagle** (7864 Santa Monica Boulevard; 213-654-3252) is a bit less dark, with hot, friendly bartenders. A more mature (chronologically, though not necessarily behaviorally) neighborhood crowd hangs at the **Gold Coast** (8228 Santa Monica Boulevard; 213-656-4879), a neighborhood cruise bar. The most popular Sunday-afternoon beer bust is at **Mother Lode** (8944 Santa Monica Boulevard; 310-659-9700). **Numbers** (8029 Sunset Boulevard; 213-656-6188) is best known as a place where older investors can meet young entrepreneurs, but a good percentage of the clientele is just looking for an quasi-elegant place to enjoy dinner or a nightcap. Over to the east in historic and hilly Silver Lake are bars suited to Levi's cruisers and Latinos. Here it's scene, not necessarily appearances, that works. **Detour** (1087 Manzanita Street; 213-664-1189) is the classic Levi's, leather, and western bar in the area, but **Gauntlet II** (4219 Santa Monica Boulevard; 213-669-9472) has become more popular, especially with the prettier "leather-lite" crowd. **Faultline** (4216 Melrose Avenue; 213-660-0889) adheres to a strict leather ethic and **Cuffs** (1941 Hyperion Avenue; 213-660-2649) caters to a kinky clientele. Salsa and Latin lovers are found at **Le Bar** (2375 Glendale Boulevard; 213-660-7595). **Dragstrip 66** (third Saturday of each month at **Rudolfo's,** 2500 Riverside Drive, Silver Lake; 213-669-1226) offers drag theme parties such as "Karen Black Valentine Ball" and the "Night of a Thousand Jans" (Jan Bradys, that is). At the beach, you'll find **Friendship** (112 W. Channel Road, Santa Monica; 310-454-6024), one of the oldest bars in L.A. County, closed for a long time to recover from the Northridge earthquake. It's not quite as popular as **Roosterfish** (1302 Abbot Kinney Boulevard, Venice; 310-392-2123), which is a lot of fun, with its divey atmosphere, pool table, and attitude-free crowd. More casual and relaxed than WeHo bars, it's packed on weekends.

WOMEN'S CLUBS AND BARS

For lesbians, **Girl Bar** is the best game in town, and it attracts a glamorous crowd. Girl Bar operates out of several locations; the current schedule includes Friday nights at **Axis,** Saturday night at the **Backlot** (657 N. Robertson Boulevard; 213-260-2531). Check the women's papers or call 213-460-2531 for additional information. **Klub Banshee** (Benvenuto Café, 8512 Santa Monica Boulevard; 310-288-1601) is a Monday-night dance party for women—no cover. Tuesday night you'll find women at **Michelle's XXX All Female Review** (Club 7969, 7969 Santa Monica Boulevard; 213-654-0280), with the show at midnight. **The Palms** (8572 Santa Monica Boulevard; 310-652-6188) has been a women's bar for the last 20 years! Other spots popular with women include **Luna Park** (665 N. Robertson Boulevard; 310-652-0611), a restaurant-bar-cabaret, and **Little Frieda's** (see below.)

COFFEEHOUSES

Beyond West Hollywood's bar scene, coffeehouses have become an alternative hangout, more comfortable, quiet, relaxed, and less smoky. The top place to watch and be watched is **The Abbey** (692 N. Robertson Boulevard; 310-289-8410), just off the infamous Santa Monica strip. With its monastery-like courtyard setting, it has become a mecca for gay men to sip iced cappuccino, munch on a fat-free muffin, and check out one another outside the dimly lit clubs. If you're alone, you can always read one of the complimentary magazines offered. For lesbians, **Little Frieda's** (8730 Santa Monica Boulevard; 310-652-6495) is fast becoming the equivalent spot for women, almost SRO on weekends. Right on the strip is **The 6 Gallery** (8861 Santa Monica Boulevard; 213-652-6040), less social but offering a better view of passing foot traffic—biceps, bust, and butt traffic, too. Down the block is **Buzz Coffee** (8200 Santa Monica Boulevard; 213-650-7742), which, like the Abbey, is always packed. Its crowd, however, tends to be a lot younger and artsy. Buzz's menu is also limited to a few expensive muffins. Silver Lake also has its own **Buzz Coffee House** (3932 Sunset Boulevard; 213-913-1021). Out at the beach, **Wednesday's** (2409 Main Street, Santa Monica; 310-452-4486) is notable for its funky living room atmosphere and very late hours.

Activities
ATHLETIC AND OUTDOOR

A lot of natives never make it to the beach, and what a pity. With fresh air, sunshine, and broad, sandy beaches, L.A.'s coastline is the best of what the city has to offer. The local color varies depending on which beach you go to. The gay beach is an obvious choice for many, but you may be more entertained by the sideshow atmosphere of Venice or the surfing crowd at Zuma. Whichever you choose, consider making a day trip. Our ideal itinerary would be breakfast at Patrick's Road House, a morning visit to the J. Paul Getty museum, lunch at the Reel Inn, and then a full afternoon at one of the following beaches. If you feel a surfer dude transformation coming on, check out our athletics listings for information on renting in-line skates or taking surfing lessons. **Will Rogers Beach** (the gay beach) has a large gay section (nicknamed Ginger Rogers), with gay women and men preening and playing in sexy swimwear fashions. You'll find it where West Channel Road meets the sea. **Venice Beach** (the carnival atmosphere beach) is quite nice, but most people come here to view the bohemian sidewalk vendors and local color. **Zuma** (the surfer dude beach) is Malibu's top surfing beach; you can reach it from Pacific Coast Highway or the Kanan-Dume Road exit off the Ventura Freeway, just like the valley girls do. **Matador** (further along beach) is smaller, quieter, and prettier than Zuma, and offers a more laid-back, scenic, and private beach experience. **Playa del Rey** (flight attendant's beach) is close enough to the airport for a quick layover tan, but it suffers from the din of jets taking off and landing just overhead.

GYMS

Working out and gay life in L.A. go almost hand in hand. It's not that there is a plethora of gyms in the area, but most Angelenos, and outsiders who just want to fit in, work out religiously. Most of the notable gyms are in West Hollywood. **World Gym West Hollywood,** formerly the New Athletic Club (8560 Santa Monica Blvd.; 310-659-6630), is the best gym for visitors, offering daily and weekly rates. It's definitely gay, with club music pumping through the extensive free weight, Nautilus, and cardio areas, as well as the canopied outdoor Hammer Strength circuit. The club's café offers tasty, healthy cuisine, and an outdoor pool and rooftop sundeck beckon for sunbathing. There are also tanning beds, an on-site chiropractor, hair salon, massage therapy, and men's sauna and steam bath, but limited changing facilities for women. The **Sports Connection** (8612 Santa Monica Boulevard; 310-652-7440) is a Bally's-affiliated gym, still very popular with a gay/lesbian crowd, but kind of rundown, dirty, and sleazy. The **Sports Connection** also has a branch in Santa Monica (2929 Thirty-first Street; 310-450-4464). Further east in Hollywood is **Gold's Gym** (1016 Cole Avenue; 213-462-7012). The area is a bit rougher, but the gym, which is basically one large workout area of free-standing weights, machines, and bikes, is gay-friendly—a little less social than World. The big boys train here. Also in Hollywood is the **Hollywood Gym** (1551 N. La Brea; 213-845-1420) with an extensive aerobics schedule, free weight and cardio areas, massage therapy, tanning, saunas, and classes in karate, boxing, and kickboxing. Other gyms include Silver Lake's recently renovated **Body Builders' Gym** (2516 Hyperion Avenue; 213-668-0802), attracting a serious but friendly crowd, and the **L.A. Women's Gym** (3407 Glendale Boulevard; 213-661-9456) a weight-training gym with free weights and cardio equipment, for women only.

AEROBICS

Voight Fitness and Dance Center (1919 Broadway; 310-453-4536), now in Santa Monica, offers world-renowned low and high impact, step, slide circuit, cardio funk, and bodysculpt aerobic classes. **Martin Henry Fitness Studio** (1106 N. La Cienega Boulevard; 310-659-9200), in West Hollywood, was opened by the former Voight superstar of the same name—his body-sculpting classes are legendary.

BIKING, RUNNING, AND ROLLER-BLADING

Despite the constantly pleasant weather, surprisingly few Angelenos run or jog. Those who do, don their running shoes near the beaches at Venice and Santa Monica or along San Vicente Boulevard in Brentwood. Bicycles, Roller-blades, and boogie boards can be rented at numerous places at the beach—one we've used is **Spokes 'n' Stuff** (4175

Admiralty Way, Marina del Rey; 310-306-3332 and 1715 Ocean Front Walk, Santa Monica; 310-395-4748). **The Annex** (3159 Los Feliz Boulevard; 213-661-6665) is one of the few bike-rental shops convenient to Griffith Park. **Frontrunners Track Club** (213-460-2554) sponsors fun runs and walks six days a week in the Los Angeles area, as well as numerous special events throughout the year.

SURFING, SAILING, AND HORSEBACK RIDING

Rent-a-Sail (13719 Fiji Way, Marina del Rey; 310-822-1868) rents a variety of sail and power boats. **Los Angeles Equestrian Center** (480 Riverside Drive, Burbank; 818-840-8401), **Malibu Riding** (33905 Pacific Coast Highway, Malibu; 310-457-9783) and **Sunset Ranch Hollywood Stable** (3400 N. Beachwood Drive, Hollywood; 469-5450) offer guided rides, lessons, and rental horses. **Boarding House** (2619 Main Street, Santa Monica; 310-392-5646) and **Zuma Jay** (22775 Pacific Coast Highway, Malibu; 310-456-8044) rent surfboards and can arrange lessons as well.

SIGHTSEEING

New Yorkers used to joke that there was more active culture in a cup of yogurt than there was in Los Angeles, and with no resident opera or ballet company, L.A.'s fine arts arena is incomplete. Still, the area boasts many world-class museums, and the city's large population of actors has been a boon for live theater, with equity-waiver houses all over the city presenting a constant supply of new and interesting productions.

MUSEUMS

The **J. Paul Getty Museum** (17985 Pacific Coast Highway; 310-458-2003) is the rich uncle of all museums. Extraordinarily endowed, the Herculaneum-style villa museum and gardens house an unrivaled collection of Greek, Roman, and European art. Unless you arrive by taxi or bus, you need to secure a parking reservation at least a week in advance. Their new complex, just off the 405 freeway, will be open soon. The ultra-modern **Museum of Contemporary Art** ("the MoCA", 250

S. Grand Avenue, downtown; 213-621-2766) boasts expansive settings for Rothko, Pollock, and the like. The **Armand Hammer Museum** (10899 Wilshire Boulevard; 310-443-7300) is known for its collection of original Da Vinci manuscripts, as well as Rembrandt, Monet, and Chagall paintings. Out at the beach, the **Social and Public Art Resource Center**—SPARC (685 Venice Boulevard; 310-822-9560) shows alternative contemporary art in a converted jail cell gallery space in the 1923 Art Deco Venice City Jail.

Pasadena is home to a number of cultural attractions. The **Norton Simon Museum** (411 W. Colorado Boulevard; 818-449-6840) houses an exceptional collection of Asian and European art. Additional Asian art can be viewed at the **Pacific Asia Museum** (46 N. Los Robles Avenue; 818-449-2742), in a Chinese palace replica. The **Gamble House** (4 Westmoreland Place; 818-793-3334), designed in 1908 by Greene and Greene for the Gambles of Procter & Gamble, is a remarkable mansion whose original furnishings stand in tribute to the refined elegance of old-world, old-money California. Finish your Pasadena tour at the **Huntington Library, Art Collections, and Botanical Gardens** (1151 Oxford Road, San Marino; 818-405-2141). Although use of the library requires scholarly approval, a number of rare-book exhibits as well as the mansion and gardens are open to the public, with afternoon tea served daily.

Exposition Park (just southwest of downtown; 213-748-6131) is home to a number of museums, including the **California Museum of Science and Industry** (213-744-7400), the **Skirball Museum** (3077 University Avenue; 213-749-3424) devoted to Judaism, the **California Afro-American Museum** (213-744-7432) devoted to black history and culture, and the **Natural History Museum of California** (213-744-3466).

The **L.A. County Museum of Art** (5905 Wilshire Boulevard; 213-857-6111) has a broad but not exceptional collection; the Japanese Pavilion, however, is beautiful and serene. The nearby **George C. Page Museum** (5801 Wilshire Boulevard; 213-936-2230), a paleontological museum, is surrounded by the **La Brea Tar Pits,** tar pools oozing history and methane gas. The **Museum of Flying** (2772 Donald Douglas Loop N., Santa Monica Airport; 310-392-8822) houses a 1924 Douglas World Cruiser (first to circle the globe) and other aviation-history artifacts.

PERFORMANCE

The **Los Angeles Music Center** (135 N. Grand Avenue, downtown; 213-972-7211) is composed of the city's three major performance venues: The **Dorothy Chandler Pavilion,** hosting opera and the symphony, the **Mark Taper Forum,** hosting contemporary drama, and the **Ahmanson Theatre,** hosting national touring productions. The **Shrine Auditorium** (665 W. Jefferson Boulevard, downtown; 213-749-5123), with 6,200 seats, hosts major music events. The **Westwood Playhouse** (10866 Le Conte Avenue, Westwood; 310-208-5454) often showcases new plays, the **Coast Playhouse** (8325 Santa Monica Boulevard, WeHo; 213-650-8507) showcases new musicals and dramas, the **Celebration Theatre** (7051-B Santa Monica Boulevard, Silver Lake; 213-957-1884) presents lesbian and gay theater, and the **Groundling Theatre** (7307 Melrose Avenue, WeHo; 213-934-9700) specializes in comedy and improv. The **Hollywood Bowl** (2301 N. Highland Avenue; 213-850-2000) offers outdoor concerts from its famous concrete band shell.

OTHER

El Pueblo de los Angeles is an outdoor museum of the city's original Spanish settlement of 1781. The **Visitor's Center** (622 N. Main Street, downtown; 213-628-1274) offers informative publications and walking tours. **The Los Angeles Conservancy** (213-623-8687) offers walking tours of downtown. **Watts Towers** (1765 E. 107th Street, Watts) are a hundred-foot, three-decade, *objets trouvés* effort by Simon Rodia, who finished the towers in 1954, left the city, and never looked back. The **Watts Towers Arts Center** (213-569-8181) features exhibits by black artists in the community. The **Museum of Tolerance** (9786 W. Pico Boulevard; 310-553-8403) uses multimedia presentations to examine the destructive force of prejudice throughout history, including an exhibit on the 1992 L.A. riots. The **Petite Elite Miniature Museum & Gallery** (1901 Avenue of the Stars, Suite 500, CC; 310-277-8101) is a collection of priceless miniature settings. **The Eighth Muse Art Gallery** (8713 Santa Monica Boulevard, WeHo; 310-659-2545) is one of only two art galleries in the country owned and operated by gay and lesbian people and featuring art created by and for gay and lesbian people. The **Max Factor Museum of Beauty** (1666 N. Highland Avenue, Hollywood; 213-463-6668) includes celebrity makeup rooms, a photo gallery, and rooms devoted to each of the major hair colors. The **Frederick's of Hollywood Lingerie Museum** (6608 Hollywood Boulevard; 213-456-8506) has relics of all eras, from Mae West to Madonna.

SHOPPING

Shopping in Los Angeles is in many ways shopping at its finest. Great shopping districts, easy parking, lots of sale events, and a full range of stores from ridiculous to sublime are the recipe for a shopper's paradise. Like California cuisine, California fashion has a unique style, tailored to the pleasant climate, outdoor living, movie glamour, and laidback attitude. It's a great place to buy and wear Lycra, linen, silk, and gauze—even all at once. With Shirley Maclaine and thousands of others like her on the loose, L.A. also supports many emporiums for crystals, aromatherapy, and other tools of the self-actualized inner child. Even the malls have reached new heights, becoming more sophisticated as malls in the rest of the country just get bigger.

West Hollywood is, not surprisingly, home to nearly all of the gay-specific stores, including the likes of **Don't Panic** and **International Male.** As gay retailing finds its way to Main Streets and mailboxes across the country, freedom rings, thong bikinis, and erotic postcards no longer denote a gay shopping mecca. But you will also find many stores with a gay sense of style and sensibility in WeHo, and throughout most of the city, especially in up-and-coming Santa Monica. You can shop all over the city, until the moment a credit card authorization terminal comes back with "stop this girl at once!" As one local friend put it, "The whole city is a shopping mall—just don't forget where you parked your car!"

SHOPPING MALLS

While L.A. has its share of typical mass-market shopping meccas (such as the **Sherman Oaks Galleria**), it is also home to some of the most unusual shopping malls in the world. The **Beverly Center** (Beverly and La Cienega Boulevards; 310-854-0070) was designed to evoke Paris's Pompidou Center, and it does—sort of. Right next to Cedar's Sinai Hospital (perfect for those who take the shop-til-you-drop mentality to its literal extreme), the center is home to many of the usual mall re-tailers, but also a high percentage of smaller, interesting, nonchain boutiques. The **Macy's (née Bullock's) Men's** store opened here to high expectations, better fulfilled by **Barneys New York** in Beverly Hills. Still, the proximity to West Hollywood makes for good shopping. The **West Side Pavilion** (Pico and Westwood Boulevards; 310-474-6255) has a similar formula, with more traditional styling and a higher percentage of heterosexuals. **Century City Shopping Center** (Santa Monica and Century Park Boulevards; 310-553-5300), with its mostly single-level, outdoor plaza design, will convert all but the most mall-dreading shop-pers. Its outdoor courtyards are particularly popular with tie-clad ju-nior executives from the adjacent office towers.

SHOPPING DISTRICTS

Santa Monica Boulevard, as it runs through West Hollywood, is as gay as shopping gets in L.A., although venues are limited mostly to gay books, toys and novelties, sportswear, gymwear, and low-end fashion. The **International Male** store (9000 Santa Monica Boulevard; 310-275-0285) has most of the fashions in their catalog, as well as some things we'd actually buy. Their big sales events at the end of August and January are worth hitting. **A Different Light** (8853 Santa Monica Boule-vard; 310-854-6601) could well be the country's premier gay book-store. Book signings and readings are frequent, and their inventory is extensive. **L.A. Sporting Club** (8592 Santa Monica Boulevard; 310-657-2858) has the area's best selection of swimwear and sportswear; the store's other half is called **Caliber,** and sells a great selection of stylish casual clothes. **Don't Panic** (802 N. San Vicente Boulevard; 310-652-3668) opened its first retail store here, stocked with a large selection of witty T-shirts. **Pavilions** (8969 Santa Monica Boulevard; 310-273-0977) is perhaps the gayest supermarket in the world; a great place to shop for dinner or for someone to make you dinner.

Melrose Avenue, formerly *the* place in L.A. for stylish boutiques, is starting to lose its cachet, as **Montana Street** in Santa Monica becomes a focal point for trendy and chic shopping. Still worth a trip, you will find a number of places to ply your plastic, though many are used-clothing stores, notable mostly for their collections of vintage 501 jeans. Our favorite is **Aardvark's** (7579 Melrose Avenue; 213-655-6769).

Parallel to Melrose, you'll find a number of interesting stores on Third Street (not to be confused with the Third Street in Santa Monica). **The Traveler's Bookcase** (8375 W. Third Street; 213-655-0575) carries a great collection of travel books and publications. The **NaNa Outlet** (8327 Third Street; 213-653-1252) has great deals on discontinued and sample styles of their punk-inspired shoes. **Freehand** (8413 W. Third Street; 213-655-2607) sells interesting art-quality crafts, jewelry, and housewares.

Out in Santa Monica, you'll find **Montana Street** and the **Third Street Promenade,** a shopping street closed to vehicular traffic and one of L.A.'s most pleasant places to amble around in. The most gorgeous women's fashions can be found at **Harari** (1406 Montana Street; 310-260-1206, also in Beverly Hills at 9646 Brighton Way; 310-859-1131). Also on Montana, you'll find **Moondance** (1530 Montana Street; 310-451-5401) for jewelry and **Only Hearts** (1407 Montana Street; 310-393-3088), a bedroom fashion kind of place with heart-theme lingerie, jewelry, and other romantic things. On the Third Street Promenade, you'll find **Jurassic Inc.** (1340 Third Street; 310-393-9622), purveyors of fossils and crystals, for decades before the movie, and **NaNa** (1228-30 Third Street; 310-394-9690), the full-price store.

Rodeo Drive in Beverly Hills remains an insanely popular tourist attraction. If you can afford to shop at Bijan and Fred Hayman, you don't need us to tell you about them. If you can't afford them, feel free to gawk at the windows—just be sure to give a wide sidewalk berth to the shopping bag–laden tourists.

SHOPPING SPECIALTIES

Barneys New York (9570 Wilshire Boulevard, Beverly Hills; 310-276-4400) is another stylish branch of this (overpriced?) New York retailer. **Fred Segal** (8106 Melrose Avenue; 213-651-4129 and 500 Broadway, Santa Monica; 310-393-4477) is a bit more Dries Van Noton than Barneys—and a fun place to shop. **Rebel** (11677 San Vicente Boulevard; 310-826-7700) in Brentwood is a good option for reasonably priced women's high fashion. The **Cinema Glamour Shop** (315 N. La Brea Boulevard; 213-933-5289) is the queen of all thrift shops, where stars bring their old stuff, including silk shirts and dinner jackets and other assorted evening wear. The **Rose Bowl Flea Market** operates the second Sunday of every month in Pasadena. It's worth the trip, but only if you get there really early (8:00 A.M.!). **Maxfield's Outlet Store** (9091 Santa Monica Boulevard; 310-275-7007) sells Armani without the markup of their Melrose store. **Clacton & Frinton** (731 N. La Cienega Boulevard; 310-652-2957) for expensive but cool clothes. **Tower Records** (8801 Sunset Boulevard, WeHo; 310-657-7300), the original Tower, has been eclipsed by the **Virgin Superstore** (8000 W. Sunset Boulevard; 310-650-8666), the *ne plus ultra* of record stores. Although we always laugh remembering their game show heritage, the selection of leather fashion at **Wilson's House of Suede & Leather** (9844 Wilshire Boulevard, Beverly Hills; 310-553-0588) is quite good.

FYI

The **LA Gay and Lesbian Community Center** (1625 N. Hudson Avenue; 213-993-7400) offers a variety of services and information. *Edge* (213-962-6994) and *Frontiers* (213-848-2222) offer the most extensive news information for men, with the *Lesbian News (LN)* (310-392-8224) offering the same for women. *fab!* (6399 Wilshire Boulevard; 213-655-5716) is the city's current club guide, with good night-by-night listings for men and women. *Los Angeles Girl Guide* (2531 Sawtelle Boulevard; 310-391-8877) covers some news, but is focused on women's entertainment.

LONG BEACH

At the southernmost point of L.A. County is Long Beach, one of the largest cities in the state. Back in the 1920s, it was known as the "Coney Island of the West." Today it boasts a huge man-made harbor, a large base of industry, a steel-and-glass-towered downtown, and a sizable gay community, although gays here tend to be the more married, suburban types. Although it is not a traditional resort destination, it is a convenient stop on the coastal route down to San Diego and has a small number of tourist attractions among its suburb-industry-downtown sprawl. The most notable of these is the *Queen Mary,* one of the last remnants of the golden age of ocean liner travel. You'll find her in the seaport, at the edge of downtown. The beach here is long (as the name implies) and wide, with a bike path, calm surf, and reasonably pretty setting, despite the industrial port activity. Most of the gay businesses are on or near East Broadway, just a few blocks from the gay section of the beach, and a few minutes drive from downtown. The Long Beach gay scene is miles away (literally and figuratively) from the high-energy, high-attitude world of West L.A. and West Hollywood. If you're looking for a kinder, gentler place to interact with the locals, put Long Beach on your Southern California itinerary.

Accommodations

QUEEN MARY 1126 Queen's Highway; 310-432-6964 or 800-437-2934; $75–180

Long Beach's one spectacular accommodation, which is a destination itself, offers the opportunity to stay in the beautifully restored cabins of this historic ocean liner. The 365 original, first-class staterooms and suites have been transformed into a floating hotel. Although some cabins are small, and portholes substitute for windows, modern amenities such as color TV and direct-dial phones have been added.

HYATT REGENCY 200 S. Pine Avenue; 310-491-1234 or 800-233-1234, fax 310-432-1972; $99–150

One of the newest and nicest of the business hotels downtown, adjacent to the convention center and convenient to the beach and gay nightlife.

Dining

Long Beach has a nice range of casual, friendly restaurants. **Two Umbrellas Café** (1538 E. Broadway; 310-495-2323; $5) offers casual daytime dining with indoor and sidewalk seating. **The Original Park Pantry** (2104 E. Broadway; 310-434-0451; $9) is gay-popular, with an eclectic menu including American, Mexican, Asian, and Italian dishes. Open for lunch and dinner, it features entertainment on Monday and Saturday nights. **The Birds of Paradise** (1800 E. Broadway; 310-590-8773; $8) is restaurant-cocktail lounge-piano bar. The **Omelette Inn** (108 W. Third Street; 310-437-5625; $5) serves breakfast and lunch, with salads, sandwiches, low-fat options, and, of course, omelets. It is gay-friendly, catering to a mixed crowd, as is **Magnolia Café** (632 Redondo Avenue; 310-433-2328; $6), serving traditional, home-style food such as pot roast and mashed potatoes. The **Haven Coffee Co.** (1708 E. Broadway; 310-436-2666; $5) serves the usual coffee-latte-espresso fare, plus pastas, salads, soups, and pastries.

Nightlife

Ripples (5101 E. Ocean Boulevard; 310-433-0357) is a popular two-level dance bar, featuring a piano bar downstairs, disco upstairs, weekend drink specials, tea dance on Sundays, go-go boys on Fridays, and women's entertainment on Saturdays. **Utopia** (145 W. Broadway; 310-432-7202) is a new weekend hot spot, popular for their beer bust on Friday nights, and Sunday-night beer bust/dance.party called Spasm. It features a restaurant and 16 pool tables. **Floyds** (2913 E. Anaheim Street; 310-433-9251) offers C&W dancing. The **Mineshaft** (1720 E. Broadway; 310-436-2433) is more hard-core, catering to a Levi's crowd. **Pistons** (2020 E. Artesia Boulevard; 310-422-1928) is a popular leather bar. The **Silver Fox** (411 Redondo Avenue; 310-439-6343) caters to an older crowd, with karaoke, darts, and a happy hour. **The Broadway** (1100 E. Broadway; 310-432-3646) is a weekend piano bar catering to a mixed-age group. **Executive Suite** (3428 E. Pacific Coast Highway; 310-597-3884) is a slick, high-tech dance bar catering to men and women. It is popular weekends and has a big lesbian night on Wednesdays. **Que Sera** (1923 E. Seventh Street; 310-599-6170) is a popular women's club, open seven nights a week with live entertainment, a pool table, friendly staff, and special events. **Dede's** (at the *Queen Mary;* 310-433-1470) is a hi-energy dance party for women, the third Saturday of each month.

Activities

ATHLETIC AND OUTDOOR

The **El Dorado Nature Center** (7550 East Spring Street; 310-421-9431) is a wildlife sanctuary inhabited by 150 bird species and offering short hikes along a lake and creek. **Whale watching** is popular from late December through mid-April. You'll find the **gay beach** off Ocean Avenue, between Orange and Esperanza avenues, in front of a tall condominium tower. The beach offers a paved bike/skate/walking path and a very calm surf.

SIGHTSEEING

The **Queen Mary** (1126 Queen's Highway; 310-435-3511) is the big tourist attraction in town. It features dioramas of the golden age of steamship travel. The **Long Beach Museum of Art** (2300 E. Ocean Boulevard; 310-439-2119) is an avant-garde museum specializing in twentieth-century art.

SHOPPING

The **AIDS Assistance Thrift Store** (2238 E. Seventh Street; 310-987-5353) has donated more than $100,000 to local AIDS agencies, open Tuesday through Sunday. **Hot Stuff** (2121 E. Broadway; 310-433-0692) sells cards, gifts and adult novelties. **Out & About on Broadway** (love the name!) (1724 E. Broadway; 310-436-9930) sells gay-popular clothing and accessories.

FYI

The **Long Beach Convention and Visitors Bureau** (1 World Trade Center; 310-436-3645) can provide general tourist information. It is located along the Promenade. The **Lesbian/Gay Center and Switchboard** (2017 E. Fourth Street; 310-434-4455) is open every day except Sunday, answering questions and providing referrals.

LAGUNA BEACH

Laguna is a cute little town on the beach about an hour south of Los Angeles. It has been a small gay enclave for decades, stuck in the middle of ultraconservative Orange County, birthplace of the John Birch Society. In the summer, downtown Laguna is just mobbed, but still retains its small-town feel, with sidewalk bistros and artsy shopping. Framed by the San Joaquin hills, its coves and bluffs have a somewhat Mediterranean feel. Here you will find a small gay paradise with some very nice restaurants, gay beaches, small hotels, and nightlife. Laguna is a frequent getaway for L.A. gays, particularly on weekends. It is also home to a large lesbian population, and therefore more attractive to women than most gay resorts. It's also popular with straights, who swell the general population to an even greater extent. There is limited nightlife here, but the real emphasis is the beach, which can be packed towel-to-towel on a sunny summer Saturday or Sunday. Located at the southern end of town, West Street Beach is a gay treasure of the California coastline. Pack yourself a picnic and a beach umbrella, and come on down.

Accommodations

Laguna has one gay hotel, and a number of gay-friendly options. Our listings are concentrated at the south end of town, close to the gay nightlife and the gay beach. Hotels/motels on the west side of Pacific Coast Highway offer ocean views and possible beach access; those on the east side of the roadway often overlook more noisy traffic than ocean. **California Riviera 800** (1400 S. Coast Highway, Suite 104; 714-376-0305 or 800-621-0500) is a helpful reservations service for local accommodations.

COAST INN 1401 S. Coast Highway; 714-494-7588 or 800-653-2697, fax 714-494-1735; $49–89

The only gay hostelry in town, offering basic rooms, some with sitting areas, outdoor patios, and ocean views. It is attached to the Boom Boom Room, Laguna's only gay nightclub, and is the definitive "heart of the action" hotel. Compared to gay hotels in other areas, it would rate one or two palms. Limited room service is available; oceanfront rooms on the lowest level are in bad shape.

SURF & SAND HOTEL 1555 S. Coast Highway; 714-497-4477 or 800-524-8621, fax 714-494-2897; $175–295

Just two doors down from the ocean, it is a deluxe, 1950s-era property, gay-friendly, but mostly straight. Almost every room has an ocean view and balcony.

CAPRI LAGUNA 1441 S. Coast Highway; 714-494-6533 or 800-225-4551, fax 714-497-6962; $70–225

Located between the Coast Inn and Surf & Sand, it offers better-than-average beach motel fare. Continental breakfast is included, and some rooms have kitchenettes and terraces.

CASA LAGUNA INN 2510 S. Coast Highway; 714-494-2996 or 800-233-0449, fax 714-494-5009; $69–205

A 21-room country inn on a terraced hillside overlooking the Pacific. The clientele is mostly straight, but the inn is gay-friendly. The landscaping is more attractive than the rooms, some of which are right on the street and suffer from noise. Casa Laguna features a pool and expanded continental breakfast.

BEST WESTERN LAGUNA BRISAS SPA HOTEL 1600 S. Coast Highway; 714-497-7272 or 800-624-4442, fax 714-497-8306; $59–169

Has a location on the east side of the coastal highway, and offers modern rooms each with a whirlpool spa bath.

CARRIAGE HOUSE B&B 1322 Catalina Street; 714-494-8945; $95–150

Gay-friendly and has a certain funky charm with six suites.

ALISO CREEK INN 31106 S. Coast Highway; 714-499-2271 or 800-223-3309, fax 714-499-4601; $78–160

This is the hotel closest to the gay beach (walking distance), and offers a par-32 golf course carved out of the canyon. The 62 units are all studios and one- or two-bedroom town houses, with full kitchens and private patios. It has a small gay following, but is also popular with families and seniors.

Dining

Laguna has a great selection of restaurants, offering some of Southern California's best menus and settings. Other than the Coast Inn Café, none of the restaurants are specifically gay, though many are gay-owned and operated, and all are gay-friendly. **Mark's** (858 S. Coast Highway; 714-494-6711; $13) is the more southerly sister of Mark's in West Hollywood. Still owned by namesake Mark Depalma, this Mark's is larger and extremely popular, serving dinner daily and Sunday brunch. **Café Zoolu** (860 Glenneyre; 714-494-6825; $17) is also gay-popular, serving dinner nightly from a California cuisine menu with great grilled fish and vegetarian options. **The Leap of Faith Café** (1440 S. Coast Highway; 714-494-8595; $5) is lesbian-owned and offers great coffee, desserts, and an outdoor heated patio. They also sport new wine bistro, serving light meals and featuring live Spanish guitar music on most weekends. The **Cottage Restaurant** (308 N. Coast Highway; 714-494-3023; $10) is an early twentieth-century bungalow, decorated with turn-of-the-century antiques and stained glass. It serves traditional fare, three meals a day. **Café 242** (242 N. Coast Highway; 714-494-2444; $5) is lesbian-owned, and has a great assortment of gourmet salads and the like. The place is tiny but serves good food. **Café Zinc** (350 Ocean Avenue; 714-494-6302; $6) is a vegetarian sidewalk café, gay-owned and gay-friendly, jammed at lunch, but great anytime for a light meal and people-watching. The clientele is mostly straight. The **Coast Inn Café** (1401 S. Coast Highway; 714-494-7588; $8) has a limited but tasty café menu. Open 8:00 A.M. to 10:00 P.M. daily. **Splashes** (1555 S. Coast Highway; 714-497-4477; $13), at the Surf & Sand Hotel, is popular with the trendy movie business crowd and is noteworthy for its umbrella-shaded terrace view of the sea. **A la Carte** (1915 S. Coast Highway; 714-497-4927) is small but popular, serving gourmet sandwiches and salads for the discriminating palate. Sit outdoors and try the Cajun Fried Chicken Salad and any of their amazing desserts. The **Coyote Grill** (31621 Coast Highway; 714-499-4033; $10) is mostly straight, but attracts plenty of gay folks, especially for summer weekend breakfasts. The wait for a table is not unpleasant in sunny weather. Try to get seated on the outdoor patio. **Sorrento Grille** (370 Glenneyre; 714-494-8686; $17) is one of the best upscale restaurants in town, an American bistro and martini bar. Not especially gay-popular, but has been on the *Los Angeles Times*'s "Best Restaurants in Los Angeles" list a couple of times, and it's not even in L.A.! Down the street you'll find **Restaurant 5´-0˝** (328 Glenneyre; 714-497-4955; $14), serving contemporary Chinese cuisine with unusual, attractive décor. **230 Forest Avenue** (230 Forest Avenue; 714-494-2545; $16) is a modern café bistro, with indoor and outdoor dining and a creative California cuisine menu. It is next door to the **Renaissance Grill** (232 Forest Avenue; 714-497-5282; $15), serving up a similar atmosphere and the best burger in town. **Shame on the Moon** (1464 S. Coast Highway; 714-497-9975; $16), Palm Springs' great gay-popular restaurant, was just opening at press time, right across from the Surf & Sand Hotel. It will have a different menu and atmosphere from their desert restaurant, but aspires to share their reputation for moderately priced, excellent food and service.

Nightlife

The **Boom Boom Room** (1401 S. Coast Highway; 714-494-7588) is the main game in town—with a dance floor, pool room, two bar areas, and a busy schedule of strippers and special events. It is busiest for Sunday tea dance and on holiday weekends, when lots of boys come down from L.A. **Main Street** (1460 S. Coast Highway; 714-494-0056) caters to the older, piano-bar crowd, with nightly entertainment. The Little Shrimp, Laguna's long-standing piano bar/restaurant has closed, but a new place called **Viktor/Viktoria** (1455 S. Coast Highway) is scheduled to open on the same spot, offering much the same fare. That's all, folks. At least you can't get lost.

Activities

ATHLETIC AND OUTDOOR

There is a small beach area just below the Boom Boom Room that often hosts a few gay sunbathers, but **West Street Beach** is definitely the main gay beach, and it is definitely not handicapped-accessible. It is a beautiful, expansive beach by California standards, great for swimming, but without enough surf for surfing. It offers no facilities other than Porta-Johns and -Janes, so bring a picnic and an umbrella. There are multiple pathways to the beach, though the easiest to spot is the paved stairway down the south side of the Laguna Royale condo complex. Hit the sand and head north toward the sea of buff, tan bodies. You can't miss it in the summer. Women gather toward the northernmost end of the beach. Parking can be difficult, so get there early, and be careful swimming as the ground slopes sharply underwater, and folks who aren't alert can be slammed pretty hard. Pickup volleyball games are popular in the summer. **Table Rock** is the next beach south (an easy-to-miss set of steps one street south of the West Street steps), a small, almost unknown cove with some topless women, a small cave, and tide pools to explore. **Main Beach** is straight, but the volleyball games make great eye-candy (there's volleyball at West Street Beach as well). For those addicted to perfect pecs who need to work out even on vacation, the gay-owned **Laguna Health Club** (870 Glenneyre; 714-494-9314; $8) is the place to pump up. It's small, with a mostly gay clientele.

SIGHTSEEING

The **Festival of the Arts and Pageant of the Masters** (650 Laguna Canyon Road; 714-494-1145) is the town's most extraordinary event, staged every summer at the Irvine Bowl. The festival is your basic local artists' affair, but the pageant is a series of tableaux vivant, in which local residents stand costumed and motionless, recreating famous works of art. It must be seen to be believed. Laguna is a good place for contemporary art viewing and buying. **The Laguna Art Museum** (307 Cliff Drive; 714-494-6531) hosts interesting exhibitions of contemporary art. There are a number of art galleries in town—**Diane Nelson Fine Art** (435 Ocean Avenue; 714-494-2440) is the most established.

SHOPPING

The Coast Highway and Ocean Avenue downtown are lined with inviting small shops, selling typical seaside stuff: kites, resort wear, knick-knacks, and the like. Across the street from the Boom Boom Room is a small gay store cleverly named **Gaymart** (168 Mountain Road; 714-

497-9108). It does not have the awesome assortment of swimwear that its ad would have you believe, but it's a good place to pick up a clean pair of underwear, or tube of water-based lubricant in case of inexplicable loss or unexpected shortage. The best gift shopping in town is at **Areo** (207 Ocean Avenue; 714-376-0535). It's gay-owned and sells a wonderful upscale selection of objets d'art, frames, one-of-a-kind jewelry, candles, cards, vases, etc. Across the street is **World Newsstand** (190 S. Coast Highway; 714-376-2029) for your getaway reading. They have a darn good selection, and the gay and lesbian magazines are right out front, including some foreign magazines. **Jewelry by Poncé** (1417 S. Coast Highway; 800-969-7464 or 714-497-4154) features fine jewelry, including much gay-theme stuff, rainbows and lambdas and the like, crystal, frames, etc. It's located just south of the Boom Boom Room. Two blocks north on the other side of the street you'll find **re•finery** (1294 S. Coast Highway; 714-376-1688) selling country-house furnishings, cards, and gifts, and the **Pottery Shack** (1212 S. Coast Highway; 714-494-1141) with an immense selection of kitchen and tablewares. **Dorothy's On Broadway** (355 Broadway; 714-494-1911) is a thrift store benefiting the AIDS Services Foundation. Shop early for Halloween, or for the excitement of finding the perfect vintage shirt or skirt. **A Different Drummer Bookshop** (1027 N. Coast Highway; 714-497-6699) is a lesbian-owned business, carrying a broad range of gay books, as well as videos and audio tapes.

FYI

You'll find Laguna Beach advertising and listings in L.A.-based *Edge* magazine. The *Orange County Blade* (714-494-4898) also covers the area, but not particularly well, considering it's based here. The **Laguna Beach Chamber of Commerce** (357 Glenneyre; 714-494-1018) can provide basic tourist information. The **Gay and Lesbian Community Services Center of Orange County** (714-534-0862) can provide referrals and information.

SAN DIEGO

San Diego offers the complete Southern California vacation: great weather, uncrowded beaches, world-class tourist attractions, nearby Tijuana, and a booming gay scene centered in the Hillcrest area. As home base to the Pacific fleet, San Diego is also populated by more navy men than the Village People could have dreamed of. Rodeo fans know the city as home to the largest event on the gay rodeo circuit, scheduled for September every year. Despite its sleepy countenance, San Diego has played an important role in California and American history. Settled in 1742, it was the birthplace of California. It was also the site of the state's first mission. Under Mexican control in the early 1800s, the city didn't start growing until the arrival of the railroad later that century. The arrival of the U.S. Navy during World War II set the stage for the growth that has defined San Diego today. The military continues to drive a large portion of the economy, although tourism and agriculture are also significant, and biotech and software companies have filled the gap left by the aerospace industry. Water activities, particularly sailing, are popular, but you'll find an abundance of any activity that calls for good sunny weather, from tennis to hang gliding. The city is easily accessed and navigated: the airport is literally minutes from downtown and most attractions are no more than a few miles off a highway (It's nearly impossible to get around without a car). The city's gay and lesbian community is visible and active, with a dense concentration of gay-owned and patronized businesses of all types in the Hillcrest neighborhood. For visitors, the greater San Diego area offers a wide variety of vacation options, with something for almost everyone. Enjoy its riches any time of the year.

Accommodations

Although it is on the Pacific, San Diego itself is not on the beach and has surprisingly few beachfront properties. San Diego Bay, Mission Bay, and communities to the north provide most of the waterfront accommodations and activities. There are a number of gay-friendly options convenient to gay nightlife and entertainment.

BALBOA PARK INN 3402 Park Boulevard; 619-298-0823 or 800-938-8181, fax 619-294-8070; $80–190

A terrific upscale B&B on the edge of Balboa Park, catering to a 50% gay clientele. Each of the 25 rooms has a different theme, like "Tara" or "Tarzan." Book well in advance.

PARK MANOR SUITES 525 Spruce Street; 619-291-0999, fax 619-291-8844; $60–160

Very gay and very convenient. Accommodations are well-equipped, spacious and nicely furnished. They have a roof-top happy hour on Fridays!

HILLCREST INN 3754 Fifth Avenue, 619-293-7078 or 800-258-2280, fax 619-293-3861; $49–55

This gay-marketed inn is well located but exceedingly basic, bordering on dumpy.

HYATT REGENCY LA JOLLA 3777 La Jolla Village Drive; 619-552-1234 or 800-423-2400, fax 619-552-6066; $124–200

The closest hotel to the gay beach, the Hyatt Regency offers some resort property facilities, including a spectacular health club, large pool with tented cabanas and plenty of lounge chairs, and a number of good restaurants. It was also one of the first Hyatt hotels to advertise in the gay press. It is about 20 minutes by car from downtown San Diego.

HOTEL DEL CORONADO 1500 Orange Avenue, Coronado; 619-435-6611 or 800-468-3533, fax 619-522-8238; $145–230

Also about 20 minutes by car from downtown San Diego, this hotel is on the peninsula across the Coronado Bridge. It's usually filled with conventioneers, but it is on the beach and rich with history and old-world elegance. Stay in a balconied room in the original building, where *Some Like It Hot* was filmed.

WYNDHAM EMERALD PLAZA formerly the Pan Pacific; 400 W. Broadway; 619-239-4500 or 800-996-3426, fax 619-239-3274; $150–190

The Wyndham is luxurious, upscale, and new; it has been the official gay-pride-weekend hotel.

LA VALENCIA HOTEL 1132 Prospect Street, La Jolla; 619-454-0771 or 800-451-0772, fax 619-456-3921; $160–600

La Valencia is in La Jolla, about 20 minutes north of town. The vintage, mission-style 1920s hotel exudes tradition and style with beautifully landscaped grounds and a sweeping view of the Pacific.

THE U.S. GRANT HOTEL 326 Broadway; 619-232-3121 or 800-334-6957, fax 619-232-3626; $135-175

San Diego's Grand Dame hotel and a celebrity address with plenty of historic charm. Across from Horton Plaza downtown, it is a calm civilized oasis with pleasant service, Queen Anne furnishings and top-notch service.

Dining

Hillcrest has enough dining options to keep you fueled for all the activity it offers. **California Cuisine** (1027 University Avenue; 619-543-0790; $14) serves just what the name implies. Artful presentation and patio dining round out the experience. **Café Eleven** (1440 University Avenue; 619-260-8023; $11) features modern country-French cuisine in an intimate setting decorated with original art by local artists—their special menu on Sunday, Tuesday, Wednesday, and Thursday is an unbeatable deal. **Montana's American Grill** (1421 University Avenue; 619-297-0722; $10) serves grilled food with a Southwestern flair. A see-and-be-seen place. **Taste of Thai** (527 University Avenue; 619-291-7525; $8) serves okay Thai food with great sightseeing. **Arrivederci** (3845 Fourth Avenue; 619-299-6282; $12) is an upscale Italian restaurant with a few outdoor tables and a mostly gay clientele. **Hamburger Mary's** (308 University Avenue; 619-491-0400; $8) recreates the successful combination of casual al-fresco dining it originated in Honolulu. The city has four popular coffee shops: **Euphoria** (1045 University Avenue; 619-295-1769) caters to a young crowd; **Quel Fromage** (523 University Avenue; 619-295-1600) is the institution, catering to a very broad clientele; **The Study** (401A University Avenue; 619-296-4847) is the upscale coffee shop, playing classical and jazz music; **David's Place** (3768 Fifth Avenue; 619-294-8908) is a nonprofit coffeehouse with outdoor seating and nightly entertainment. Popular with a friendly, older crowd, it donates all its profits to AIDS charities.

Nightlife

Rich's (1051 University Avenue; 619-295-2195) is the reigning dance club. Its playlist leans toward house/techno music. It is straight on Thursday nights. **Flicks** (1017 University Avenue; 619-297-2056) is your basic video bar just a few doors away from Rich's, and a good place to hang pre- or post-dancing. Shoot pool in the smoky blue video haze. **Kickers** (308 University Avenue; 619-491-0400) is the C&W club. Nightly two-stepping and a friendly, slightly older crowd make this a fun place even if you're not a big country fan. **The Flame** (3780 Park Boulevard; 619-295-4163) is San Diego's hot lesbian bar/club/hangout—highly recommended. Tuesday night is mixed men and women. **Club Bombay** (3175 India Street; 619-296-6789) caters to a more upscale women's crowd; Friday night is big. The **Eagle** (3040 North Park Way; 619-295-8072) is the popular leather/Levi's bar until midnight, when the crowd moves en masse to **Wolf's** (3404 Thirtieth Street; 619-291-3730). **The Hole** (2820 Lytton Street; 619-226-9019) is more sleazy Levi's than leather, and only popular (but amazingly so) on Sunday afternoons, particularly in good weather. The **Matador** (4633 Mission Boulevard, Pacific Beach; 619-483-6943) is packed on Sunday evenings (dead the rest of the week), a popular transition from Black's Beach.

Activities

ATHLETIC AND OUTDOOR

The north end of **Black's Beach** is the major gay beach, located in La Jolla just north of San Diego. Two cautions there: The path from parking lot to the beach is very steep, unnavigable without sure footing and some stamina, and the police sometimes crack down on nudity and the heavy cruising that occurs in the bushes above the beach. (Take the Genessee exit off I-5, head west, cross Torrey Pines, and go right at the glider port sign.) **Hillcrest Gym** (142 University Avenue; 619-299-PUMP; $12/day) is the city's only gay-owned-and-operated gym. Serious free weights and an assortment of cardiovascular equipment; a Jacuzzi and sauna are new additions. **The Athletic Center** (1747 Hancock Street; 619-299-2639; $7/day) has some straight clientele, but a mostly gay atmosphere. **Bally's Total Fitness** (405 Camino Del Rio S.; 619-297-6062) is a big gym with a lot of bodily distractions—the city's premier gay workout scene. They don't sell day passes, but many hotels offer access. **Gold's** (2949 Garnet Avenue; 619-272-3400; $7/day) is the least gay of the four, but still somewhat gay-popular, particularly in the morning.

SIGHTSEEING

Balboa Park contains the **San Diego Zoo,** the **Fleet Space Center,** three different art galleries, ten museums, and many breathtakingly sculpted gardens. Leave a lot of time. **Sea World** is fun and educational. Finally, if you must, head south to **Tijuana** (check your car rental agreement for insurance restrictions first). This town offers little more than tourist junk and fairly impoverished conditions. But it is Mexico and less than an hour away.

SHOPPING

San Diego is possibly the best and easiest place to shop for a wardrobe of California-style clothes. And of course the Hillcrest doesn't disappoint. Everything from a huge **International Male** store to the funky and quirky can be found on the streets shooting off of University Avenue. **California Man** (3930 Fifth Avenue; 619-294-9108) specializes in trendy California wear. **Obelisk** (1029 University Avenue; 619-297-4171) sells gay books. **Laguna Trends** (1092 University Avenue; 619-298-2555) sells gay gifts and cards. There is a small but thriving art scene in the downtown area, not far from the harbor. **Horton Plaza** is downtown San Diego's huge and whimsical mall. And if you're feeling adventurous (or want a break from the sun at Black's Beach) head up to Del Mar (just north of La Jolla) and check out the **Del Mar Plaza** shopping center. It is an exquisite shopping-dining-gallery complex set in an indoor/outdoor plaza.

FYI

General tourist information is available from the **San Diego Convention and Visitors Bureau** (619-232-3101). For gay-specific assistance, call the **Lesbian & Gay Center** (619-692-GAYS). For the latest information on the nightlife scene, pick up *Update* (619-225-0282) or *The Gay & Lesbian Times* (619-299-6397), the major gay papers.

Hawaiian Islands

Hawaii's imagery is indelibly etched in the minds of anyone who has ever oohed and aahed over game-show prizes, lived through Pearl Harbor, or watched any of Elvis's Hawaii movies. But Hawaii is much more than hula skirts and aloha shirts, cool Mai Tais and warm ocean breezes. To understand Hawaii, you need to see Waikiki, the world's most famous beach. To love Hawaii, you need to venture beyond Waikiki, to the less-touristy pleasures of Oahu's north shore and the outer islands: Kauai, Maui, and the Big Island. Many of these pleasures are beaches, and you'll find them with white sand, black sand, even green and red sand; you'll find beaches for surfing, beaches for swimming and snorkeling, beaches where you'll meet other gay people, and beaches where you won't see another soul. But Hawaii is also much more than sandy shores, for here are waterfalls and rain forests, active volcanoes and phenomenal golf courses, fields of cane and gardens full of orchids. Hawaii is unique, and you will be constantly amazed by its beauty and entertained by its variety.

THIS LAND IS YOUR LAND

A Hawaiian vacation can be as individual as you are. Custom craft a trip from numerous easily combined options: Hike a volcano at sunrise, swim with dolphins, sleep on an outdoor waterbed, have tea under an ancient banyan tree, disco the night away, learn to surf, indulge in spa luxury, play golf, eat sushi, wear a grass skirt. With its multicultural history and its U.S.–Pacific Rim crossroads location, Hawaii is a true vacation paradise, tarnished only by the consequences of its deserved popularity. If the Hawaii you dream of is unspoiled and unhurried, you'll be glad to know there is plenty of it left, and you don't need to spend $350 a night to find it. More and more Hawaiian visitors are bypassing Honolulu entirely, connecting directly to Kauai, Lanai, Molokai, and especially Maui (which has its own overdevelopment problems). But Honolulu deserves a visit of a few days. It makes an ideal stopover to or from the Pacific basin, and a great way to ease in or out of the laid-back life of the outer islands.

The gay "scene" in Hawaii is unusual, populated more by visitors than by locals. Discos, bars, and clubs are limited almost entirely to Waikiki, though you will find an occasional gay bar or gay-popular nude beach on the outer islands. You may encounter some homophobia on the streets of Waikiki, but in general you'll find Hawaii a tolerant and friendly place. Single men may find playmates on the beach or in the few clubs, but if you're looking for a singles scene, stay in Waikiki or visit someplace else. Hawaii is an ideal place for couples. It could become even more so if the landmark decision by Hawaii's Supreme Court in May 1993 establishes the legality of same-sex marriage. In the meantime, you'll just have to enjoy the honeymoon first. It's a harsh sentence, but you won't find a more perfect place to carry it out.

When to Go and How to Get There

Hawaii is a five-hour flight from the West Coast, nine from Atlanta, nonstop, and is well situated for a stopover en route to Australia or the Pacific Rim. With many different scheduled carriers and charters, it is a surprisingly inexpensive destination. Once there, you'll want to schedule a few days on Oahu before moving on. How many islands you visit depends entirely on how much time you have and how much packing, flying, and driving you want to do. We recommend three days to a week per island. So settle into your seat, get comfortable, and let us unfold your Hawaii vacation. Our coverage of each of the four major islands will help you decide which to visit and where to stay. When to go is really up to you. Although Hawaii is busiest around Christmas and over school holidays and often less expensive in the summer, there's really no specific high and low season.

TWO TICKETS TO PARADISE

Under most circumstances, Hawaiian vacations are best booked through tour wholesalers. Accessible through any travel agent, wholesalers offer group discounts to individual travelers by contracting services in bulk. Because wholesale operations dominate Hawaiian tourism, they generally offer the best rates on airfare, hotels, car rental, interisland airfare, and more. Usually, a minimum three-night hotel booking on one island is all you need to avail yourself of the full array of optional tour elements, so even if you are using frequent-flyer miles for your transpacific airfare and hotel vouchers for most of your stay, one hotel booking can allow you to buy all of your interisland flights and car rentals at discount prices.

Ask your travel agent to compare rates from different wholesalers for each island—prices vary, and you can use more than one whole-saler per trip (and you'll get lei'd more if you do). Gay-owned and op-erated **Pacific Ocean Holidays** (808-923-2400 or 800-735-6600, fax 808-923-2499) offers packages similar to mainstream wholesalers, but also offers gay-specific accommodations, as well as a gay-hosted wel-come and orientation breakfast and their gay *Pocket Guide to Hawaii.* **Men on Vacation** (619-641-7085 or 800-959-4636, fax 619-641-7088) has added Hawaii to their roster of group vacation destinations and can offer some wholesale assistance in booking individual itineraries.

A NOTE ON ACCOMMODATIONS

Hale is the Hawaiian word for *house* or *home,* and you'll see the word in many guest-house names. You'll also see many different kinds of lodging, from towering modern hotels to thatched cottages. Many of the deluxe hotels are part of large resort developments including golf courses, private residences, and other hotels. Some achieve an isolated retreat atmosphere, but others are one on top of the other, on strips like Waikiki and Kaanapali, Maui. Hawaii's gay-specific lodging is lim-ited and in a constant state of flux. Many "gay guest houses" you may find advertised are a couple of rooms of someone's home or even just a rental condo unit. Only some are exclusively gay, many are not even gay-owned. Ownership, management, and clientele can and do change often, sometimes with dramatic effects. Although only the **Hotel Hon-olulu** (see Oahu) and **R.B.R. Farms** (see the Big Island) feel very gay, many of the gay-marketed properties offer unique settings and friendly management at affordable prices.

The shorter your stay, the less likely you'll be to venture beyond your resort, so picking the right one is important. The large resorts we've listed offer extraordinary facilities or atmospheres—places worth splurging on. The vast majority of hotels, particularly in Waikiki, are midrange properties with few distinguishing characteristics. We've only made recommendations in this category for Waikiki, where some of these properties have an edge for the gay traveler in terms of their amenities or clientele. Prices listed are rack rate; steep discounts are often available at most properties other than the **Halekulani** on Waikiki, and the small guest houses. Wholesalers and frequent-flyer program awards are the best sources for bargain room rates. All listed properties cater to a mixed gay/straight clientele, unless otherwise noted.

𝓕𝓨𝓘

We recommend two guidebooks for the Hawaiian Islands. *Hidden Hawaii* (Ulysses Press) is the best general guide for a sophisticated traveler. Specializing in out-of-the-way special places, we find their restaurant listings and sightseeing descriptions to be particularly useful. The *Hawaii Handbook* (Moon Publications) is especially good for flora and fauna lovers, with great emphasis on Hawaii's natural attractions. The **University of Hawaii Press** publishes the best topographic road maps. Widely available, they are appropriately titled "Map of Oahu," "Map of Maui," etc. There are a few local gay publications: *Island Lifestyle* (2851A Kihei Place, Honolulu 96816; 808-737-6400) is the largest monthly, covering news, culture, community events, and the club scene. You can obtain a copy in advance of your trip by sending $4. **Pacific Ocean Holidays** (P.O. Box 88245, Honolulu, HI 96830; 808-923-2400) publishes *Pocket Guide to Hawaii*, a biannual gay pocket guide to the islands. You can obtain a copy in advance of your trip by sending $5. *Odyssey Magazine Hawaii* covers nightlife. *Out in Maui* is a relatively new monthly covering gay life in Maui. It is published by **Both Sides Now,** whose info line (808-872-6061) offers up-to-date events information, and whose web site can be accessed at http://www.maui.net/-glom/index/html. A **Maui Women's Events Hotline** can be reached at 808-573-3077. The **Gay/Lesbian Community Center** (808-926-1000) in Honolulu also offers 24-hour information. **Lambda Aloha** (808-828-0426) is an informal information resource for women on Maui. **The Hawaii Visitor's Bureau** (808-923-1811) can provide general tourist information. Computer junkies can order the Visitor's Bureau *Official Travel Planner on CD-ROM* for $8.95 (send check to VCT, P.O. Box 61297 Dept. A, Honolulu, HI 96839, specify Mac or Windows).

Information on hiking trails and campsites can be obtained from the **Department of Land and Natural Resources** (808-587-0300 for state parks; 808-587-0166 for reserves and trails). Note that camping permits are required for all camping, and rental-car contracts are valid only on paved roads. As hard as it is not to be a tourist in Honolulu, you won't have to worry about seeming an obnoxious tourist—the competition for that title is just too fierce. Learn a few Hawaiian words—everyone knows *aloha,* but surprisingly few know *mahalo* (thank you).

OAHU

Just 100 years ago, Honolulu was under the rule of Queen Liliuokalani, a foreign monarchy with a distinctly South Pacific culture. Today, it remains America's most foreign city, although it resembles a Tokyo shopping center by the sea more than Margaret Mead's Samoa. The Japanese have become the dominant force in the Hawaiian economy, from real estate development to the throngs of young women waiting five deep to use their JCB cards at Chanel, Tiffany, and Louis Vuitton. Tourism has eclipsed both the military and agriculture as the dominant industry in Hawaii, and nowhere is this more apparent than on Waikiki Beach, which has the highest concentration of hotel rooms in the world. Honolulu is not the island paradise of our pineapple-scented dreams. That Hawaii still exists, but it is the province of the outer islands, where wide unspoiled beaches and thatched-hut hotel cottages still exist. Instead, Honolulu is a vibrant city, with glittering high-rise towers, expansive shopping malls, traffic problems, and nightlife. It is the first port of entry for all international and most mainland flights, and it offers at least a taste of all things Hawaiian, hidden beneath its veneer of T-shirt shops. Although parking in Waikiki can be expensive, a rental car makes sightseeing easier. Without one, you'll find **The Bus** system is inexpensive (85¢) and efficient. For route information call 808-848-5555 between 5:30 A.M. and 10:00 P.M., or call 808-296-1818 and enter code 8287 for recorded route information for 50 places of interest. You can also avail yourself of **Island Pride** (808-732-6518, fax 808-739-1435), Honolulu's superfriendly gay-owned/operated taxi and driver/guide service.

Accommodations

There is little to distinguish one middle-ground hotel in Waikiki from the next. You get what you pay for, with bargain-price rooms being dumpy, and beachfront accommodations commanding a premium. We have listed some middle-ground hotels that offer something that is close to gay nightlife or the gay beach, or otherwise appeals to our gay sensibilities. Although you may run into other gay tourists at these places, you are more likely to be staying with Asian tour groups, as you would be at any Honolulu hotel.

GAY-MARKETED

HOTEL HONOLULU 376 Kaiolu Street; 808-926-2766 or 800-426-2766; $79–115

Hawaii's only gay hotel is in the heart of Waikiki's small gay business zone. Available are rooms, comfortable studios, and one-bedroom suites, each with a full kitchen and bath and different design theme; all are clean. Although there is no pool and common areas are not remarkably attractive (other than the greenhouselike entrance hall), the staff wins high praise for unusually warm, friendly service. Unless you require the amenities of a large hotel, we would recommend it over comparably priced mainstream hotels.

MANGO HOUSE 2087 Iholena Street; 808-595-6682 or 800-77-MANGO; $60–85

Caters mostly to women, in a quiet, safe residential neighborhood 15 minutes from Waikiki. The house has a panoramic view of downtown and the ocean, and four mango trees in the backyard—yielding fruit for the mango jam you'll enjoy on the homemade bread each morning.

NOTABLE MAINSTREAM HOTELS

HALEKULANI 2199 Kalia Road; 808-923-2311 or 800-367-2343; $290–470

Consistently voted one of the best hotels in the world. With a AAA 5-diamond rating for both the hotel and its signature restaurant La Mer,

it is the preeminent address in town. You won't find better service anywhere, but note that the hotel has virtually no beach directly in front
of it and is a modern, though beautiful, building.

SHERATON MOANA SURFRIDER 2365 Kalakaua Avenue; 808-922-3111 or 800-STAY-ITT; $230–365

Waikiki's first hotel, and it remains an elegant and genteel oasis from
the surrounding hubbub. The historic rooms in the oldest (middle) section are spacious and delightful. Even if you don't stay here, it's worth
a visit to imagine what Waikiki was like before the advent of the jet plane.

ROYAL HAWAIIAN 2259 Kalakaua Avenue; 808-931-8425 or 800-STAY-ITT; $275–505

Known for years as the Pink Palace, the hotel is decidedly pink and
palatial. Its large lawn and outdoor café add to the oasis-like atmosphere. Rooms in the tower have better views but less charm. Some historic rooms are small, and it's worth the premium for a better room if
you're going to stay here. The beach right in front is known as a gayish alternative to Queen's Surf.

IHILANI Ko'Olina Resort; 808-679-0079 or 800-626-4446; $275–550

A deluxe resort and spa set alone in a new development west of the
airport.

MIDDLE GROUND

WAIKIKI JOY HOTEL 320 Lewers Street; 808-923-2300 or 800-336-5599; $125–255

A boutique hotel featuring JVC/Bose stereo systems, refrigerators,
and Jacuzzi bathtubs in every room. More expensive rooms have wet
bars or kitchens. A coffee bar and karaoke studio help make up for the
tiny pool. It is very close to the nightlife, and we know many gay travel
agents who send their clients here.

ROYAL GARDEN 440 Olohana Street; 808-943-0202 or 800-367-5666; $120–500

Newly acquired and renovated, the hotel features a lot of surface
luxe: marble lobby, plush rooms, terraced gardens, and two pools. Their

free continental breakfast and shuttle service to the beach and Ala Moana are nice touches. Located within walking distance of the gay nightlife.

PARK SHORE 2586 Kalakaua Avenue; 808-923-0411; $135–190

Rooms here are a bit frumpy, but their location is unbeatable, offering the only unobstructed views of Waikiki and Diamond Head. Just steps away from the gay beach, the hotel has a nice pool, and the only ocean-view Denny's restaurant we've ever seen.

NEW OTANI KAIMANA BEACH HOTEL 2863 Kalakaua Avenue; 808-923-1555 or 800-356-8264; $99–575

The only hotel on the other side of the gay beach from the rest of Waikiki, with rooms that are very nice, and a beautiful beach, which is uncrowded and slightly gay. The staff is friendly, and there are two excellent restaurants, one Japanese, and the other literally on the beach.

HILTON HAWAIIAN VILLAGE 2005 Kalia Road, 808-949-4321 or 800-HILTONS; $280–340

Waikiki's only true resort hotel, with spacious grounds populated with exotic flora and fauna and an expansive, undercrowded beach. It is the only place in Waikiki that doesn't feel crowded by other hotels and T-shirt stores. Although the hotel is much upgraded from its tacky origins and offers ultradeluxe accommodations in its Ali'i Tower, it still appeals primarily to a straight, family market.

WAIKIKI TERRACE HOTEL 2045 Kalakaua Avenue; 808-955-6000 or 800-922-7866; $125–175

Typical of the nicer three-star generic high-rise hotels, distinguished only by its convenient location to the gay bars and a marketing effort aimed at gay travelers.

Dining

One well-kept dining secret is the hors d'oeuvres buffet served 6:00 P.M. to 10:00 P.M. daily on the terrace of the **Moana Surfrider Hotel.** For just $11.95 and a one-drink minimum, you can enjoy an elaborate salad and hors d'oeuvre buffet in an elegant beachfront setting. One of the best local restaurants is **Roy's** (6600 Kalanianaole Highway; 808-396-7697; $22), located about 20 minutes from downtown in Hawaii Kai and serving transpacific cuisine. The best Japanese food in town is at **Izakaya Nonbei** (3108 Olu Street; 808-734-5573; $9), serving authentic Japanese bistro food—no sushi but nightly karaoke. **John Dominis** (43 Ahui Street; 808-523-0955; $37) serves local seafood in a dramatic waterside setting. **Hula's Restaurant** (2103 Kuhio Avenue; 808-941-0424; $6) serves burgers and the like until 2:00 A.M. in a gay-festive environment. **Keo's** (625 Kapahulu Street; 808-737-8240; $13) is a gay-popular restaurant serving good, moderately priced Thai food. The **Tahitian Lanai** (1811 Ala Moana Boulevard; 808-946-6541; $20) features seaside dining in a tropical setting—we love it for great breakfasts. **Café Valentino** (2139 Kuhio Avenue; 808-926-2623) is a gay-popular coffee shop. **Caffe Guccini** (2139 Kuhio Avenue; 808-922-5287; $12) and **Jungle** (311 Lewers Street; 808-922-7808; $9) also cater to a gay clientele, and have decent food. If you're stuck in the Ala Moana shopping center and need sustenance, grab some good Chinese food at **Patti's Chinese Kitchen** (808-946-5002).

Nightlife

Waikiki's main bar scene for men is **Hula's Bar & Lei Stand** (2103 Kuhio Avenue; 808-923-0669), with a small dance floor and large outdoor bar. It's packed most nights of the week. You may try other places, but you'll always end up back here. In 1995, it expanded by taking over the space previously occupied by Hamburger Mary's and Dirty Mary's. **Fusion** (2260 Kuhio Avenue; 808-924-2422) is popular for its "Men of Fusion" strip show on Tuesday, Friday, and Saturday at 11:45 P.M., and for after-hours dancing, one of only two bars open until 4:00 A.M. The piano bar **Windows on Eaton Square** (444 Hobron Lane; 808-946-4422) caters to a quieter and older crowd. **Metropolis** (611 Cooke Street; 808-593-2717) is the women's bar, with C&W dancing on Fridays, and more men on Thursdays.

Activities

ATHLETIC AND OUTDOOR

Waikiki Beach is crowded, but a good place for novice surfers—a number of the hotels offer surfboard rental and instruction. The main gay beach is appropriately named **Queen's Surf,** and is located at the Diamond Head end of Waikiki, near the lifeguard stand before the showers. The beach in front of the Royal Hawaiian hotel is a gayish alternative. You may recognize **Hanauma Beach** as the famous surf tryst locale in *From Here to Eternity.* **The Gym** (435 Keawe Street; 808-533-7111; $10/day) is the gay-friendly gym. It's about 15 minutes from Waikiki. **Gold's Gym** (2490 Kalakaua Avenue; 808-971-4653; $20/$10 for some hotel guests) in Waikiki is reasonably gay-popular and very convenient.

SIGHTSEEING

Oahu is more than just Waikiki. **Pearl Harbor, Diamond Head, Chinatown,** the **Honolulu Zoo, Iolani Palace,** and the **North Shore** are Oahu's greatest attractions. Gay-friendly taxi services include **City Taxi** (808-524-2121) and **Island Pride Taxi & Tour** (808-732-6518). **Diamond Head** (808-548-7455), with its 760-foot volcanic crater, has hiking trails up to its summit. The **Fort DeRussy Army Museum** (Kalia Road; 808-955-9552) has an interesting collection of ancient Hawaiian weapons, weapons captured from the Japanese, and newspaper accounts of World War II. **Bishop Museum** (1525 Bernice Street; 808-847-3511) houses the world's finest collection of Polynesian art. **Foster Botanic Garden** (180 N. Vineyard Boulevard; 808-522-7066) features an incredible orchid collection. **Iolani Palace** (Richard and King Streets; 808-522-0832) is the only palace ever built on U.S. soil—its last resident, Queen Liliuokalani was imprisoned here. Tours are available Wednesday through Sunday, concerts are given Friday afternoons. The Mormon-managed **Polynesian Cultural Center** is a skippable Epcotesque Polynesian theme village. Go to **Pearl Harbor** as early as possible in the morning. Once the Japanese tour busses begin to arrive, the wait becomes hours long. Your first sunset must be spent drinking a daiquiri and gazing at the Pacific from the beach bar at the Royal Hawaiian Hotel.

SHOPPING

Kuhio Avenue, the gay main drag, is home to many gay-popular businesses. Two of the gayest are **Down Under** (2139 Kuhio Avenue; 808-922-9299), selling men's underwear and swimwear, and **80% Straight** (2139 Kuhio Avenue, second floor; 808-923-9996) selling the same, plus cards, novelties and the usual gay-mart stuff. There are surprisingly few places to find really nice Hawaiian shirts, new or used. (There are plenty of places to buy tacky Hawaiian shirts—you don't even have to go to Hawaii to find them.) Used shirts can cost hundreds of dollars, having achieved collector status. **Bailey's Antiques & Aloha Shirts** (517 Kapahulu Avenue, Honolulu; 808-734-7628) is the best place to find them. New shirts made with retro designs from the 1940s and 1950s can be found in Waikiki at **Newt** (Royal Hawaiian hotel, 2259 Kalakaua Avenue; 808-922-0062). The **International Marketplace** (2330 Kalakaua Avenue; 808-923-9871) is a great place to pick up souvenirs. The **Ala Moana Shopping Center** (Ala Moana Boulevard across from Ala Moana Park; 808-946-2811) is a large open-air mall—Honolulu's most important shopping venue since 1959. Nearby **Ward Center** and **Ward Warehouse** (Ala Moana Boulevard across from Kewalo Boat Basin) are home to more upscale boutiques and galleries. The studio of **Douglas Simonson** (4614 Kilauea Avenue, #330; 808-737-6275), known for his homo-exotic art, is open by appointment.

MAUI

We'd call Maui the driving island, because you need to do a lot of it to see all the island has to offer. From historic **Lahaina** to heavenly **Hana**, there is a lot of ground to cover. Fifty-five miles of it are the Hana Highway, a seemingly endless series of switchback curves and one-lane bridges through spectacular scenery. If you're not a squeamish driver you should definitely do it . . . once. Nature lovers shouldn't miss sunrise at the summit of **Mount Haleakala,** or **whale watching** from December through March. Lahaina town is touristy-quaint, a lot like Key West or Provincetown. Most of Hawaii's most lavish resorts have been built here, and while they have begun crowding each other, Maui still offers unparalleled options for those who want to lead the resort life. Maui has a small share of gay nightlife—a quantum leap down from Oahu, but a quantum leap up from Kauai and the Big Island. Maui claims the same middle ground with regard to chain restaurants and stores, and while the place hasn't been the same since **Planet Hollywood** fell out of orbit and landed in Lahaina, you can still find enough indigenous shopping and dining not to forget you're in Hawaii.

Accommodations

Maui has a broad and interesting range of accommodations. Some of the world's best resorts are here, built around golf courses in planned developments. Most of these developments are a minimum 20-minute drive from the towns of Wailuku, Kihei, and Lahaina, where you will find nightlife, restaurants, and shopping. Be prepared to be driving daily, or held hostage to the options and amenities at your chosen resort. Way over at Maui's east end is Hana, accessible by air or the Hana Highway, a beautiful but twisted 50-mile piece of road that takes about 2½ hours to deliver you from the main airport or back. Many of the gay-specific properties are on the road to Hana. They benefit from spectacular settings, but are really secluded, and best chosen by couples or groups of friends who really want to get away from it all.

GAY-MARKETED

HANA PLANTATION HOUSES P.O. Box 249, Hana; 808-248-7868 or 800-228-HANA; $70–150

A collection of well-furnished and well-maintained rental properties around Hana, also referred to as Blair's Original Hana Plantation Houses. Beware of a different company trading under the Hana Plantation Houses name. Blair is a great host who knows the island, owns the Hana Gardenland and Café, and will make sure your stay is an enjoyable one. Clientele is mixed.

GOLDEN BAMBOO RANCH 1205 Kaupakalua Road, Haiku; 808-572-7824; $69–80

Opened by former owners of Key West's Oasis Guest House, it reflects a similar attention to style and detail. Views of the ocean through horse pasture and forests are unobstructed. The units all have a private bath, TV, VCR, and telephone. Hosts live on the property in a separate house and are available for assistance. On the road to Hana, only 20 minutes from Kahului airport. Clientele is mixed.

HALE O WAHINE 277-B105 S. Kihei Road, Kihei; 808-874-5148 or 800-369-6696; $75–125

Caters mostly to women, with lesbian-hosted condos in a residential complex on or close to the beach. Although the accommodations are not particularly noteworthy, women who have an interest in socializing at all with the local community will find it possible here.

HUELO POINT FLOWER FARMS P.O. Box 1195, Paia; 808-572-1850; $95–215

Offers spectacular cliff views. The main house may be rented by the week; the cottages and carriage house are available for shorter stays. Cottage accommodations are a bit small, but well furnished and maintained. Facilities include a pool with waterfall, sauna, and three hot tubs. Gay-owned and managed, the clientele is mixed and breakfast is included for short stays.

THE TRIPLE LEI P.O. Box 593, Kihei; 808-874-8645; $85–165

A four-room house surrounded by Ironwood pines affording privacy. All rooms have refrigerators; the suite has a private bath and sauna. The clothing-optional pool is popular with their mostly male clientele.

KAILUA MAUI GARDENS SR Box 9, Haiku; 808-572-9726 or 800-258-8588; $55–200

Consists of five units set in dense, tropical gardens. From the simple "Love Shack," a one-room cottage with an ocean view and outdoor shower, to the three-bedroom Kailua House, with its own pool, each unit has the feel of being tucked away in a jungle retreat. Shaded pathways and bridges connect the cottages to a common spa and barbecue area. Gay-owned and managed, clientele is mixed.

HALFWAY TO HANA HOUSE P.O. Box 675, Haiku; 808-572-1176; $50–65

A redwood house in peaceful surroundings with a 180-degree ocean view. Located on the road to Hana (but not quite halfway), the studio unit has its own entrance, a private bath, and a minikitchen. A tropical breakfast including homemade coconut pudding is included. Clientele is mixed.

NAPULANI O'HANA P.O. Box 118, Hana; 808-248-8935; $55–75

Located just above Hana Gardenland and Café, on the road to Hana just before town. The units are very spacious, designed for couples or large groups. There are some nice touches, such as hand-painted tile work, but overall the furnishings, setting, and atmosphere pale significantly in comparison to other accommodations in the area. Clientele is mixed.

CAMP KULA P.O. Box 111, Kula; 808-878-2528; $42–78

The only guest house that refused to let us inspect the property, claiming that it would compromise the privacy of their guests. We have heard some good reports about the place and its resident owner, but we've also heard it may be closing or changing hands. Located on the lush slopes of Mount Haleakala, the clientele is gay/lesbian and a tropical breakfast is included.

NOTABLE MAINSTREAM RESORTS

KAPALUA BAY HOTEL & VILLAS One Bay Drive, Kapalua; 808-669-5656 or 800-367-8000; $260–495

Just beyond Kaanapali, this is one of the first deluxe, secluded resorts built in the islands. Luxurious beyond its time 16 years ago, the place stands up well to newer competition with sophisticated service and spacious, simple, yet elegant rooms and grounds. Lower-category rooms look out on more ocean than you pay for. Guests can rent their Cliff House for private picnic dining or snorkeling.

GRAND WAILEA Wailea Resort; 808-875-1234 or 800-888-6100; $380–580

The most expensive resort ever built, and it shows in every opulent, tasteful detail. The spa facilities and pools are unrivaled in the state. Even base-rate rooms are spectacular, lacking only a view. If you like large resorts, this place sets the standard worldwide.

MAUI PRINCE 5400 Makena Alanui; 808-874-1111 or 800-321-6284; $230–840

The closest resort hotel to the gay beach, which is within walking distance from the hotel. Overshadowed and outshown by the resorts of Wailea, this resort is often available at discount prices.

HOTEL HANA-MAUI Hana Ranch; 808-248-8211 or 800-321-4262; $395–795

An oasis of seclusion and understated elegance. Hotel rooms and sea cottages offer refuge for those who would rather read than watch TV.

PLANTATION INN 174 Lahainaluna Road; 667-9225 or 800-433-6815; $104–219

Looks like a deluxe Key West inn, and offers great value with charming rooms surrounding a garden pool and spa in its downtown Lahaina location. Breakfast and parking are included.

Dining

Try one of Maui's top-rated restaurants, **Gerard's** (174 Lahainaluna Road; 808-661-8939; $25), serving French cuisine incorporating Hawaiian produce. **David Paul's Lahaina Grill** (127 Lahainaluna Road; 808-667-5117; $28) serves truly excellent innovative Pacific Rim fare. **Roy's Kahana Grill** (4405 Honoapilliana Highway; 808-669-6999; $22) is another world-class dining experience. **A Pacific Café Maui** (1279 S. Kihei Road; 808-879-0069; $22) is a new outpost of Kauai's popular fine restaurant. If you've ever wondered what would happen if you crossed Hawaii's Pacific Rim cuisine with Mexican and Italian influences, you can find the answer at **Joe's Bar & Grill** (131 Wailea Ekike Place; 808-875-7767; $22) in the Wailea resort. For more casual fare, try **Cheeseburger in Paradise** (811 Front Street, Lahaina; 808-661-4855; $6) for the best burgers on the island. Another casual option is **Alexander's** (1913 S. Kihei Road; 808-874-0788; $6), known for its great fish and chips. Head next door to **Tobi's** (1913 S. Kihei Road; 808-879-7294) for a shave ice with one of their 27 syrup flavors, including tropical flavors such as guava, mango, and passion fruit.

Nightlife

Maui nightlife is currently limited to two venues. **Blue Tropix** (900 Front Street; 808-667-5309) in Lahaina is gay on Sunday afternoon and night, with a drag show at 9:30 P.M. All other nights, it's **Hamburger Mary's** (2010 Main Street at the corner of Market Street; 808-244-7776) in Wailuku. Saturday night is busiest; Tuesday and Thursday nights are also popular for their "shipwreck" parties, hosting gay crew and passengers from the American Hawaii cruise ships docked down the road on those evenings. For us, the minimum 20-minute drive from anywhere worth staying puts a bit of a damper on the place.

Activities

ATHLETIC AND OUTDOOR

Maui's gayest beach is **Little Beach,** located south of Wailea, one mile past the Maui Prince Hotel. Just past the large hill on the right is a paved-road turnoff leading to Makena Beach. Hike over the promontory at the right end of the beach to reach Little Beach. The **Maui Surfing School** (808-875-0625) may be the only gay and lesbian surfing school in the world. They specialize in beginners, cowards, and non-swimmers. **Mount Halekala** ("The House of the Sun") **National Park** (808-572-9306) is home to the world's largest dormant crater, 19 square miles and 3,000 feet deep. The park offers horseback riding, hiking, and cabin rentals for overnight stays. Early morning and late afternoon are best, sunrise excursions are popular, and warm clothes are necessary at the summit, no matter how warm it is at sea level.

SIGHTSEEING

Maui's best sights are all outdoors, but history buffs may enjoy a trip to the **Maui Historical Society Museum** (2375A Main Street; 808-244-3326) on Highway 32 near Wailuku.

SHOPPING

Find authentic, new Aloha shirts based on original designs from the 1940s and 1950s in Wailuku at **Gilbert's Formal Wear** (104 Market Street; 808-244-4017), three blocks down from Hamburger Mary's. **Sweet Maui onions** are some of the tastiest souvenirs you can bring home, and it's most convenient to buy them at the Kahului airport.

KAUAI

Beautiful Kauai was devastated by hurricane Iniki in 1992, and while some vegetation and the economy are still in recovery, the island is our favorite of the chain. To put it simply, Kauai feels more like the Hawaii most mainland visitors dream of. Remarkably beautiful and a little sleepy, Kauai is meant to be enjoyed on a lazy itinerary. Scenic vistas, hidden beaches, and lush, verdant jungles create a spectacular environment that has not (yet) been overdeveloped or commercially exploited. The northern, windward side of the island is one of the wettest places on earth, but the sunny southern coast delivers dependable, warm, sunny weather. Because the northernmost part of the island is impassable by car, most visitors explore the island in two trips: south and west to **Poipu Beach** and **Waimea Canyon,** then east and north to quaint **Kapaa,** the dramatic **Na Pali Coast,** and lovely **Hanalei.** If you're going to pick just one island for a helicopter flight-seeing tour, this is the one. Kauai's limited gay gathering places are beside the point: Kauai's unsurpassed beauty appeals to gay travelers in a special, sensuous way. If the allure of sand, sea, and nature are calling you to Hawaii, you'll find the Hawaii of your dreams on the island of Kauai.

Accommodations

Kauai has a number of guest houses and one of our favorite resort properties anywhere. The guest houses tend to be concentrated near Kapaa, which is convenient to shopping, dining, and nightlife (such as it is), and central to all of the natural attractions.

GAY-MARKETED

PALI KAI P.O. Box 450, Kilauea; 808-828-6691; $80–135

Offers spectacular views from a beautiful garden setting. Rooms are spacious and attractively furnished, and the hosts are sophisticated and professional, yet down-to-earth and friendly. The Kalihiwai River and beach are within walking distance and the hot tub is great after a day of hiking, kayaking, windsurfing, or just lying on the beach. Tropical breakfasts, beach towels, and picnic coolers are all provided. Clientele is primarily female.

OLA HOU GUEST RETREAT 332 Aina Loli Place, Kapaa; 808-822-0109 or 800-772-4567; $90–125

An attractively furnished and beautifully landscaped home in a new residential development above Kapaa. With a spacious, clothing-optional pool and a multistation exercise machine, the hosts cater to a primarily gay male clientele. Road bikes are available for exploring the nearby terrain, and four-wheel drive tours can be arranged.

MAHINA KAI 4933 Aliomanu Road, Anahola; 808-822-9451; $115

A beautiful Japanese-style farmhouse with Western amenities, a view of the ocean, pretty landscaping and a great lagoon swimming pool, hot tub, and Japanese garden. Currently lesbian-owned, the place has a mixed clientele.

HALE KAHAWAI 185 Kahawai Place, Kapaa; 808-822-1031; $60–90

A redwood home with appropriately stylish furnishings on a tropically landscaped plot with spa. A tropical breakfast is served in the living room or on the lanai. Following a change of management in 1995, it is no longer exclusively gay, but still gay-friendly.

ALOHA KAUAI 156 Lihau Street, Kapaa; 808-822-6966 or 800-ANAHOLA; $60–85

A new location for the former hosts of the Anahola Beach Club, who get high marks for friendliness from returning guests. The house has a pool and three bedrooms, one with private bath. Breakfast and afternoon refreshments are included. Clientele is almost exclusively gay male.

NOTABLE MAINSTREAM RESORTS

HYATT REGENCY KAUAI 1571 Poipu Road; 808-742-1234 or 800-233-1234; $275–465

Our favorite of the deluxe resorts on any island. Designed to emulate Hawaiian resort style of the 1930s, the low-rise open-lobby architecture blends harmoniously with the elaborate landscaping, belying the size of the resort and capturing the essence of our Hawaiian dreams. Great restaurants, a complete spa, an exceptional library bar, attentive service, and terrific pool and beach spaces make this everything a great resort should be.

PRINCEVILLE HOTEL Princeville Resort; 808-826-9644 or 800-STAY-ITT; $250–450

This hotel was gutted and rebuilt as one of Hawaii's most deluxe resorts, maximizing the extraordinary views of its north shore location. It is one of the most breathtaking settings in the world.

Dining

Pack a picnic and head to one of the island's small beaches, such as **Donkey Beach** or **Secret Beach**. For dinner, **A Pacific Café** (4-138 Kuhio Highway, Kapaa; 808-822-0013; $22) is located in a strip mall but offers the finest food and service on the island. If you have a yen for Japanese cuisine, **Kintaro** (14-370 Kuhio Highway, Kapaa; 808-822-3341; $18) is the best in town.

Nightlife

Sideout (4-1330 Kuhio Highway, Kapaa; 808-822-7330) is a divey bar where you'll find gay people as well as characters of all other persuasions. They have a $1 draft happy hour and a full kitchen.

Activities

ATHLETIC AND OUTDOOR

Donkey Beach is the gay beach. Reach it by finding the cane road off Highway 56 between mile markers 11 and 12. Walk toward the ocean on the wide sugar cane field access road and then down through the ironwood trees to the beach. **Waimeia Canyon**, the Grand Canyon of Hawaii; offers spectacular vistas and glorious day-hikes.

SIGHTSEEING

Kilohana (3-2087 Kaumualii Highway; 808-245-5608) is a legendary plantation estate built in the 1930s by Kauai's sugarcane king, Gaylord Wilcox. Tours through the estate by horse-drawn carriages are offered daily. The **Kauai Musuem** (4428 Rice Street; 808-245-6931) chronicles the island's history, and houses an interesting collection of missionary memorabilia. More missionary memorabilia is on display at the **Waioli Mission House** (Hanalei Town; 808-245-3202), built by New Englanders in 1846, open Tuesday, Thursday, and Saturday. A helicopter ride here offers the drama of the Na Pali Coast and numerous extinct volcanoes.

SHOPPING

The gift shop at **Kilohana** (see above) has a nice selection of native products.

HAWAII

You'll be amazed by the dramatically different environments you'll see on Hawaii, the Hawaiian Island known as the Big Island. From the orchid-laden rainforest of the east shore, to the lunarlike lava surface of the east shore, to the desert climate up north, the terrain changes before your eyes. Most visitors head to the resorts on the sunny Kahala and Kona coasts, but the Hilo side of the Island is home to more native beauty. We recommend flying into Hilo and out of Kona, with at least a night spent near Volcanoes National Park. The drive around the island is scenic and easy.

Accommodations

The Big Island is home to Hawaii's most unusual and attractive hostelries. With as wide a range of climates as accommodations, you may be tempted to stay in more than one. The island's large area and easily navigated roads make this both feasible and recommended.

GAY-MARKETED

SAMURAI HOUSE 82-5929 Mamalahoa Highway, Captain Cook; 808-328-9210; $65–85

An authentic samurai house imported from Japan. The serene architecture is complemented by the spectacular view of Kealekekua Bay from the spacious lanai. Both Japanese tatami and Western-style accommodations are available.

THE PAAUHAU PLANTATION HOUSE P.O. Box 1375, Honokaa; 808-775-7222; $75–140

Built in 1920 as an owner's residence, the house retains the aura of its gracious past. Hawaiian décor includes a large living room with grand piano, a Queen Anne dining room set, and a hand-carved koa pool table. The 5,000-square-foot house is set on five beautifully landscaped acres, with rental cottages and a tennis and basketball court in the rear yard. The whole main house (two garden bedrooms and one master suite) can be rented for $400 a night—the perfect location for a new family-values Thanksgiving or a Big Chill reunion. Management is straight, clientele is mixed.

HALE OHIA COTTAGES P.O. Box 758, Volcano Village; 808-967-7986 or 800-455-3803; $75–95

Set on several acres of exquisitely landscaped grounds, just one mile from the entrance to Volcanoes National Park (and a 25-minute-drive from the active lava flow), the suites and cottages offer privacy and comfort, with pretty interiors and access to the garden hot tub. Limited and full kitchen facilities allow cottage guests to eat in. Charming gay owner-hosts provide sightseeing and dining recommendations, as well as a tropical breakfast to a mixed clientele.

BUTTERFLY INN P.O. Box 6010, Kurtistown; 808-966-7936 or 800-54-MAGIC; $45–60

A small, homey inn on a lushly planted acre catering to women travelers, the inn has a secluded setting that includes an outdoor steam house and Jacuzzi hot tub. Rates include a tropical breakfast, coffees and teas all day, and use of the full kitchen for other meals. With a massage therapist on call and a work-for-housing swap program, the place promotes a sisterly, healing, and relaxing environment.

HULIAULE'A P.O. Box 1030, Pahoa; 808-965-9175; $40–75

Not accessible when we visited, but we have heard mixed reports about the facilities (rustic and remote), and great comments about the very friendly and knowledgeable gay host.

WOOD VALLEY BED & BREAKFAST P.O. Box 37, Pahala; 808-928-8212 or 800-854-6754; $35–55

A delightful plantation shack surrounded by 12 acres of pastureland and gardens. Although the interior space and furnishings are of a lower standard than we generally recommend, the place exudes a rare simplicity and charm, in great part because of the aura of Jessie Hillinger, its proprietor. If you don't mind shared baths, you'll love the outdoor facility here. Breakfast includes fruit from the orchards and eggs from the coop; a wood-burning steam bath and lomilomi massage are available for an additional charge.

R.B.R. FARMS P.O. Box 930, Captain Cook; 808-328-9212 or 800-328-9212; $60–175

Still a working coffee and macadamia nut plantation, the Farms offer the only exclusively gay guest house experience on the islands, comparable to a Key West–type house. The place is very private, and while there is some sexual energy, especially in and around the clothing-optional pool, the overall experience is that of a high-quality B&B. Full breakfast is served by the pool off a printed menu, and turn-down service is provided nightly. Clientele is mostly male, but women are warmly welcomed.

THE DRAGONFLY RANCH P.O. Box 675, Honaunau; 808-328-9570 or 800-487-2159; $60–160

Offers tropical fantasy lodging, very nature oriented and romantic. Their honeymoon suite features an outdoor waterbed with a pavilion roof and a private outdoor bathing area with claw-foot bathtub surrounded by banana trees. Accommodations are not luxurious, but truly unique. Breakfast is included, clientele is mixed, owner management is straight, but gay-friendly enough to promote same-sex marriages on property.

NOTABLE MAINSTREAM RESORTS

KONA VILLAGE Kaupulehu; 808-325-5555 or 800-367-5290; $395–680

Genuine Hawaiiana, with 125 deluxe thatched-roof cottages on 82 acres that have charmed honeymooners for years. The place is very straight-couple and family oriented, but still highly recommended. Room rates include daily meals. Their Friday (and sometimes Monday) night luaus are known as some of the best and most authentic in the islands—open to nonguests if there is space available.

THE ORCHID AT MAUNA LANI I N. Kaniku Drive, Kamuela; 808-885-2000 or 800-782-9488; $285–475)

This hotel retains the nineteenth-century chandelier and oil-painting elegance of its former life as a Ritz-Carlton.

HILTON WAIKOLOA VILLAGE Waikoloa Beach Resort; 808-885-1234 or 800-HILTONS; $200–375

Sort of a hybrid deluxe resort and theme park. A monorail and canal boats provide transportation from one end of the resort to the other. A dolphin experience is offered on property. Definitely an E-ticket.

ROYAL WAIKOLOAN Waikoloa Beach Resort; 808-885-6789 or 800-688-7444; $120–750

Offers a better beach than its Hilton neighbor. Known for its quality staff, the place is more low-key than its flashy neighbors.

HAPUNA BEACH PRINCE HOTEL 62-100 Kauna'oa Drive; 808-880-1111 or 800-882-6060; $325–900

A new hotel in the famous Mauna Kea Resort, offering deluxe accommodations, a pristine beach, and a unique, environmentally sensitive Arnold Palmer golf course.

Dining

There are few restaurants outside of the hotels on the Kohala/Kona coast. **Merriman's** (Opelo Plaza, Opelo Road at Highway 19; 808-885-6822; $21) serves the best food on the island, contemporary cuisine from fresh local ingredients. The restaurant at **Kilauea Lodge** (Old Volcano Road, Volcano Village; 808-967-7366; $19) has a romantic, alpine-like atmosphere with a great stone fireplace and a menu that includes continental and Polynesian-inspired entrées. **Kona Village** (Kaupulehu-Kona; 808-325-5555; $63/luau/person) has one of the best luaus in the islands. Call ahead for schedule, availability, and reservations.

Nightlife

Mask (75-5660 Kopiko Street; 808-329-8558) is the only gay bar on the Big Island of Hawaii. It's in the Kopiko Plaza shopping center next to Domino's Pizza. Other than that, you're on your own, so bring a great lover and/or a good book.

Activities

ATHLETIC AND OUTDOOR

Honokohau is the gay beach on Highway 19 between Kailua and the Kona Airport. Turn onto the road to the Honokohau Boat Harbor, take the first right, and drive around the boat storage area to the north side. Follow the trail that leads north and then to the left through a thicket. At the ocean, head to the far right end. **Kahena** is the other gay beach, a fine black-sand beach south of Pahoa. Reach it by hiking down a lava rock trail, from Highway 137 near mile marker 19. **Eco•Adventures** (75-5744 Alii Drive; Kailua-Kona; 808-329-7116 or 800-949-DIVE) is a gay-owned snorkel, surf, and dive shop offering high-quality watersports programs, instruction, and custom packages, including accommodations. You can actually ski on Mauna Kea from December through April. Call **Ski Guides Hawaii** (808-885-4188) for information. Golf is a big deal here—try the **Mauna Kea Beach Golf Course** (808-882-7222), the **Hapuna Golf Course** (808-882-1035), the **Waikoloa Village Golf Course** (808-883-9621), the **Waikoloa Beach Resort Golf Course** (808-885-6789) or the **Waikoloa Kings' Golf Club** (808-885-4647).

SIGHTSEEING

Don't miss the live lava flow at the bottom of Chain of Craters Road in **Volcanoes National Park** (808-967-7311)—go at night and take a flashlight. The nearby **Akatsuka Orchid Gardens** are a treat for flower lovers, as are the numerous orchid nurseries around Hilo. The **City of Refuge National Park** (808-328-2326) is a sacred ground where fugitives who survived the treacherous swim across Honaunau Bay were granted pardons in the sixteenth century. The grounds are home to temples, recreated sixteenth-century *tikis,* and craftsmen who carve wooden canoes with traditional tools. **Parker Ranch** (Kamuela; 808-885-7655) is one of the Big Island's unexpected contrasts: a 225,000-acre cattle ranch with rolling hills. A museum and tours are available.

SHOPPING

Kealakekua's Grass Shack (Mamalahoa Highway, Kealakekua; 808-323-2877) sells all sorts Hawaiian crafts by natives of all ethnicities.

LANAI AND MOLOKAI

Molokai, "The Friendly Island," is the least touristy island, known mostly for its leper-colony history, the vestiges of which are its biggest tourist attraction. But Molokai is also home to some of Hawaii's most pristine scenery. Rain forests, waterfalls, and miles of secluded uninhabited beaches offer a Hawaiian paradise that most tourists only dream about. Although there is nothing gay on the island, **Blair's Hana Plantation Houses** (808-248-7868 or 800-228-HANA; $70–164) offers condo rental properties. The **Molokai Mule Ride** (808- or 800-567-7550) resumed operation in 1995, after a two-year hiatus. The full-day tour costs $120, and includes lunch and a ground tour of the leper colony, which is still home to more than 70 former patients. Lanai, "The Private Island," was the world's largest pineapple plantation, owned almost entirely by the Dole Food Company. Now that pineapple is farmed mostly in Central America, Lanai has entered the tourism business with two deluxe Rockresorts, the **Lodge at Koele** (808-565-7300 or 800-321-4666, fax 808-565-6477; $250–2,000) and **The Manele Bay Hotel** (808-565-7700 or 800-223-7637; $250–2,000). The Lodge is a manorial upcountry hotel, while Manele Bay is a Mediterranean Villa nine miles away on the shore. The quaint 10-room **Hotel Lanai** (828 Lanai Avenue; 808-565-4700 or 800-321-4666; $95) was built in 1923 to house important visitors to the island. Recently renovated, it offers more modest accommodations. Visitors to the island rarely run into each other exploring the diverse terrain and untouched beaches on this 13-by-18-mile island.

The Caribbean

The Caribbean's appeal is easy to understand: beautiful beaches, near-perfect year-round weather, and easy access from most of the United States. Home to many different indigenous and imposed cultures, the islands that stretch from the Florida Keys to South America offer a wide variety of beach vacations, from familiar to exotic. Whether it's the stylish European sophistication of St. Barts, the sultry sensuality of Trinidad at Carnival time, or the American glamour of the U.S. Virgin Islands, the Caribbean offers a warm-weather retreat for just about every taste. The area beckons gay travelers in need of rest and relaxation and the simple pleasures of sun and surf. Come here to trade your winter blues for the clear blue Caribbean sky and water. Come to escape the trappings of the city and indulge in a slow-paced way of life.

BIRDS NOT OF A FEATHER

Although we refer to the Caribbean islands as a group, they actually comprise a broad range of destinations (frequently including two Atlantic ocean destinations—Bermuda and the Bahamas—that aren't even in the Caribbean Sea). Puerto Rico is the only destination in the entire region with enough gay nightlife and accommodations to qualify as a gay destination, although a lack of gay-specific venues has not stopped St. Barts from becoming very gay-popular, attracting a stylish crowd from New York and Paris. The U.S. Virgin Islands are home to a smattering of businesses catering to gay travelers, and Trinidad's Carnival is the biggest gay event in the region. Beyond these islands, there is virtually no gay presence to speak of in the Caribbean. No bars, discos, or hotels cater explicitly to gays, and few could even be pegged as places where you're likely to meet other gays. This gay invisibility has less to do with discrimination or a lack of welcome or popularity than with the geography and ambiance of the islands themselves. Even for straight travelers, nightlife is scarce here. If you're looking to party, stay in Miami. If you're in need of lazy days and some good nights' sleep, come on down.

THE GAY CARIBBEAN

Although many native Caribbean people engage in homosexual sex, being gay is not well accepted or understood in much of the area. The British left behind harsh, though largely unenforced, antigay laws in all of their former colonies, and religious parochialism reigns on others. Most natives who do engage in same-sex activities don't identify themselves as bisexual, let alone gay, and most island populations are too small to support social groups or liberation movements. While homophobia may be a problem for natives, it is rarely so for visitors, since tourist dollars speak loudly. If you're willing to draw the line of discretion at hand holding and similarly mild forms public display, most of the Caribbean islands will welcome you. Those that are more sophisticated, or less British, or rife with isolated beaches and private resorts may be the perfect spots for a romantic gay getaway. While most hotels are indifferent to gay couples (unless you arrive as the Hat Sisters or Mrs. & Mrs. Leather), you may encounter a little difficulty getting a room with one bed. The good news is that more and more lodging establishments are selling to the gay market, gay nightlife is on the rise, and local gay organizations are coming into existence. We've provided extensive information on the gay-popular Caribbean islands. Other islands that might have a particularly noteworthy gay-friendly guest house or some kind of gay-specific appeal have more limited information presented.

When to Go and How to Get There

The Caribbean has relatively consistent weather. While Palm Springs gets beastly hot in the summer and Florida gets uncomfortably humid, the Caribbean stays comfortable year round. Fall is hurricane season, and with the increasing storm activity of the past few years, the possibility of violent weather can't be ignored. The deep Caribbean—Barbados, the Grenadines, and the Netherland Antilles—are fairly well out of the hurricane belt and a much safer bet for fall vacations. Where there are nonstop flights, you can get from the East Coast to anywhere in the Caribbean in less than five hours, but it can take all day to get to islands with limited air service. American Airlines has dominated

Caribbean commercial aviation since the demise of PanAm and Eastern Airlines. Most destinations are served through Miami or San Juan, with additional nonstops servicing major destinations, particularly from the East Coast. Other U.S. and Caribbean-based carriers serve the area and code-share programs are helping provide competitive fares and connections. Local transport by small plane and boat rounds out the transportation options.

Your Own Private Caribbean

Although it might strike you as a little too *Lifestyles of the Rich & Famous,* many travelers have discovered that renting a villa or chartering a yacht can be a very affordable way to vacation in the Caribbean. For gay and lesbian travelers, the privacy offered by a villa or yacht vacation can be a welcome bonus, allowing a more free expression of your romantic and sexual orientation, or simply an escape from the heterosexual single- and couple-oriented resorts. While many companies arrange villas and yachts, only a few market specifically to the gay and lesbian communities. Using these businesses, you needn't feel uncomfortable about your orientation, and you can be confident that your boat captain or house staff will be gay-friendly.

RENTING A VILLA

VHR (800-633-3284 or 201-767-9393) is one of the most active and respected villa-rental companies operating in the Caribbean. They don't mark up homeowner rates, and they are members of the IGTA, as well as ASTA and the Caribbean Tourist Organization. **LaCure** (800-387-2726 or 416-968-2374, fax 416-968-9435), based in Canada, is also an IGTA member, marketing to gay travelers, with a high-end lineup of villas and yachts, which can be viewed in their "World Book" brochure, or on their Website: *http://www.lacure.com.*

CHARTERING A YACHT

Journeys by Sea (800-825-3632, fax 954-630-9266 or 800-825-5956) offers gay-owned and -operated and gay-friendly yacht charters worldwide, with friendly service and very comprehensive brochures and documentation. Even if you have never been on a yacht, you can book with confidence and understanding. Scuba diving, windsurfing, and kayaking can be arranged in conjunction with your yacht. **Whitney Yacht Charters** (800-223-1426 or 941-927-0108) is one of the oldest crewed yacht charter brokers in the country and also offers gay and gay-friendly charters. In addition, they can book individual singles and couples into ad-hoc groups on the *Endless Summer II*.

FYI

Island Underground (809-775-5245) is a gay publication covering the entire Caribbean in bimonthly issues, although the emphasis is on the U.S. Virgin Islands. *Puerto Rico Breeze* (809-268-5101) is Puerto Rico's gay publication, with news and nightlife information. For general guide-books, we recommend *Birnbaum's Caribbean* (HarperCollins) and the *Fielding's Caribbean* (Fielding Worldwide). The **Caribbean Tourism Organization** (212-682-0435, fax 212-697-4258) provides information on the entire region, but most of the Caribbean islands have U.S.-based tourist offices: **Anguilla** (516-271-2600 or 800-553-4939, fax 516-425-0903), **Antigua and Barbuda** (212-541-4117, fax 212-757-1607), **Aruba** (201-330-0800 or 800-862-7822, fax 201-330-8757), **The Bahamas** (305-932-0051), **Barbados** (212-986-6516 or 800-221-9831), **Belize** (212-563-6011, fax 212-563-6033), **Bermuda** (212-818-9800), **Bonaire** (212-956-5911 or 800-826-6247, fax 212-956-5913), **British Virgin Islands** (212-696-0400 or 800-835-8530, fax 212-949-8254), **Cayman Islands** (212-682-5582, fax 212-986-5123), **Cuba** (416-362-0700), **Curaçao** (305-374-5811 or 800-445-8266, fax 305-374-6741), **Dominica** (809-448-2351, fax 809-448-5840), **French West Indies** (900-990-0040 at 50¢/minute, 212-315-0888), **Jamaica** (212-856-9727), **Martinique** (212-315-0888 or 800-391-4909), **Montserrat** (809-491-2230 or 800-646-2002), **Puerto Rico** (212-599-6262 or 800-223-6530), **St. Barthélémy** (212-315-0888), **St. Eustatius-Saba** (407-394-8580 or 407-722-2394), **St. Kitts-Nevis** (212-535-1234 or 800-582-6208), **St. Lucia** (212-867-2950 or 800-456-3984, fax 212-370-7867), **Sint Maarten** (212-953-2084), **St. Martin** (212-315-0888), **St. Vincent and the Grenadines** (212-687-4981 or 800-729-1726, fax

212-949-5946), **Trinidad and Tobago** (201-662-3403 or 800-748-4224, fax 201-869-7628), **Turks and Caicos** (809-946-2321 or 800-241-0824, fax 809-946-2733), **U.S. Virgin Islands** (212-332-2222, fax 212-332-2223).

ANGUILLA

Originally known as Malliouhana by its Indian inhabitants, *Anguilla* comes from the Spanish word for "eel," the creature whose shape is likened to that of the island. The lack of casinos and limited nightlife, shopping, and historical sights keep most tourists and cruise ships away—even Christopher Columbus didn't visit. Flat and dry, Anguilla's 30 beaches, surrounded by crystal clear water and coral reefs, are the premier places for a restful vacation of reading, swimming, and sunning. Anguilla is reached by air or by 20-minute ferry from St. Martin.

Accommodations

LA SIRENA 809-497-6827 or 800-331-9358; $110–295

For affordable accommodations, this is well-run and just a two-minute walk from Mead's Bay.

THE MALLIOUHANA Mead's Bay; 809-497-6111 or 800-44-UTELL, fax 809-497-6011; $240–610

Frequently listed as one of the world's top resorts, it may be a bit stuffy and formal for most gay couples. It houses a romantic, elegant restaurant serving classic French cuisine, but the dining room is open only to resident guests during high season dinners.

THE CINNAMON REEF BEACH CLUB ON LITTLE HARBOR BEACH 809-497-2727 or 800-223-1108; $175–400.

Of the deluxe resorts, this one is one of the most laid-back and friendly.

RENDEZVOUS BAY HOTEL 809-497-6549 or 800-274-4893; $90–450

Offers clean and simple rooms as well as villa accommodations, on 60 acres of coconut groves and sandy beaches.

Dining

Some local-favorite restaurants include **Aquarium** (809-497-2720; $14), **Short Curve** (809-497-6600; $8), and **The Old House** (George Hill; 809-497-2228; $18), all serving West Indian–style cuisine.

Activities

ATHLETIC AND OUTDOOR

Best isolated beaches are Cove Bay, Mimi Bay, and Captain's Bay, the latter reachable only with four-wheel drive. Shoal Bay, Rendezvous Bay, and Maunday's Bay are more popular, and offer food, drink, and other concessions.

ANTIGUA

Despite its very quiet gay scene and a slight degree of homophobia (Antiguans were flabbergasted into silence by past visits of RSVP cruises), Antigua is still very much worth a visit. Its 365 white sand beaches include some of the finest in the region. Pounded during the 1995 hurricane season, many of island's tourist venues were still being repaired as this book went to press.

Accommodations

Antigua has a number of recommended gay-friendly accommodations:

BARRYMORE BEACH APARTMENTS Runaway Bay; 809-462-4101, fax 809-462-4101; $72–355

Spacious rooms and suites in cottages on the beach within walking distance of other hotels, restaurants, and water sports are some of the features offered here. Rooms have ceiling fans, telephones, and TVs by request.

TRADE WINDS HOTEL Halcyon Heights above Dickenson Bay; 809-462-1223; $125–185

Houses the British Airways flight crews, making it the gayest hostelry on the island. (It was still closed for hurricane repairs at press time.) It features a pool and excellent restaurant; only four of the comfortable, air-conditioned, and recently renovated rooms are available to the general public. Ten minutes to the beach by foot.

JUMBY BAY 809-462-6000 or 800-421-9016, fax 809-462-6020; $645–990

One of the most exclusive and deluxe resorts in all of the Caribbean—rates include all meals.

HAWKSBILL BEACH RESORT 809-462-0301 or 800-223-6510, fax 809-462-1515; $175–450

Has Antigua's only clothing-optional beach (one of four beaches on the 37-acre property), and offers most water sports at no charge.

Dining

Many people leave Half Moon Bay at 3:00 P.M. and head up to **Shirley Heights** (809-460-1785; $21), near English Harbor, for light West Indian fare daily, and their weekly barbecue on Sunday. With spectacular views, live reggae and steel-band music, near-lethal rum punch, and a party crowd, it's one of the best weekly fetes in the islands. November through May, you might want to head down to **G & T Pizza** (English Harbor; 809-460-3278; $13) for a slice and more drinking with the sailors. On rare occasions a different version of Spin-the-Bottle has been played and patrons have been known to climb on tables to watch the losers strip. **Alberto's** (Willoughby Bay; 809-460-3007; $28) offers upscale Italian dining in a large gazebo, with good food and friendly service; it's very popular; dinner only. **Abracadabra** (English Harbor; 809-462-1732; $20) serves moderately priced Italian food in an attractive setting, with a bar, music, and good sailor watching. **Chez Pascal** (St. Johns; 809-462-3232; $25) is located in an Antiguan house with wonderful, moderately priced French bistro food. **The Wardroom** (Nelson's Dockyard; 809-460-1058; $24) in the Copper & Lumber Hotel features an international menu in a more formal setting. **Coconut Grove** (Dickenson Bay; 809-462-1538; $22) serves West Indian/continental cuisine with a romantic setting of palms on the beach. **La Dolce Vita** (Redcliff Quay, St. Johns; 809-462-2016; $11) offers a quiet setting and friendly service with homemade pastas and pizzas. Veranda dining is available at the lovely **La Perruche** (English Harbor; 809-460-3040; $26), serving West Indian/French/Cajun cuisine. **Home Restaurant** (Lower Gambles, near St. Johns; 809-461-7651; $12) offers creatively prepared West Indian cuisine served in a charming local home, with friendly service and moderate prices.

Nightlife

The **Copper & Lumber Pub** (Nelson's Dockyard; 809-460-1058) offers 2-for-1 drinks on Tuesdays and Fridays until 8:00 P.M., then great music until late. It's not gay, but it is someplace to go after dinner.

Activities

ATHLETIC AND OUTDOOR

Dickenson Bay and **Runaway Bay** are hotel-lined with lots of watersports options. For complete seclusion, rent a four-wheel-drive jeep and go to **Rendezvous Bay** (between Falmouth and Old Road Town). Driving there is at your own risk, since it violates your rental contract. If you tell the rental agency you are planning to go to Rendezvous Bay, they won't rent to you. Ask for directions to the track road in Falmouth. Don't go if you're not prepared to be responsible for the contract violation. More accessible is **Freyes's Beach,** but it gets crowded with families on the weekend. The **Fourth Beach** at the Hawksbill Hotel is the only official nude beach on the island, and the hotel provides lounge chairs. The best beach on the island is **Half Moon Bay,** with a lovely setting on the east coast. Those who aren't content to lounge for a week will be glad to find **The Fitness Shack** (Dickenson Bay; 809-462-5223) with free weights, bikes, stairs, and aerobics, but no air conditioning; open Monday through Saturday, 6:00 A.M. to noon and 3:00 P.M. to 9:00 P.M.

SIGHTSEEING

Nelson's Dockyard is a restored eighteenth-century working dockyard and the center of Antigua's charter-yacht industry. **Antigua Sailing Week** (the last week in April) is one of the largest regattas in the Caribbean. You can see the drunken sailors every night in the bars, but to see the actual races (or enjoy an off-land experience any time of year), charter the *Sentio* (809-464-7127), a 45-foot gay-friendly sailboat, or call **Nicholson Yacht Charters** (809-460-1530), which can set you up with a gay-friendly captain and crew.

SHOPPING

Base (Redcliff Quay, St. Johns; 809-460-2500) is a very gay-friendly shop selling body-conscious clothing for women and the best T-shirts for all.

BARBADOS

Barbados boasts a wide array of activities, and the greatest percentage of return visitors of any island in the Caribbean. The island is fairly welcoming of gay visitors, and heard an open dialog on homosexuality at the arrival of a lesbian group a few years ago, but gay venues remain elusive. In addition to good surfing, windsurfing and wreck diving, Barbados offers some nightlife, including jazz bars and discos where you will occasionally see gay people comfortably enjoying themselves.

Accommodations

SANDY LANE St. James Beach; 809-432-1311 or 800-44-UTELL, fax 809-432-2954; $495–1000

Although the Sandy Lane is Barbados's long-standing class act, it's very straight and stuffy.

GLITTER BAY 809-422-4111 and ROYAL PAVILION 809-422-5555 or 800-283-8666; $200–330

Equally luxurious but a bit more informal than Sandy Lane.

ROMAN'S BEACH APARTMENTS 809-428-7635; $40–60

Friendly and comfortable, located on a beautiful beach.

SANDY BEACH HOTEL 809-435-8000 or 800-44-UTELL, fax 809-435-8053; $95–410

Offers solid midrange accommodations on a good swimming beach.

OCEAN VIEW HOTEL 809-427-7821, fax 809-427-7826; $55–225

The island's oldest hotel, celebrating its 100th birthday in 1998, is located on a busy street. It's funky, old-fashioned, and convenient to Bridgetown.

Dining

Barbados has as good a selection of restaurants as is available anywhere in the Caribbean. Bajan cuisine incorporates West Indian, British, and African influences, and much of it features the native flying fish. **Koko's** (Prospect House, St. James; 809-424-4557; $17) offers local cuisine served in an attractive beach setting. **The Fathoms** (Paynes Bay, St. James; 809-432-2568; $22 dinner/$7 lunch) is a small restaurant specializing in seafood. Casual lunches and romantic dinners are enhanced by the ocean views and sound effects. The **Waterfront Café** (The Careenage, Bridgetown; 809-427-0093; $18) is popular with a hip, young crowd. Located on an inlet, it's a casual restaurant serving light meals. It has a bar, music nightly, and outdoor tables facing the water.

BEQUIA

The largest of the 36 Grenadine Islands, Bequia has not yet been developed for tourism and attracts an eclectic group of world travelers, artists, writers, and yachties. You can reach Bequia by air from Barbados (**Air Mustique,** 809-456-4586, leaves Barbados at 4:00 P.M., returns at 1:00 P.M. in high season) or by ferry or boat charter ($80) from St. Vincent. The ferry usually leaves late enough to allow same-day connections from the eastern United States.

Accommodations

THE OLD FORT HOTEL 809-458-3440; $130–160
A seventeenth-century farmhouse hideaway on a magnificent cliffside setting.

THE FRANGIPANI 809-458-3255, fax 809-458-3824; $30–55
Offers comfortable accommodations in the original house and 10 newer cottages. The bar here is *the* local gathering spot, and the Thursday-night barbecue and "jump-up" steel band dance actually draws a crowd of tourists and locals.

LOWER BAY GUEST HOUSE 809-458-3675; $20–30
Located on Lower Bay, this lodging is quiet and friendly. The front corner room is best.

KEEGAN'S GUEST HOUSE 809-458-3254; $65–80
Front rooms with balcony are best at this quiet, friendly place.

Dining

Recommended dining includes **Mac's Pizza** (809-458-3474; $7–30) for great casual terrace dining, **Le Petit Jardin** (809-458-3318; $32) serving elegant French/Creole cuisine, and **The Old Fort** (809-458-3440; $34) serving gourmet dinners in a location with a gorgeous view. Reservations are recommended for dinner at all, even Mac's. **De Reef** (809-458-3641; $28) is the place for Sunday brunch.

Nightlife

The bar at **The Frangipani** (see above) is it.

Activities

ATHLETIC AND OUTDOOR

Hope Beach offers seclusion (be sure to arrange a return time with your taxi), nude sunbathing, and breaking waves for body surfing. **Industry Bay** offers near seclusion, beautiful views, and food and drink from the Crescent Bay Lodge. **Friendship** and **Spring Bays** offer good snorkeling and diving, **Princess Margaret Beach** offers windsurfing, and numerous roads and footpaths offer good walking and bird watching.

BONAIRE

Often considered a place for divers only, this boomerang-shaped arid island has enough attractions above sea level to be of interest to any traveler. With barely 10 inches of rainfall annually, low humidity, and pleasant trade winds outside of the hurricane belt, the weather here is unsurpassed. "Discovered" and named (*bonnah,* from the Arawak for "lowland") by Italian Amerigo Vespucci, the island is now Dutch governed, though the popular language is Papiamento—a combination of Dutch, English, Spanish, Portuguese, and French. Despite its brutal colonization, Bonaire is now known as the friendliest island in the Caribbean. ALM offers the best service to the island, with direct flights from Miami and Atlanta, and a *Visit Caribbean Pass,* making day trips or overnights to Aruba or Curaçao easy and affordable.

Accommodations

OCEAN VIEW VILLAS Kaya Statius Van Eps 6; 011-599-7-4309, fax 011-599-7-4309; $80–140

Bonaire's only gay-owned and -operated accommodations, with a studio and two-bedroom apartment, each offering a fully equipped kitchen, private, walled rear patio, indoor and outdoor showers, and cable TV. Friendly hosts provide helpful guidance to the island's activities.

HARBOUR VILLAGE 011-599-7-7500 or 800-424-0004, fax 011-599-7-7507; $265–695

The nicest resort for the nondiver. Its amenities include a sand beach, water sports, a fitness center and an excellent, affordable dining room.

THE SOROBON BEACH RESORT 011-599-7-8080 or 800-828-9356, fax 011-599-7-8080; $135–225

A gay-friendly, European-style "naturalist" resort, with mediocre rooms but the island's nicest beach ("clothes optional" and open to the public for $15/day).

Dining

Richard's Waterfront (60 J.A. Abraham Boulevard; 011-599-7-5263; $21) sits on the sea and serves excellent local seafood as well as traditional continental cuisine. **Beefeater Garden Restaurant** (Kaya Grandi 12; 011-599-7-7776; $15) specializes in fresh fish and local cuisine, has a large tropical garden, and is decorated with local handicrafts and paintings, which are for sale. **Green Parrot Restaurant** (at the Sand Dollar Beach Club; 011-599-7-5454; $12) has a great waterfront location and a casual atmosphere, making it a great place for a burger or salad at sunset. Saturday night, they feature a BBQ buffet ($17) and entertainment by a local trio. **Rendez Vous Restaurant** (Kaya L.D. Gerharts #3; 011-599-8454; $14) features a cozy, relaxed atmosphere and an outdoor terrace, making this a nice place to enjoy local seafood and freshly baked French bread.

Activities

ATHLETIC AND OUTDOOR

Diving is the biggest attraction here. The excellent, gay-friendly staff at **Bon Bini Divers** (at the Coral Regency Resort; 011-599-7-5425) can arrange state-of-the-art equipment rental, training, in addition to shore, boat and night dives. Bonaire's beaches are not the idyllic white sand oases of Aruba, but **Pink Beach, Boca Slagbaai** and the clothes-optional beach at **Sorobon Resort** should keep most sun worshipers happy. Great wildlife viewing, including iguanas, parrots and pink flamingos.

SIGHTSEEING

Petroglyphs from the original Arawak populations who were removed to Hispaniola by Spanish colonists can be found off a side road north of Rincon, Bonaire's oldest village.

SHOPPING

This is not a shopping destination, but if you must, stroll down Kralendijk's **Kaya Grandi,** where you'll find an assortment of gift shops.

BRITISH VIRGIN ISLANDS

The British Virgin Islands are mostly uninhabited, known for good diving and great sailing. **Virgin Gorda** has a large protected wildlife area with big boulders called the Baths. **Tortola** is the commercial and political center of the BVIs. **Salt Island** is home to the most famous diving site in the area, the wreck of *The Rhone.* **Norman Island, Jost Van Dyke, Great Dog,** and **Beef Island** are just some of the others. The BVIs are remote and easygoing, popular with a sophisticated crowd that wants to escape the masses. With little air service and no big cruise ship travel, the BVIs offer some the best of the Caribbean without extensive commercialization.

Accommodations

LONG BAY BEACH RESORT Tortola; 54252 or 800-729-9599; $120–420

A delightful hillside complex overlooking a spectacular beach—the oceanfront rooms and cabanas are much nicer than the units up the hill.

FORT RECOVERY ESTATES Tortola; 809-495-4354 or 800-367-8455, fax 809-495-4036; $125–629

Offers gay-friendly luxury villa rentals with a spa program, yoga, and massage.

COOPER ISLAND BEACH CLUB Cooper Island; 800-542-4624; $75–145

Best suited for travelers looking to get away. Cooper Island, less than 1 square mile in area, has no roads, nightclubs, or McDonald's. Twelve simple rooms on the beach, with kitchens and a beachfront restaurant and bar.

Virgin Gorda is home to two ultra deluxe resorts:

LITTLE DIX BAY 809-495-5555 or 800-928-3000; $225–1,000

Offers 98 deluxe wood cottages on a 500-acre estate.

BIRAS CREEK HOTEL 809-494-3555 or 800-223-1108; $340–840

33 suite rooms on 150 acres, with pampering service and an excellent restaurant.

Dining

The Sugar Mill (at the Sugar Mill Hotel, Apple Bay; 809-495-4355; $23/dinner) offers the most intriguing (though limited) menus in the

BVIs. Run by former *Bon Appetit* magazine columnists, the food is world class. Lunch is à la carte, dinner prix fixe. **Biras Creek** (see above; $40/dinner) serves a five-course set meal with an extraordinary wine list and amazing views.

Nightlife

Bomba's Surfside Shack (Cappoon's Bay; 809-495-4148) has local bands on Wednesday nights and Sunday afternoons, and a big party every full moon.

Activities

ATHLETIC AND OUTDOOR

The BVIs are an ideal spot for sailing, fishing, snorkeling, and scuba diving. The beaches are among the best in the Caribbean. Bring plenty of sunscreen, you won't be sitting in your room!

SIGHTSEEING

The Baths (Lee Road, South Shore) are Virgin Gorda's most popular feature—saltwater grottoes formed by immense boulders.

SHOPPING

On Tortola, the **Sunny Caribee and Spice Company** and **Sunny Caribee Gallery** offer a great selection of spices, plus handicrafts, furniture, and fine artwork.

DOMINICAN REPUBLIC

The Dominican Republic is home to a few gay businesses; unfortunately, they open, close, and change names faster than anyone can keep up with. Many travelers have shied away from the Dominican Republic in recent years, because it shares its island land mass, Hispaniola, with Haiti. Despite the cartological connection, they are two distinct countries, and the border between them is nearly impassable.

Accommodations

JARAGUA 367 Avenue George Washington; 809-221-2222 or 800-468-3571, fax 809-686-0528; $80–900

Of the tourist resorts, this one is your best bet for facilities and location.

Nightlife

The big disco is **The Penthouse,** at the corner of Seibo and Twentieth Streets, but don't attempt to find it on your own—get a taxi driver or guide who knows where he's going. **Le Pousse Bar** (19 de Marzo) in the Colonial zone is a small, crowded, sweaty, and friendly dance bar without a lot of prostitution.

JAMAICA

Despite its reputation as one of the most dangerous and least gay-friendly islands in the Caribbean, Jamaica's beautiful beaches and affordable prices are an enticing draw, even for gay travelers. Marijuana-infused **Negril** is relatively comfortable, maybe because so many locals and visitors are too stoned to care. We are hard-pressed to recommend the island at all, except for the accomodations listed below, and the fact that you can rent a villa here and be totally secluded. Jamaica is home to more rental villas than any other island in the Caribbean; the privacy they offer makes them an attractive option for couples and groups who want to be completely comfortable. We haven't heard of any problems regarding homophobic house staff, but be sure to voice any concerns to your rental agency.

Accommodations

SEAGRAPE VILLAS 800-637-3608; $1,800–2,500/week
This is one villa complex marketing specifically to the gay market, with three four-bedroom houses on the sea in Ocho Rios.

HALF-MOON CLUB Montego Bay; 809-953-2211 or 800-237-3237; $145–680
A sophisticated, upscale country club–like resort that has a small, devoted gay following.

MUSTIQUE

The vacation home of Jagger, Bowie, and Princess Margaret, Mustique is reached via Barbados, and offers the simple beach life for the jet set. With a picnic and your mule (a glorified mini-moke vehicle, not an animal), drive along roads with spectacular views to one of the dozen or so beaches that ring the island.

Accommodations

COTTON HOUSE 809-456-4777; $225–760 MAP-AP
Choices here are very simple: Either rent a house or stay at this very gay-friendly hotel, which offers spacious and attractive cottages nestled around an eighteenth-century plantation house, pool, and beach.

MUSTIQUE VILLAS 809-458-4621, fax 809-456-4565; two-bedroom villas, $2,800–5,700/week
This rental agency offers properties of all styles, sizes, and locations. Yes, you can even rent Princess Margaret's house.

Dining

At night, the **Cotton House** serves excellent dinners on the veranda. The other choice is **Basil's Bar** (see below).

Nightlife

Basil's Bar (809-458-4621) is famous for late-night cocktails, but it also offers good food in a great setting over Brittania Bay. This is it for entertainment, and if you hang here long enough, you'll get to see everyone on the island, including celebrities and royalty.

Activities

ATHLETIC AND OUTDOOR

Busiest and best is **Marconi Beach,** but farther down the same coast is wide, scenic, scarcely populated, clothing-optional **Pasture Beach.** Beware of swimming from October to May as the currents can be treacherous.

SIGHTSEEING

Bring your telephoto lens—you never know who you might spot on the beach.

SHOPPING

Charter a jet and fly to Saint Thomas.

PUERTO RICO

Puerto Rico is the gayest spot in the Caribbean, with much to offer the gay traveler. Its sunny shores are U.S. soil, so there are no customs formalities for travelers from the mainland. In addition, the large number of flights from many gateways means convenient, inexpensive access. **Old San Juan** is scenic, with interesting sightseeing and shopping. **The Condado** section offers many first-class and deluxe beach resorts and casinos, as well as most of the gay nightlife. The city's status as a major cruise port brings large and often unsightly crowds, but the heavy traffic is what brought about the infrastructure that supports gay businesses. In addition to a host of bars and clubs, you'll find a gay hotel, two gay-popular beaches, a few gay guest houses, some gay-popular restaurants, and even a Condomania store. San Juan is really the only destination in the entire Caribbean that offers extensive gay nightlife.

Accommodations

Although you can party all night in San Juan, at some point you'll probably want a bed to sleep in, and the city offers many options. The Condado section is most convenient to nightlife. The gay-marketed accommodations are acceptable, but anyone desiring true resort amenities and style should stay at a mainstream hotel.

OCEAN WALK GUEST HOUSE Calle Atlantic #1, Ocean Park; 809-728-0855; $55–130

This is the nicest of the gay accommodations, a Spanish-style resort complex of 40 rooms on the beach with a courtyard pool, bar, and grill. Catering to a mixed gay/straight clientele, their rooms vary greatly in size. All are clean, but in need of renovation.

ATLANTIC BEACH HOTEL Calle Vendig #1, Condado; 809-721-6900; $75–140

Also on the beach, this gay hotel has 37 private and shared-bath rooms, high sexual temperature and a large, popular bar and restaurant. It does not have a pool, and its beachfront is public and mixed, but happy hour here is popular, and the terrace restaurant gets high marks for food. Their bustling tea dance and bar can make the hotel too busy for some potential guests, but those looking for action shouldn't stay anywhere else.

OCEAN PARK BEACH INN Calle Elena #3, Ocean Park; 809-728-7418; $40–120

Exclusively gay/lesbian, this inn offers simple, affordable accommodations just 50 feet from the beach in the residential neighborhood of Ocean Park.

THE MARRIOTT 1309 Ashford Avenue, Condado; 809-722-7000 or 800-223-6388; $149–400

A new hotel in the Condado, the Marriott is located on the beach just two buildings down from the Atlantic Beach Hotel. It is the best deluxe option nearest to the gay nightlife.

On the other side of the Atlantic Beach are the Condado Beach Trio, including:

LA CONCHA Ashford Avenue, Condado; 809-721-6090 or 800-468-2822, fax 809-724-1650; $137–294 and
CONDADO BEACH HOTELS Ashford Avenue, Condado; 809-721-6090 or 800-468-2775, fax 809-724-7222; $142–457

Under the joint management of Carnival Hotels & Casinos, La Concha offers rooms with oceanfront views, most with terraces, and also small bungalows around the pool. Unfortunately, the place has been rundown for a few years, with resources shifted to the Condado Beach, part of which used to be the old Vanderbilt mansion in the early 1900s. Both hotels are very gay-friendly and within walking distance of many of the gay hot spots.

EL SAN JUAN HOTEL AND CASINO Isla Verde Road, Isla Verde; 809-791-1000 or 800-468-2818; $320–465

Offers the island's most stylish and elegant surroundings, located in Isla Verde, about a 10-minute ride from the gay beach and nightlife.

RADISSON NORMANDIE HOTEL Muñoz Rivera Rosales; 809-729-2929 or 800-333-3333; $125–275

Offers stylish and affordable Art Deco lodgings—be sure to ask for their package rates.

EL CANARIO 1317 Ashford Avenue, Condado; 809-722-3861 or 800-742-4276; $75–85

A small, affordable hotel near the beach and nightlife in the Condado. While we know a number of gay people who have stayed here comfortably for years, we have had one significant complaint of homophobia from a travel agent booking a room for two men and can no longer recommend the place without that caveat.

Dining

Latin American food is the order of the day (or night) in San Juan, although you may be surprised by the variety of cuisines represented and the sophisticated menus you will encounter. **Amadeus** (Calle San Sebastián, Old San Juan; 809-722-8635; $12) is a modern café serving Latin American food. Reservations are recommended for the back dining room. **Ramiro's** (Avenida Magdalena 1106, Condado; 809-721-9049; $28) serves creative Spanish cuisine in a posh atmosphere. **Al Dente** (Calle Recinto Sur, Old San Juan; 809-723-7303; $13) is an unpretentious Italian restaurant in a historic building.

Nightlife

Krash (1257 Ponce de León, Santurce; 809-722-1131) is the most popular disco, with strippers and shows—its biggest nights are Fridays and Saturdays; Wednesdays are also popular. Thursdays the crowd splits between here and **Laser Discothèque** (also referred to as "Abbey Discothèque"; Calle Cruz #251, Old San Juan; 809-725-2581), which is gay and very popular on Sunday nights as well. **Tabú** (Calle Loiza 1753, Santurce; 809-268-5737) is a popular women's dance bar, which is men-only on Tuesday nights, with salsa and merengue music. **CUPS** (1708 Calle San Mateo, Santurce; 809-268-3570) and **CUPS 2** at the beach are the other popular women's bars. Monday night is gay at **Sky Dance. The Atlantic Beach Bar** (Calle Vendig #1, Condado; 809-721-6900) at the Atlantic Beach Hotel is open 11:00 A.M. to 1:00 A.M., with happy hour nightly and a very popular tea dance on Sunday. Also at the beach is the **Barefoot Bar** (Calle Vendig #2, Condado; 809-724-7230), open 9:00 A.M. to 2:00 A.M., to 3:00 A.M. on weekends. **La Laguna** (53 Calle Barranquitos, Condado) is a popular after-hours club, open daily from 11:00 P.M. Show and strippers at 2:00 A.M., late show Thursday through Sunday at 4:00 A.M. Next door is **Vibration** (51 Barranquitas, Condado), very cruisy and a bit sleazy.

Activities

ATHLETIC AND OUTDOOR

You'll find other gay women and men on the beach in front of the Atlantic Beach Hotel and at the quieter Ocean Park beach. San Juan has a great new gay-friendly gym called **Fitness City** (1959 Calle Loiza, entrance on Ocean Park; 809-268-7773; $10/day, $25/week) located in Ocean Park on the fourth floor above the post office, with striking beach views, new equipment, free weights, and aerobics classes. The **Caribbean National Forest,** known locally as **El Yunque,** is easily accessible from San Juan and offers 28,000 acres of trails through four types of forest, including the low-elevation, high-canopied rain forest. The **Hyatt Resorts** in **Dorado** and **Cerromar** (796-1234) offer two **18-hole Robert Trent Jones golf courses.**

SIGHTSEEING

While your image of San Juan may have been influenced by *West Side Story*'s musical disparagement, the town of **Old San Juan** is as charming and impressive as any you might encounter in the Caribbean. Its structures date back as far as the sixteenth century, and many have been lovingly restored. The dramatic **Fuerte San Felipe del Morro** (Calle Norzagray; 809-729-6960), or **El Morro** as it is called locally, guards the entrance to San Juan Bay. Take a guided tour, or freely explore its dungeons, vaults, barracks, and lookouts on your own. The **Museo de Pablo Casals** (Calle San Sebastián 101, Old San Juan; 809-723-9185) houses memorabilia from the last 20 years of the famous cellist's life.

SHOPPING

Casa Méndez Suárez (251 San Justo) has been selling Panama hats since 1886. Cristo and San José streets are lined with art galleries. **Galería Botello** (208 Cristo) is a particularly good choice for local artists.

SABA

Saba is 5 square miles of towering volcanic island, virtually ignored by tourists because of its lack of beaches. Lilliputian villages, a well-protected marine park for diving, and a botanically rich rain forest are what to see here.

Accommodations

CAPTAIN'S QUARTERS Windwardside; 011-599-4-62377; $85–130

An old wooden home built in 1832, it has 10 rooms (4 in the original structure), spectacular views, swimming pool, good restaurant, and a significant gay following from marketing efforts in the gay press.

ST. BARTS

Very French, St. Barts (St. Barthélémy is its rarely used formal name) offers superb cuisine, excellent beaches, and a very hip, relaxed atmosphere. Although it was once a Swedish island, there are only trace reminders of that history, as well as of West Indian culture. Haute cuisine and high fashion meet here on the beach, where wealthy, sophisticated, and somewhat reclusive gays wage their campaign against winter. There are no gay-specific businesses, but an increasingly visible regular, trendy crowd who take comfort, though not necessarily pleasure in each other's company. St. Jean, east of Gustavia, has become the tourist center of the island, replete with chi-chi bistros and boutiques, but farther east is **L'Orient,** an increasingly gay cove and probably the gayest beach on the island. St. Barts is reached primarily by plane and boat from St. Martin.

Accommodations

CARL GUSTAF Gustavia, 011-590-27-82-83; $490–1200

This charming hotel caters to high-end queens, with posh rooms and a gay-friendly atmosphere.

HOTEL CHRISTOPHER 011-590-27-6363 or 800-221-4542, fax 011-590-27-92-92; $190–290

With 40 comfortable rooms at the island's northern tip, the hotel also has a pool, fitness center, 2 restaurants and 3 bars.

ST. BARTS BEACH HOTEL Grand Cul de Sac; 011-590-27-60-70; $155–350

Family owned and managed, this 44-unit resort offers beachfront rooms and villas.

VILLAGE ST. JEAN 011-590-27-61-39 or 800-633-7411; $89–300

This spot offers 24 units, including some kitchen-equipped cottages, all with partial ocean view. Modestly furnished, some units are noisy, so be sure to ask.

CLUB LA BANANE 011-590-27-68-25, fax 011-590-27-68-44; $115–500

Accomodations in L'Orient are limited to this deluxe hotel, a three-minute walk from the beach. With only 9 units, reserve well in advance.

Villa rentals are popular in St. Barts.

LE TOINY 011-590-27-88-88; $450–720

A very elegant collection of villas—though we can't imagine anyone needing that much space at the beach.

Sibarth, represented in the United States by **Wimco** (800-932-3222 or 401-849-8012) has a broader selection of villas all over the island.

Dining

Some of the best meals anywhere in the region are served at the waterfront **Chez Maya** (Public Beach, Public; 011-590-27-73-61; $31) featuring Creole and American cuisine and at the **François Plantation** (Colombier; 011-590-27-78-82; $28), serving haute French. Gay-popular and less expensive are **Newborn Restaurant** (Anse de Caye; 011-590-27-67-07; $18) and **Eddie's Ghetto** (Gustavia; no phone; $17), serving good food; the former French/Creole and the latter basic Creole. **L'Escale** (La Pointe; 011-590-27-70-33; $20) is recommended for its change-of-pace Italian cuisine and happening bar.

Nightlife

Nightlife here is limited to the well-known **Le Sélect** (Gustavia; 011-590-27-86-87), with its West Indian atmosphere (go after 11:00 P.M.) and the small but elegant **American Bar** (aka Escale Bar, Gustavia), which happens to serve Italian food (go figure, and go after 1:00 A.M.).

Activities

ATHLETIC AND OUTDOOR

St. Barts has seven beautiful beaches. **L'Orient** is the gayest. **Anse Grande Saline** is gay on the right side, and clothing-optional, as is **Anse Gouverneur**. **St. Jean** is topless.

SIGHTSEEING

The **Municipal Museum** in Gustavia is the island's only museum, with displays chronicling the island's history. If you hit three days of rain you might want to consider going.

SHOPPING

On the southwestern coast, you'll find **Corossol,** an old fishing village whose straw hat–selling stalls are far removed from the tony shops of Gustavia.

ST. KITTS AND NEVIS

Named St. Christopher (after Columbus) until 1988, St. Kitts was the "mother colony" of the West Indies, as it was from here that the English and French settled other islands. Today, St. Kitts and Nevis are an independent nation, best known for their combination of natural, undeveloped beauty and historical sights. Central mountains surrounded by sugarcane fields dominate the scenery on these two small and charming islands. Old sugar-plantation houses have been turned into some of the island's best inns, and the old plantation roads make excellent trails for walking and horseback riding. The island topography is varied, including rain forest and mountains, which are home to the green velvet monkeys, brought by French settlers for no apparent reason. The two capitals of Basseterre in St. Kitts and Charlestown in Nevis are both lovely, the latter having some fine eighteenth-century architecture—Alexander Hamilton's birthplace is splendid. Nevis can be easily visited on a day trip by ferry from Basseterre to Charlestown, a 40-minute commute.

Accommodations

OTTLEY'S PLANTATION Ottley's; 809-465-7234; $240–385

Upscale lodging on St. Kitts is best found at this gracious plantation, with its spacious antique-furnished rooms, a pool built into the ruins of a sugar factory, and one of the best restaurants on the island.

THE GOLDEN LEMON INN & VILLAS 809-465-7260 or 800-633-7411; $175–950

Created by Arthur Leaman, former editor of *House and Garden,* the inn and villas are frequented by the glitterati of Hollywood and Washington, who enjoy its elegant, house-party atmosphere. Rates include breakfast, high tea, and dinner.

FAIRVIEW INN 809-465-2472 or 800-223-9815; $100–170
A cluster of mountainside cottages near Basseterre, functionally furnished and situated around an eighteenth-century plantation house with a pool and an excellent dining room.

TIMOTHY BEACH RESORTS Frigate Bay, 3 miles from Basseterre, 809-465-8597 or 800-777-1700, fax 809-465-7723; $65–360 has 60 rooms and suites on an extensive beach, plus a good restaurant and water sports.

FOUR SEASONS RESORT Pinney's Beach; 809-469-1111 or 800-332-3442; $300–550 offers an ultradeluxe gay-friendly refuge on tiny Nevis.

Dining

In addition to **Ottley's Plantation** (see above), other good places to dine include the elegant **Rawlins Plantation** (Mount Pleasant; 809-465-6221; $23/full lunch, $35/full dinner) with prix-fixe menus of Creole specialties and international cuisine. Other local favorites include **Ballyhoo** (Fort Street, Basseterre; 809-465-4197; $40) and **Chef's Place** (Church Street, St. Kitts; 809-465-6176; $13), both serving West Indian specialties.

Nightlife

You'll also find weekend nightlife with an attractive, mostly straight crowd at the **Kittitian Monkey Bar** (Timothy Beach; 809-465-8050). After midnight, try the **Why Not** (Fort Street, Basseterre; 809-465-2858) bar in Basseterre, a small, local, and sometimes cruisy video bar where the crowd pours out onto the street.

Activities

ATHLETIC AND OUTDOOR

For the best beaches on St. Kitts, the south peninsula is the place to go. Here you may see some of the island's population of wild green monkeys. Frigate Bay and Salt Pond offer white-sand beaches, with the best beaches—Banana, Cockleshell, Major's, and Mosquito bays—only recently accessible by car.

SIGHTSEEING

Brimstone Hill, the "Gibraltar of the Caribbean" on St. Kitts, is a must for the panoramic views from its eighteenth-century fortifications.

SHOPPING

At the **Caribelle Boutique** (Old Town Road; 809-465-6253) at Romney Manor you can see batiks being made in a lovely house surrounded by lush gardens. Half of the island's stores can be found at **Pelican Mall.**

ST. MARTIN/SINT MAARTEN

Split between the French and the Dutch, St. Martin offers a quintessential Caribbean experience: beautiful beaches, good food, duty-free shopping, casinos, and nightlife. Like other heavily touristy islands, this island suffers its share of overdevelopment, crime, and cruise-ship crowds. A car is highly recommended for exploring the real beauty here—37 powdery white-sand beaches. St. Martin/Sint Maarten was hit hard by the 1995 hurricane and will be recovering for many years.

Accommodations

MAHO BAY HOTEL AND CASINO Maho Bay; 011-5995-52115 or 800-223-0757; $155–590

While the big resorts have their appeal of activities, Maho Bay Hotel has stuff aplenty to keep active vacationers busy.

LE MERIDIEN L'HABITATION Anse Marcel; 011-590-876700 or 800-543-4300; $160–450

Le Meridien and its new luxury wing, **La Domaine,** offer sophisticated and charming accommodations, with a 1,600-foot beach and exquisite landscaping.

GREEN CAY VILLAGE Orient Bay; 011-590-873636 or 800-832-2302; $229–543

Offers luxurious and private villas.

ORIENT BAY Mont Vernon; 011-590-873-1110 or 800-223-5695; $105–185

This hotel is recommended for its inexpensive, newly built studio and apartment units set amid lush foliage.

CLUB ORIENT Orient Bay; 011-590-873385 or 800-452-9016; $115–315

This was a naturalist resort, with basic prefab pine chalets with kitchens and living rooms but no TVs or telephones. It was destroyed in the 1995 hurricane but should be rebuilt by 1997.

ALIZEA Mont Vernon; 011-590-877030; $126–191

Near Orient Beach—small and gingerbready, with great views, a swimming pool, and a very good restaurant.

HOLLAND HOUSE Philipsburg; 011-599-522572, fax 011-599-524673; $79–195

Right on the beach and adjacent to Philipsburg's shopping, the hotel has a simple décor and a small gay following.

Dining

For great dining, try **Rainbow** (Grand Case; 011-590-875-580; $24), with a chef imported from New York's Greenwich Village, a menu that includes cross-cultural creative cuisine, and a terraced dining room overlooking Grand Case Beach. It is open for lunch and dinner in season, reservations required. More moderate fare with a French flair can be had at **Le Pressoir** (011-590-877662; $18), in a charming old house—reservations recommended. On the Dutch side, **Paradise Café** (Mullet Bay; 011-5995-52842; $12) offers informal, inexpensive al fresco dining across from the Maho Beach Resort.

Nightlife

The Greenhouse (Bobby's Marina, Philipsburg; 011-599-5-22941) is a popular bar and restaurant with a dance floor and pool table. Very gay on some nights. There is no exclusively gay nightlife, but there are three places with a gay following: **L'Atmosphère** (011-590-875024), a chic disco on the marina in Marigot; **Cheri's Café** (next to Maho Beach Resort; 011-599-5-53361), serving up live reggae and Latin music nightly in Maho, and the **Music News Café,** a popular bar in Simpson Bay.

Activities

ATHLETIC AND OUTDOOR

Clothing-optional beaches that attract some gay visitors include the beach in front of Club Orient and the farthest Cupecoy Beach.

SIGHTSEEING

The **Simartin Museum** (111 Frontstreet, Philipsburg) is a small museum with changing exhibits on the island's history and culture. The nineteenth-century cottage also houses some small stores. If you're too sunburned to go outside, this might distract you for an hour.

SHOPPING

French Marigot has more stylish shopping than Dutch Philipsburg, whose shopping is mostly limited to the main street. The best shops in Marigot are at the **Marina Royale,** but visitors looking for a more native experience should go to the **Early Morning Market.**

TRINIDAD AND TOBAGO

Just off the coast of South America, Trinidad and Tobago are at the geographic bottom of the Caribbean chain. As one of the largest oil producers in the western hemisphere, Trinidad has an African heritage, a cosmopolitan, fun-loving, and friendly population, 700 species of orchids, and a carnival rivaling Rio and New Orleans. Tobago is the quieter island, hence the local saying, "Tobago is paradise, Trinidad is New York." The gay community here is relatively uncloseted, and a gay rights group was organized in 1994. Gays play an important role in the social fabric of the country, especially in the arts and in Carnival, resulting in a unique island experience: sophisticated, multiracial, and culturally rich. The islands are at their gayest, figuratively and literally, during the weeks prior to Ash Wednesday. Carnival is a week-long celebration, far smaller and safer than Rio's, and far more participatory than that of New Orleans. Fabulous costumes, hot dancing to Soca music, and local Carib beer keep energy levels high. The king/queen show on Friday night is a feathers-and-sequins extravaganza. The panorama finals on Saturday night, a steel-drum competition, is the Trinidadian equivalent to our Super Bowl in terms of energy and enthusiasm. The Sunday night before Ash Wednesday you will find yourself at one of the numerous parties organized around town before hitting the streets just before dawn to partake in *J'Ouvert* (joo-vay). Be prepared to be covered in mud, sometimes dyed green or blue, by bucket-toting strangers as you follow 40-foot sound trucks and dance through the streets of Port of Spain to welcome the final countdown of Carnival. Playing *Mas* on Monday and Tuesday will bring you back to the streets in costume.

Accommodations

TRINIDAD HILTON Lady Young Road, Port of Spain; 809-624-3111 or 800-HILTONS; $141–180; $237 Carnival week
Recently refurbished, the Hilton is still the best hotel in town and within walking distance of the Carnival festivities. The poolside is very gay, available to locals by membership, and to nonguests for a daily fee. The Hilton is a good base for gay tourists any time of the year.

Recommended hotels on Tobago include:

GRAFTON BEACH HOTEL Black Rock; 809-639-0191; $162–252
A new and very attractive large, gay-friendly hotel with pool, beach, AC, TV, and good West Indian food.

KARIWAK VILLAGE Crown Point; 809-639-8442; $50–90
Near the beach, a long-time gay-popular small resort with excellent food. Air-conditioned cottages surround a pool.

Dining

Veni Mange (67 Ariapita Avenue, Woodbrook; 809-624-4597; $10) is the place for lunch, run by a local TV talk-show host. On Tobago, try **Rouselles** (Bacolet Street, Scarborough; 809-639-4738; $12), serving excellent West Indian and international cuisine in a charming house with lovely views—gay women and men are very welcome.

Nightlife

On Trinidad, you'll find other gays at **Smoky & Bunty** (Western Main Road; St. James), the most popular mixed bar in town—small and simple but open late—or the **Pelican Pub** (2-4 Coblentz Avenue, Port of Spain, next to the Hilton; 809-624-7486), the oldest gay hangout in town, now more mixed and less popular. On Saturday nights, you should find a gay party at one of these clubs: **Cocoa House** (46 Ariapita Avenue, Port of Spain; 809-628-3176), **Gayelle** (Cipriani Boulevard, Port of Spain), **The Attic** (Maraval Shopping Center, Maraval), or **Pier One** (Chaguanas; 809-634-4472), a very popular mixed seaside bar that can have a gay crowd on weekends.

Activities

ATHLETIC AND OUTDOOR

Bird watching is a popular activity on Trinidad, and the **Asa Wright Nature Center** (Spring Hill Estate; 809-667-4655) is home to more than 100 species on 191 acres, two hours from Port of Spain. With 20 guest rooms, you can spend the night. The **Caroni Bird Sanctuary** (Butler Highway) is best at sunset, when the scarlet ibis comes back to this mangrove swampland. If your Trinidad experience is more Carnival bacchanalia than birding, head to Tobago, sleepy and incredibly beautiful with lush scenery. **Back Bay Beach** is the best of the beaches, and is usually deserted. Find it on the West Coast Road between the Mount Irvine Hotel and Grafton Beach. Access is via the dirt road through the coconut plantation opposite Gleneagles Drive. Discreet nudity is okay.

SIGHTSEEING

If you want to participate in Carnival instead of just watching, your hotel can probably help to arrange a costume with one of the Masquerade Camps. "Poison" is one of the best Mas Camps, with minimal costumes and a high percentage of gays in their 5,000-member group. A costume and entry should run about $100. You'll need to make reservations two to five months in advance for hotel rooms and Poison costumes. On Tobago, **Fort King George** offers sweeping vistas and some historical relics.

SHOPPING

Trinidad is the place to buy fabrics, and you'll find a great selection of silks and cottons in downtown Port of Spain on Frederick Street near Independence Square.

U.S. VIRGIN ISLANDS:
ST. CROIX, ST. JOHN, AND ST. THOMAS

The U.S. Virgin Islands are the Caribbean at its best and worst. **ST. JOHN,** with the majority of its land conserved in national parkland, remains relatively sleepy, underdeveloped, and unspoiled. Gay life begins and pretty much ends at Solomon Bay, the gay beach. The appeal here is not the gay scene but the natural beauty and laid-back rhythm. **ST. THOMAS** is a shopping paradise, besieged by cruise ships and a small crime problem. Downtown Charlotte Amalie remains fairly quaint, despite the fast-food outlets and the one million *Love Boat* passengers set loose here each year. Use streetwise caution at night, don't leave valuables in a parked rental car, and be careful where you choose to make a display of same-sex affection. You'll probably be too busy with shopping bags to hold hands anyway. **ST. CROIX** has struggled with hurricane recovery and tense race relations, but it remains in many ways the most appealing of the three U.S. Virgins for a gay visitor. It has beautiful rugged scenery and powder-white beaches (like St. John, but maybe more so), gay-specific attractions (like St. Thomas, only less so), and lower prices that go hand-in-hand with fewer tourists, both good news.

Accommodations

Choices on St. John are limited. Choose either of the deluxe but very straight resorts, rent a private house, or stay at the "luxury campgrounds" at Maho Bay.

HYATT REGENCY VIRGIN GRAND St. John; 809-776-7171 or 800-233-1234; $295–520
Deluxe, family-oriented resort.

CANEEL BAY St. John; 809-776-6111 or 800-928-8889; $250 and up
Deluxe, couple-oriented resort.

MAHO BAY in the Virgin Islands National Park, St. John; 809-776-6240 or 212-472-9453 or 800-392-9004; $95
Platform tent accommodations are luxurious, for a campground.

HARMONY same as Maho Bay; $150–170

Harmony is an eco-resort luxury campground built entirely from recycled materials and minimizing environmental impact.

SUNSET POINTE St. John; 809-773-8100

Offers two rental residences with great views just a few minutes from the beach, shopping, and dining.

BLACKBEARD'S CASTLE St. Thomas; 809-776-1234 or 800-344-5771; $110–190

Gay-owned and operated since 1985, this hotel used to be the most popular gay-friendly lodging option, although it was still partially closed at press time because of hurricane damage.

DANISH CHALET INN St. Thomas; 809-774-5764, fax 809-777-4886; $60–95

A 10-room inn within walking distance of downtown. Gay-friendly, some rooms have shared baths.

HOTEL 1829 St. Thomas, Government Hill; 809-776-1829 or 800-524-2002; $60–230

Small and charming hotel, with attractive rooms, a sunny courtyard, and small pool.

MARRIOTT FRENCHMAN'S REEF HOTEL St. Thomas; 809-776-8500 or 800-524-2000; $225–395

Closest to gay/lesbian-popular **Morningstar Beach.**

ON THE BEACH formerly the King Frederick; Frederiksted, St. Croix; 809-772-1205 or 800-524-2018; $50–180

Offers accommodations for gay women and men on a nice, white sandy beach with a restaurant, Jacuzzi, pool, and beachfront bar.

Dining

On St. John, **Paradiso** (Mongoose Junction; 809-779-4422; $21) offers trendy, Northern Italian bistro fare. The best food on the island is found at **Asolare** (Route 20, Cruz Bay; 809-779-4747; $22), specializing in spicy, Asian-influenced food. **Le Chateau de Bordeaux** (Junction 10, Centerline Road; 809-779-4078; $23) offers great food, a romantic atmosphere, and spectacular views from its mountainside location. The all-you-can-eat dinner buffet at the **Hyatt Virgin Grand** (see above) is a good value for big eaters looking in an elegant environment; **Barracuda Bistro** (809-779-4944; $6) in Wharfside Village satisfies big appetites with huge portions, reasonable prices, and good "greasy spoon" diner food. **The Lime Inn** (Cruz Bay; 809-776-6425; $12) is a good choice for seafood, popular with locals and tourists, especially on all-the-shrimp-you-can-eat Wednesdays. Get there early. The **Café Normandie** (Rue de St. Barthélémy, Frenchtown; 774-1622; $31) is an elegant French restaurant, expensive but exceptional. On St. Croix, **Café Madeleine** (Teague Bay; 809-773-8141; $22) serves up great Italian/Continental cuisine in a plantation-house atmosphere. **Kendrick's** (52 King Street; 809-773-9199; $20) is the trendy spot, serving French cuisine with Caribbean influences.

Nightlife

While the U.S. Virgin Islands have almost always had some gay nightlife, it was unfortunately all in transition as we went to press. Ask around at the gay beaches or one of the gay-friendly hotels. It won't be hard to find out about the limited offerings, when there are some. On St. Croix, a gay bar was set to open as we went to press. **The Last Hurrah** (57 King Street) might still be there by the time you read this.

Activities

ATHLETIC AND OUTDOOR

Solomon Bay is the gay beach on St. John, reached by heading out of town on Route 20, and turning left at the Park Service sign about 1/4 mile past the Visitor's Center. Park at the end of the cul-de-sac and walk the 10-minute trail down to the sea. (You can also pick up the trail from Caneel Bay or Cruz Bay.) Solomon is one of the nicest of St. John's beautiful beaches—if you arrive there early in the morning you may have it to yourself. On St. Thomas, **Morningstar Beach,** just down from the **Marriott Frenchman's Reef Hotel** is popular with gay men and lesbians, as is **Little Magen's,** a secluded clothing-optional beach. Find it by parking at Magen's Bay and walking right along the rocks, climbing over or around the pile of rocks marking the end of the beach.

SIGHTSEEING

On St. John, the **Virgin Islands National Park** (Cruz Bay; 809-776-6201) is the primary attraction, with 20 miles of trails, ruins of a 1780s sugar plantation, and petroglyphs. On St. Thomas, you'll find the **St. Thomas Synagogue** (Synagogue Hill; 809-774-4312), the second oldest synagogue in the western hemisphere. Its sand floor symbolizes the desert through which Moses led the Jews on their exodus from Egypt. On St. Croix, the **St. George Village Botanical Gardens** (Kingshill; 809-772-3874) is a 17-acre paradise with 850 species of plants, as well as restored buildings from its previous incarnation as a plantation workers' village.

SHOPPING

The U.S. Virgin Islands are a duty-free shopping paradise. Note that the customs allowance for travelers returning from these islands is $1,200/person, double the standard allowance. St. Thomas has the greatest variety and number of stores. We like some of the unusual shops in convenient **Havensight Mall** (near the dock, all ashore!) for souvenirs. On St. John, **Mongoose Junction** has a small but interesting array of stores. On St. Croix, Christiansted's **Gallows Bay** is the place to bring your Visa card.

VIEQUES

This tiny island eight miles off the east coast of Puerto Rico is reached by ferry from Fajardo (arrive in San Juan by 2:00 P.M. to catch the 4:30 P.M. departure; 809-741-4761), or by air from San Juan International

(Isla Nena in the Delta Terminal; 809-741-6362; $90 r/t or Vieques Air Link from a small airport near Old San Juan; 809-723-9882; $66 round trip). Sleepy is an understatement, but the island attracts a nice mix of tourists and Puerto Ricans. Vieques is becoming popular with the sophisticated end of the *Condé Nast Traveler* crowd, and no longer the "secret getaway" it once was. Yet the island is not commercially developed, and there are still wide-open spaces, country roads, rolling hills, and beautiful beaches that are mostly deserted. There are no nightclubs or movie theaters, few stores or diversions. There's a very small and discreet population of gay women and men on the island, and two gay-popular accommodations that draw an equally small and discreet population of gay tourists. If you're looking to get away to a sophisticated yet simple island where gay people are completely welcome but not at all obvious, Vieques is your haven.

Accommodations

NEW DAWN 809-741-0495; $40–50

A six-bedroom guest house on a five-acre country setting overlooking the Caribbean, just three miles from one of over 40 deserted beaches. The guest house caters to groups and individuals who don't require a lot of amenities. With a large female following, New Dawn offers a remote, rustic retreat.

INN OF THE BLUE HORIZON 809-741-3318 or 800-468-4325; $140–175

A stylish old country inn with three antique furnished rooms, open-air reading room, a breathtaking pool on the sea, a pristine crescent beach, and a restaurant and bar on the premises. Three two-bedroom cottages are planned.

Dining

The **Café Blu** (at the Inn of the Blue Horizon; see above; $19) is the best restaurant on the island, serving fresh local seafood as well as steaks and chops, prepared in a new American-Caribbean fusion style. It is open December to April, but not for every lunch and dinner, so be sure to check the schedule. **Crow's Nest** (809-741-0011; $15) is less fancy, but the food is just as good. **Carmen's** (at the New Dawn, see above; $12) serves local and American food with an emphasis on vegetarian meals. For casual, local meals try **Taverna Española** (809-741-1175; $15) or **Posada Vistamar** (809-741-2900; $13).

Nightlife

Don't fool yourself. But if you need to get out for a drink, try the eight-sided **Blu Bar** (at the Inn of the Blue Horizon, see above), which also serves a bar menu in the summer months.

Activities

ATHLETIC AND OUTDOOR

Vieques is known for its **bioluminescent (phosphorescent) bay** (Sharon 809-741-3751 and Clark 809-741-8600 offer trips), and playing in the water at night is a popular activity. **Horseback riding** (Eddie 809-741-0668), **scuba diving** and **snorkeling** (Blue Caribe 809-741-2522 or Richard 809-741-1980), and **bicycle rentals** (DYMC 809-741-3042) are all available.

SIGHTSEEING

Vieques has a few museums and art galleries, but that's not why you're here.

SHOPPING

Stop in at **Caribbean Kites** (809-741-3260) and buy a kite to fly on the beach.

Mexico

Mexico is a perennial favorite travel destination for many reasons. Its pre-Columbian cultural legacy, natural wonders, and many locales for adventure and escape make it a true vacation wonderland. It boasts fascinating museums, clean and exceptional colonial cities, and beautiful beaches on two coasts. And, with the recent currency devaluation, Mexico is once again a wonderful travel bargain. As evidenced in numerous news reports, Mexico is currently undergoing a profound transformation. Gay men and women are also emerging from years of repression and silence to demand a more just society, and gaining good results. Slowly but surely, a unique gay community will set an example for the rest of Latin America and be acknowledged as among the biggest in the world.

A gay vacation in Mexico can be many things. Mexico has been very popular for gay group vacations. Atlantis, RSVP, and Olivia all charter resort villages here a week at a time for exclusively gay groups. Acapulco remains a popular Thanksgiving gathering point for hundreds of gay men. Independent gay and lesbian travelers to Mexico have many options. Most tourists come to Mexico for its sunny beaches, and with good reason: Mexico's Caribbean and Pacific coasts offer some of the world's great resorts, easily accessible and quite affordable. Mexico's inland colonial towns offer culture, history, and art reflecting the country's rich history. Mexico City is filled with world-class museums, colorful markets, and an active gay nightlife. You don't need to know a lick of Spanish to get around here, but of course it helps.

When to Go and How to Get There

Many airlines fly direct from major U.S. gateways to all of Mexico's tourist destinations. Additional charter departures are available in season. Be sure to reconfirm your return flight on arrival, and get to the airport early, as flights are frequently overbooked, especially during peak travel seasons. Mexico's high season runs from mid-December through Easter/spring break. Thanksgiving is also a very popular time, particularly with gay travelers, who have a history of coming here in droves from Texas and California. Summers can be rather wet, as well as very hot and humid, but if you can stand the heat, hotel and airfare bargains abound. Resort towns are best avoided during school holidays, particularly spring break and New Year's week. During these times, the resort cities are filled not only with tourists, but a lot of drunk 18-to-21-year-olds (the legal drinking age is only 18). Late spring and fall are often the most pleasant times weatherwise, and off-season bargains are usually available.

Although airfares and prices in big hotels keep adjusting to the changing exchange rate, most local expenses such as food and souvenirs are very inexpensive. The exchange rate has gone from three pesos/$1 in 1993, to more than eight pesos/$1 at the end of 1995. Long taxi rides for $3, a lobster dinner for $12, and big margaritas for $1.50 were typical prices at press time.

Americans are required to present **proof of citizenship** when entering Mexico. A driver's license is not sufficient. You need a passport, original birth certificate, or notarized copy (either with raised seal) along with photo ID. You'll also need a tourist card, which will be given to you on arrival by the airline or customs officials. Guard this like your passport; you'll need it to leave the country.

SEX AND SENSIBILITY

Though Mexico has a Latin/Catholic influence that often breeds homophobia, many Mexican men are what we would consider either gay or bisexual. You can meet locals at the beach, the discos, on the street, and in the evenings at the *zócalo* (the church-anchored squares found in the center of all Mexican towns, large and small). While many of these men have wives or girlfriends and wouldn't define themselves as gay, they do have sex with other men. After a while you get the feeling that everybody is available and sexuality is like legality in Mexico— amorphous and more dependent on the peso than morality. The resort towns (especially Acapulco) are home to large numbers of *chichifos* or *mallates,* men that sell their favors.

If you are planning to be sexually active in Mexico, note that locals often don't like to use condoms and probably won't have one on them, since they are expensive. Good lubricants are even more of a problem, as they are generally unavailable in Mexico. Bring an ample supply of both with you, and be sure to have them on you when you go out for the night (or afternoon, or morning . . .).

NO GUESTS AT THE INN

Most hotels here won't allow you to bring guests to your room. They cite security reasons and in reality, it makes sense for them to control access. So if you want to spend time with someone who is not going to register with you on arrival, a gay guest house or villa is your best option. Be sure to inquire about guest policies when booking if this is a concern for you. Outside of the big touristy mainstream hotels, most hotels, apartments, and villas provide few (if any) amenities such as shampoo and even soap, so plan accordingly. Kitchens have *no* condiments (not even salt), and towels tend to come in only one size— large—no washcloths and rarely a hand towel.

DON'T DRINK THE WATER

Although many big hotels and restaurants now have water purification systems, the best advice is still to stay away from tap water, and anything it may be in or lingering on (ice cubes, lettuce, unpeelable fruits, etc.). Use bottled water for everything, even brushing your teeth. As for other risks, common sense prevails in Mexico, as it does at most tourist destinations. Bring and use plenty of sunscreen, especially during your first few days of exposure. Carry traveler's checks or use readily available ATMs for cash. In the evenings, take taxis back to where you're staying if you have any concerns about walking alone. Acapulco and Puerto Vallarta have a lot of tourist police in white uniforms and safari hats. They all speak some English and their job is to help you should you need it. Carry a copy of your passport for identification and leave the real thing at your hotel. Bribes and scams are not uncommon, and tourists are likely targets. If the bribe requester is an official, ignore the request or pretend not to understand, or in some way become an annoyance without being insulting and you may get off. If not, keep a supply of small bills on hand, preferably separate from your wallet. Get prices in writing before agreeing to services such as shoe shines, and always count your change. Women traveling alone are often subjected to nosy questions. Saying you're married with children and traveling with friends will cut most inquiries short.

MEXICO CITY

Mexico City is well known as the world's most densely populated city. It is BIG! Located in a valley in the central region of the country, Mexico City offers convenient access by air and comfortable ground transportation by bus to nearby cities. Travel within Mexico City is best done by taxi, via its efficient Metro, or with the assistance of an experienced local guide. Because of its size (1,500 square kilometers—approximately 575 square miles!), complexity (remember Rome?), and differences (language and customs), you should have some idea of what you want to see and do in advance of your arrival. Mexico City, as the capital and center of power, is an important place to visit for both Mexican and international tourists. Residents are justifiably proud of their numerous museums, scattered over the city and containing historical, scientific, and artistic works.

Accommodations

Mexico City has no gay-specific accommodations to recommend, but a wide range of mainstream choices to choose from.

HOTEL FOUR SEASONS Reforma 500; 011-52-5-230-1818 or 800-332-3442, fax 011-52-5-230-1808; $220–375
You can't go wrong at this elegant hacienda-style building surrounding a beautiful interior courtyard. With large, beautiful rooms and excellent service, the hotel is a deluxe oasis at the western edge of the Zona Rosa.

HOTEL MARQUIS REFORMA Reforma 465; 011-52-5-211-3600 or 800-525-4800, fax 011-52-5-211-5561; $185–410
Right across the street from and half the size of the Four Seasons, this hotel is very much its equal in terms of amenities and service.

HOTEL CALINDA GENEVE QUALITY INN Londres 130; 011-52-5-211-0071 or 800-228-5151, fax 011-52-5-208-7422; $123–136

Travelers on more moderate budgets may prefer this comfortable and popular hotel with a perfect location.

HOTEL REGENTE París 9; 011-52-5-566-8933, fax 011-52-5-593-5794; $35–45

This recently renovated hotel is a good budget option within walking distance of the Zona Rosa.

Dining

The city's only "out" restaurant is **Fonda San Francisco,** or **Casa Paco,** (Joaquín Velázquez de León 126, Colonia San Rafael; 5-546-4060; $12). It features continental dishes, and traditional Mexican specialties, all at very reasonable prices. Reservations are advised on weekends. The crowd is not always gay enough to be a real draw, and those seeking memorable food and atmosphere should head to some of the better restaurants in the Zona Rosa. You may also see other gays eating at **La Opera** (Calle Cinco de Mayo 10; 5-512-8959; $9), an elegant cantina open from 1:00 P.M. The city has two chain restaurants, **Sanborn's** and **VIPS,** dull but reliable. **Sanborn's Diana** (Paseo de la Reforma 506; $6) adjacent to Chapúltepec Park and the **VIPS** (Paseo de la Reforma and Avenida Florencia or Zona Rosa a few blocks north of the Chapúltepec Metro station; $6) are sometimes gay-frequented. **Cicero Centenario** (Londres 195; 5-533-3800; $27) is one of the city's most elegant restaurants, serving a menu of international and modern Mexican dishes. Open only for dinner; reservations are recommended. **Café Tacuba** (Tacuba 28; 5-512-8482; $10) near the zócalo is a popular restaurant with a colonial feel and live entertainment during dinner on weekends. A less expensive option nearby is the **Café Cinco de Mayo** (Cinco de Mayo 57; 5-510-1995; $5), low on atmosphere, but serving good food all day at very affordable prices.

Nightlife

Tourists staying at one of the numerous hotels in the **Zona Rosa** can enjoy a casual walk on Reforma, the city's tree-lined boulevard. The Zona Rosa (or "Pink Zone") is frequented by gays and lesbians most anytime. On weekends, the area becomes a loud, raucous party zone. Yet the only gay bars in the area are the popular, subterranean **El Taller** (Florencia 37; 5-533-4984) and its newly opened, more casual **Almacén** at street level. Tuesdays they host a community meeting for local activist group Guerilla Gay. Both are closed on Mondays. They'll be very happy to give you a copy of *Ser Gay,* a local guide to nightlife. For dancing, nearby **Anyway–Exacto–The Doors** (Monterrey 47; 5-533-1691) is fun and crowded. This three-level venue has something for everyone. Anyway for men, Exacto for women (both with shows), and The Doors, a restaurant and later a mixed after-hours bar. Open seven days a week. A recent welcome addition is **Dolce Vita** (Orizaba 146, Colonia Roma; 5-585-7406). Transformed from a private villa into an elegant, hip club, Dolce is where Mexico City's beautiful people go to dance, drink, and relax. The inside features salons in a variety of bold, elegant styles while the outside has a large dance floor under a tall oak. The music playing is current faves, and the surrounding tables are candlelit. A visit is highly encouraged. In the south of the city, you'll find **Tom's Bar** (Insurgentes Sur 357) for leather, **El Vaquero** (Insurgentes Sur 1231) for mustache lovers, and **Privata** (Universidad 1909; 5-661-5939) for young Latinos.

Activities

ATHLETIC AND OUTDOOR

Known for its congestion and pollution, Mexico City is not the place to go for outdoor activities. Head to either coast, and enjoy the country's fabulous seashores.

SIGHTSEEING

Not to miss are the famous **National Museum of Anthropology, Museum of Modern Art,** and **Rufino Tamayo Museum** in family-filled **Chapúltepec Park.** In the **Centro Histórico** (Historic Center, or Downtown), you'll find the ruins of the **Templo Mayor** (spiritual center of the Aztecs) adjacent to the **Cathedral** and **National Palace** (containing murals by Diego Rivera, commissioned to celebrate Mexican culture and history), all facing the world's largest public square, the **Zócalo.** Popular with gays, the Centro Histórico has numerous places to explore, shop, and people-watch. It's worth a day's visit, starting at the Zócalo and meandering down **Avenida Cinco de Mayo** toward the **National Museum of Art** and its lovely plaza. Lunch at **Café Tacuba** (on Calle Tacuba) or **Los Girasoles** (in front of the museum's plaza) are recommended. Nearby **Alameda Park,** still a green space and vendor-filled after 400 years, is anchored by **Bellas Artes,** the Art Deco opera house and art gallery. (You'll find fabulous gifts in the museum shop and delicious food in its café.) In the south of the city lie **Coyoacán** and **San Angel,** once small villages. Coyoacán boasts the museum-homes of Leon Trotsky and Frida Kahlo, and in San Angel, art aficionados can visit the studio of Diego Rivera.

SHOPPING

The neighborhoods of Coyoacán and San Angel contain small boutiques, but those in search of native handicrafts should try to visit the **Plaza de San Jacinto** on a Saturday for the best open marketplace. The **Zona Rosa** offers stylish, upscale shopping—the Fifth Avenue of Mexico City.

GETTING OUT OF THE CITY

If you have time to travel to **Cuernavaca,** stay at **Nido de Amor** (private address; 011-52-73-18-0631), a guest home run by an American ex-patriot. Decorated throughout with Mexican artworks, suites are large, comfortable, and private. Conveniently located to the Zócalo and nightclub **Shadee** (Adolfo López Mateos; 73-12-4367), you can have a romantic visit here and enjoy scenic, colonial Cuernavaca. Don't forget to tour **Brady House,** museum-home of an eccentric gay heir to the Phelps Dodge fortune. Cuernavaca is a popular weekend retreat for residents of Mexico City, and also increasingly famous as a center of Spanish language studies. Touring sites outside of Mexico City should also include **Taxco, Puebla,** and the pyramids at **Teotihuacán.**

ACAPULCO

Acapulco is readily accessible to Mexico City, has a permanent population of between 1.5 and 2 million people, and has been a major resort for decades. The result is that it has a resident gay population that is accustomed to gay travelers. Unlike some of the other resorts in Mexico (Cancún, Puerto Vallarta), Acapulco's long history gives the city a little more character than the instant resorts. Its long history has also taken a toll on its popularity, with a large share of its glamorous gay devotees having moved on to new and different resorts. It is a bit sleazier than Puerto Vallarta, and no longer "happening," but still offers an affordable Pacific beach vacation and an established, accessible gay scene.

Unfortunately, addresses don't really mean a lot in Acapulco. Avenida Costera Miguel Alemán, more commonly known as "La Costera," is the main avenue running along the beach, but you won't find any addresses listed on its buildings. Even if you have numbers on the streets they don't go in any order. Buses are extremely cheap and offer a lot of atmosphere. If you go to the less touristy Pie de la Cuesta Beach for the afternoon you might get to ride with a pig.

Accommodations

THE FIESTA AMERICANA CONDESA ACAPULCO Costera Miguel Alemán 1220; 011-52-74-842355 or 800-223-2332, fax 011-52-74-841828; $135–155

A large luxury hotel towering over the gay beach. Each room has a private terrace and ocean view, with upper floors offering the best views. The pool has a spectacular view, and the hotel is very gay-popular because of its location.

QUALITY INN CALINDA BEACH Costera Miguel Alemán 1260; 011-52-74-840410 or 800-221-2222, fax 011-52-74-844676; $100–115

A more moderately priced option near the Fiesta Americana is this cylindrically shaped inn, with large, comfortable rooms and two pools.

LAS BRISAS 011-52-74-841580 or 800-223-6800, fax 011-52-74-842269; $150–540

A pink landmark, this self-contained luxury resort is built into the terraced hillside overlooking the bay. Most rooms feature their own private pool. If you don't mind (or prefer) being far removed from town, this is the place to stay.

Dining

Café Tres Amigos is a nice restaurant right off the zócalo, serving traditional Mexican food. (Once you're in the zócalo, ask someone where it is as the street address is useless.) The owners, a married couple, speak English and are gracious and friendly. The upscale, gay-owned **Le Bistroquet** (Andrea Doria 5; 74-846860; $10) serves international cuisine. The English-speaking staff is very friendly, and they have outdoor dining under an enormous rubber tree. They are located away from Condesa Beach toward Las Brisas. Another upscale gay-owned restaurant is **The Kookaburra** (Carretera Escénica, Marina Las Brisas; 74-841448 or 844418; $12), with a beautiful view of the bay, overlooking the wealthy Las Brisas section. Their cuisine is international with an okay wine list. **Madeiras** (Carretera Escénica 33; 74-844378; $35/prix fixe) is east of town near Las Brisas, serving elegant meals with a stunning view. Reservations are required for the fixed-price dinner, featuring Mexican and continental specialties. Another great view can be found at **Su Casa/La Margarita** (Avenida Anahuac 110; 74-844350; $10), on a hillside above the convention center. The margaritas are tops and the menu constantly changes, offering grilled fish, meats, and other lighter Mexican fare. **Jovitos** (on the Costera right across from the Fiesta Americana Condesa) offers tacos and other traditional Mexican fare. Be sure to try the vegetarian flautas, which are served with chips and about a dozen different chili sauces.

Nightlife

The best way to see all that Acapulco has to offer is to start your evening with dinner on the zócalo (the plaza around the cathedral). Wait until the sun goes down: This is when the locals come out and the temperature cools. Walk around the zócalo before dinner and you'll see a lot of locals and tourists on the make. Acapulco is very friendly and you don't need to worry about coming on to the wrong person. If the person isn't interested, you'll figure it out. The bars in Acapulco are all fairly close to each other. At many of them you'll be directed to sit at a table and a waiter will take your order. Tips are expected to be around 10 to 12%. Don't be a mark; always keep track of your tab, especially if you are buying drinks for new friends.

   Open House (74-847285) is located in the back of the Condesa Plaza complex right across the street from the Fiesta Americana Condesa. Keep walking up the sets of stairs until you see the sign or hear the music. Open House has a small dance floor that picks up about 11:00 P.M., but most people go there to meet local "working" boys and have a few drinks before moving on to the other discos. The strippers take everything off and, aroused, make their way through the crowd. This is customary in Acapulco. You'll be reminded that you aren't in Kansas anymore. On the other side of Condesa Plaza is **Bar La Malinche** (74-811147), which is accessible through a gate (sometimes closed) near Open House or from the street behind Condesa Plaza—Privada Piedra Picuda. La Malinche has strippers beginning around midnight, with a shower in the bar; if you are so inclined, you can shower with one of the strippers, providing entertainment for the entire bar. A disco is upstairs. On the same street as La Malinche (toward La Costera) is **Disco Demás** (74-841370), more of a dance club than Open House or La Malinche. Demás starts hopping around 1:00 A.M. It has a bar as well as cocktail tables and a nice dance floor with good sound and lights and high ceilings. It's located about a block from Open House and La Malinche, very near the landmark restaurant **Carlos 'n Charlie's,** and features strippers and female impersonators. Just a short walk along La

Costera on Lomas del Mar a few feet away from Denny's restaurant is **Relax** (74-840421), a wonderful dance club like Demás, only more intimate. It's the most American-feeling of the gay discos, and things keep hopping until the wee hours of the morning on busy nights. They sometimes have strippers and female impersonators. Downstairs is a quieter bar with erotic videos. If you're still going at 5:00 A.M., try the after-hours bars **Kos** and **Faces.** These places have cheaper drinks, attract a more mixed clientele (uh . . . say sailors, drag queens, *mallates*, and straights). Ask someone at one of the gay bars how to get there.

Activities

ATHLETIC AND OUTDOOR

Condesa Beach (right by the Condesa Fiesta Americana Hotel) is the gay beach. You can rent a *palapa* for 10 to 20 pesos, have lunch, drink, sleep, and watch the crowd go by. During busy periods it sometimes becomes necessary to reserve a palapa in advance. The rocks down by the beach are a place where gay tourists and locals meet right after sundown. Most of the **parasailing** operators work right on Condesa Beach. If you want to go deep-sea fishing, book your trip with the **Boat Cooperative** (74-821099), located in a pale pink building opposite the zócalo. You'll save about $50 over booking through a travel agent.

SIGHTSEEING

The famed **Acapulco cliff divers** dive at 12:45 P.M., and at half-past the hour from 7:30 to 10:30 P.M. Follow (climb) Calzada la Quebrada about 15 minutes from the zócalo. Arrive early for a good position (pay the $1.50 to use the viewing platform), or watch from the bar ($10 drink minimum) or restaurant ($35 buffet, reservations recommended) at the **Playa Las Glorias Hotel** (Quebrada 74; 74-831155).

SHOPPING

Acapulco has limited shopping opportunities. The **Costera Alemán** is lined with clothing boutiques that sometimes have good deals on lightweight sportswear. The **Mercado Parazal** or **Mercado de Artesanías** (Calle Velásquez de León near Cinco de Mayo) is a large crafts market open daily. You'll need to walk away from most purchases to get down to a final price.

CANCÚN

It was not long ago that Cancún was just a small island with a minor fishing village nearby, although there are few reminders of that today. In the early 1970s, the Mexican government conducted a study to find the best location for a modern planned tourist resort. The government began building the first hotel in 1974, and the construction hasn't stopped since. Cancún was designed for tourists, Americans specifically, and you'll find them here in droves. With incredibly cheap charter packages and a lower drinking age than most of the United States, Cancún attracts a disappointingly disproportionate number of drunken teenagers and rowdy spring breakers looking for trouble. Nonetheless, Cancún is tourist-friendly (if not gay-friendly), has 12 miles of sandy beaches, and is ideally situated for excursions to fantastic Maya ruins. Cancún consists of the city (Ciudad Cancún) and the hotel zone (Zona Hotelera). The hotel zone is essentially a sandy Caribbean island, separated from the mainland by a lagoon and connected by a causeway. The island has one main street, Kukulcán Boulevard (Paseo Kukulcán), lined with moderate to luxury beach resorts, one after another. There is no undeveloped beachfront, but since all of the beaches are public, you do not need to be a hotel guest to use them. There is not an appreciable gay presence here. And while Cancún is not particularly homophobic, it is not the place to go if a gay scene or nightlife are at all important to you. Crime is not a big problem, but don't flash around a lot of cash or jewelry (leave that tiara at home). Come for the virtually guaranteed good weather, remarkably affordable air/hotel packages, and nearby ruins, and you won't be disappointed.

Accommodations

Cancún has an overabundance of new hotels, sprawling complexes with glistening pools and modern amenities. While prices here are the highest in Mexico, they are inexpensive by Caribbean standards, and many budget choices exist, particularly in town.

THE RITZ-CARLTON Paseo Kukulcán; 011-52-98-85-0808; $260–515
Cancún's first superluxurious, AAA Five-Diamond resort.

THE MELIÁ CANCÚN Paseo Kukulcán; 011-52-98-85-1114 or 800-336-3542, fax 011-52-98-85-1263; $190–365
Glamorous and huge.

CAMINO REAL Paseo Kukulcán; 011-52-98-83-0100 or 800-722-6466, fax 011-52-98-83-1730; $110–215
Old but not faded, surrounded by water on 3 sides.

CLUB MED Paseo Kukulcán; 011-52-98-85-2300 or 800-CLUB-MED, fax 011-52-98-85-2290; $130–175/person
The all-inclusive Club Med is as close to secluded as one can get here (when it was built, there was not another hotel in sight).

HOTEL ANTILLANO Claveles 37; 011-52-98-84-1532, fax 011-52-98-84-1878; $35–50
Located downtown, this hotel is a good value, with a pool, across from the Rosa Mexicana restaurant.

HOTEL AMERICA CANCÚN Avenida Tulum y Brisa; 011-52-98-84-7500 or 800-44-UTELL, fax 011-52-98-84-1953; $55–80
Has a pool, rooms with terraces, and its own beach shuttle.

PLAYA DEL SOL Avenida Yaxchilán 31; 011-52-98-84-3690; $65–95
This hotel also has its own beach shuttle. It's a more intimate place with a Mexican flavor.

Dining

Dining in the Zona Hotelera is a testament to American franchising. Denny's, Taco Bell, McDonald's, the Hard Rock Café, and the very popular Planet Hollywood are all here. The hotel restaurants offer an array of good dining—most notable are **Blue Bayou** (Hyatt Cancún Caribe, Paseo Kukulcán; 011-52-98-83-0044; $25/meal), featuring Cajun and Creole cuisine in a lush tropical environment, and **Bogart's** (Hotel Krystal Cancún, Paseo Kukulcán; 011-52-98-83-1133; $35/meal), serving international cuisine in Moroccan surroundings. **El Caribeño** (Presidente Inter-Continental Hotel; Paseo Kukulcán; 011-52-98-83-0200; $10) has a spectacular breakfast buffet, right on the beach with a great view of the water. Cancún City offers good Mexican food and less expensive prices than the hotel zone. The restaurants along Avenida Yaxchilán seem less touristy than the ones on Avenida Tulum. Most have menus posted and a friendly employee outside to entice you in. Walk around and check out a few before making a choice. **100% Natural** (6 Sunyaxchen; 011-52-98-84-1617; $7) serves salads, sandwiches, and fresh fruit shakes in a tiled-floor, open-porch California environment. **Super Deli** (Avenida Tulum at Xcaret; 011-52-98-84-1412; $6) is a takeout and sit-down deli with all of the American favorites. Two favorites you may want to return to more than once are **El Pescador** (Tulipanes 28; 011-52-98-84-2673; $15) serving great seafood, as well as Mexican specialties. Be prepared for a short wait. **La Dolce Vita** (Avenida Cobá 87; 011-52-98-84-1384; $17) has a great Italian menu and a casually elegant atmosphere. Cancún also has some international fine dining options. **Maxime** (Paseo Kukulcán; 011-52-98-83-0704; $16) is an elegant former mayor's home serving continental cuisine; jackets optional, shorts and sandals not permitted.

Nightlife

Cancún had one gay club at press time—**Picante** (Plaza Galerías, 20 Avenida Tulum), with a nice though small dance floor. It is located in the Plaza Galerías on Avenida Tulum past the bus station and close to McDonald's (you *do* deserve a break today!). Take a cab there the first time—they all know where it is. And while the gay nightlife in Cancún is nothing to write home about, the straight clubs are not all exclusively straight either. Though you might be a bit confused, you'll find some of them can be fun. The **Parque de las Palapas,** near the Cine Blanquita, is a popular meeting place. It is the place to go to hook up with locals and find out the most current nightlife information. Look for a copy of *Gay Cancún Info-Notes*. It is available at bars and in a number of languages.

Activities

ATHLETIC AND OUTDOOR

The beach and related sports activities are the prime activities here. Although there is no specifically gay beach, local gays recommend the **Mirador,** a long and strikingly beautiful stretch of beach almost at the end of the Hotel Zone, across from the Ruinas del Rey. The beach at Club Med is great, but don't stray into the resort, as you will promptly be escorted off. The beach in front of the sprawling Sheraton Hotel is popular with Americans, and you are less likely to be chased away for jumping in their pool. **Playa Chac Mool** is popular with local families because the water is calmer here than elsewhere. Scuba diving, sailing, deep-sea fishing, and snorkeling can be arranged at any number of sports centers or any of the major hotels. Golf at the Robert Trent Jones–designed **Pok-Ta-Pok** (011-52-98-83-0871) features a stunning setting and its own restored Mayan ruin. A number of the hotels have workout facilities, but for the fitness fanatic, there is **Gold's Gym** (Plaza Flamingo, Avenida Kuk; 011-52-98-83-2933) right in the Hotel Zone.

SIGHTSEEING

People watching along the streets in town is great fun. Try Avenida Tulum or Yaxchilán in the early or late evening. Walk down the west side, not the Town Hall side. Bullfights, for those who don't find them repugnant, happen every Wednesday at the Plaza de Toros.

SHOPPING

Along with the sleek hotels, Cancún is home to a number of sophisticated shopping malls—air-conditioned retreats from *la playa*. Avenida
Tulum downtown is also lined with stores. If you're adventurous and/or
thrifty, try exploring the side streets, or the malls down Avenida Tulum
about a mile past the bus station. Here the prices are even lower, and
the clientele is less touristy and more local. Though the area is more
authentic, it is also less safe, so don't stray too far. Even in the touristy
shops, you can find good deals on handwoven rugs, hammocks, and
varied handicrafts, in addition to tacky T-shirts and souvenirs. The
Plaza Mexico (Avenida Tulum) is a mall specializing in Mexican handicrafts. More of the same can be found in Cancún's two crafts markets,
Coral Negro, next to the Convention Center and **Ki Huic** (Avenida
Tulum) downtown. Another market, **Plaza Garibaldi** (Uxmal South
and Avenida Tulum) has tablecloths, clothing, and the like. Be wary of
poor quality and be sure to bargain in the markets. Stall merchants may
quote prices marked up 300% if you appear an easy target.

SIGHTSEEING

Cancún can serve as a base for many day trips or short excursions. The
choices fall primarily into two categories: other beaches that are less
crowded/expensive than Cancún; and magnificent Mayan ruins inland.
They can be organized through your hotel, a Cancún travel agency, or
you can take the local buses. **Chichén Itzá** is located about 125 miles
from Cancún and offers stunning ruins of what was a major Mayan metropolis in the seventh and eighth centuries. It is by far the most popular excursion from Cancún and is a place that you will not soon forget. Be prepared for very hot and humid weather even in winter and
dress for a lot of walking and climbing. If you climb up the high pyra-
mid, you have to be able to come down too. **Cozumel,** Mexico's largest
island, is about 40 minutes from Cancún and can be reached by ferry
from Playa del Carmen on the mainland or by plane from Cancún airport. Once a sacred Mayan site, Cozumel was developed as a tourist
destination before Cancún but is still undeveloped and features large
nature reserves. There are a few Mayan ruins spread throughout the island. The calmest waters are found on the island's west side. There are

only a few beaches. The most beautiful for swimming or snorkeling are **Chancanaab Lagoon** and **Playa San Francisco.** If you spend more than a day here, a rental car or the more popular moped is recommended, because there are no buses outside of the island's only town. Taxis are available and can take you everywhere; everything in town is within easy walking distance. **Isla Mujeres** (Island of Women) is a quiet getaway about 10 miles from Cancún. Ferries depart from Puerto Juárez right outside of Cancún. There are both a passenger and a car ferry. Prices are lower here than in Cancún, with hotel costs running moderate to cheap. **Tulum** (City of Dawn), located 80 miles from Cancún, attracts herds of tour buses from Cancún by midday. The ruins, perched on a cliff overlooking beautiful beaches and clear water, were the first Mayan structure sighted by the Spanish in the sixteenth century. Tulum is thought to have been a trading center. Consider an overnight stay for the tranquility this site affords once the tour buses go home. There is none of the development of Cancún here. Tulum has only a few small hotels scattered near the ruins and along the beach. Accommodations are basic. The stars at night are so bright, you almost need sunglasses.

PUERTO VALLARTA

Located on the Pacific coast side of Mexico, inside the Bay of Banderas, Mexico's largest bay, Puerto Vallarta, or Vallarta as those "in the know" call it (and never PV!), was discovered in 1541, but wasn't on the tourist map until Elizabeth Taylor-Hilton-Wilding-Todd-Fisher carried on a scandalous affair with Richard Burton during the filming of John Huston's *Night of the Iguana,* which was shot south of town in Mismaloya. This 28-mile stretch of near-white sand beaches and deep-blue water became famous as the backdrop to the film and romance.

Although the town has been greatly developed, there is still some native charm to be found in the cobblestone streets and red-tiled roofs of the Mismaloya area 20 minutes south of downtown. Wandering through Old Vallarta, down the breezy malecón to the lively zócalo along the seafront drive, Paseo Díaz Ordaz, you can fall in love with this magical resort town.

Accommodations

Doin' It Right Travel (415-621-3576 or 800-936-DOIN, fax 415-621-3576) out of San Francisco is a good source for hotel and villa bookings, specializing in gay-owned villas. They are the exclusive reservation agents for the first two hotels listed.

PACO PACO DESCANSO DEL SOL Pino Suárez 583; 322-30277; fax 322-26767; $40–120

A gay-exclusive (mostly men) 24-room hotel, managed by Paco and David of the Club Paco Paco, it features rooms and multiroom suites, a rooftop pool and bar, and 24-hour front desk. All rooms have ocean or jungle views, TV, and phone; some have kitchen facilities. There's no elevator—be prepared for stairs.

VALLARTA CORA Calle Pilitas 174; 322-26058; $45

A gay-exclusive hotel/apartment in Vallarta, it is one-half block behind the Tropicana Hotel and beach, just a few blocks to Blue Chairs (the gay beach). It has 15 rooms on four floors (no elevator), all one-bedroom, 1 1/2 bath suites with equipped kitchens, but no TVs, phones, or ocean views. It is rustic though newly painted and has a clothing-optional pool.

VILLA FELIZ B&B 011-52-322-20798 or 714-752-5464 ext. 277; $60–95

A wonderful, exclusively gay B&B with five very clean rooms, a pool, and bar. Hosts are very service oriented, and unobtrusive. It is located up on the hill in Conchas Chinas.

CASA PANORÁMICA B&B Carretera Mismaloya; 011-52-322-23656 or 800-745-7805; $75–98

A heavily advertised B&B with a mixed clientele, it has seven guest rooms on five levels, four separate dining areas, two outdoor bars, and a dipping pool. Although it is an impressive villa, it requires a good deal of steep step climbing, and we have heard reports of poor upkeep and management.

LOS CUATRO VIENTOS Matamoros 520; 011-52-322-20161, fax 011-52-322-22831; $45

A cheerful budget property, catering to a mixed straight/gay clientele with rooms decorated with Mexican furnishings and crafts. The rooftop sundeck has a view of the city. Located five steep blocks from the central plaza, the hotel runs several week-long women's getaways each year.

BEL AIR RESORT Pelicanos 311, Marina Vallarta; 011-52-5-322-10800 or 800-457-7676, fax 011-52-5-322-10801; $135–290

A deluxe resort, with rooms, villas, and a pool set on a golf course. The villas each have private pools, and use of a beach club is provided for all guests.

CAMINO REAL Playa de las Estacas; 011-52-322-15000 or 800-722-6466, fax 011-52-322-16000; $130–210

A large hotel relatively close to the gay beach (2 miles south of town), set on its own beach cove and offering some sense of exclusivity. Two pools, lighted tennis courts, and seven restaurants and bars round out the facilities.

Dining

Many of these restaurants are gay-owned, but not everyone is "out." Puerto Vallarta has a good number of upscale dining establishments. **Café des Artistes** (Guadalupe Sánchez 740; 011-52-322-23228; $18) ranks for us as the best restaurant in town. Great décor and a French menu with Mexican touches makes this a unique experience. **Bombo's** (Matamoros 327 at Corona; 011-52-322-25164) is a great spot for seafood, featuring gourmet dining, bay views, and tableside cooking. **El Palomar de los Gonzáles** (Aguacate 425; 011-52-322-20795; $20) serves up one of the most spectacular views in all of Vallarta. Expensive and hard to find, but worth the effort for its seafood and Mexican cuisine, and elegant, romantic setting. **Le Bistro** (Isla Río Cuale 16-A; 011-52-322-20283; $14) is also worth the expense for its international cuisine, romantic Art Deco dining on an island in the middle of the River Cuale at the old (upper) bridge. **Quiza** (Isla Río Cuale Locale 3; 011-52-322-25646) is under the same ownership and across the street from Le Bistro, and features pasta, steak, seafood, chicken, ribs, and live jazz with dinner, harp and flute music with lunch. **Chef Roger** (Avenida Rodríguez 267; 011-52-322-25900; $11), at the entrance to

Old Town, serves continental cuisine on an outdoor balcony or in the lovely indoor dining room. Puerto Vallarta also has plenty of casual restaurants to choose from. **Adobe Café** (Basilo Badillo 252; 011-52-322-26720 or 322-31925; $10) serves good chicken, beef, and Mexican dishes, with Southwestern-style décor and more moderate prices. **La Palapa** (Amapas at Pulpito; $7) serves up some of best seafood in town with daily drink special and great music on beach. **Night of the Iguana Palapa** (across from La Jolla de la Mismaloya Hotel; $7) or *La Noche de la Iguana,* is our favorite beach palapa, closest to the river at Mismaloya. If you stayed too long at the fair, catch all-day breakfast at **Memo's Pancake House** (Basilo Badillo 289; 011-52-322-26272; $4). Make your own tacos at **Mama Mias** (Díaz Ordaz 840 at Basilo Badillo; no phone; $5), which features live South American music nightly. **De' Claire's** (Basilo Badia 269) is a great place for breakfast or lunch, serving great pizza and fantastic pastries, with dining in the garden.

Nightlife

Bar hopping is *the* thing to do, and you have four spots to choose from! Every club has stripper shows, and some have drag shows on the weekend. Be forewarned—most bars have straight employees. **Los Balcones** (Avenida Juárez 182 at Libertad; 011-52-322-24671) is the most popular with tourists, with a West-Hollywoodish atmosphere. If you get there early enough, snag a balcony table—there are only three. **Club Paco Paco** (Ignacio L. Vallarta 278; 011-52-322-21899) attracts more of a mixed tourist/local crowd than Los Balcones, with the locals out after midnight. Its new, bigger location is proving to be very popular. Downstairs is more upscale, with dancing; upstairs has a pool table and video games. It also attracts more women than other clubs. **Zotano** (Morelos 101 Plaza Rio, north of bridge) is a club in a basement with an undergroundish feel, playing more "alternative music" to a mixed gay/straight crowd. You can enjoy the sunset during happy hour at **Hotel Paco Paco Descanso del Sol** (see Accommodations), featuring free hors d'oeuvres (6:00 to 9:00 P.M.) at their rooftop pool/bar.

Activities

ATHLETIC AND OUTDOOR

The gay beach is known as **Blue Chairs** because of the blue chairs there. Locals and tourists come together on this section of Playa de los Muertos in front of the Vallarta Beach Hotel, near El Dorado Condos. **Amadeus Tours** (Mario; 011-52-322-32815) is a gay-run company offering a number of tours, some seasonal. They include a **Gay Day Bay Cruise** ($45), with snorkeling equipment, continental breakfast, lunch, light dinner, open "national" bar, and trip to a deserted beach. **Jungle horseback riding** ($25/3 hours), **scuba diving** ($50/tank) on Fridays, and a **Sunset Bay Cruise** ($30) on Saturday. These all-gay tours are based on a minimum number of participants and space is limited. Book early, as they are often sold out, or canceled. Mario has an office at the Vallarta Cora Hotel, but you'll also find him at bars and the beach promoting his tours. Club Paco Paco runs a **Gay Evening Hot Springs BBQ;** ask at the club for schedule information. **Mountain Bike Tours** (Badillo 381; 011-52-322-20080) is a mainstream operator offering trips to outlying areas.

SIGHTSEEING

The Taylor-Hilton-Wilding-Todd-Fisher–Burton villa **Casa Kimberly** (Calle Zaragoza 445; 011-52-322-21336) can be toured for $5.

SHOPPING

Although the prices are usually higher here than in other parts of Mexico, Puerto Vallarta has an excellent selection of indigenous merchandise. The **Mercado** (Libertad and Avenida Rodríguez) sells crafts and T-shirts. You'll find great Mexican blown glass at **La Rosa de Cristal Vidrio Soplado Artesanías** (Insurgentes 272; 011-52-322-25698). The **Olinala Gallery** (Cárdenas 274; 011-52-322-24995) is the best place for high-quality crafts and folk art.

OTHER PACIFIC COAST DESTINATIONS

One of the Pacific coast's most famous resorts is **Las Hadas** (Santiago Peninsula; 011-52-333-30000 or 800-722-6466, fax 011-52-333-41950; $182–420) in **Manzanillo.** You may remember it from the Bo Derek movie *10.* Situated on a peninsula facing the sunrise, it is quite lovely and somewhat gay-popular. By late afternoon, the air begins to cool comfortably as the sun disappears. Just over the hill from Las Hadas is the little-known **Villas La Leyenda** (Club de Yates 12; 011-52-333-30281 or 800-232-VIVA, fax 011-52-333-40924). Its spacious, exclusive villa setting features large, stylish suites complete with kitchens, gay hospitality, and indulgent tropical surroundings. You can tan on your own terrace, share a drink under the palapa, or snuggle in the Jacuzzi. If you're seeking a more bohemian beach retreat, escape to **Zipolite.** Its location, in the southern state of Oaxaca (between, and less than 100 km from, either Huatulco or Puerto Escondido), is popular because it is more unspoiled than Acapulco or Puerto Vallarta. If you like inexpensive beer, can live on fresh seafood and local beef, and enjoy restful starry nights, you are sure to like Zipolite. You'll find many gays here, Mexicans as well as Europeans, indulging in the freedom of the local nudist beaches.

FYI

The **Mexico Tourist Board** (800-44-MEXICO) has a hotline for general information and tourist brochures. For more complicated inquiries, local tourist offices may be more helpful. New York: 212-755-7261; Chicago: 312-565-2778; Los Angeles: 310-203-8191; Houston: 713-880-5153; Miami: 305-443-9160.

If you're interested in traveling with a group, **Doin' It Right Travel** (see Accommodations) runs several small group departures. **Club RSVP** (800-328-RSVP) calls Puerto Vallarta's Royal Maeva resort home, chartering the resort by the week; call for schedule information.

Costa Rica

The buzz about Costa Rica gets louder all the time. This little strip of Central America was scarcely mentioned as little as ten years ago. Suddenly the eco-traveler set began talking. And before you knew it, Costa Rica seemed to be on the itinerary of every adventurous gay traveler looking for someplace new. How could a place become so hot in such a short time? Could Costa Rica really be gay paradise found? In a word, yes. Costa Rica is everything a gay traveler could desire: extraordinary physical beauty, biodiversity rivaled by few places on earth, a surprisingly well-developed tourist infrastructure, friendlier people than you thought existed (outside of the Magic Kingdom), and a gay scene in San José that is lively, sexy, and tons of fun. In this compact little land you will see rain forests, cloud forests, active volcanoes, white water rivers, beaches, mountains, and an amazing wealth of plant, insect and animal life. All you need to pack is a sense of adventure and a love of natural beauty.

SWITZERLAND IN CENTRAL AMERICA

Costa Rica's proudly touted lack of any armed forces and its neutrality in a part of the world often known for thugs, political upheaval, and worse have earned it the nickname "Switzerland of Central America." But this name could just as easily derive from its physical beauty. Drive 20 minutes from the center of San José and you're in lush hills and valleys once covered with forest but now harvested for crops or grazed upon by dairy cows, sheep and goats. You might think you're in the Alps, but take a closer look at the beautiful scenes in front of you and you'll see that the crops are coffee, bananas, and pineapples. The signs are in Spanish. The smiling faces are that special Latin American mix of Indian, European, African, and Caribbean. And you know that Switzerland doesn't have so many different birds and butterflies. Costa Rica was discovered by Columbus during his fourth visit to the Americas. Though he named it Costa Rica or "rich coast," the Spaniards pretty much abandoned the land because it had too small an indigenous population to exploit (for labor) or convert (to Catholicism). Gaining its independence in 1821, and realizing relative economic prosperity through harvesting coffee and bananas, Costa Rica has entered its true golden age in the 1990s by recognizing perhaps its greatest asset—its physical beauty.

The hardest part about planning a trip to Costa Rica is choosing which of its treasures to squeeze into your limited vacation time (unless, of course, you're planning to join the growing flow of ex-pats who have moved there for good). Ideally, allot two full weeks for your trip. If that's not possible, you can still take a wonderful "best of Costa Rica" tour in seven to ten days. Using a map and our suggested highlights, you're on your way. After deciding what you want to see and do, you must decide how to structure your vacation. There are basically three different ways. First, you can take an organized tour, in which your itinerary will be preplanned to include many highlights and most lodging and transportation arrangements. The second way to structure your trip is to base yourself in the capital of San José and take day trips (or longer) out of town using one of several tour companies you can book in advance or through your hotel when you arrive. Your hotel will have relationships with reliable outfitters, and you can generally feel confident with its arrangements. This option has the advantage of letting you keep one base while exploring the diversity of Costa Rica, most of which is within fairly easy reach of San José. The third option, and the best if you are a true adventurer, is to rent a four-wheel drive and explore the country yourself. You will get a thorough feel for the land, stay in many terrific places, and really get to know the people. The breadth of choices for a trip to Costa Rica is overwhelming, which you will learn as soon as you open any guidebook. Its geography simply offers too many wonderful choices. Our recommendation for your first trip to Costa Rica includes a short visit to **San José** (mostly to meet the *Ticos* and sample their wonderful gay nightlife); an overnight visit to the **Arenal Volcano,** exploring and hiking through a **cloud forest and/or rain forest;** a few days on the beaches of **Manuel Antonio National Park;** a couple of days exploring **Tortuguero;** and a day of **white water rafting.** Should you have more time, consult one of our recommended guidebooks to help you choose among the many options.

When to Go and How to Get There

Only 10 degrees north of the equator, Costa Rica has a dozen climate zones, with little variation from the average temperature of 72 degrees, except on the coasts where it can be hotter, and on the mountain tops, where cooler air prevails year round. Travel to Costa Rica during its wet (or "green") season of May to mid-November offers the advantage of lower prices, fewer crowds, and more natural adventuring through the country's ecostructure. Even in the rainy season the mornings are usually bright and clear, with a shower in the afternoon and heavier rains at night. The best weather is from Christmas through Easter, but there are some exceptions and variation between the coasts. In general, here's what you can expect: **Pacific Coast:** November–April, dry; May–June, rain; July, Indian summer; late August–November, heavy rain. **Caribbean Coast:** November–March, slight rain; April–July, heavy rain; August–September, heavy to slight rain; October, dry. The bottom line is: prepare to get wet, and you'll have a great time.

All international flights arrive and depart San José airport, with most direct service through Miami. Lasca, American Airlines and Continental (via Houston) are the primary carriers. You'll often find better rates and availability booking through the tour operators and travel arrangers listed below.

FYI

Two highly recommended gay-run group tour operators are **Toto Tours** and **Mariah Wilderness Expeditions** (See Organized Gay Cruise, Tour, and Resort-Based Vacations chapter) which offer several trips a year. More mainstream tour companies than we can list here offer Costa Rica tours. Some reputable ones include **Mountain Travel-Sobek** (800-227-2384 or 510-527-8100), and **Overseas Adventure Travel** (800-221-0814). If you're planning an independent trip, **Southern Horizons Travel** (800-333-9361 or 818-980-7011), **Costa Rica Connection** (800-345-7422 or 805-543-8823), and **Steppingstone** (800-874-8484) can help you. For the best rates, rent your car before you head to Costa Rica. Try **National Interrent** (800-227-7368), which has easy airport pickup.

Many excellent guidebooks are devoted solely to exploring Costa Rica. Among the best are *The Costa Rica Traveler* by Ellen Searby, and Lonely Planet's *Costa Rica Travel Survival Kit,* both extensive in their coverage of every corner of the country; *Frommer's Costa Rica,* which provides excellent coverage of the highlights, and solid hotel and restaurant recommendations; *Hidden Costa Rica* (Ulysses Press) and *The Essential Road Guide for Costa Rica,* which is helpful if you plan to drive yourself. There is a gay/lesbian guide to Costa Rica called *Pura Vida,* by Joseph Itiel. The phrase literally translates to "pure life" and is used to mean "far out" or "awesome." Unfortunately, the book is anything but. It reads more as tedious stories of the author's own extended stay in Costa Rica, and if you don't share his proclivities, you're unlikely to find it very useful.

SAN JOSÉ

Accommodations

It's no surprise that you've never seen a San José hotel on a World's 10 Best list. There simply are no world-class accommodations in Costa Rica's capital. But there are several very good options, including two that are gay-owned and -operated. If you expect to bring "new friends" back to your room, be sure to check hotel policies on unregistered guests at time of booking. San José addresses are denoted by indicating the location on the grid of interlocking avenidas and calles. Any taxi driver will know how to get to most of the places listed below, or will be able to call in for directions. San José has two gay-run, gay-popular choices:

COLOURS GUEST RESIDENCE 800-277-4825, fax 305-534-0362; $70–109

Located a quick ten-minute/$4 cab ride from the center of San José, Colours features comfortable rooms (shared or private bath), a beautiful swimming pool, delicious daily breakfast and afternoon cocktails, and one of the friendliest, most in-the-know staffs you'll find. If you plan to base yourself in San José for several days, Colours is an excellent choice and a great way to tap into local gay and lesbian life. The slightly out-of-the-way location is not really a drawback, as it provides a quieter location than most city center hotels and is an easy back and forth trip.

JOLUVA GUESTHOUSE Calle 3b, between Aves. 9 and 11; 800-298-2418; $18–$45

This in-town spot provides a far more spartan accommodation than Colours. The rooms and common space are fairly basic. What it offers is a central location within walking distance of most sights, restaurants, and clubs and a friendly management that will help you find your way. Clientele is gay women and men; breakfast is included.

The Barrio Amon is one of downtown San José's nicest areas, featuring many old mansions and within easy walking distance of major sights. A number of lodging options here are recommendable.

TAYLOR'S INN 011-506-257-4333, fax 011-506-221-1475; $60.

A comfortable, quiet, historic inn featuring ten double rooms surrounding a central interior courtyard; rates include breakfast.

THE BRITANNIA 011-506-223-6667, fax 011-506-223-6411; $85–$108

A classical Victorian mansion, with a quiet, turn-of-the-century atmosphere. The rooms are modern, though, and feel more like a business hotel than a small inn; rates include breakfast.

AMSTEL AMON 800-575-1253, fax 011-506-257-0284; $105

One of the nicest larger hotels in San José. Unlike some of the older, center-of-town hotels, which are showing their age, the Amstel Amon boasts very modern rooms, a friendly and efficient staff, and a quiet location.

DON CARLOS 011-506-221-6707, fax 011-506-255-0828; $50–60

A charming property with a feeling of old San José. Three colonial homes were combined to create a lovely space, featuring clean, spacious rooms, live music in the lobby and (don't laugh) one of the best souvenir stores in San José. A real find, it's refreshingly quiet and rates include breakfast.

L'AMBIANCE 011-506-222-6702, fax 011-506-223-0481; $90

On a quiet street near the center of town, this is one of the most luxurious spots there. It's built in a restored colonial building, featuring tiled floors and a lovely central courtyard—you can't go wrong here.

There are several choices for those desiring a complete resort as their base for a Costa Rica visit. While farther from San José's center, these resorts offer swimming pools, gardens, and more spacious grounds for relaxation. Both of the choices listed below are located between the airport and downtown San José

CARIARI HOTEL & COUNTRY CLUB 800-227-4274, fax 011-506-239-2803; $125–165

This large resort complex is a good choice for golfers.

HOTEL HERRADURA 011-506-239-0033, fax 011-506-239-2292; $125–180

With over 250 rooms, this resort is known for its attentive staff and beautiful landscaping.

Dining

Though Costa Rica is not known for gourmet cuisine, San José offers many excellent and affordable eateries. Service is included in virtually all restaurant tabs, and tipping is not the custom in most circumstances (taxis, hotels, etc.). Many establishments in Costa Rica note that their water is safe to drink, but we strongly suggest (as always when traveling south of the border) to stick to bottled water and drink lots of liquids. The culinary stars of Costa Rican cooking are its seafood and beef dishes, and they are usually simply prepared.

Cocina de Lena (011-506-255-1360; $12) is an excellent choice for well-prepared, typical Costa Rican foods. It is located in the **El Puebla** area, a stomping ground of upscale restaurants, shopping, and nightlife frequented by wealthier Costa Rican locals and ex-pats. **Luka's** (011-

506-233-8145; $13) is also in El Puebla, and known for its high-quality steaks and seafood. **Hotel Grano de Oro** (011-506-255-3322; $13), located in the B&B that carries its name, excels in adding inventive touches to typical Costa Rican dishes. **Nimbe** (011-506-281-173; $12) is in the well-to-do suburb of Escazu, a ten-minute drive from town. Built in a historic colonial home, the food offers an excellent and wide range of international specialties, many featuring seafood. **Café de Teatro Nacional** (011-506-223-4488), located in the lobby of the Teatro Nacional, is a quiet, sophisticated spot for lunch, coffee, and people-watching. **Vishnu Vegetarian Restaurant** (Avenida 1, between calles 3 and 1; $5) is bustling with locals and features excellent, affordable choices.

Nightlife

Perhaps the greatest treat in San José is the nightlife, which is unsurprisingly lively but quite surprisingly gay. There are several terrific clubs that will keep you very entertained and bring you in close touch with the wonderful tico/tica spirit. (*Tico*, by the way, is the way natives refer to themselves. It derives from their unique dialectic use of "tico/tica" for diminutive descriptions.) **Déjà Vu** (Calle 2, between avenidas 14 and 16) is San José's most American-style club. The music tends toward U.S./U.K. dance club hits and features male strippers (Friday nights), two dance floors, flashing lights and all-you-can-drink beer on Friday and Saturday nights. By U.S. standards, Déjà Vu is decidedly low tech, but everyone always seems to be having a great time here. **La Avispa,** "The Wasp" (Calle 1, between avenidas 8 and 10) is a terrific Latino dance club that you really must visit. It is especially popular on Sunday afternoons and evenings (starting at 5:30), Tuesdays (10 P.M.–2 A.M.) and Saturday nights from 9. The club has two large dance areas, featuring predominantly Latin music and an infectious energy generated by gay and lesbian couples. Upstairs are a huge video screen, pool table, and sitting area. You can have a good time here participating or just watching. Other clubs/bars worth considering are **Los Cuchorones** (Calle 6, between avenidas Central and Primera), also featuring Latin music and dancing, with a more down and dirty crowd (best Wednesday through Sunday), or **La Taberna** (Avenida 9, between calles Central and 1), a local bar drawing young Costa Rican professionals who all seem to know one another but are happy to see a new face (best on Mondays and weekends).

Activities

ATHLETIC AND OUTDOOR

Ojo de Agua is a swimming resort on the outskirts of San José which attracts many local gays and can be cruisy. If you have free time in San José and want some sun and a pool, give it a try. Finally, if you are a real daredevil, try **bungee jumping,** arranged by **Tropical Bungee** (011-506-233-6455; $45 for first jump, $25 for second). The jump location, about 20 minutes out of San José, is awesome, and just watching is a thrill.

SIGHTSEEING

Some traditional sightseeing exists in San José, but it is limited. Accept right from the start that San José is not one of Latin America's most beautiful cities. There is little in the way of glorious architecture or rich history—Costa Rica was neither a major colonial capital nor home to a rich pre-Columbian culture, and earthquakes through the ages have felled many of the more notable buildings. The most beautiful part of San José is its setting, surrounded by lush mountains, easily viewed over the (mostly) one- and two-story buildings. Still, San José offers a number of worthy tourist sights, most of which you could manage in a single day. You might want to check out the **Gold Museum,** housing the Americas' largest collection of pre-Columbian gold jewelry; the **Serpentarium,** one of several nearby butterfly gardens; the **Teatro Nacional** (the glorious national opera house, offering performances most nights); and the **Central Market,** with its bustling trade of foods, spices, home goods and other of life's necessities. A short trip (14 miles) to neighboring **Cartago** is well worth the time, as the town boasts lovely gardens and churches, most notably its **Basilica,** perhaps the most beautiful church edifice in Costa Rica.

SHOPPING

Colombian emeralds brought in duty free and set in gold are an excellent buy in San José, as are 18k reproductions of pre-Columbian and Aztec gold items. The **Emerald House** on the Irazú Highway is an excellent and reliable source. Also outstanding is the leather of **Del Río,** whose products, exported under a number of couture labels, are available in their several shops in tourist areas, or direct from the factory (call to arrange a visit: 011-506-238-2881) at a 50% discount.

MANUEL ANTONIO NATIONAL PARK (AND NEARBY TOWN OF QUEPOS):

Accommodations

Accommodations near Manuel Antonio National Park are plentiful and surprisingly good, with many new properties constructed during the past two to three years. The majority of hotels are built high in the jungle on the road connecting Quepos (the main town near the park) and the entrance to the park. This three-mile road winds through the jungle several hundred feet above the ocean, affording many of the properties' spectacular views. Get one if you can. All properties listed below are marked with signs, as there are no numbered addresses. We feel comfortable recommending each of them, both in terms of quality and gay friendliness. [Note: All properties listed have swimming pools and all rates include breakfast.]

SÍ COMO NO 011-506-777-1250 or 800-237-8201, fax 011-506-777-1250; **$85–210**

Recently built by a former Disney exec, with obvious loving care and a keen appreciation for the nature surrounding it. This place is tops. Rooms have fabulous views, are beautifully decorated with jungle patterns, and are immersed in lush grounds with pool and Jacuzzi.

MAKANDA BY THE SEA 011-506-777-0442, fax 011-506-777-1032; $85–125

A terrific property, with seven rooms, each a beauty. It is surrounded by dense jungle, yet each room provides excellent views. One of the prettiest pools and Jacuzzis we've seen. A true private oasis.

EL PARADOR 800-451-4398, fax 011-506-777-1437; $88–450

Brand new and certainly the largest place in Manuel Antonio, really a "mega-resort," complete with tennis, large swimming pool, mini-golf and a fitness center. This is not for everyone, but it's hard not to relax here. The pool is an "infinity" pool, appearing to spill over into the Pacific, providing a real fantasy swim. It's the closest thing to a Hyatt resort that the country has to offer.

LA MARIPOSA 800-268-0424; fax 011-506-777-0050; $140–240

Long considered the best option available, it has slipped some since a recent change in ownership. Each private villa on this property commands an exceptional view, and the grounds are beautifully sculpted. Rates are steep and while they include breakfast *and* dinner, the restaurant has seen better days. You might be better off simply visiting the bar and enjoying the spectacular sunset for the price of a cocktail.

PLINIO 011-506-777-0055, fax 011-506-777-0558; $45–75

A great bargain choice, with rooms that are older than the others listed here but are well-appointed and feature an outpost jungle feel. The property sits in dense jungle (which, unfortunately, limits the views) including 30 acres for guests to explore. Management is quite friendly and its restaurant is a hub of activity.

VILLAS EL PARQUE 011-506-777-0096, fax 011-506-777-0538; $55–75

A solid, affordable choice, well-integrated into its jungle surroundings and is a bit more rustic than the others listed. Each room has a spectacular view, hammocks for lazing in the sun, terra cotta floors and very nice appointments. It also has a terrific pool.

CASA BLANCA 011-506-777-0253, fax 011-506-777-0253; $40–80

The gay hotel in Manuel Antonio. Though not as luxurious as the other properties listed above, it is a solid choice in many respects. The rooms with views (excellent views, at that) are simple yet comfortable, and far preferable to the rooms connected to the main house. The real plus here is the social aspect and the congenial staff, which outweigh its shortcomings for travelers who enjoy a completely gay environment. Almost all reports from Casa Blanca guests are raves.

Dining

This is a short list of recommendations from the myriad of options around the park. Ask around for others; none are too expensive. **Barba Roja** (011-506-777-0331) for excellent daily fish specials. **Plinio** (011-506-777-0055) for Italian specialties, the friendly crowd, and the warm atmosphere. **Vela Bar** (011-506-777-0413) for seafood and vegetarian specialties. **Karola's** (011-506-777-0424) for their wonderful seafood specials. **Mary Sombra** is right on the beach at Manuel Antonio. Known for typical Costa Rican seafood, a beautiful view, great people-watching, and frequent visits by a local troop of monkeys.

Nightlife

In Quepos town, near Manuel Antonio, you'll find **Arco Iris,** a mixed gay/straight disco. It's very large, and can be mostly empty midweek or in the low season, but it gets going on weekends, especially in high season.

Activities

ATHLETIC AND OUTDOOR

Manuel Antonio sits on a beautiful stretch of Pacific coast. You can get here by plane (less than 30 minutes from San José, on Travelair or Sansa), or you can drive, which will take you roughly four hours on some very rough roads which should be driven only in daylight hours. The drive is beautiful and, if you have the time, worth taking. The national park itself is an oceanfront jungle offering easy trails to explore and the chance to see natural rain forest vegetation and an abundance of wildlife (monkeys, parrots, sloths, and more). Many ticos wait at the park entrance to offer guided excursions. These are generally inexpensive and can greatly enrich your visit if you are unfamiliar with the terrain.

The main reason visitors flock to Manuel Antonio is to spend time on the beach. And what a beach it is! This small sweep of the Pacific features a jungle behind you, dramatic, jutting rocks to the north and south, and a warm, clear Pacific facing west. There is also a gay beach. To get to it, simply go to the entrance of the park (by bus, taxi or foot, depending where you're staying), turn right on the beach, then walk about ten minutes until you face a large rock outcropping. Cross these rocks (sandals or sneakers a must) and there you are: on a glorious, private beach peopled (usually sparsely) by gay men and women. Note that nudity is officially not permitted, and the police do occasionally come by, point, frown, and wait for you to put your suit back on. Also, you cannot safely walk to the gay beach at high tide because of the rock outcroppings. Plan ahead. Though you will hear people say that Manuel Antonio has been overdeveloped, relax. There are no high-rises, and nothing on the beach except hidden bungalows. The many new hotels are discreetly set in the jungle cliffs above the Pacific, offering seclusion, private beaches, and spectacular views. You won't be by yourself here, but the people you meet will, like you, appreciate the beauty and solitude of this special place. Plus, many of them will be gay.

OTHER AREA HIGHLIGHTS

Accommodations

ARENAL VOLCANO AND TABACÓN:

You can book a visit to Arenal as a day trip, but we strongly suggest staying overnight, and if at all possible, at the **Arenal Lodge** (011-506-228-3189, fax 011-506-289-6798; $95). This property offers unparalleled views of the volcano (you must request a volcano-view room), and it is terrifically designed, with the warm feel of a mountain lodge and an open structure connecting a library, billiard room, dining room, and long viewing patio. It is a class operation throughout.

MONTEVERDE CLOUD FOREST:

The place to stay here is the top-end **Monteverde Lodge** (011-506-257-0766, fax 011-506-257-1665; $78).

LOS ANGELES CLOUD FOREST:

The **Hotel Villablanca** (011-506-228-4603, fax 011-506-228-4004; $90) is *the* place to stay. Its rooms are private casitas and feature fireplaces and views of the surrounding cloud-covered hills.

TORTUGUERO NATIONAL PARK:

The top place to stay is the **Tortuga Lodge** (011-506-257-0766, fax 011-506-257-1665; $466 double, for 2 days, one night, all meals, air transportation from San José, and two three-hour boat tours), run by experienced tour operator **Costa Rica Expeditions.** It's expensive, but worth it for the staff's overall experience. Other options include the **Jungle Lodge** (011-506-233-0133, fax 011-506-222-0778; $176 double, 2 days, 1 night, transportation and meals included) and the **Mawamba Lodge** (011-506-223-7490, fax 011-506-255-4039; $402 double, 2 days, 1 night, transportation and meals included), on the opposite side of the canal from the other two, allowing easy access to the Caribbean beach.

Activities

ATHLETIC AND OUTDOOR

Costa Rica is an outdoor paradise, and you will find an extraordinary array of environments to explore. We have listed the major tourist destinations and their attractions here.

ARENAL VOLCANO AND TABACÓN:

A major highlight of any trip to Costa Rica is heading north of San José to the Arenal Volcano. Arenal delivers exactly what you desire from a volcano: It is shaped like a cone, it is very, very big, and it erupts—virtually every hour. You can book a visit to Arenal as a day trip, but we strongly suggest staying overnight. The thrills of a trip to Arenal are threefold: exploring the mountain and its jungle environs (by foot or horseback), which can include fishing or wind surfing on nearby Arenal Lake; hearing and seeing the volcano erupt, which is an incredible experience (you can hear it by day, but the drama of the eruption is only possible at night); and, finally, the not-to-be-missed volcanic water park called **Tabacón Hot Spring** (011-506-222-1072, fax 011-506-221-3075; located 7 miles west of the town of La Fortuna on the way to Arenal Lake; open 10 A.M.–10 P.M.). Only two years old, Tabacón consists of several acres of super-heated water (thanks to the aforementioned volcano) that flows in streams, waterfalls and, finally, into several large swimming pools, all for your soaking enjoyment. It's an all-natural spa set in the middle of the jungle (with sound effects), complete with pool bar, restaurant, massage and mud mask (the latter two a modest $27.50). Admission costs just $13. Everyone who comes here loves it. You will too, so plan to spend a few hours.

RAIN OR CLOUD FOREST TREKS

If you've never been in a jungle, Costa Rica offers you a golden opportunity to explore this fascinating natural environment. Large sections of the country are covered with varying types of rain forest, including eerily beautiful primeval cloud forests that are high-elevation rain forests shrouded in clouds. Cloud forests host a wide diversity of plant and animal life, much of which you can observe during even a short visit. The largest and perhaps most spectacular of these is the **Monteverde Cloud Forest,** located in northern Costa Rica's Tilarán mountains. You'll need close to a full day to travel to and from Monteverde, plus at least a day there. Park attendance is limited to one hundred people at a time, but you can purchase your entrance pass the day before you enter. We suggest hiring a guide to enhance your understanding and enjoyment of this unique environment. In addition to the actual reserve are a hummingbird gallery and a butterfly garden, both worth a visit. Easier to get to and similarly beautiful is the **Los Angeles Cloud Forest,** only a few hours' drive from San José. You can visit Los Angeles as a day trip, which provides adequate time to discover this environment, but we recommend an overnight stay. The forest is actually a private reserve owned by ex-president of Costa Rica Rodrigo Carazo Odio, and offers several short and long trails. Guides can be hired through the hotel.

TORTUGUERO NATIONAL PARK

Named after the giant green sea turtles who nest here each July through September, Tortuguero National Park is located on Costa Rica's remote and far less visited Caribbean coast. The only city on the Caribbean coast is **Limón,** approximately 37 miles south of Tortuguero. Visitors come here to see the turtles nesting at night and, in non-nesting months, to explore the dense rain forests of this region. The area has a series of canals and rivers that parallel the sea and can be explored by boat, offering a jungle exploration not unlike a cruise down the Amazon. It's different from the experience of seeing the jungle by foot, yet equally fascinating. Getting to and from Tortuguero is best achieved by air (65 minutes from San José), and many of the accommodations in the area offer packages that include airfare and meals in their prices. The lodges will also arrange your exploration of the park, as well as fishing and other activities.

WHITE WATER RAFTING

For a travel adventure that you are unlikely to forget, spend a full day white water rafting. By far the best option is the **Pacuare River,** a clean, sweeping waterway which cascades through awesome jungle canyons, passing abundant wildlife and many waterfalls along the way. The experience of riding the rapids surrounded by such verdant beauty is heart-pounding and soul-stirring. Trips can be organized by your hotel travel desk or concierge, and cost roughly $90 for a full day, including breakfast and lunch. Two of the best operators are **Costa Rica Expeditions** (011-506-257-0766) and **Ríos Tropicales** (011-506-233-6455), though there are many other reputable companies. Your hotel should have a well-established relationship with one of them. There are other rivers to raft, some with less powerful rapids than the Pacuare. Choose one that fits your confidence level, but choose the Pacuare for a day to remember.

SHOPPING

Costa Rican handicrafts make excellent souvenirs. **Sarchi** (about one hour from San José) is the handicrafts capital—a great place to buy wood carvings, pottery, weavings, rocking chairs, and miniature ox carts, available in various sizes for use as patio bars. The chairs fold, and the ox carts come apart for easier portage. In Monteverde, there is a women's craft cooperative selling embroidered and hand-painted clothing. The handicraft shop at **Poás Volcano,** Tienda de la Naturaleza, sells handicrafts from the local population.

SPA VACATIONS

*B*ubbling waters. Soothing massages. Healthy food. Just thinking about the curative properties of a spa vacation makes us start to relax. Picture an early morning hike through the forest. Or a quiet hour of meditation in a Japanese garden. Or a vigorous aerobics class followed by a manicure, pedicure, and purifying facial. Of course it sounds good—and probably just the thing your body needs after moving your stuff into your girlfriend's apartment, or after a Saint Party binge.

SPAS FOR GAYS

Gay interest in spa vacations is growing rapidly. Whether it's because of our health and fitness fixation or the added stress of living in a straight world, gay women and men are booking more and more spa stays, and spas are beginning to address our particular needs and sensitivities. We've received numerous requests for spa information from our subscribers, and some positive Reporter-at-Large recommendations. Considering the number of gay women and men interested in fitness, an all-gay spa may well be looming in the near future.

In the meantime, we polled 271 spa and fitness programs and asked them whether they had any experience with gay and lesbian travelers, and whether they would describe their program as a welcoming and friendly place for gay couples and singles. We've combined the responses with our (limited) first- and secondhand knowledge to provide this guide to spa vacations.

SPAS FOR DAYS

Our listings run the gamut, from luxurious pampering experiences to rustic basic escapes. Spas are one arena where programs for women are more available and evolved than programs for men. Some women-only spas, like Golden Door, have added men-only and co-ed weeks, and others, like La Costa, have put in separate treatment areas for men, who might feel uncomfortable in a women's salon. Some spas offer specific extensive programs geared to those who are looking to impart a new fitness consciousness to their lives, while others concentrate on salon services in a resort environment. Meditation, education, and spiritual programs are as integral to some as fine dining and championship golf are to others. List your priorities, check your budget, and be sure to plan well in advance for many of the well-known programs. When you book, be sure to inquire about scheduling activities in advance.

Booking a Spa Vacation

None of the spas listed cater specifically to gay women and men, but all of them are relatively comfortable and at least gay-neutral, if not gay-friendly. **Spa-Finders** is the world's largest travel service dedicated solely to health and fitness vacations. They publish an annual resource guide ($6.95, including shipping) and quarterly newsletters. We asked their president, Frank van Putten, which spas he would recommend for gay and lesbian clientele and marked his recommendations (•SP√). Spa-Finders works with travel agents, or you may call them directly at 212-924-6800 or 800-255-7727.

AEGIS THE ABODE RD 1, Box 1030D, New Lebanon, NY 12125; 518-794-8095; $30–40/night, including simple vegetarian meals

AEGIS is a small Sufi community in the Berkshire Hills, offering private and group spiritual retreats. You need not be an initiate of the Sufi order, or even know anything about Sufism, to feel welcomed in this eclectic community. The main residence is located in an original Shaker community, with 450 acres for long peaceful walks in the woods. A schedule of specific retreats is available, but many visitors just come for an inexpensive, peaceful getaway.

CANYON RANCH IN THE BERKSHIRES (•SP√) Kemble Street, Lenox, MA 02140; 413-637-4100 or 800-621-9777; three-night programs start at $984 per person, including meals and three spa services

The New England sister to the Canyon Ranch in Tucson, this 120-acre converted Berkshire estate includes an indoor track, enclosed swimming pool, and racquetball, squash, and basketball courts. Outdoor facilities include another pool, tennis courts, and miles of trails for biking, hiking, and cross-country skiing.

CANYON RANCH SPA (•SP√) 8600 East Rockcliff Road, Tucson, AZ 85715; 602-749-9000 or 800-742-9000; four-night packages start at $1,460

A modern deluxe spa on 60 acres of desert, Canyon Ranch is well-known for its recreational facilities, pampering service, innovative programs, and fine food. Catering to a well-heeled, sophisticated crowd, the place is popular with stressed-out CEO types. Stress reduction, smoking cessation, and plastic surgery post-op recovery are some of their specialties, but anyone desiring a healthy, luxurious retreat will be happy here.

DEERFIELD MANOR SPA 650 Resica Falls Road, East Stroudsburg, PA 18301; 717-223-0160 or 800-852-4494; two-night minimum packages start at $290 per person, double occupancy, including meals and classes but not personal services or massage

Located just 1½ hours from New York City, Deerfield is a nice cozy place, open April–October. The program takes an individualized approach to diet and nutrition, stressing moderate exercise and diet. The warm, supportive environment encourages a family feel among the men and women there to unwind and shape up.

DORAL RESORT (•SP√) 8755 N.W. Thirty-sixth Street, Miami, FL 33178; 305-593-6030 or 800-331-7768; room rates start at $155

A Tuscan-style spa just minutes from South Beach nightlife, Doral is luxurious and sports oriented, with five championship golf courses,

15 tennis courts, an equestrian center, and organized volleyball, basketball, croquet, and *boccie* games.

FORT RECOVERY Box 239, Road Town, Tortola, British Virgin Islands; 800-367-8455—Pam Jacobson; $1,166–2,145/week, includes meals, classes, three half-hour massages, and a full-day boat excursion

A beachfront villa in the Virgin Islands, Fort Recovery offers the usual villa rental program, combined with a spa-type weight-loss program. Three low-calorie meals are served in your villa each day, and yoga and meditation classes, individual health discussions, and massage are available. Accommodations range from one-bedroom villas to four-bedroom houses.

THE GOLDEN DOOR (•SP√) P.O. Box 1567, Escondido, CA 92025; 619-744-5777 or 800-424-0777; seven-day programs start at $4,250, all-inclusive

One of the most expensive and exclusive spas, the Golden Door offers a Japanese country inn setting and a program designed for the health conscious in need of quiet meditation and challenging exercise. Catering primarily to women, a few weeks every year are designated as men-only and co-ed. Each of the single-occupancy rooms (no double occupancy!) has a private Japanese garden.

HOTEL HANA-MAUI WELLNESS CENTER Hana, Maui, HI 96713; 808-248-8211 or 800-321-4262; room rates are $305–795

Part of the luxurious, remote, and renowned Hotel Hana, the Wellness Center Program offers a variety of hiking, exercise, and massage opportunities, and serves healthy gourmet cuisine. Activities are offered on an à la carte basis to all hotel guests.

THE INN AT MANITOU (•SP√) McKellar, Ontario, Canada P0G 1C0; 705-389-2171; in winter: 416-967-3466; three-day packages start at Canadian $599

A tennis clinic turned full-service spa, the Inn at Manitou offers cross-training and luxury pampering, with an emphasis on private sports instruction and personal service. Horseback riding, kayaking, canoeing, windsurfing, and swimming instruction are all offered; use of tennis courts, mountain bikes, and water sports equipment is complimentary. A member of Relais and Chateaux, the menu includes classic French cuisine and gourmet spa menus.

JIMMY LESAGE'S NEW LIFE FITNESS VACATIONS Inn of the Six Mountains, P.O. Box 395, Killington, VT 05751; 802-422-4302; $200–230/day includes accommodations, three meals daily, all exercise classes, hiking program, and one massage

Affordable weekly programs are designed to push participants to the next level of well-being through fitness activities, healthy food, education, and overall body-mind awareness. Operating out of the AAA four-diamond Inn of the Six Mountains, the program combines resort-based spa activities such as massage and studio exercise classes. Hiking is the principle outdoor activity—golf, tennis, swimming, and biking are also included. Five-night and weekend programs are available.

LA COSTA HOTEL & SPA (•SP√) Costa Del Mar Road, Carlsbad, CA 92008; 619-438-9111 or 800-854-5000; room rates start at $295

Located between L.A. and San Diego, La Costa is popular with film-industry types looking to escape the city without forsaking comfort. Facilities include two 18-hole championship golf courses, 23 racquetball courts, and 23 tennis courts. Spa services are also extensive (with separate treatment facilities for men), and there is a wide range of excellent dining choices, including spa and gourmet cuisine.

LAKE AUSTIN RESORT (•SP√) 1705 Quinlan Park Road, Austin, TX 78732; 512-266-2444 or 800-847-5637; two-night programs start at $424, spa services extra

On the shores of Lake Austin in Texas hill country, this resort offers a week-long program combining rest, relaxation, exercise, and education. Lake views from the gym and guest rooms create a peaceful atmosphere in which to build a better foundation of well-being.

NEW AGE HEALTH SPA (•SP√) Route 55, Neversink, NY 12765; 914-985-7601 or 800-682-4348; $114–227/night includes accommodations, meals, spa facilities, and daily activities

A truly holistic approach to health and very moderate prices have made New Age popular. A wide selection of body treatments and consultations are offered à la carte, from astrological charting to colonic irrigation. The core schedule includes a lineup of exercise, meditation, lectures, and meals, with a juice-fasting option.

THE OMEGA INSTITUTE FOR HOLISTIC STUDIES 260 Lake Drive, Rhinebeck, NY 12572; 914-266-4301; workshops average $260; accommodations and meals start at $49/night for dormitory housing; tent campsites are also available

The Omega Institute offers a lakeside campus, gardens, sports facilities, a spirited community of staff and participants, good food, and a wellness center. Accommodations range from dormitories to comfortable cabins with private baths. Workshops include holistic health, martial arts, recovery programs, gender, relationship, and family programs, arts, creativity, and sports, nature, society, and spiritual understanding. A few workshops are gay-specific; past offerings have included Art as Awareness for Gay and Bisexual Men, a Lesbian Writer's Workshop, and a Gay Men's Retreat.

THE PHOENICIAN CENTRE FOR WELL-BEING (•SP√) 6000 E. Camelback Road, Scottsdale, AZ 85251; 602-941-8200 or 800-888-8234; $275–435

On 130 acres of manicured desert, the Phoenician offers elegant accommodations, a wide range of spa services, and a wellness center. Oversize guest rooms, an attention to service, and elegant public areas make the Phoenician a good choice for those who wish to combine a resort stay with a spa experience. Seven pools, 11 tennis courts, and a golf course top the long list of sports activities.

QUALTON CLUB AND SPA VALLARTA K.M. 2.5 Avenida de las Palmas s/n, Puerto Vallarta, Jalisco, Mexico; 011-52-322-4-44-46; packages run $289–589 per person

On the beach where the sea meets the mountains, the Qualton offers an all-inclusive resort experience (meals, entertainment, cocktails, nonmotorized watersports, entertainment) and spa facilities including workout room, aerobics, sauna, Jacuzzi, and steam room. Three-night spa packages include a massage, facial or hair treatment, and herbal wrap or manicure/pedicure, and 20% discount on additional spa services.

RANCHO LA PUERTA (•SP√) P.O. Box 2548, Escondido, CA 92025; 619-295-3144 or 800-443-7565; $1,350–1,700

Located in Tecate, Mexico, just 1 1/4 hours southeast of San Diego, Rancho La Puerta has extensive fitness facilities, reasonable prices, and a spa and modified vegetarian menu. Because it is very popular, your stay should be booked well in advance, and massage and facial appointments should be booked immediately upon arrival, or even beforehand. Program runs Saturday to Saturday.

SKYLONDA FITNESS RETREAT (•SP√) 16350 Skyline Boulevard, Woodside, CA 94062; 415-851-4500; rates start at $300/day

With a spectacular view of the redwoods, Skylonda offers a seven-day all-inclusive program incorporating hiking, yoga, meditation, weight training, aerobics, and massage. Opened by Golden Door veterans, the program stresses vigorous activity and inner reflection. A glass-enclosed swimming pool and outdoor Jacuzzi add to the elegant country-lodge feel.

SONOMA MISSION INN AND SPA P.O. Box 1447, Sonoma, CA 95476-1447; 707-938-9000 or 800-862-4945; prices start at $129/night, per person, double occupancy, including accommodations in a historic inn room, daily spa admission, one spa treatment/person/night, and unlimited fitness classes

Just 45 minutes from San Francisco, the Sonoma Mission Inn and Spa attracts a large number of Bay Area couples, gay and straight. This pretty pink Spanish colonial is a romantic wine-country inn, with a full-service spa building down a short path from the inn. The Spa offers an outdoor mineral water exercise pool, exercise equipment, tennis courts, hiking, and daily classes in aerobics, yoga, step, stretch, and body work. Spa services include 40 different types of massage, facials, wraps, and salon services.

SPA HOTEL AND MINERAL SPRINGS 100 N. Indian Avenue, Palm Springs, CA 92262; 619-778-1772 or 800-854-1279; $155 includes room, two meals, and one spa service

Built on the site of hot mineral springs, the Spa Hotel offers a fitness program based on its natural water source. The contemporary facility was recently renovated, offering attractive, moderately priced accommodations. Located in downtown Palm Springs, the hotel is a short drive from gay nightlife and just steps from the Marquis Hotel, which hosts the Easter White Party.

TWO BUNCH PALMS 6742 Two Bunch Parkway, Desert Hot Springs, CA 92240; 619-329-8791 or 800-472-4334; $110–450

This is the luxury desert hideaway for Hollywood types. Very private, intimate, and luxurious, the place offers a mineral water pool, extensive body work, and beauty services. Al Capone built the original place, which explains the rock walls, the Art Deco dining room (originally a casino), and the bullet hole in a mirror in two-bedroom suite #14. All services are à la carte.

ORGANIZED GAY CRUISE, TOUR, AND RESORT-BASED VACATIONS

*A*lthough travel is extremely popular among gay people, most gay men and lesbians have never been on an organized "gay vacation." True, many straight travelers have never been on an organized travel experience, and, gay or straight, some people never should. But there are a lot of gays and lesbians out there (you may be one of them) who have eschewed organized gay vacations out of ignorance or misconception. This chapter will help dispel false assumptions and misinformation. After reading it, you may still choose only independent travel, but at least you'll choose it for all the right reasons. More likely, you may decide to try a gay vacation for your next trip. Find one that's right for you, and you will experience a new level of comfort and satisfaction from your vacation.

WHAT IS A GAY VACATION?

There is no single definition for a "gay vacation." Some trips, such as an RSVP cruise, have grown so popular that they have become synonymous with the concept of gay travel. But even RSVP offers several different kinds of vacations, and each has specific and different appeals. If you're gay and you go on vacation, that may be gay vacation enough for you. Certainly, if you're RuPaul, every vacation is a gay vacation. For the purposes of this book, we've defined gay vacations as "existing, organized tours, cruises, or other travel experiences that you join *as a member."* This differentiates them from independent travel, which is planned for you specifically. Sometimes the same people and companies that arrange gay groups also arrange independent travel, and we've listed these companies, along with a number of firms that provide only independent travel arrangements.

WHY GO AWAY GAY?

Everyone goes on vacation to have a good time, relax, explore, indulge, and escape. Gay vacations fulfill these desires with many of the same elements as straight ones: beautiful beaches, room service, exotic destinations, and so on. But people who go on gay vacations cite five overriding reasons to go on a gay trip:

1. *Romance.* Even in the straight world, meeting new friends for romantic encounters ranks high on the list of choices for vacations—look at Hedonism II and Singleworld Cruises as prime examples. For gays, sexual motivation may play an even bigger role in travel choices, since the romantic opportunities of our everyday world are more limited.

2. *To escape the straight world.* People who feel oppressed by the straightness of their everyday existence enjoy the liberation of a gay environment. Just as Club Med's TV-phone-clock-newspaper void helps create an "Antidote for Civilization," the heterosexual-majority void of a gay vacation helps relieve the stress of living and/or working in a straight environment.

3. *To escape the opposite sex.* Although the percentage of gay travel experiences for gay women and men together continues to grow dramatically, the strongest appeal remains in trips that are mostly or exclusively one sex or the other. Some of that appeal goes back to romance. But there's more to it. For women, an all-female environment allows the consciousness-raising and feminist/feminine community bonding that is fundamental to many lesbians. Those same women are often the object of abject vitriol from men who really don't want to see or hear them on their vacations. Politically correct or not, being away from the opposite sex is a big part of gay vacations.

4. *To meet other gay people.* Romance aside, meeting new people and making new friends are popular attractions of a vacation. Choosing a gay vacation ensures that you'll have something major in common with your fellow vacationers.

5. *For the gay entertainment and activity.* Gay vacations tend to feature gay recreation. Although many vacation activities don't have gay-specific versions, many do. Dancing, pool games, cabaret entertainment, and costume parties are never as much fun on a straight vacation.

WHAT IS A "GAY ENVIRONMENT," ANYWAY?

The gay-environment vacation is the most visible and most popular of gay vacations, and a number of companies have joined industry leader **RSVP** in creating and marketing gay-environment trips. In the realm of gay travel, these are "mass-market" vacations, our version of a Disney World vacation or a Carnival cruise. (In fact, RSVP actually chartered its first Carnival ships in 1995 and 1996.) **Atlantis Events** brought the gay environment to Club Med, and **Olivia** brought both land and sea concepts to the women's market.

More important than the destinations they travel to is the all-gay atmosphere these companies create. For many people it's a dream come true, and, indeed, RSVP for a while took to calling itself a "purveyor of dreams." For others, the thought of "being stuck on a boat with 700 queens" is a nightmare. The reality of these vacations is that they are enormously popular, and even people with strong reservations about going usually end up having a great time. Being in an idyllic environment with hundreds of other gay people is exciting and liberating in a way that ordinary vacations can't be.

While gay-environment trips dominate the gay-vacation landscape, they are not the only options. A growing number of companies are offering gay cruises and tours with different vacation agendas. Most of these companies fall into two types, with a number of hybrid variations. One type is the customized tour, offering a travel experience with gay-specific interest. This type of tour offers a decidedly gay composition and generally appeals to a niche market among gay travelers. The other kind is a mainstream-type tour with minimal customization, but marketed as an all-gay departure. These tours offer mainstream tour opportunities, in the company of gay traveling companions, on the premise that you'll have a better time sightseeing with a bus full of other gay people than you would in a bus full of straight people. For many gay women and men, that is unquestionably true. But some gay travelers would actually rather travel with straight people, risking the company of homophobes and forfeiting the romantic comfort, to avoid being in a group that labels itself as gay. Many gay-travel entrepreneurs do not consider these travelers when making overly ambitious business projections.

WHY THE "GAY MARKUP"?

The concept of a price markup for a gay trip versus a straight one angers many potential vacationers. In reality, it's a fallacious concept, even though many gay vacations are priced at a premium in comparison with their straight counterparts. Most gay cruises are sold at the cruise lines' brochure rates, without the steep discounts that are offered on almost every other departure of the chartered ships. A week at Club Med purchased from Olivia or Atlantis is often more expensive than the week preceding or following it purchased directly from Club Med. There are two primary reasons for the price discrepancy. The most salient is that RSVP, Atlantis, and Olivia all augment the standard cruise or resort experience with activities, entertainment, and staff. RSVP is not selling the same Carnival Cruise experience that Kathie Lee Gifford is (and thank God for that, although now that Carnival has Richard Simmons singing along, we're a bit confused). The other reason is that the annual marketing, reservations, and operations expenses of a company like Olivia are spread over four trips, whereas Club Med's overhead is spread over hundreds of trips. The "premium" that gay tour operators charge is the premium cost of creating a gay environment. It is not profiteering on the resale of services. Our Family Abroad is the only large gay tour operator without a markup. Although it does not substantially customize the subcontracted tours it sells, all of its tours are offered at the exact same price as those of the mainstream operators it works with.

THE TOUR THAT GOT AWAY

Canceled departures are a dirty little secret of the tour business in general. The right to cancel is often in very fine print, and tour cancellation victims are often completely unaware of the possibility until it happens. The percentage of tours a company cancels is often a telling number, because it offers clear indication of the tours' popularity and the company's success in marketing them. A high number is not always bad, but it calls for caution and some proactive questioning and action, especially if you are locked into specific travel dates. When planning a tour vacation, ask if a departure is guaranteed, and if not, how many passengers it requires to depart, how many are currently booked, and whether other departures are more heavily booked or are more likely to operate. If you're booking early, it behooves you to put down a deposit early, because your deposit makes your chosen departure more likely to operate, and will in turn attract even more bookings.

BIRDS OF A FEATHER

So much of your experience on a gay trip, good or bad, will be based on your enjoyment of your fellow tour members. During downtime and travel time, *they* are your entertainment. While actually touring, sightseeing, or engaging in other activities, they are the ones you'll be sharing your excitement and discoveries with. If you really like a good percentage of your fellow tour members, you'll have a great time, even if the tour is less than wonderful. But even the best tour can be ruined if you don't get along with your fellow travelers. This is the crux of group travel, and often the reason why one hears such different opinions from different travelers. After choosing a trip that best reflects your personal style, the best way to ensure you'll like your fellow participants is to book your travel with a friend or group of friends. This will ensure you have someone to talk to on bus rides or at dinner. Many experienced gay vacationers end up planning future trips with people they have met on past travels.

JUST ONE OF THE BOYS

While most women's tour operators do not accept male passengers on their trips, the biggest men's tour operators accept women. Most women who go on men's trips have no interest in traveling on a women's trip—they make no bones about preferring to "hang out with the boys," and those that prefer to be left alone claim that there is no better environment to achieve that. Because they're a minority and are not inclined to promote the political or social subtext of a women's trip, most men barely notice their presence.

TAKING THE PLUNGE

Request information and brochures from the listed companies whose offerings sound intriguing. Ask a travel agent for opinions and assistance. Prepare a list of questions (see our list on p. 350)—you can learn a lot about a trip if you ask the right questions. Many of the firms listed are one-woman/one-man operations, without fancy brochures or on-line Web sites. Be sure to buy travel insurance, and bring something good to read, as well as an open mind. Depart with realistic expectations and a willingness to go with the flow, and your gay vacation will be a trip to remember.

For each company, we've listed phone and fax numbers, as well as e-mail and street addresses. (As always, we encourage you to book through a professional travel agent.) The "Clientele" listing will tell you to what percent and age group the company caters, but note that the composition of individual trips may vary. Price range, tour length, and group size and composition reflect the full range of a company's offerings but may not be indicative of a specific trip. And away we go . . .

ABOVE & BEYOND TOURS 330 Townsend Street, #107, San Francisco, CA 94107; 415-284-1666 or 800-397-2681, fax 415-284-1660

CLIENTELE: 98%G/85%M, 50% couples; ages 25–65   PRICE RANGE: $200–7,500   TOUR LENGTH: 3–25 days   NUMBER OF DEPARTURES: 27   DESTINATIONS: South Pacific, Brazil, Europe   GROUP SIZE: avg. 50

Above & Beyond's group departures are scheduled around gay-popular events such as Carnival in Rio and Sydney Mardi Gras. They feature component options and very few scheduled activities—tour members are mostly on their own. The company is a recognized tour operator for Qantas, Air New Zealand, Varig, and Alitalia, and is affiliated with Destination Down Under, Australia's largest gay tour operator. They are professional, thorough, and knowledgeable.

ADVENTURE BOUND EXPEDITIONS 711 Walnut Street, Boulder, CO 80302; 303-449-0990, fax 303-449-9038

CLIENTELE: EG/100%M, all ages and relationship affinities   PRICE RANGE: $1,600–3,500   TOUR LENGTH: 2–3 weeks   NUMBER OF DEPARTURES: 1   DESTINATIONS: International   GROUP SIZE: 7

Started in 1987, the company takes small groups to remote parts of the globe to share thrilling outdoor experiences.

ADVANCE DAMRON VACATIONS 10700 Northwest Freeway, #160, Houston, TX 77092; 713-682-2002 or 800-695-0880, fax 713-680-3200, e-mail: adv@advance-damron.com

CLIENTELE: EG/90%M, 50% singles; ages 35–45   PRICE RANGE: $700–2,000   TOUR LENGTH: 1 week   NUMBER OF DEPARTURES: 3   DESTINATIONS: Caribbean Windjammers, Whistler Gay Ski Week   GROUP SIZE: 130–150

A founding member of the IGTA, with over a decade of experience in running gay trips, including 20 Windjammer cruises. Advance Damron is also a full-service travel agency.

ALLEGRO ENTERPRISES 900 West End Avenue, #12C, New York, NY 10025; 212-666-6700 or 800-666-3553, fax 212-666-7451

CLIENTELE: some EG, most 60–70%G, mostly couples   PRICE RANGE: $600–4,995   TOUR LENGTH: 4–15 days   NUMBER OF DEPARTURES: 22   DESTINATIONS: Russia, Italy, Egypt, Scandinavia   GROUP SIZE: 10–15

Allegro is the North American agent for the Kirov Mariinsky Theatre in St. Petersburg, the Bolshoi Theatre in Moscow, and the Finnish National Opera, with advance schedules and guaranteed orchestra seating. Their tour programs are built around cultural events, including these venues. Some departures are escorted; individual tickets for the above-listed venues are also available.

ALYSON ADVENTURES P.O. Box 181223, Boston, MA 02118; 617-247-8170 or 800-825-9766, fax 617-542-9189, e-mail: alyventure@aol.com

CLIENTELE: 90%G/75%M, 80% single; ages 25–60   PRICE RANGE: $1,095–2,550   TOUR LENGTH: 5–11 days   NUMBER OF DEPARTURES: 15   DESTINATIONS: France, Australia, Caribbean, Switzerland, Wyoming   GROUP SIZE: 5–12

An outgrowth of gay book publisher Alyson Publications, this young company provides active, adventurous trips that include hiking, biking, climbing, and skiing.

ATLANTIS EVENTS 9060 Santa Monica Boulevard, #310, West Hollywood, CA 90069; 310-281-5450 or 800-6-ATLANTIS, fax 310-281-5455, e-mail: atlantiskr@aol.com

CLIENTELE: EG/95%M, 60% singles; avg. ages 30–35   **PRICE RANGE:** $895–2,195   **TOUR LENGTH:** 7–10 days   **NUMBER OF DEPARTURES:** 6   **DESTINATIONS:** Mexican and Caribbean all-inclusive resorts, Mediterranean cruise   **GROUP SIZE:** 200–600

Atlantis charters Club Med villages and other all-inclusive resorts and remarkets them as gay resorts. They also run occasional cruises. They were a 1994 *Out & About* Editor's Choice Award winner.

BY EXPOSURE P.O. Box 27373, Los Angeles, CA 90027; 213-913-1300, fax 213-913-1333
   CLIENTELE: EG/75%M, 80% couples; ages 35–60   **PRICE RANGE:** $2,795–3,995   **TOUR LENGTH:** 9–11 days   **NUMBER OF DEPARTURES:** 4   **DESTINATIONS:** Kenya, Tanzania, Malaysia, Egypt

Dedicated to the premise that global acceptance is the product of de-sensitization (by all) and exposure (to all), and that travel is the best way to accomplish that. Started in 1994, the company's all-gay tours offer a certain personal and emotional comfort level while exploring remote regions of the world.

CLUB LE BON 76 Main Street, Woodbridge, NJ 07095; 800-836-8687, fax 908-826-1577, e-mail: clublebon@aol.com
   CLIENTELE: Either: 100%W, 75% couples, avg. age 35; or: 20%M, 30%W, 50% kids   **PRICE RANGE:** $595–2,500   **TOUR LENGTH:** 1–2 weeks   **NUMBER OF DEPARTURES:** 6   **DESTINATIONS:** Caribbean, Latin America, Europe, Africa   **GROUP SIZE:** 30–50

Trips are all women, or gay parents and their kids. Most are all- or semi-inclusive, and include interaction with the local gay community.

DESTINATION DISCOVERY P.O. Drawer 659, Rutherford, CA 94573; 707-963-4160 or 800-954-5543, fax 707-963-4160, e-mail: ddiscovery@aol.com
   CLIENTELE: HIV+   **PRICE RANGE:** $1,680   **TOUR LENGTH:** 7–10 days   **NUMBER OF DEPARTURES:** 3   **DESTINATIONS:** Maui   **GROUP SIZE:** 16

Started in 1994, the company runs wellness vacations for HIV+ men. Activities include an à la carte menu of "playshops" and seminars on relaxation, stress management, meditation, communication, and healing.

DIFFERENT DRUMMER TOURS P.O. Box 528, Glen Ellyn, IL 60137; 800-645-1275, fax 708-530-0059

CLIENTELE: EG, mostly single men; avg. age 35   PRICE RANGE: $1,025–2,360   TOUR LENGTH: 7–15 days   NUMBER OF DEPARTURES: 12   DESTINATIONS: worldwide   GROUP SIZE: 6–12

Different Drummer promotes upscale, small, gay-designed international tours with mostly gay local guides.

ECO-EXPLORATIONS P.O. Box 339, Felton, CA 95018; 408-335-7199, fax 408-335-3375, e-mail: Eco-Explor@aol.com

CLIENTELE: 60%G/50%W, some all-gay, some women-only; ages 30–60   PRICE RANGE: $60–1,200   TOUR LENGTH: 1/2 day–2 weeks   NUMBER OF DEPARTURES: 9   DESTINATIONS: Monterey Bay, Calif., and warm-water sites around the globe   GROUP SIZE: 2–14

Lesbian-owned and operated by a professional naturalist and master dive instructor and specializing in aquatic destinations, activities, and instruction.

EMBASSY TRAVEL 906 N. Harper Avenue, #13, Los Angeles, CA 90046; 213-656-0743 or 800-227-6668, fax 213-650-6968

CLIENTELE: EG/75%M, 60% single; ages 35–65   PRICE RANGE: $3,000–7,000   TOUR LENGTH: 2 weeks   NUMBER OF DEPARTURES: 2   DESTINATIONS: South Africa   GROUP SIZE: 10–15

These tours to South Africa are planned and escorted by a gay South African now living in the United States. The tour escort has full knowledge of gay life in South Africa and arranges parties in Johannesburg and Cape Town to complement the sightseeing highlights of the country.

FIESTA TOURS 323 Geary Street, #619, San Francisco, CA 94102; 415-986-1134 or 800-200-0582, fax 415-986-3029, e-mail: brazusa@sf.net

CLIENTELE: 50%G/50%M, 75% single; ages 25–55   PRICE RANGE: $999–2,500   TOUR LENGTH: 10–14 days   NUMBER OF DEPARTURES: 2   DESTINATIONS: Brazil   GROUP SIZE: 15 people

Fiesta Tours has 15 years experience in booking Latin America and does mostly customized itineraries. They run two scheduled tours per year—New Year's and Carnival in Rio.

FLORIDA ADVENTURES P.O. Box 677923, Orlando, FL 32867; 407-677-0655, fax 407-677-0238

CLIENTELE: 70%G but not mixed: tours are men *or* women *or* straight, all ages **PRICE RANGE:** $465–1,475 **TOUR LENGTH:** 1 week **NUMBER OF DEPARTURES:** 2 **DESTINATIONS:** Florida, Outer Bahamas, Caribbean **GROUP SIZE:** 2–6 persons

Unique, affordable vacations off the coast of Florida, exploring undiscovered cays. Most of their business is customized trips including a 15-cabin ship, private island rentals, and yacht sailing and instruction.

FRAUEN UNTERWEGS E.V. Potsdamerstrasse 139, Berlin 10783 Germany; 011-49-30-215-1022, fax 011-49-30-216-9852

CLIENTELE: 100%W **PRICE RANGE:** $300–6,000 **TOUR LENGTH:** 1–2 weeks **NUMBER OF DEPARTURES:** n/a **DESTINATIONS:** Europe, Gambia, New Zealand, Thailand **GROUP SIZE:** 8–16

Frauen Unterwegs is Europe's largest women-only tour operator. They specialize in relaxing holidays, study tours, workshops, and sport travel, including sailing, skiing, hiking, and canoeing.

GAY 'N' GRAY PARTNERS IN TRAVEL P.O. Box 726, Atkinson, NH 03811; 603-362-5011

CLIENTELE: EG/100%M 40 years and over **PRICE RANGE:** $1,500–5,000 **TOUR LENGTH:** 2–3 weeks **NUMBER OF DEPARTURES:** 1–2 **DESTINATIONS:** Africa, Alaska, Hawaii, Australia, Caribbean **GROUP SIZE:** 10–24

Gay 'n' Gray offers one or two annual trips geared to mature gay males who are young at heart. They are a good choice for men looking for like-minded traveling companions, but not emphasizing hot spots and the bar scene.

GAYVENTURES 12769 N. Kendall Drive, Miami, FL 33186-1701; 305-382-7757 or 800-940-7757, fax 305-388-5259

CLIENTELE: EG/20%W, 75% couples; ages 30–50   **PRICE RANGE:** $995–1,485   **TOUR LENGTH:** 7–12 days   **NUMBER OF DEPARTURES:** 1   **DESTINATIONS:** Costa Rica   **GROUP SIZE:** 7–12

Specializing in Costa Rica, this company runs men-only and women-only tours, and also arranges independent travel.

HANNS EBENSTEN TRAVEL, INC. 513 Flemming Street, Key West, FL 33040; 305-294-8174, fax 305-292-9665

CLIENTELE: 90% gay men; 2 tours/year, mixed gay-straight; ages 29–75   **PRICE RANGE:** $2,985–5,300   **TOUR LENGTH:** 10–16 days   **NUMBER OF DEPARTURES:** 14   **DESTINATIONS:** worldwide, exotic and unusual   **GROUP SIZE:** 6–14

Mr. Ebensten has been escorting gay tours for more than 20 years. His tours combine luxury, such as the *Orient Express*, with adventurous activities, such as sailing down the Nile in felucca sailboats. The tour ambiance is often reserved, formal, and old-fashioned. The destinations read like a trip-of-a-lifetime wish list: Easter Island, the Galapagos Islands, Morocco, Turkey, etc. Mr. Ebensten's book *Volleyball with the Cuna Indians* gives an in-depth profile of touring, Ebensten-style, and Mr. Ebensten himself was the first recipient of the *Out & About* Editor's Choice Hall of Fame award.

HAWK, I'M YOUR SISTER P.O. Box 9109, Santa Fe, NM 87504; 505-984-2268

CLIENTELE: 50%G/50%W, 90% single; ages 20–75   **PRICE RANGE:** $1,000–2,500   **TOUR LENGTH:** 9–21 days   **NUMBER OF DEPARTURES:** 6   **DESTINATIONS:** United States, Russia, Peru, Bahamas   **GROUP SIZE:** 14

Wilderness trips, mostly women (some co-ed trips), and mostly canoeing, with some writing retreats. Trips are drug/alcohol free and emphasize a reverence for the earth and an understanding of the language of forests, canyons, deserts, lakes, rivers, and the sea.

HER WILD SONG P.O. Box 515, Brunswick, ME 04101; 207-721-9005, fax 207-721-0235

CLIENTELE: 100%W/50–60% lesbian, some couples; ages 25–75   **PRICE RANGE:** $215–895   **TOUR LENGTH:** 2–10 days   **NUMBER OF DE-**

PARTURES: 10   **DESTINATIONS:** Maine, Caribbean, Southwest   **GROUP SIZE:** 8–12

Founded in 1990, the company fosters spiritual awareness in the outdoors. Tours combine adventure activities such as sea kayaking and dogsledding with light-handed meditation, Buddhist and feminist practices.

MARIAH WILDERNESS EXPEDITIONS P.O. Box 248, Port Richmond, CA 94807; 510-233-2303 or 800-462-7424, fax 510-233-0956
  CLIENTELE: 20%G/60%W, 70% couples; ages 25–75   **PRICE RANGE:** $220–1,320   **TOUR LENGTH:** 1–13 days   **NUMBER OF DEPARTURES:** 20   **DESTINATIONS:** California, Costa Rica, Baja, Sea of Cortez   **GROUP SIZE:** 10–100

California's only women-owned white-water rafting and adventure travel company includes all-gay and women-only tours in its lineup. Now in its fifteenth year, they are known for well-run, eco-sensitive quality tours focusing on the active exploration of native environments and cultures.

MEN ON VACATION 4715 Thirtieth Street, #6, San Diego, CA 92116; 619-641-7085 or 800-959-4636, fax 619-641-7088, e-mail: menonvacat @aol.com
  CLIENTELE: EG/97%M; ages 20–75   **PRICE RANGE:** $219–6,000   **TOUR LENGTH:** 5–14 days   **NUMBER OF DEPARTURES:** 12   **DESTINATIONS:** Australia, New Zealand, Fiji, Hawaii, Russia, Spain   **GROUP SIZE:** avg. 20

With independent, escorted, and customizable group packages, MOV offers a wide range of tour options. Originally marketing just Sydney Mardi Gras, the company has expanded into tours that are more about travel and less about partying. Good value, and a hip, younger sensibility remain the company's calling cards. A new partnership with Certified Tours offers worldwide independent vacation packages.

OLIVIA CRUISES & RESORTS 4400 Market Street, Oakland, CA 94608; 510-655-0354 or 800-631-6277, fax 510-655-4334)
  CLIENTELE: 99%G/ 100%W; 80% couples; avg. age 35   **PRICE RANGE:** $1,095–4,195   **TOUR LENGTH:** 7 days   **NUMBER OF DEPARTURES:** 4   **DES-**

TINATIONS: Alaska, Caribbean, Mediterranean cruises; Club Med Ixtapa **GROUP SIZE:** 500–600

Women-owned and women-focused for more than 20 years, Olivia ventured into travel six years ago, and customizes the resort and cruise experience by bringing along a staff of up to 50 women on each trip. The company won an *Out & About* Editor's Choice Award for its exceptional customization of popular travel experiences.

OUR FAMILY ABROAD 40 W. Fifty-seventh Street, New York, NY 10019; 212-459-1800 or 800-999-5500, fax 212-581-3756
   CLIENTELE: EG/85%M, 60% couples; avg. age 42   **PRICE RANGE:** $768–3,998   **TOUR LENGTH:** 9–17 days   **NUMBER OF DEPARTURES:** 22
   DESTINATIONS: Mostly Europe, also Egypt, Morocco, Asia   **GROUP SIZE:** 35

Entering its fourth season, Our Family Abroad has brought the realm of first class motorcoach touring to a gay environment. Tours are subcontracted from mainstream suppliers (Globus is the primary contractor), and remarketed as exclusively gay tours, sold at the same price as the mainstream tours are sold. Quality is high, with the emphasis on creating a gay-friendly environment, not gay-specific tour content. The company was a 1995 *Out & About* Editor's Choice Award winner.

OUT WEST ADVENTURES P.O. Box 8451, Missoula, MT 59807; 406-543-0262 or 800-743-0458, fax 406-543-0262, e-mail: outwestadv@aol.com
   CLIENTELE: EG/75%M, 80% singles, ages 25–45   **PRICE RANGE:** $650–1,650   **TOUR LENGTH:** 7–20 days   **NUMBER OF DEPARTURES:** 10
   DESTINATIONS: Rocky Mountains—mostly Montana, Wyoming, Utah   **GROUP SIZE:** 8–18

A new company offering active, outdoor vacations in the Rocky Mountains, featuring rafting, skiing, hiking, mountain biking, backpacking, ranch stays and national park tours.

PASSPORT TRAVEL & TOURS 415 E. Golf Road, #111, Arlington Heights, IL 60005; 708-364-0634 or 800-549-8687, fax 708-364-1813
CLIENTELE: EG/80%M, 80% singles; ages 30–40   PRICE RANGE: $1,000–1,700   TOUR LENGTH: 8–9 days   NUMBER OF DEPARTURES: 6   DESTINATIONS: Europe   GROUP SIZE: 20

Upscale, entertaining tours with a focus on history and culture from a general and gay perspective. Gay history tours focus on London, Amsterdam, Berlin, Rome, Copenhagen, and Paris.

PIED PIPER 330 W. Forty-second Street, #1804, New York, NY 10036; 212-239-2412 or 800-TRIP-312, fax 212-239-2275, e-mail: 73170,1410@compuserve.com)
CLIENTELE: 90%G/80%M, 50% couples; ages 20–70   PRICE RANGE: $795–12,580   TOUR LENGTH: 2–15 days   NUMBER OF DEPARTURES: 9   DESTINATIONS: United States, Canada, Europe, Bermuda, Hawaii   GROUP SIZE: 30–35

Pied Piper has specialized in escorted groups on the *Queen Elizabeth 2* ocean liner for more than five years. Every group is personally escorted, and the trips include private parties and shore excursions. While many companies are attempting to sell gay groups on large cruise ships, Pied Piper won an *Out & About* Editor's Choice Award for its dedication to and success in the market.

PINK TRIANGLE ADVENTURES P.O. Box 14298, Berkeley, CA 94712; 510-843-0181, fax 510-843-4066, e-mail: 72774.3451@compuserve.com
CLIENTELE: EG/60%M, 40% couples; ages 30–50   PRICE RANGE: $1,900–3,900   TOUR LENGTH: 2 weeks   NUMBER OF DEPARTURES: 2   DESTINATIONS: Australia, Ireland, Scotland   GROUP SIZE: 30

Pink Triangle owner John Paul has organized square dancing trips to Russia, Latvia, and Australia. His 1997 tour lineup includes Australia for Mardi Gras, Ireland and Scotland tours that feature sightseeing, excursions, and social events including C&W and square dancing. Accommodations include home stays with local hosts.

PROGRESSIVE TRAVELS 224 West Galer, Suite C, Seattle, WA 98119; 206-285-1987 or 800-245-2229, fax 206-285-1988
CLIENTELE: 97% straight; 3% exclusively gay departures   PRICE RANGE: $1,295–2,890   TOUR LENGTH: avg. 7 days   NUMBER OF DEPARTURES: 3   DESTINATIONS: France, Italy, Portugal, Pacific Northwest   GROUP SIZE: avg. 10

One of the leading straight bicycle/walking tour companies, Progressive Travels selects a few all-gay departures each year. The company offers luxury and standard guided tours, fully van-supported, and emphasizing elegance, charm, and local flavor.

RSVP TRAVEL PRODUCTIONS 2800 University Avenue S.E., Minneapolis, MN 55414; 612-379-4697 or 800-328-RSVP, fax 612-379-0484
CLIENTELE: EG/75–90%M; 50% couples; avg. age 35   PRICE RANGE: $695–2,495   TOUR LENGTH: 7 days   NUMBER OF DEPARTURES: 9   DESTINATIONS: Mexico, Caribbean, French Canada, Mediterranean   GROUP SIZE: 400–1,500

RSVP is currently marketing a number of vacation types: large ship-cruise charters, Club RSVP, a resort-based vacation, clipper-ship charters, and PLAAnet RSVP independent vacation packages. Although RSVP flags itself as a community-inclusive vacation company, its clientele is heavily male (more so on ships than resorts). The first "gay environment" purveyor, RSVP has won an *Out & About* Editor's Choice Award for their production, especially in the operations and entertainment realm, and founder Kevin Mossier was honored with an Editor's Choice Hall of Fame award.

SKYLINK WOMEN'S TRAVEL 2560 West 3rd Street #215, Santa Rosa, CA 95401; 310-452-0506 or 707-570-0105 or 800-225-5759, fax 707-570-0107, e-mail: Skylinktvl@aol.com
CLIENTELE: 100% lesbian, avg. age 42   PRICE RANGE: $535–5,000   TOUR LENGTH: 7–17 days   NUMBER OF DEPARTURES: 12   DESTINATIONS: United States, Africa, Hawaii, Europe, Fiji   GROUP SIZE: 40–100

Skylink caters to women travelers with low-cost, air-inclusive packages. All tours are escorted, with special care given to singles traveling alone.

SPIRIT JOURNEYS P.O. Box 5307, Santa Fe, NM 87502; 505-351-4004 or 800-490-3684, fax 505-351-4999

CLIENTELE: EG/100%M, 75% singles; ages 26–72 PRICE RANGE: $375–1,425 TOUR LENGTH: 3–8 days NUMBER OF DEPARTURES: 16 DESTINATIONS: United States, esp. Southwest; Bahamas GROUP SIZE: 15

Weekend workshops, retreats, and adventure-travel opportunities that foster self-discovery, intimacy, brotherhood, and vision.

TOTO TOURS 1326 W. Albion Avenue, #3-W, Chicago, IL 60626; 312-274-8686 or 800-565-1241, fax 312-274-8695, e-mail: TotoTours@aol.com

CLIENTELE: EG/mostly men, several men-only trips, slightly more singles than couples, increasingly non-American; ages 27–74 PRICE RANGE: $1,100–6,750 TOUR LENGTH: 7–22 days NUMBER OF DEPARTURES: 21 DESTINATIONS: worldwide, exotic, and unusual GROUP SIZE: 10–25

Toto's name and tours were inspired to some extent by the movie *The Wizard of Oz*, and by the fact that some gay people referred to themselves as "Friends of Dorothy." Their mission is as much about bringing people together and creating a "family" of tour members as it is about showing them exotic destinations and creating exciting adventures. Tour accommodations are never deluxe but usually better than average, and activities range from easy to rigorous.

TRAVEL KEYS TOURS P.O. Box 162266, Sacramento, CA 95816; 916-452-5200, fax 916-452-5200

CLIENTELE: Antiques—25%G, Dungeons—EG/100%M PRICE RANGE: $1,990–2,990 TOUR LENGTH: 13–15 days NUMBER OF DEPARTURES: 3 DESTINATIONS: Europe GROUP SIZE: 3–20

Travel Keys offers two different tours: the Antiques Fairs & Flea Markets of Europe for antique collectors and dealers, and Dungeons and Castles of Europe, geared to leathermen and timed to include Munich's Oktoberfest.

TRAVELMAN Im Hainchen 18, Konigstein 6240 Germany; 011-49-6174-22029, fax 011-49-6174-25290

CLIENTELE: 90% gay men, 80% singles; ages 25–60 PRICE RANGE: DM 2,900–7,900 TOUR LENGTH: 14–25 days NUMBER OF DEPAR-

TURES: 22 **DESTINATIONS:** South Pacific, Asia, Australia/New Zealand **GROUP SIZE:** 15–25

A German tour operator offering gay men the opportunity to explore a country's history and culture in comfortable company.

UNDERSEA EXPEDITIONS 4950 Lamont Street, San Diego, CA 92109; 619-270-2900 or 800-669-0310, fax 619-490-1002, e-mail: underseax@aol.com
   CLIENTELE: 95%G/70% M; avg. age 35 **PRICE RANGE:** $499–5,000 **TOUR LENGTH:** 7–14 days **NUMBER OF DEPARTURES:** 7 **DESTINATIONS:** worldwide warm-water diving and snorkeling destinations **GROUP SIZE:** 15–25

Provides a gay-friendly venue and place for gay/lesbian divers to meet new dive buddies in a "safe" environment. By pre-screening dive operators and accommodations, and chartering live-aboard boats, Undersea Expeditions has been successful in creating a gay-friendly niche in this often homophobic sport. They won a 1994 *Out & About* Editor's Choice Award.

VOYAGES & EXPEDITIONS 8323 Southwest Freeway, #800, Houston, TX 77074; 713-776-3438 or 800-818-2877, fax 713-771-9761
   CLIENTELE: mixed straight/gay **PRICE RANGE:** about $200/person/day **TOUR LENGTH:** 7–21 days **NUMBER OF DEPARTURES:** 15 **DESTINATIONS:** worldwide **GROUP SIZE:** 2–30

Voyages & Expeditions is a division of Cruise & Expedition Planners International, which has promoted group offerings on deluxe, exotic cruise ships. While some scheduled departures actually materialize as gay groups, many clients end up traveling as individuals on group rates. The company is upfront about informing potential travelers of this situation.

WOODSWOMEN 25 West Diamond Lake Road, Minneapolis, MN 55419; 612-822-3809, fax 612-822-3814
   CLIENTELE: 100%W, very lesbian-friendly **PRICE RANGE:** $24–5,145 **TOUR LENGTH:** 1–21 days **NUMBER OF DEPARTURES:** 70 **DESTINATIONS:** United States and 10 other countries **GROUP SIZE:** 6–25

Woodswomen is a nonprofit service organization encouraging the spirit of adventure in women focusing on relaxation, fun, personal growth, and skill and leadership building. Over 7,000 women and 1,000 children have traveled with Woodswomen in its 18-year history.

WHAT'S YOUR STYLE?

Gay vacations, like gay vacationers, come in all different styles—and matching the style of a tour to your own style is perhaps the most critical measure you'll need to consider to ensure your enjoyment. Here are some vacation styles and recommended purveyors for each:

FANCY
Hanns Ebensten
Voyages & Expeditions

SIMPLE
Hawk, I'm Your Sister

LEISURELY
Our Family Abroad

WATER SPORTS-ORIENTED
Undersea Expeditions
Eco-Explorations

ADVENTUROUS
Toto Tours
Mariah Wilderness
   Expeditions

CULTURED
Allegro Tours
Passport Travel & Tours

SPIRITUAL
Spirit Journeys
Her Wild Song
Hawk, I'm Your Sister

THEMATIC
Toto Tours
Pink Triangle Adventures
Travel Keys Tours
Club Le Bon

PARTY-ORIENTED
Above & Beyond Tours
Fiesta Tours
Men on Vacation
Atlantis
RSVP

TEN QUESTIONS TO ASK ABOUT
YOUR FIRST GAY VACATION

1. Who else will be on the trip?

2. What is not included in the trip price?

3. What elements of the trip have past passengers complained about?

4. What elements of the trip have past passengers been most pleased with?

5. Are any of the trip services being subcontracted to other operators, and if so, who are they?

6. Has the person booking your trip been on one like it? Will he or she be on this one?

7. Are there any past participants in your hometown you could talk to?

8. How do the food/rooms/activities compare with other vacations you've been on?

9. Is the departure guaranteed? If not, how likely is it to operate?

10. Is travel insurance included or available?

OUT & ABOUT
CALENDAR OF ANNUAL EVENTS

W hile the rest of the world gets only a few holiday weekends to let loose and celebrate, the gay and lesbian community has its own celebration schedule to keep a festive, pride-filled spirit alive year-round. Groups around the world sponsor parties, events, and parades where gay men and lesbians gather to celebrate being out, being proud, and being a community.

Some of the events listed below are built around the long-established traditions celebrated by the entire population. Mardi Gras and Carnival, for instance, have been popular for centuries. These naturally flamboyant and sensual events are perfect for adaptation and embellishment by the gay community. But the gay community has also crafted many celebratory events of its own. These often involve a street fair and a large dance party as their focus, and a portion of the revenues raised are typically earmarked for a gay-related charity. Many of these festivities have become known as "Circuit Events," since so many of the same people (often derogatorily referred to as "circuit queens") show up at consecutive celebrations in different cities.

The more established of the gay events can be so much fun that you might consider building a vacation around them. Let Sydney's Mardi Gras provide the excuse you've needed to head Down Under. Or why not build a romantic autumn weekend around Montreal's Black & Blue Party? And what better reason to plan that long overdue visit to Chicago's Art Institute than the International Mr. Leather Contest in late May? Because the exact dates for the events listed below change each year, we have provided numbers for specific information where available, but be aware that these, too, change often. Try calling the host city's local gay publication or community center to get the details for a given event, or ask an IGTA-affiliated travel agent. Or check *Out & About*, which provides information on upcoming mega-events for each month, including that year's dates and contact numbers.

January—March

The Blue Ball, Philadelphia
A weekend of dances and parties benefiting the AIDS Information Network. The venue changes annually. Call 215-575-1110 for info.

Hero, The Party, Auckland, New Zealand
Even New Zealand has jumped on the circuit party bandwagon. It's a long way to go, but it might be worth the trip. Check with Men on Vacation (800-959-4636) for details.

Aspen Gay Ski Week
This is the largest and most well-attended of the country's gay ski events. Thousands descend for a week of parties and activities organized by a broad range of groups, including ski clubs, AIDS charities, and for-profit promoters. A different Aspen-area mountain is designated each day as the official gay ski area. Call the Aspen Gay and Lesbian Community at 303-925-9249.

The Hearts Party, Chicago
Traditionally scheduled on the Saturday before Valentine's Day, Chicago's Hearts Party provides a warm respite from Chicago's chilly winter. Weekend events revolve around a large dance on the Saturday night, and funds raised benefit regional AIDS charities. For info, call 312-472-6397.

Carnival, Rio de Janeiro
One of the world's greatest parties, whatever your sexual orientation. This is the busiest time of the year to visit Rio, but the floats, parties,

and general mayhem make it one of the best. Gay tour operator Above & Beyond (800-397-2681) has been offering escorted trips to Carnival for several years.

Trinidad Carnival, Trinidad

A week-long celebration of festivities, parades, and music that is smaller and safer than Rio's and more participatory than the Mardi Gras in New Orleans. This incredible week is full of wonderful costumes, hot dancing, a massive steel-drum competition, and parties galore. It's an event around which you might plan a full Caribbean vacation, and is held during the week prior to Ash Wednesday.

Whistler Gay Ski Week, Whistler, British Columbia

This increasingly popular gay ski week takes place in one of Canada's premier ski resorts. A full slate of events and parties is arranged, including horse-drawn sleigh rides, charity auctions, and slope-side picnics. Call 604-938-0772.

The Purple Party, Atlanta

A new twist on the monochromatic circuit party theme, the Purple Party has grown to be a major event for Atlanta, attracting thousands to the Atlanta Apparel Mart. It's a benefit for Project Open Hand, Atlanta's food-delivery program for people with AIDS. Call 404-525-4620.

Saint-at-Large, White Party, New York City

The four annual Saint-at-Large parties (Halloween, New Year's Eve, White, and Black Parties) carry on the grand tradition of the Saint, New York City's legendary disco palace of the 1980s. The Saint parties draw crowds of revelers (as many as 8,000!), who come to dance from late at night until well into the next day. Attendees dress in the appropriate attire for each of the four events. The White Party is held over President's Weekend. Call 212-674-8541.

Mardi Gras, New Orleans

One of the world's great parties, Mardi Gras is known for revelry (especially of the drunken kind) among all its participants, gay or straight. But a whole slate of parties and events for gay and lesbian participants overlaps the general festivities. Call the New Orleans Convention & Visitors Bureau (504-566-5011) for information.

Sydney Gay & Lesbian Mardi Gras, Sydney, Australia

The Sydney Gay & Lesbian Mardi Gras celebration is far and away the largest non-U.S. gay party, attracting thousands of Australians, Europeans, and Americans to the gay-populated streets of Sydney. A month-long festival of theater, film, comedy, exhibitions, and sporting events culminates with the annual Mardi Gras parade and party. The parade itself crosses glitzy Las Vegas production values with an old fashioned gay pride parade—including dykes on bikes, fully decorated thematic floats, every variation of drag, and endless legions of muscle boys marching in step to "I'm Every Woman." The entire city comes to a screeching halt, with a half-million spectators lining the streets to watch the spectacle, which is also broadcast live on Australian television. Following the parade, the largest all-night party in the world takes place at the Royal Show grounds, which encompasses five different pavilions, each with different DJs and entertainment. In the main hall, three live shows punctuate the evening, each a fully staged production number worthy of Radio City Music Hall. Several gay tour operators put together packages around the Mardi Gras events, including Above & Beyond (800-397-2681), Men on Vacation (800-959-4636) and Atlantis (800-6-ATLANTIS).

Winter Party, South Beach

Second only to the Thanksgiving Vizcaya Weekend on the South Beach social calendar is the Winter Party, taking place in early March. It is less exclusive but more elaborately designed than the GMHC Morning Party on Fire Island, and it attracts thousands of winter-weary travelers looking for a hot escape. Proceeds benefit the Dade Human Rights Foundation, a grass-roots advocacy group. Call 305-460-3115 for information.

Saint-at-Large Black Party, New York City

The Black Party is the highlight of the New York City circuit party scene, drawing thousands of dancers annually to this leather-themed, all-night bash. Though dancing is the raison d'être for the Black Party, sex, leather, and other forms of conspicuous consumption play a big

role in this very late evening (how about 4:00 P.M. the next day for late?).
If you can take the crowds and are inclined to dance among a sea of
leather-clad men, this event is worth at least one visit. Call 212-674-
8541.

Academy of Friends Oscar Night Party, San Francisco
If you can't get a ticket to the actual Oscars in L.A. by all means fly to
San Francisco for this annual fund-raiser, drawing thousands for its lav-
ish food, drink, décor and, oh yeah, the Oscars. All proceeds go to local
AIDS service groups. A great reason to plan a trip to the Bay Area. For
information call 415-252-0713.

April—June

Dinah Shore Weekend, Palm Springs
Glamour girls from around the country (but especially from L.A. and
San Francisco) flock to this annual celebration of fun, sun, and golf.
The weekend (which has turned into a full week) is full of parties, performances, and athletics in the desert. Dinah Shore Weekend is perhaps the premier women's party event of the year. Get information at
310-281-1715.

White Party Weekend, Palm Springs
This annual party in the Palm Springs desert is one of the longer-
running circuit parties. Though attended by thousands from across the
country, it is particularly popular with the southern California gym-
boy set. Dance parties fill the weekend agenda. For information call
310-659-3555.

Cherry Jubilee Weekend, Washington, D.C.
A new entrant to the circuit in 1996, the Cherry Jubilee weekend of
parties benefits several D.C. charities and organizations. Through its
careful choice of a spring weekend in the heart of cherry blossom season, this party is expected to become a perennial favorite. Call 202-
797-4639.

The Queen's Birthday, Amsterdam

The gay and lesbian community of Amsterdam hosts an enormous national celebration of street fairs, theater, and partying. Try Above & Beyond for tour information at 800-397-2681.

Geared for Life, Detroit

One of the newer parties on the circuit, this is Motor City's entry to the fundraising, dance-your-tires-off game. Call 313-581-2238 for information.

PrideFest, Philadelphia

A weekend of lectures, panels, workshops, and parties in the City of Brotherly Love. Philadelphia has worked hard to carve itself a place on the gay map, in the shadows of neighboring New York City and Washington, D.C. PrideFest is a step in the right direction. Reach them at 215-732-3378.

Memorial Day at the Beach, Pensacola

Though an unlikely spot for a gay trip, Memorial Day in Pensacola has become bigger each year. The weekend is capped by a huge dance party (of course), but features a lot of fun, sun, and socializing with boys (mostly) from all over the Southeast. (There's no official organizer for this event.)

International Mr. Leather Weekend, Chicago

Throughout the year, many cities hold contests for local or regional Mr. Leather designations, but Chicago's (held Memorial Day weekend) is one of the largest. The international gathering showcases the best of the leather best, and provides an occasion for partying with leathermen of all shapes, sizes, and accessories. Try calling 800-545-6753 for more information.

Gay Day at Disney World, Orlando

Started in 1991 and held the first weekend in June, this event, which is not officially sanctioned by Disney, is a terrific way to share the excitement of the Magic Kingdom. Disney World remains open to the general public on Gay Day, but the thousands of gay folks are easily noticed, and there are many formally and informally designed parties and events throughout the weekend. For more information, check their Web page: *http://www.gayday.com/index.html.*

Gay Arts Festival, Key West

Known for its many galleries as well as for its more sybaritic pleasures, Key West began this arts festival a few years back, and it receives strong support from the local gay business community. A good reason to visit in June. Call 800-833-2299.

July—September

Halsted Street Fair

Chicago's long-standing, midsummer street festival cuts through the heart of the Second City's gay area. The fair consists of street vendors, concerts, and parties. The usual mix in a great city to be gay. Call the Chicago Convention & Tourism Bureau (312-567-8500) for dates.

Women in Paradise, Key West

This is the week that women rule the gay paradise of Key West. All sorts of events, parties, and activities take place. Call the Key West Business Guild at 305-294-4603.

Hillcrest Fair, San Diego

The charming, eclectic Hillcrest area (the Greenwich Village of San Diego) plays host to a terrific street fair in late July. The gay and lesbian crowds take to the streets and parks for one of the friendliest, largest weekends on the Southern California schedule. Call the San Diego Convention & Visitor's Bureau (619-236-1212) for information.

Hotlanta River Expo, Atlanta

There is nothing comparable to floating down the Chattahoochee River with a few thousand genetically fabulous and/or chemically altered gay men. The Hotlanta River Expo is one of the grand-daddies of tailor-made gay events, and it's hard (impossible, maybe) not to have a great time here. The massive river float is the main event, but the weekend is packed full of nightly parties. Call 404-874-3976.

Provincetown Carnival, Provincetown

The biggest weekend of the year in P'town is held in mid-August. The week features a big parade, numerous parties, and a plethora of dances and performances. You must book early to find room at the inn. Call the Provincetown Business Guild at 508-487-2313.

GMHC Morning Party, Fire Island

One of the loveliest parties imaginable. Set directly on the beach between Fire Island Pines and Cherry Grove, the Morning Party pulls in thousands for a day of beachside dancing, beautiful men and women, wonderful design, and bittersweet memories, all to raise funds for New York's Gay Men's Health Crisis. Most attendees have shares on the beach or visit for the week, but many day-trip across the bay for this special day. For information call 212-255-1109.

Southern Decadence Weekend, New Orleans

A gay mini–Mardi Gras over Labor Day weekend, this circuit event gets bigger every year. Call 504-529-2860 for information.

Wigstock, New York City

Labor Day Sunday brings out the best wigs in the world, all in honor of Wigstock, the drag festival extraordinaire started by the Lady Bunny and grown into an event big enough to justify its own movie. Join thousands for a day of hair finery and hours of world-class drag entertainment. A spectacle! Call the Lesbian/Gay Services Center (212-620-7310) for information. The event was cancelled in 1996 due to organization/venue/funding problems.

Last Splash Weekend, Austin

Now some ten years old, Last Splash weekend is highlighted by the annual Sunday pilgrimage to nearby Travis Lake for sunning, gawking, splashing, and just about everything else that people do in the wild. It's a fitting farewell to summer, and a great reason to visit this Texas city. Parties take place all weekend. Call 512-476-3611 for information.

Womyn's Music Festival, near Hart, Michigan

One of the largest gatherings of women each year, this rural Michigan music festival draws thousands of participants seeking an all-women environment to celebrate their lives, discuss their issues, and enjoy music, camping, and the great outdoors. Call 616-757-4766 for information.

Folsom Street Fair
A huge gathering of leather women, men, and their admirers on the streets of San Francisco. A fantastic weekend of some of the best real-life theater you'll ever witness. Call 415-861-3247 for information.

Castro Street Fair
This early fall festival is a cleaner-cut version of the Folsom Street Fair a few weeks before. It's a traditional street fair winding its way through the Castro and down San Francisco's Market Street. Call 415-467-3354 for information.

Rudely Elegant Red Party, Columbus
Considered to be one of the first circuit parties, this is the Midwest's most fabulous theme-colored party, the color being red. It is an extremely creative party whose theme the attendees do their best to carry throughout. Held in a large event space near the Columbus airport late each September, this is the oldest ongoing large-scale dance event in the U.S., begun in 1977. For information, call 614-294-8309.

October—November

Sleaze Ball, Sydney, Australia
Officially a fundraiser for Sydney's Gay & Lesbian Mardi Gras, the Sleaze Ball is Australia's second party extravaganza. Tour operators Above & Beyond (800-397-2681) and Men on Vacation (800-959-4636) offer trips.

Black & Blue Weekend, Montreal
The Black & Blue Weekend is Canada's main party event, and one of the best reasons yet to visit beautiful, romantic Montreal. An entire Columbus Day Weekend of parties and events surrounds the massive Saturday-night dance-cum-fundraiser. More than 10,000 people have

attended in the past, and all seem to have a great time. Call 514-393-9500 for more information.

Halloween, New Orleans

The capital of debauchery lets loose almost as much on Halloween as it does for Mardi Gras. An entire slate of gay parties and activities are organized to support local helping organizations. For information call 800-523-9338.

Women's Week in Provincetown

P'town knows what the girls like, as the community has always been shaped by a strong lesbian presence. Women's Week brings that spirit to its peak, and it is definitely worth saving a spot on your calendar for this soirée. Call the Provincetown Business Guild (800-637-8696) for information.

Fantasy Fest, Key West

Key West's Halloween celebration has been a favorite for years. Where else would you expect such an embracing of the decadent? Call the Key West Business Guild at 305-294-4603.

Fire & Ice Party, Phoenix

Ice in the desert? Well, anything goes when it comes to circuit parties, and Phoenix has recently joined the circuit. Call 602-955-4673 for information.

Vizcaya White Party, Miami

This annual drop-dead fabulous benefit party at the opulent Vizcaya estate in Coral Gables is one of the jewels in the crown of gay happenings. Since 1985, Thanksgiving weekend in South Beach has evolved into one of the biggest gay party weekends in the United States, with over a dozen organized events (including several for women) surrounding the legendary Sunday night White Party at Vizcaya. Tickets to the main event are limited to far fewer than the number of visitors over the weekend, but many officially sanctioned and unofficial events take place throughout the long weekend. Call 305-759-6181.

December

Do you really need another big party or event to keep you celebrating during a month that hosts Christmas, Chanukah, Kwanzaa, New Year's Eve, and one-too-many office parties? We suggest you save your energy for important tasks, like shopping for gifts and fighting for space in the overhead bin.

INDEX

~~~~~~~

Billy Kolber-Stuart holds a B.S. in Biology from Yale University, and well over 1,000,000 frequent flyer miles. He and his hyphenate unpack their suitcases in Los Angeles and Water Island, NY, where Billy's Banana Cream Pie took First Prize in the 1996 Bake-Off.

David Alport grew up in St. Louis, graduated from Brown University in Providence, set up home in New York City, and left behind three years in advertising and five years at American Express to start *Out & About*. He has never looked back, or stopped moving.